APPLIED COST–BENEFIT ANALYSIS

To Elizabeth, Adam and Matthew

Applied Cost–Benefit Analysis

Robert J. Brent

Professor of Economics, Fordham University, USA

Edward Elgar
Cheltenham, UK • Lyme, US

Published by
Edward Elgar Publishing Limited
8 Lansdown Place
Cheltenham
Glos GL50 2HU
UK

Edward Elgar Publishing, Inc.
1 Pinnacle Hill Road
Lyme
NH 03768
US

Paperback edition 1997
Paperback edition reprinted 1997

British Library Cataloguing in Publication Data
Brent, Robert J.
  Applied Cost–benefit Analysis
  I. Title
  339.41

Library of Congress Cataloguing in Publication Data
Brent, Robert J., 1946–
    Applied cost–benefit analysis/Robert Brent.
      p. cm.
    Includes index
    1. Cost effectiveness. I. Title.
HD47.4.B74 1995
658.15'54—dc20   95–13485
                                                           CIP

ISBN 1 85898 285 5
      1 85898 338 X (paperback)

Printed and bound in Great Britain by
Biddles Limited, Guildford and King's Lynn

Contents

PART IV

PART V

Tables

Abbreviations

AF	Annuity Factor
AC	Average Cost
AR	Average Revenue
B	Benefit
C	Cost
CBA	Cost–Benefit Analysis
CEA	Cost-Effectiveness Analysis
CM	Cost Minimization
CS	Consumer Surplus
CUA	Cost-Utility Analysis
I	Indifference Curve
IRR	Internal Rate of Return
L	Financial Loss
LEDR	Life Expectancy Discount Rate
MB	Marginal Benefit
MC	Marginal Cost
MCF	Marginal Cost of Public Funds
MEB	Marginal Excess Burden
MR	Marginal Revenue
MRS	Marginal Rate of Substitution
MRT	Marginal Rate of Transformation
MSC	Marginal Social Cost
MU	Marginal Utility
N	Number of People
NPV	Net Present Value
Q	Quantity
QALY	Quality Adjusted Life Year
R	Repayments or Revenues
SDR	Social Discount Rate
SOCR	Social Opportunity Cost Rate
STPR	Social Time Preference Rate
U	Utility
V	Maximum Value Function
W	Social Welfare
WTA	Willingness to Accept
WTP	Willingness to Pay
Y	Income

Preface

The title of the book *Applied Cost–Benefit Analysis* was chosen to highlight a major limitation in the existing literature on Cost–Benefit Analysis (CBA), namely the gap between theory and applications in this field. Many texts cover theory and applications. But there is very little correspondence between what the theory specifies and what the applications cover. In part, this is a reflection of the fact that often the practice of CBA does depart from the theory. But it does not have to be that way. CBA was developed as a subject in order to be a practical guide to social decision-making. If the usefulness of the theory were made apparent, there would be a greater chance that the theory and practice of CBA would coincide.

My conception of applied economics generally, and applied CBA in particular, is this. One starts with the theory, one applies it, and on the basis of the results, one goes back to modify the theory to include the important aspects that practice deems relevant, but theory originally neglected. There is this constant to-and-fro from the theory and the practice until, hopefully, there is (for a while) a strong correspondence between the two. The world is constantly changing and our framework for thinking about these changes must be expanded at the same time.

This book does not pretend to be a 'hands-on', step-by-step guide how to do a CBA. At this stage of the art of CBA, it is more important that practitioners get acquainted with the basic principles of CBA than follow some alleged 'masterplan'. If one knows what one should be doing, one can (perhaps) find a way of implementing those principles. In any case, it is clear that there is no one, single way of proceeding. Certain components must be present. But the manner in which they are assembled can vary. The availability of reliable and relevant data will, into the foreseeable future, continue to be one of the main factors that determine how a CBA will actually be undertaken.

What the book does attempt is a unified statement of the principles of CBA. I have adopted the benchmark that 'less is more'. Unlike some encyclopedic texts that cover everything that could possibly be applied, I have focused only on those parts of theory that are fundamental and have been usefully incorporated into actual applications. The discussion of the applications is to show the relevance of the theory. Note, that by 'an application' I do not simply mean that I have made up some numbers to illustrate a particular model. The case studies I have chosen all deal with an important and concrete public policy issue analysed using real data. The intention is that the book provides a unified course in the principles of CBA rather than a set of disconnected topics. On this basis the reader should be able to appreciate the main strengths and weaknesses of actual studies in the field.

The book is geared to upper-level undergraduate or beginning graduate students. The applied nature of the course should make this of interest not only to traditional economics students, but also those in professional programmes, especially those connected with studies in transport, the environment and health care. Students in Eastern Europe would find the subject matter especially relevant.

I would like to thank a decade or more of graduate students at Fordham University who participated in the public policy courses on which this text was based. They taught me the need to provide applications in this area. I am grateful also to Fordham University for giving me a semester off to write the book, and Columbia University who arranged for me to visit the economics department while I wrote and taught some of the chapter material. I would also like to thank Professor Robert Millward who taught me my first course in public expenditure economics, Professor Peter Hammond who introduced me to the modern theory of public sector economics, and to Professor Edwin West for getting me started and supporting me over the years.

Acknowledgements

The author wishes to thank the following who have kindly given permission for the use of copyright material.

American Economic Association for Table 7.3 first published in Hirschleifer and Riley, 'The Analytics of Uncertainty and Information: An Expository Survey', *Journal of Economic Literature*, **17**, 1979; for Table 7.6 first published in Cropper et al., 'Rates of Time Preference for Saving Lives', *American Economic Review*, **82**, 1992; for Table 8.6 first published in Brookshire et al., 'Valuing Public Goods: A Comparison of Survey and Hedonic Approaches', *American Economic Review*, **72**, 1982; for Table 9.1 first published in Browning, 'On the Marginal Welfare Cost of Taxation', *American Economic Review*, **77**, 1987.

American Journal of Agricultural Economics for Table 6.3 first published in Bowker and Stoll, 'Use of Dichotomous Choice Nonmarket Methods to Value the Whooping Crane Resource', *American Journal of Agricultural Economics*, **71**, 1988.

American Medical Association for Tables 4.3 and 4.4 first published in Hsiao et al., 'Results, Potential Effects, and Implementation Issues of the Resource-Based Relative Value Scale', *Journal of the American Medical Association*, **260**, 1988a.

American Society of Tropical Medicine and Hygiene for Table 11.3 first published in Cohn, 'Assessment of Malaria Eradication: Costs and Benefits', *American Journal of Tropical Medicine and Hygiene,* **21**, 1972.

Basil Blackwell Ltd for Table 3.2 first published in Foster and Beesley, 'Estimating the Social Benefits of Constructing an Underground Railway in London', *Journal of the Royal Statistical Society*, **Series A**, 1963.

Brookings Institution for Table 2.1 first published in Weisbrod, 'Income Redistribution Effects and Benefit–Cost Analysis', in Chase (ed.), *Problems of Public Expenditure Analysis*, 1968.

Canadian Public Policy for Table 9.2 first published in Constantatos and West, 'Measuring Returns from Education: Some Neglected Factors', *Canadian Public Policy*, **17**, 1991

Elsevier Science Publishers B.V. for Table 2.2 first published in Cordes and Weisbrod, 'Governmental Behavior in Response to Compensation Requirements', *Journal of Public Economics*, **11**, 1979; for Table 6.2 first published in Bohm, 'Estimating Demand for Public Goods: An Experiment', *European Economic Review*, **3**, 1972; for Table 8.5 first published in Brown and Mendelsohn, 'The Hedonic Travel Cost Method', *Review of Economics and Statistics*, **66**, 1984; for Table 9.3 first published in Fullerton and Henderson, 'The Marginal Excess Burden of Different Capital Tax Instruments', *Review of Economics and Statistics*, **71**, 1989.

Hanley and Belfus Inc. for Table 10.2 first published in Thompson et al., 'Feasibility of Willingness to Pay Measurement in Chronic Arthritis', *Medical Decision Making*, **4**, 1984.

Harper Collins for Table 11.1 first published in Staats, 'Survey of Use by Federal Agencies of the Discounting Technique in Evaluating Future Programs', in Hinricks and Taylor (eds), *Program Budgeting and Benefit–Cost Analysis*, California: Goodyear 1969.

Houghton Mifflin Co. for Table 10.1 first published in Loury, 'Efficiency and Equity Impacts of Natural Gas Regulation', in Haveman and Margolis (eds), *Public Expenditure and Policy Analysis*, 1983.

Johns Hopkins University Press for Table 8.1 first published in Clawson, *Economics of Outdoor Recreation*, 1966.

Journal of Transport Economics and Policy for Table 3.4 first published in Hau, 'Distributional Cost–Benefit Analysis in Discrete Choice', *Journal of Transport Economics and Policy*, **20**, 1986; for Tables 4.1 and 4.2 first published in Morrison, 'The Structure of Landing Fees at Uncongested Airports', *Journal of Transport Economics and Policy*, **16**, 1982.

Lancet Ltd. for Table 1.2 first published in Lowson et al., 'Costing New Services: Long-term Domiciliary Oxygen Therapy', *Lancet*, **i**, 1981.

Massachusetts Medical Society for Table 1.3 first published in Boyle at al., 'Economic Evaluation of Neonatal Intensive Care of Very Low Birth-Weight Infants', *New England Journal of Medicine*, **308**, 1983; for Table 7.4 first published in McNeil et al., 'Fallacy of the Five-Year Survival in Lung Cancer', *New England Journal of Medicine*, **299**, 1978.

Oxford University Press for Table 1.1 first published in Drummond et al., 'Methods for the Economic Evaluation of Health Care Programmes', 1987; for

Table 9.4 first published in Ahmad and Stern, 'Alternative Sources of Government Revenue: Illustrations from India, 1979–80', in Newbury and Stern (eds), *The Theory of Taxation for Developing Countries*, 1987; for Table 10.3 first published in Hughes, 'The Incidence of Fuel Taxes: A Comparative Study of Three Countries', in Newbury and Stern (eds), *The Theory of Taxation for Developing Countries*, 1987.

Pergamon Press Ltd for Table 3.4 first published in Hau, 'Using a Hicksian Approach to Cost–Benefit Analysis in Discrete Choice: An Empirical Analysis of a Transportation Corridor Model', *Transportation Research*, **21B**, 1987.

Sage Publications Inc. for Table 8.4 first published in Haynes and Larsen, 'Financial Consequences of Incarceration and Alternatives: Burglary', *Crime and Delinquency*, **30**, 1984.

Scandinavian University Press for Table 5.1 first published in Swint and Nelson, 'The Application of Economic Analysis to Evaluation of Alcoholism Rehabilitation Programs', *Inquiry*, **14**, 1977.

Southern Economic Journal for Table 8.2 first published in Forester et al., 'A Cost–Benefit Analysis of the 55 MPH Speed Limit', *Southern Economic Journal*, **50**, 1984.

University of Chicago Press for Table 3.1 first published in Whittington et al., 'Estimating the Willingness to Pay for Water Services in Developing Countries', *Economic Development and Cultural Change*, **38**, 1990; for Table 12.1 first published in Thobani, 'Charging User Fees for Social Services: Education in Malawi', *Comparative Education Review*, **28**, 1984.

University of Texas Press for Table 8.3 first published in Gray and Olson, 'A Cost–Benefit Analysis of the Sentencing Decision for Burglars', *Social Science Quarterly*, **70**, 1989.

University of Winsconsin Press for Table 12.4 first published in Mwabu et al., 'Quality of Medical Care and Choice of Medical Treatment in Kenya', *Journal of Human Resources*, **28**, 1994.

Every effort has been made to trace all the copyright holders but if any have been inadvertently overlooked the publishers will be pleased to make the necessary arrangements at the first opportunity.

PART I

1 Introduction to CBA

1.1 Introduction

We start by stating the Cost–Benefit Analysis (hereafter CBA) approach to public policy. Then we provide a definition and identify the crucial issues that need to be resolved in general terms. Next we discuss the role of discounting in CBA. This is followed by an explanation of the particular model that will be used throughout the book. To illustrate the different approaches to economic evaluation, we present applications of the main methods that have been used in the health-care field. An explanation of the basic methodology for estimating the policy parameters is provided, together with an outline of the theoretical content of the book. This introductory chapter closes with a summary and problems section.

1.1.1 The cost–benefit approach

Economic theory has been founded on the notion of a rational individual, that is, a person who makes decisions on the basis of a comparison of benefits and costs. CBA, or strictly *social* CBA, extends this to the area of government decision-making by replacing private benefits and costs with social benefits and costs (to be defined below). Although we will talk in terms of a public project (such as building a highway or discontinuing a railway line) the scope of the analysis is very wide. It relates to *any* public decision that has an implication for the use of resources. Thus, giving a labour subsidy or restricting an activity by regulation (e.g., the 55 mph speed limit in the United States) are within the purview of CBA. That is, if the activity is worth subsidizing, the benefits must be greater than the costs; and if it is necessary to restrict an activity, the costs must be greater than the benefits.

The purpose of this book is to show that there is nothing esoteric about the subject matter of CBA. Welfare economics is at the heart of public policy and hence at the core of CBA. One cannot avoid making value judgements when making social decisions. The choice is only whether one makes these judgements explicitly or implicitly. Since there is nothing 'scientific' about making the value judgements implicitly, and it obscures understanding, all the necessary value judgements will be made explicitly. Apart from showing that there are a unified set of principles that can govern public expenditure decisions, this book will attempt to present applications of all the theoretical concepts. This entails providing the institutional context for the decisions and discussing in detail how the value parameters can be obtained in practice.

1.1.2   The general cost–benefit model

To introduce the subject, let us use the definition of the CBA process given by Prest and Turvey (1968): 'Maximize the present value of all benefits less that of all costs, subject to specified constraints'. They break this down to four inter-related questions:

a. Which costs and which benefits are to be included?
b. How are the costs and benefits to be evaluated?
c. At what interest rate are future benefits and costs to be discounted to obtain the present value (the equivalent value that one is receiving or giving up today when the decision is being made)?
d. What are the relevant constraints?

How one answers these questions depends on whose welfare is to be maximized. For example, let us first present the answers that would be given by a private firm making an investment decision.

a. Only the private benefits and costs that can be measured in financial terms are to be included.
b. Benefits and costs are the financial receipts and outlays as measured by market prices. The difference between them is reflected in the firm's profits.
c. The market rate of interest is to be used for discounting the annual profit stream.
d. The main constraint is the funds constraint imposed on the expenditure department.

For a social CBA, the scope is wider and the time horizon may be longer.

a. *All* benefits and costs are to be included, consisting of private and social, direct and indirect, tangible and intangible.
b. Benefits and costs are given by the standard principles of welfare economics. Benefits are based on the consumer's willingness to pay for the project. Costs are what the losers are willing to receive as compensation for giving up the resources.
c. The social discount rate (which includes the preferences of future genera-tions) is to be used for discounting the annual net-benefit stream.
d. Constraints are not allowed for separately, but are included in the objective function. For example, income distribution considerations are to be included by weighting the consumer's willingness to pay according to an individual's ability to pay. A fund's constraint is handled by using a premium on the cost of capital, that is, the social price of capital is calculated which would be different from its market price.

The word *social* is used in the literature to refer to three different aspects of a CBA. Firstly, it is used to denote the idea that included in the evaluation are the effects of the project on all the individuals in society, not just the parties directly involved (the consumers and the producers of the project). For example, everyone would be affected if the project caused any environmental impacts. Secondly, it is used to recognize that distributional effects are being included with the efficiency effects. Without the distributional effects one is making an economic rather than a social evaluation. Lastly the word social is used to emphasize that market prices are not always good indices of individual willingness to pay. A social price would therefore mean that the market price was being adjusted to include effects that the market does not record, or records imperfectly.

The second use of the word social just outlined, that is, the use of distribution considerations to supplement efficiency effects, warrants elaboration. Some major authors, such as Mishan (1976) and Harberger (1978), consider that distribution should not be a part of CBA. We will not follow this approach. It is one thing to argue that it is better to use the tax transfer system for distribution. But, what relevance does this have if the tax system has not been (or cannot be) employed to set incomes optimally. We take the view that CBA is more useful if it recognizes from the outset that social policy-makers *are* concerned with distribution. It should therefore try to ensure that the theory and practice of CBA reflects this concern. A full discussion of the distribution issue will be covered later in the book.

In all three aspects, it is important to emphasize that the word social does *not* imply the existence of an organistic view of the state, that is, an entity that has preferences different from individual valuations. Rather the word is used to stress that one is attempting to give full expression to the preferences of all individuals, whether they be rich or poor, or directly or indirectly affected by the project.

We conclude this section by considering two questions that are often raised in connection with CBA. How scientific is CBA? Is it better than using the political mechanism? (see Williams, 1983). The main points to note are:

a. The subject is no more or less scientific than any policy area of economics, such as international economics or labour economics. The strengths and weaknesses are those of welfare economics itself.
b. One needs to use CBA for some government decisions because it is too administratively costly to hold an election every time a public decision needs to be made.
c. Providing the objectives are the same for all projects, and measured in a consistent fashion, there is no necessary bias by using CBA. For example, if environmental factors are considered to be important for one project decision, they must be considered to be important for all project decisions.

This guards against a policy-maker bringing in special factors that raise the net benefits only for those particular projects that are personally preferred by the policy-maker.

1.2   The particular cost–benefit model

In this section we give an outline of the main ingredients that make up the particular cost–benefit model that will be used throughout the book. Each ingredient will be examined later in a separate chapter. The aim here is simply to identify the key concepts and to show how they fit together. Once one knows what the 'puzzle' looks like, the individual pieces will then start to have some significance. All the numbers in this section are illustrative only. They have been chosen to keep the arithmetic simple, ignore currency units and, at this introductory stage, avoid the need to make precise specifications of the benefit and cost categories .

The basic idea behind the model (first started by Marglin (1968) and later developed in a series of papers by the author that are listed in the references) is to: (a) take the benefits and costs and disaggregate them into their constituent parts, and then (b) apply unequal weights to those components that have a different social significance from others. The level of complexity involved is equivalent to using a weighted average rather than an unweighted average to summarize the typical effect in statistics.

1.2.1   Economic efficiency

As the general model points out, the aim is to maximize the difference between benefits B and costs C:

$$B - C \qquad\qquad (1.1)$$

The difference is the efficiency effect of the project. It can be regarded as the additional resources that are now available, or in Marglin's words, it shows the increase in the 'size of the economic pie'. The greater the difference, the greater the contribution of the project. (Chapter 2 makes explicit the assumptions on which an efficiency calculation is based.)

When no constraints other than production possibilities exist, all projects with a positive difference should be approved. For example, if a project has a B of 100 and a C of 60, it should be approved; while if C were instead 120, the project should be rejected. When only one project can be accepted (as in the case where there is just one particular site on which to build a project), one should choose the project with the highest net benefits. (For a discussion of investment criteria with and without budget constraints, see Brent (1990, ch. 2) and Vinod (1988).)

1.2.2   Redistribution when the benefits are in cash

Society is concerned not only with the total size of the pie, but how it is distributed. To accommodate income distributional factors one can distinguish the group that gets the benefits (group 2) from those that incur the costs (group 1). One can assume that group 2 is a poor group living in the rural areas, while group 1 represents rich urban taxpayers. Let a_1 be the social value of a unit of benefits to group 1, and let a_2 be the value for group 2. It is natural to judge that a unit to a poor person is worth more in social terms than one to a rich person, so we would expect that a policy-maker would give a value for a_2 that is larger than for a_1. The cost–benefit calculation allowing for both efficiency and distribution is:

$$a_2B - a_1C \qquad (1.2)$$

Think of the a coefficients, or distributional weights, as numbers that centre around unity. (How these can be estimated will be explained in full in Chapter 10.) If, for example, $a_2 = 1.4$ and $a_1 = 0.6$, then a project that has benefits one half the size of costs would still be approved, i.e., $1.4(100) > 0.6(200)$. This means that society would be willing to make the rich group forgo resources equal to an additional 50 per cent of the costs of the project provided that the poor group are made better off.

Although inefficient projects may be approved, there is no policy contradiction implied. Weighted benefits exceed weighted costs and therefore society is better off with the project. The weights reflect the trade-off between efficiency and distribution. This trade-off is at the heart of public policy. One cannot always expect that policies will be both efficient *and* distributionally fair. Specifying the weights makes explicit the value judgements regarding the priority of objectives.

Note that those who suggest that distributional considerations should be excluded from the formal criteria deciding projects are effectively setting *unit* weights in equation (1.2). It is not possible to avoid using distribution weights even if one wishes to ignore distribution as a separate CBA objective.

1.2.3   *Redistribution when the benefits are in-kind*

Marglin also stresses that society may be concerned with how one 'slices the pie'. People who are giving up the resources that are being redistributed have preferences about what the poor spend their assistance on. These preferences may entail the requirement that the poor work for their assistance, or that the poor be encouraged to spend their assistance on designated items, such as food and education.

Equation (1.2) assumes that group 2 receives the benefits free of charge. More generally, there will be some repayment R. R has the effect of transferring some of the gain from the beneficiary group back to the taxpaying group. The gain to group 2 will be net of R, i.e., $B - R$, while the cost to the taxpayers is also reduced to $C - R$. Since this latter term, $C - R$, is the financial loss L involved with the public investment, equation (1.2) then becomes:

$$a_2 B - a_2 R - a_1 L \qquad (1.3)$$

Note that B in (1.3), a dollar or pound of benefits in-kind (for example, food consumption), is given the same value as for R, a dollar or pound of benefits in cash (e.g., a social security payment). However, people may volunteer to contribute to the poor's food consumption (as in the US Food Stamps Program), but be reluctant to assist the poor with cash handouts that can be spent on such things as alcohol. Because of this, one has to put a higher social value on benefits in-kind (B) than for benefits in money terms (R):

$$a_{2.k} B - a_{2.m} R - a_{1.m} L \qquad (1.4)$$

where $a_{2.k}$ is the social value of benefits in-kind and $a_{2.m}$ is the social value of benefits that are received in money income form. The financial loss term is also in money income terms and it therefore has the weight $a_{1.m}$.

Equation (1.4) has B and R with opposite signs because the beneficiaries have to give up cash in order to receive the benefits in-kind. For example, the beneficiaries of an irrigation project may receive positive benefits from the water, but they may have to pay for it. We can make a simple cash versus in-kind comparison by considering a positive cash transfer as a separate project whereby repayments R are *reduced*. In terms of equation (1.4) therefore, one can compare an in-kind project that gives $+a_{2.k} B$ with a cash subsidy project that gives $+a_{2.m} R$. Thus, even if B were equal to R (the beneficiary was indifferent between the two projects), and L were the same for both projects, the in-kind one would be ranked higher because the weight would be greater ($a_{2.k} > a_{2.m}$). This means that the taxpayers would feel better off. They pay the same amount L, but the benefits are in a form that they prefer. (The way that donor preferences impact on social decisions is developed in greater detail in Chapter 6.)

1.2.4   Marginal social cost of public funds

In order to finance the loss incurred by the project, taxes may have to be raised. In practical terms, there is no way of raising taxes that does not affect adversely the choices that individuals make over their use of resources. There is therefore an additional (or excess) burden of taxes over and above the (direct) financial burden entailed in paying the taxes themselves. This difference between the direct and excess cost is seen clearest in the case where a tax is levied on a product (such as cigarettes) which induces consumers to cease purchasing it (that is, they quit smoking). Here there is no tax revenue (no direct cost). But there is an excess burden caused by losing the satisfaction from consuming the product (the pleasure from smoking the cigarette). This excess burden from financing the project needs to be included as a part of the CBA criterion.

The marginal cost of public funds *MCF* is the sum of the direct and excess costs per unit of finance required by the project. This needs to be applied to the financial loss term in equation (1.4) to produce

$$a_{2.k}B - a_{2.m}R - a_{1.m}(MCF)L \qquad (1.5)$$

Once more, unity is the benchmark to keep in mind when considering a value for the *MCF* term. For if there were no excess burden *MCF* = 1. The role of the *MCF* in CBA is to give a premium to any net receipts that go to the government (say from employing user fees for the public project). These receipts mean that taxes do not need to be raised, or can be lowered, thereby avoiding the excess burden. (Chapter 9 is devoted to analyzing and estimating the MCF.)

1.2.5   Time discounting
So far all the criteria relate to a particular point in time. Take equation (1.1), *B* – *C*, for reference. Any investment decision has a time dimension because it involves sacrificing current consumption for future satisfaction. Thus in equation (1.1), *C* is in the current period while *B* is in the future. To make the two comparable, we need to discount the benefits to express everything in current value terms. Redefine *B* to be a fixed amount of benefits that accrue every year. The annuity form of discounting is now appropriate, and the current value for benefits would be *B/i*, where *i* is the social discount rate. (This annuity formula, and the subsequent equation (1.7) on which it is based, is derived in full in the appendix. The process of discounting is explained in the next section.) Equation (1.1) should therefore be replaced by

$$B/i - C \qquad (1.6)$$

and all the disaggregating and weighting should take place from this base.

1.3   Discounting and cost–benefit analysis
First we explain the discounting process and how it leads to a net present value (NPV) figure which is to help determine the fate of the project. Then we show how to convert a capital sum into a stream of annual capital costs.

1.3.1   Discounting and the net present value
Given a choice, individuals would prefer to have a unit of benefits today rather than in the future. This could be because individuals may not live to experience the future benefits. But more general is the fact that interest can be earned on the current unit. By the time the future arrives, the cumulated interest will

mean that there will be more than one future unit to enjoy. Thus, if the interest rate i is 10 per cent (0.10) per annum and we are comparing a unit today with a unit next year, the current unit will be preferred because it will amount to 1.10 next year (i.e., $1 + i$). The process of multiplying current year units by $(1 + i)$ to yield next year amounts is called compounding.

Saying that a unit today is worth more than a unit next year is equivalent to saying that a unit next year is worth *less* than a unit this year. In other words, the future unit has to be *discounted* to make it comparable to a current unit. Discounting is compounding in reverse. We know that one unit today amounts to $(1 + i)$ next year. How much is $(1 + i)$ next year worth today? Obviously, it is worth one unit, because that is what we are starting out with. Hence next year's amounts must be *divided* by $(1 + i)$ to obtain the current or present value, that is, the NPV.

In a two-period setting, we can consider a project as sacrificing current consumption for additional consumption next year. Say the sacrifice is 100 and the return next year is 120. Is this project worthwhile? We cannot just subtract the 100 from the 120 to obtain a net figure of +20. This is because the 120 comes next year, and we have just seen that this is worth less than it would if obtained today. This means that the 120 must be divided by $(1 + i)$ to be comparable in *today-value terms*. If i is 10 per cent, $(1 + i) = 1.10$, and 1 unit next year is worth 1/1.10 or 0.9091. One hundred and twenty units would therefore have a present value of 120 (0.9091), which is 109.0909. The cost is 100 today, so its present value is clearly 100. With future benefits discounted, both figures are in present value terms and can be compared. The net result is that the current year equivalent benefit of 109.0909 minus the current cost of 100 leads to an NPV of +9.0909.

The decision rule that is to be used to decide whether a project is worthwhile is that the NPV must be greater than zero. (For other decision rules, such as the internal rate of return or the benefit–cost ratio, see Brent, 1990, ch. 2.) A positive NPV figure means that the project is producing more benefits in present value terms than the current costs and so there is a positive contribution left over. At an interest rate of 10 per cent therefore, the +9.0909 signifies a worthwhile project.

Clearly, the outcome of a project is very much dependent on the interest rate used. For example, if the interest rate were 25 per cent, the present value of 120 next year would be only 96. When current costs of 100 were subtracted, this would make the NPV equal to –4, and the project now would not be worthwhile.

The important issue of what determines the social interest rate is covered in Chapter 11. But, given the interest rate, discounting is a straightforward computational exercise. The only point to remember is that every year's benefits must be discounted for each year that they are in the future. So 1 unit next year is worth $1/(1 + i)$ today; 1 unit in two years' time is worth $1/(1 + i)^2$; and so on until the terminal year of the project, designated by T, where the present value of 1 unit is $1/(1 + i)^T$. A stream of benefits (or costs) of 1 unit from next year ($t = 1$) to the end of the project ($t = T$) can therefore be summarized as

$$\frac{1}{(1+i)} + \frac{1}{(1+i)^2} + \cdots + \frac{1}{(1+i)^T} = \sum_{t=1}^{t=T} \frac{1}{(1+i)^t} \tag{1.7}$$

1.3.2 Converting a capital stock to a flow

Most of the applications referred to in this book will consist of benefits and costs on a recurring annual basis. That is, the B and the C are fixed amounts per year. If net benefits are positive in any one year then they will be positive in all years. This usually occurs because data on the benefits are difficult to collect. Once it is obtained for one year, expediency leads to it being assumed that the benefits are constant throughout the life of the project.

Consequently, benefit estimates are normally expressed as an annual flow. Operating expenses are also in the nature of a flow. However, a capital expenditure, especially the initial sum needed to initiate the project, is a one-time payment. The issue to be tackled here is: how to convert this capital stock into a flow, so that it can be combined with the operating expenses and deducted from the flow of benefits?

The conversion of the capital cost into a flow is achieved by utilizing the notion of an 'annuity factor' AF. Let C_0 represent the initial capital sum. If E is the equivalent annual cost of the capital (the flow amount we are trying to find), then the relation between stocks and flow is given by

$$C_0 = E.AF \tag{1.8}$$

The annuity factor is just the sum expressed in equation (1.7). That is, it is the present value of a unit stream of effects (benefits or costs, or net benefits). We can see in equation (1.7) that the value of AF depends on two factors, namely: (a) how long the stream is presumed to take place T, and (b) the interest rate i. Sets of tables exist for all combinations of time horizons and interest rates. The simplest case is when an infinite horizon for the project is assumed. For then the AF is the reciprocal of the interest rate: $AF = 1/i$. This was the annuity (strictly, 'perpetuity') case represented in equation (1.6) when discounting was introduced into the particular CBA model in section 1.2.5.

To see how this capital conversion works in practice, consider Hau's (1990) evaluation of the Hong Kong electronic road-pricing system. (This issue will be covered in greater detail in Chapter 5.) All value figures are in 1985 HK dollars (HK\$7.8 = US\$1). Hong Kong experienced severe road congestion during peak periods. Between 1983–85, private vehicles were required to fit a video-cassette-sized electronic number plate. This enabled one to record the number of times a vehicle passed various toll sites. Thus charges could be assessed on those vehicles that contribute most to the congestion.

The annual operating costs of the road-pricing system were $20 million. To establish the toll sites and purchase the electronic number plates involved a one-time capital expenditure of $240 million. To find the total annual cost, the capital expenditure had to be converted to an annual flow. In terms of equation (1.8), C_0 = $240 million. i was effectively set by Hau at 0.125 which made the AF = 8 using the annuity formulation (i.e., 1/0.125). Equation (1.8) can be rearranged to state that $E = C_0/AF$. Since C_0/AF = $240/8 million, the annual capital equivalent E was $30 million. The annual capital charge added to the operating expenses made the total annual cost of the road-pricing scheme $50 million.

1.4   Applications: health-care evaluations

In this section, we present applications that relate just to the simplest version of CBA as set out in the two equations (1.1) and (1.6). That is, we look at the difference between (discounted) benefits and costs, while ignoring distribution and the social cost of public funds. (Ignoring these issues means setting the weights and the *MCF* equal to one.) All of these other issues will have applications in subsequent chapters. The simplest, economic efficiency, case is in fact the norm in the field of health care evaluations. So it makes sense to start with applications in this area. In the process we can cover and compare the different ways of carrying out an economic evaluation. (This section relies heavily on Drummond et al., 1987.)

An economic evaluation tries to assess the efficiency of a programme relative to some other alternative. If no other alternative is being considered, then the programme is being described, but not evaluated. Prior to an evaluation, one must always check the effectiveness of the programmes. That is, does the treatment actually have an effect on the complaint. As Drummond et al. emphasize, 'there is no point in carrying out an ineffective programme efficiently'.

Table 1.1   Categories of costs and consequences

Costs	Effects	Utilities	Benefits
1. Direct	Health effects	Health effects	1. Direct
2. Indirect	in natural	in quality-	2. Indirect
3. Intangible	units	adjusted life	3. Intangible
		years	

Source: Drummond et al. (1987)

A health-care programme transforms resources consumed into health improvements. The resources consumed are the costs (C). The health improvements are the consequences, and these are expressed in terms of either effects (E), utilities (U) or benefits (B). Schematically the pattern is represented in Table 1.1.

With these categories as ingredients, we can now explain the four main types of technique used in health-care evaluations.

1.4.1 Cost minimization (CM)

A measurement of the costs is the common ingredient in all the four evaluation methods. Costs are usually measured by market prices. The main non-market cost involves volunteer labour. Direct costs are the health-care costs (though health administrators often use the term direct to refer to operating costs and use the term indirect costs to refer to shared overheads). Indirect costs are the production losses (forgone income). (Whether to include indirect costs or not is a controversial issue in health-care evaluations. This explains, to a certain extent, why there is more than one evaluation method.) Current practice in the *New England Journal of Medicine* is typically to discount costs using a 5 per cent rate (within a range which has 0 per cent as a lower bound and 10 per cent as an upper bound). The evaluations are usually presented in constant costs.

There are two main issues on the cost side:

i. How to allocate overheads. Overheads (hospital administration, laundry, medical records, cleaning, power, and so on) are usually allocated by some formula related to the usage by the particular programme under review. For instance, the hospital patient days attributable to the programme (as a proportion of the total number of hospital days) can be applied to total hospital expenditures to obtain the hospital cost of the programme.

ii. How to deal with capital costs. The best method of allowing for capital costs was explained in section 1.3.2. That is, they can be converted into an equivalent annual basis, by using the formula in equation (1.8). To illustrate the method once again, but this time where the time horizon is not infinite, consider the evaluation of long-term oxygen treatments by Lowsen et al. (1981). The general formula for the *AF* (the sum of the series represented by equation (1.7)) is

$$AF = \frac{1-(1+i)^{-T}}{i} \qquad (1.9)$$

With a five-year time horizon ($T = 5$) and a discount rate of 7 per cent ($i = 0.07$), the annuity factor that results from equation (1.9) is 4.1002. The cost of buying the liquid oxygen delivery system was £2 153. So, using equation

(1.8), E = £2 153/4.1002 = £525 per annum. With operating costs of £662, the total annual cost for liquid oxygen was £1 187 (in 1978 UK prices).

A cost-minimization study involves judging/assuming that the effects of different health treatments are the same, and then finding the cost of each treatment. One then selects the method that produces the effect for the lowest cost. We illustrate cost minimization by considering the full Lowson et al. study of long-term, at-home oxygen therapy.

There were three main methods of long-term treatment with oxygen in the home. The three methods of delivery were: cylinder oxygen, liquid oxygen, and oxygen from concentrators. Lowson reported that each seemed to be equally effective. Capital costs were converted to an equivalent annual basis. There were two sizes of cylinder to consider. Concentrators were more capital intensive and, because of the fixed cost of maintenance, sensitive to the number of patients served. Two sets of assumption were adopted for the maintenance of the concentrators. Assumption A assumed full capacity in the workshop, and B assumed spare capacity. The cost per patient of all methods (and all variants) is shown below in Table 1.2 (in 1980 prices).

Table 1.2   Annual costs per patient for oxygen (in pounds)

Number of patients	Cylinders		Liquid oxygen	Concentrators	
	Small	Large		A	B
1	3 640	2 215	1 486	16 069	9 072
5	3 640	2 215	1 486	3 545	2 145
10	3 640	2 215	1 486	1 982	1 279
20	3 640	2 215	1 486	1 196	846

Source: Lowson et al. (1981)

All treatment modes had constant costs per patient except for concentrators. The results show that the number of patients being served is one of the key influences of the relative costs of the delivery methods. Liquid oxygen was the cheapest method for less than 8 patients, concentrators serviced by alternative B for 8 to 13 patients, and concentrators (irrespective of the method of servicing) for any number above 13. The National Health System was at that time using small cylinders, the most expensive method!

1.4.2   Cost-effectiveness analysis (CEA)

This looks at both the consequences as well as the costs. On the consequences side programmes must either have a main objective in common (for example, detection of a disease) or have many objectives achieved to the same extent.

Unlike CM, one can compare across programmes. Moreover, one can allow for the fact that different programmes achieve their objectives to different degrees. Thus, for instance, the cost per case detected can be used to make comparisons. So if one screening programme can detect more cases than another, this is allowed for in the comparison. For CM one must have a given/fixed level of output. The consequence can be an input (frequency that medication is taken) or a final output (year of life gained).

Stason and Weinstein (1977) imply that there are some in the health-care field who are unsure whether the consequences should be discounted or not. But, clearly, discounting should take place. Stason and Weinstein make the case for discounting on consistency grounds. Costs are being discounted. Not to discount on the output side would distort the constancy assumed between dollars and health benefits in any year. Moreover, Drummond et al. (1987) make the point that if a programme gives $1 benefits each year into perpetuity, then this would be desirable whatever the size of the initial capital sum. As this cannot be correct, they also conclude that discounting of consequences must take place.

This technique, and the other two remaining methods, will be illustrated by Boyle et al.'s (1983) study of neo-natal intensive care in Canada. (All monetary figures cited are in Canadian dollars.) The provision of neo-natal intensive care involves increased current capital expenditures (to control the respiratory, nutritional and environmental circumstances of the baby) in order to increase a baby's future survival chances. The cost and consequences for babies with birth weight 1 000–1 499 gm are listed in Table 1.3 below (all figures are undiscounted).

Table 1.3   Evaluation of neo-natal intensive care treatment

Cost or consequence	Before intensive care	With intensive care	Incremental cost or effect
1. Cost per live birth (to hospital discharge)	$5 400	$14 200	$8 800
2. Cost per live birth (to death)	$92 500	$100 100	$7 600
3. Survival rate (to hospital discharge)	62.4%	77.2%	14.8%
4. Survival time (per live birth):			
a. Life-years	38.8	47.7	8.9
b. QALYs	27.4	36.0	8.6
5. Earnings per live birth (to death)	$122 200	$154 500	$32 300

Source: Boyle et al. (1983)

The cost effectiveness of neo-natal intensive care can be indicated in a number of forms, depending on how one specifies the unit of output, that is, the increased survival chances. If one measures output by looking at the increased number of survivors, then the CE ratio would be $8 800/0.148 = $59 459. This is obtained by dividing line 1 by line 3 in the table. An incremental cost of $8 800 leads to a 14.8 per cent chance of saving the baby's life to hospital discharge (roughly, a 1 in 7 chance). It would therefore cost almost 7 times as much as $8 800 to ensure the certain survival of a baby, and this is what the $59 459 represents.

Alternatively, one can look at the number of extra years that a baby is expected to live/survive including the period after hospital discharge (that is, till death). In which case the CE ratio would be $7 600/8.9 = $853.9. For this figure, line 2 was divided by line 4a. Line 4a shows a baby would live on average an extra 8.9 years if it were given treatment in an intensive care unit. The additional cost to death (including services given at home as well as at the hospital initially) was $7 600. This sum spread out over the 8.9 years produced the $853.9 cost per life year saved amount. (Incidently, the discounted CE ratio (at a 5 per cent rate) was $2 900 per life year saved.)

1.4.3   cost-utility analysis (CUA)

A CUA can be viewed as a CEA that has output measured in only one kind of dimension, a quality adjusted life year (QALY). We have just seen with the neo-natal intensive care study that this treatment increased a baby's expected life by 8.9 years. A CUA attempts to adjust these years for the average utility of each year. This is usually done on a scale of 1 (the utility from a year of normal health) to 0 (the utility from being dead). Negative values would indicate a state worse than being dead. Boyle et al.'s (1983) adjustment effectively averaged out to around 0.7. (This was obtained by using method 1 described below.) The change in quality adjusted life years was 8.6 years (see line 4b) and the cost was $7 600 (see line 2). The (undiscounted) CU ratio was therefore $7 600/8.6 = $883.7. (The discounted CU ratio was $3 200 per quality adjusted life year saved.)

One can obtain the utility values in three main ways:

1. By reference to the literature. An important study was by Torrance et al. (1982). They classified health states by four attributes, each with a given number of levels: physical function (6 levels), role function (5 levels), social–emotional (4 levels) and health problem (8 levels). Overall, there were 960 possible health states. The utility level for a health state is obtained by multiplying the 4 utility levels that correspond to each attribute level. That is, the utility level is given by the formula:

$$U = 1.42(m_1, m_2, m_3, m_4) - 0.42 \qquad (1.10)$$

where U is the utility of a health state, and m_i is the utility for the level of attribute i. If the individual has the highest health level for all four attributes, then each $m_i = 1$ and the utility level would be 1 ($1.42 - 0.42$). If all attributes are zero, then the utility level would be -0.42, which means that the individual would be in so much pain that it was worse than being dead. (Note that a negative value was actually assigned to some babies in the Boyle et al. study, although the average value was plus 0.7.)

2. By the analyst making a personal judgement. For example, in the hypertension study by Stason and Weinstein (1977), they adjusted life years saved by 1 per cent for the adverse side-effects that taking medication imposes.

3. By measuring the utility for the particular study itself. The three main methods are: a rating scale, a standard gamble and a time trade-off. All three rely on individual answers to a questionnaire. For the first, the individual is asked (on a scale of normal health being 1, and the worst state being 0) where the individual places a particular health state (for example, being confined to bed for 3 months with a kidney machine). The second is the von Neumann–Morgenstern test, where the individual rates a particular health state, which is considered to be certain, against the probability of winning a lottery where normal health is the main prize (valued at 1) and death is the loss (valued at 0). Say the individual judges that s/he would accept an 80 per cent chance of living normally (and thereby accepting a 20 per cent chance of dying) as equivalent in satisfaction to living with arthritis that could not be treated. The 0.8 probability would then mean that the utility value of living with arthritis was 0.8. This follows because living normally is valued at 1.0 and an 80 per cent chance of having this equals 0.8. For the third method, the individual is asked to equate months of normal health against a full year with a particular health state. If the individual would equate a year having diabetes with 10 months of normal health then the utility value of living a year with diabetes would be 10 over 12 (or, 0.83).

The advantage of a CUA is that it is well suited to deal with the quantity/quality of life issue in treatments. That is, a treatment may prolong life, but with unpleasant consequences. Many environmental effects of a project are really quality of life issues and to date these effects have often been ignored in economic evaluations. But, the disadvantage is that one cannot say from a CUA whether a treatment is socially worthwhile. For example, the result of the intensive care treatment was that a quality adjusted year of life could be saved for $3 200 (discounted). Only by a comparison with other kinds of treatments can one say whether this is a high or a low value.

1.4.4   Cost–benefit analysis (CBA)

In this method the consequences are expressed in monetary terms. They are thereby made commensurate with the costs. This means that one can calculate the net benefits of the procedure. Hence only CBA can ascertain whether a project should be undertaken. However, there has been a tendency to measure only those effects that one can easily measure in monetary terms, such as the earnings of those affected (to measure the indirect benefits). Consequently intangibles are often ignored.

Under the human capital approach, one's earnings are meant to reflect a person's productivity. A health intervention by restoring a person's productivity thereby provides a benefit to society. This approach ignores the preferences of the individual him/herself, and clearly does not fit in with the usual welfare economic base behind CBA which is based on an individual's willingness to pay. Nonetheless, this is the main method for measuring the benefits used in the health-care field. We will adopt this approach here just in order to compare it with the other forms of evaluation.

For the neo-natal intensive care treatment, the benefits were the extra earnings that accrued from the 8.9 years of extra life. This amounted to $32 300 (see line 5 of Table 1.3). The costs were $7 600 (from line 2), which meant that the net benefits were +$24 700 when undiscounted. However, when discounted at 5 per cent, the net-benefits were –$2 600. This result was basically due to the fact that the benefits accrue after 27.4 years have elapsed (the life expectancy in the absence of intensive care treatment) and are therefore worth less in today-value terms, while the costs were incurred immediately. The treatment was therefore not socially worthwhile.

To summarize: when the consequence is identical for different treatments, then cost minimization is the appropriate technique. When the consequence is the same type of effect, but varies in magnitude among alternatives, then a cost-effectiveness analysis is valid. For treatments that have a common effect that is expressed in terms of a quality adjusted life year, a cost-utility analysis should be used. Finally, if one wishes to know not only which treatment is most cost effective, but whether any of them are socially worthwhile, then a CBA is necessary. In this case, a method must be found for expressing both benefits and costs in monetary terms in order to see which is larger.

The health-care field has worked with a variety of non-CBA techniques because there are misgivings about the standard way of putting monetary values on benefits. But, that is not an inherent weakness of CBA. On the whole (and some exceptions will be highlighted later in the book) the willingness-to-pay approach is a more suitable valuation methodology than the human capital approach. Which is, of course, not to say that there are no measurement and valuation problems in CBA. We emphasize only that: (a) there is no alternative to using CBA if one wishes to tell whether any project is worthwhile even if it is cost effective, and (b) there are alternative methods available for placing monetary values on the benefits and they will be illustrated extensively throughout the book.

1.5 Overview of the book
Many of the applications used in the book will draw from the revealed preference approach to estimation. We begin therefore with an outline of the fundamentals of this approach. Then we list the main theoretical concepts that will be covered and indicate briefly how they fit together to form a unified approach to public policy decision-making.

1.5.1 *Revealed preference applications*
To estimate the unknowns in the CBA model, whether they be value parameters or measures of the costs and benefits themselves, the revealed preference approach will be the main approach to estimation. Since this will appear in a number of the applications throughout the book, it is useful to explain the basic ideas behind this methodology. We do this by first showing that the approach is a standard one to parameter estimation in applied microeconomics generally. Then we extend the approach to the policy sphere.

A core topic in applied economics is demand estimation (see, for example, Deaton and Muellbauer, 1980). Say Q is the quantity purchased of a particular commodity, P is the price consumers paid, and Y is their income. The theoretical specification of the demand curve may appear as:

$$Q = \beta_0 + \beta_1 P + \beta_2 Y \tag{1.11}$$

On the basis of data on Q, P and Y, an appropriate statistical technique can be used to derive estimates of the β coefficients. Focus on the coefficient attached to the price variable, that is, β_1. If both P and Q were entered in log form, β_1 would indicate the (own) price elasticity of demand.

A useful way of interpreting the demand estimation process is to suggest that, through the purchasing choices made, the behaviour of consumers *reveals* their preferences (see Ben-Akiva and Lerman, 1985). The price elasticity of demand is thereby revealed from the data on the actual purchases made by consumers. Another way of expressing the same idea is to say that the coefficient reflect the preferences implicit in market behaviour.

Using this same interpretation of statistical estimation, we can treat choices made by government decision-makers as revealing their preferences. For example, if we take the CBA model expressed in equation (1.2) and postulate that government decisions D were based on this criterion, then the following relationship can be specified:

$$D = a_2B - a_1C \qquad (1.12)$$

With data on the past decisions made, and measures of B and C, estimation now reveals the values of the distribution weights that were implicit in those past decisions. Alternatively, if we can construct a formula for the weights, then B and C would then be the unknowns. Estimation this time would reveal the implicit values of the benefit and cost categories.

The revealed preference approach is therefore very general. The only real difference between its use in policy analysis (from its standard use in microeconomics) is that the dependent variable will usually be qualitative rather than continuously variable. That is, D will be a categorical variable that takes the value 1 when a project has been approved in the past, and takes a value of 0 when the project was rejected. This is in contrast to the standard case where purchasing decisions can be any number (provided that it is a non-negative integer). This difference is not a problem, however, as statistical techniques (such as Logit and Probit) for dealing with categorical dependent variables are well established. The advantages and disadvantages of the revealed preference approach will be discussed as the applications are presented.

1.5.2   Chapter content

The book is divided into five parts. The first, consisting of the introductory Chapter 1, has just been presented. Part II covers the welfare economic base to CBA. Chapter 2 covers the efficiency-based compensation test that attempts to identify when a potential welfare improvement will result from the introduction of a public project. The test is based on the willingness to pay of project beneficiaries and losers and, for small projects, these can be measured by market prices (if a market exists). Certain well-known inconsistencies of the test are then exposed. In recognition of the fact that willingness to pay is partially dependent upon ability to pay, distributional weights need to be attached to the willingness to pay of the various groups affected. But, even with these weights, the tests are still concerned only with potential rather than actual welfare improvements. This raises the issue whether the compensation tests need to be extended further to incorporate a third social objective – the number of uncompensated losers. Chapter 3 recognizes that, for large projects, market prices understate willingness to pay. Consumer (and producer) surpluses need to be added. The different kinds of surplus are then explained and once more distributional weights are added.

Part III deals with all the cases where market prices are inadequate reflections of social value. Chapter 4 presents the general principles for using social (or, shadow) prices rather than market prices. The emphasis is on measuring social values directly, without reference to market prices. The subsequent chapters then focus on cases where clearly identified special problems with using market prices are recognized. In these cases, market prices are to be adjusted or supplemented, but not necessarily completely replaced. Chapter 5 explains that when external effects are present, there are third parties involved. Their willingness to pay must be considered alongside the direct beneficiaries and losers. Linked to the idea of an externality is the presence of pure public goods and this is covered in Chapter 6. By treating income redistribution as a pure public good we show that third-party preferences also need to be consulted when deciding whether to redistribute income in-kind rather than cash. Externalities, in all the many forms, thus provide one of the main reasons why market prices diverge from social values.

The next two cases where market prices are poor indicators of social value occur when markets are 'missing'. There are incomplete markets for state contingent claims (outcomes that are dependent on states of nature outside our control). Chapter 7 therefore examines the question as to how to allow for uncertainty when making public investment decisions. Again, for projects that produce intangible benefits or costs, there are no markets to use even if one wanted to use them. Chapter 8 shows the main techniques available for valuing intangibles. There is no more fundamental intangible valuation issue than how to value a life that may be lost as a byproduct of undertaking a public project. The various ways of valuing a human life are detailed and an alternative approach based on replacing monetary values with time units is outlined. The last case requiring adjustment to market prices is because there are costs involved with raising the revenue to pay for projects, in addition to those directly related to the project itself. An analysis is therefore provided in Chapter 9 of the welfare cost of raising public funds.

Part IV, is devoted to the meaning, determination and usefulness of the distributional weights. This area is a controversial one and thus all views on the issue will be represented. Chapter 10 deals with weights in an intragenerational context (rich versus poor). Chapter 11 covers the weights in an intergenerational context (consumption today versus consumption in the future) which is the social discount rate issue.

Part V completes the book by looking at how the basic CBA model can be extended. We relax the assumption that repayments are outside the control of the person responsible for making the public investment decision. There is a great deal of current interest in employing user prices as a way of financing public projects. The implications of this will be fully analysed in the final chapter.

1.6 Final comments
We conclude this chapter (and all others in the book) with a summary and a set of problems.

1.6.1 Summary
We began by setting out the basic cost–benefit model and provided an overview of the particular CBA model that will be used extensively throughout the book.

The main ingredients of a CBA are the benefits B, the costs C, the set of distribution weights (represented by the a's), the marginal cost of public funds MCF and the social discount rate i. All of these ingredients will be given individual attention later in the book.

A knowledge of discounting is an important background skill in CBA, so this introductory chapter gave it special emphasis. We presented the discounting process from first principles. Then we explained how it plays a crucial role in converting a capital sum into a flow. This conversion is necessary to put the capital expenditures in comparable units to the other main component of total costs, that is, the operating expenses.

The applications part of the chapter covered the four main techniques of economic evaluation used in the area of health care evaluations. These applications were chosen because: (a) they highlighted only some of the necessary ingredients for a CBA, and thus required only the minimum exposure to the theory behind CBA, yet (b) they nonetheless did illustrate the many different ways economic evaluations can be carried out in practice.

The chapter closed with an overview of the rest of the book. Many of the applications rely on the revealed preference approach and this method was sketched out. Basically, in a statistical equation where the dependent variable is past decisions, and the independent variables are determinants of decisions, the coefficients in these equations estimate the unknowns, whether they be value parameters (such as the distribution weights) or implicit values of the benefits and costs themselves. Finally, a list was given of how the analysis of the main ingredients of a CBA are spread out over the next 11 chapters. Chapters 2–9 identify how to estimate the B and C. Chapter 10 covers the a's, and Chapter 11 deals with i. The last chapter deals with situations where the main ingredients have to be reassembled to correspond to different decision-making settings.

1.6.2   Problems

The following three problems relate to one of the main themes stressed in this chapter, namely discounting. We wish to highlight the three equations that were used to explain discounting, that is, (1.6), (1.8) and (1.9).

1.   By observing equation (1.6) (or by considering the difference it made to the NPV in section 1.3.1 when a discount rate of 25 per cent was used instead of 10 per cent), what is the relation between the NPV and i? How does this relationship explain why there is so much controversy over the size of the social discount rate? (Hint: if you were a politician who favoured private rather than public investment, would you prefer a large or a small value for i to be used in the evaluation of public investment projects?)
2.   Use equation (1.9) to confirm the formulation given in (1.6), that if the time horizon for a public project is infinite, then the AF is $1/i$ and the NPV of

the benefit stream is therefore B/i. (Hint: what happens to the value of $(1 + i)^{-T}$ as T gets larger and larger?)

3. Consult the figures for the capital expenditures conversion application related to the Lowson et al. (1981) evaluation of the liquid oxygen system given in section 1.4.1. If instead of converting the capital expenditures to a flow, one were to convert the operating costs of £662 to a stock, what would be the present value of the total cost stream? (Hint: use equation (1.8), but this time treat the operating expenses as if they were the flow variable E and C_0 were the present value of the operating expenses. Then add the present value of the operating expenses to the capital expenditure figure.)

1.7 Appendix

The task is to derive equation (1.6) from first principles. In the process, we show how equations (1.7) and (1.9) fit into the discounting process.

Assume that the costs C occur in the current period ($t = 0$) and that there are a stream of benefits of B_t, where t is from years $t = 1$ to the terminal year $t = T$. The sum of discounted net benefits (the NPV) would be

$$NPV = -C + \frac{B_1}{(1+i)} + \frac{B_2}{(1+i)^2} + \cdots + \frac{B_T}{(1+i)^T} \qquad (1.13)$$

Now let the benefits be the same in each year, equal to B. The NPV becomes

$$NPV = -C + \frac{B}{(1+i)} + \frac{B}{(1+i)^2} + \cdots + \frac{B}{(1+i)^T} \qquad (1.14)$$

which, by collecting terms in B, simplifies to

$$NPV = -C + B\left[\frac{1}{(1+i)} + \frac{1}{(1+i)^2} + \cdots + \frac{1}{(1+i)^T}\right] \qquad (1.15)$$

The term in the square brackets of equation (1.15) is equation (1.7) in the text. Call this sum S. That is

$$S = \frac{1}{(1+i)} + \frac{1}{(1+i)^2} + \cdots + \frac{1}{(1+i)^T} \qquad (1.16)$$

Using S, equation (1.15) reduces to

$$NPV = -C + B[S] \qquad (1.17)$$

So all we need to do now is solve for S. Multiply both sides of equation (1.16) by $1/(1 + i)$ to get

$$S\left[\frac{1}{(1+i)}\right] = \frac{1}{(1+i)^2} + \frac{1}{(1+i)^3} + \cdots + \frac{1}{(1+i)^{T+1}} \qquad (1.18)$$

Subtracting (1.18) from (1.16) produces

$$S\left[1 - \frac{1}{(1+i)}\right] = \frac{1}{(1+i)} - \frac{1}{(1+i)^{T+1}} \qquad (1.19)$$

Dividing both sides of this equation by $1 - [1/(1 + i)]$ results in

$$S = \frac{1}{i} - \frac{1}{i.(1+i)^T} \qquad (1.20)$$

The right-hand side of (1.20) is exactly the annuity factor AF given by equation (1.9) in the text. The perpetuity case is when T is large (it approaches infinity). Then $1/(1 + i)^T$ approaches zero and equation (1.20) becomes

$$S = \frac{1}{i} \qquad (1.21)$$

Substituting for (1.21) in (1.17) produces the perpetuity case, which is equation (1.6) in the text.

PART II

2 Compensation tests

2.1 Introduction

As emphasized in Chapter 1, it is impossible to make public policy decisions without making value judgements. Economists typically rely on the idea of a Pareto improvement. The first task in the introductory section will be to explain fully the strengths, weaknesses and implications of adopting the Paretian value judgements. When Pareto improvements exist, it is possible to compensate all losers from projects. Hence, there is a strong link between applying compensation tests when evaluating public projects and adopting the Paretian value judgements of traditional welfare economics. The rationale of compensation tests is therefore the next topic covered. When the explanations concerning Pareto improvements and compensation tests are complete, one should have a clear understanding of what economists mean when they say that a policy change is 'efficient'.

The second section analyses compensation tests and the distribution of income. In practice, actual compensation can not always be carried out. The 'new' welfare economists tried to extend the Pareto framework to deal with situations where compensation would be hypothetical only; compensation could take place, but need not actually occur to sanction the project. The modern literature takes exception to this extension. If compensation does not occur, and the losers are low income, then the distribution of income could get worse. This would constitute a distributional argument against the project. The fate of the project, in the modern view, depends on trading off the distributional loss against the efficiency gain. The trade-off is achieved by setting, and applying, the distribution weights. The modern approach therefore requires working with a two-social-objectives criterion for CBA.

Even with distributional and efficiency factors, the list of necessary value judgements for CBA is not yet complete. Weights do address the distributional issue; but they do not deal with the absence of compensation *per se*. In most cases (and, ironically, there is no provision to compensate *at all* in the modern approach) there will be losers. Since it is socially undesirable to have losers, whether these losers be poor or not, the final section of the theory for this chapter further extends the CBA criterion. The number of uncompensated losers from a project is to be a third social objective, in addition to efficiency and distribution.

The applications focus mainly on the efficiency aspects of the theory. We first see how one study proceeded when, as often occurs in the health-care field, one of the main Paretian value judgements is questionable. In the next two applications, we try to get an appreciation of why compensation can not always be expected to be carried out. The last application presents a case where the number of uncompensated losers did influence actual CBA decisions.

2.1.1   Pareto improvements

Mishan (1976, p. 101) has written that 'Cost–Benefit Analysis has been founded on the principle of a virtual Pareto improvement'. Although we will reinterpret this to state that *traditional* CBA has been founded on this principle, a Pareto improvement *is* fundamental to CBA because it helps to define an efficient project. Distribution is an additional objective in the 'modern' approach (Irvin (1978), calls his CBA text *Modern Cost–Benefit Methods*). But the distribution weights are applied to the efficiency effects and therefore these efficiency effects are still the starting point for a project evaluation.

Millward (1971) explains that there are really four Pareto value judgements that underlie the concept of a Pareto improvement:

i.   an individualistic conception of social welfare;
ii.   non-economic causes of welfare can be ignored;
iii. consumer sovereignty;
iv.   Pareto optimality.

We will explain and discuss each of these value judgements in turn.

An individualistic conception of social welfare   We want the project to make society better off, that is, increase social welfare. The first Pareto value judgement states that to make society better off, one must first make individuals better off. This individualistic postulate seems obvious and is ingrained in the Western way of thinking. But not all societies have endorsed this view of social welfare. A communist country would postulate the existence of a 'state' that is separate from the individuals who comprise that country. In such a country, planners try to give expression to the state's preferences.

In this book, we follow the mainstream and accept the first Paretian value judgement. This is true even when we incorporate distributional considerations. The distributional weights will originate from interdependent individual utility functions. It is because individuals have preferences for redistribution that we will be incorporating this as a social objective.

Non-economic causes of welfare can be ignored   If it is necessary to make individuals better off in order to make society better off, the next step is to find out how to make these individuals better off. In economics, it is standard to state that a person's level of satisfaction (i.e., utility) is determined only by the set of goods and services that are consumed. Non-economic factors are either assumed to change and have a small impact on utility; or they have a potentially large impact, but are assumed not to change. The extent of freedom and democracy is not something that economists usually need to consider when evaluating a project.

In the past, the World Bank have been involved with financing large dams in a number of developing countries. These dams have displaced many people from their homes and have had numerous adverse effects on the environment. Due to much recent political opposition to these large-scale dams, psychologists, environmentalists, sociologists and others are now to be integrated into the review process (see World Bank, 1990). Clearly, large-scale dams are one area where the economist's assumption concerning the utility function is not acceptable. But CBA always works best when one is working in a partial equilibrium setting. Here the project does not affect the prices of other goods and one does not need to record the reverse (feedback) impact of a changed economy on the inputs and outputs of the project.

Consumer sovereignty 'Consumer sovereignty' requires that individuals are to be the best judge of their own welfare. Thus, the goods and services that affect individual utility functions are to be chosen by them (not, chosen for them). Mooney (1986) argues that three questions have to be answered in the affirmative for consumer sovereignty to be valid.

i.   Do individuals *accept* that they are the best person to judge their own welfare?
ii. Are individuals *able* to judge their own welfare?
iii. Do individuals *want* to make the appropriate judgements?

In the context of health care in which Mooney was discussing matters, consumer sovereignty is not obviously desirable. When individuals are not the best judge, then someone else has to make the judgements. In health care there is a ready alternative to the individual, namely, the doctor. Thus some people think that the 'doctor knows best'. In which case they do not accept their own judgements. Also, the doctor knows more about medicine than the individual, and so some individuals might think they lack the ability to make informed judgements. Finally, some individuals would prefer that the doctor make the judgements even when they accept that they are able to make the judgements. This might occur when unpleasant choices need to be made (such as whether to remove a life-support system from a brain-dead relative).

Later in this chapter we will cover the case of mental patients. Certainly the law does not accept that they are the best judge of their welfare. We will therefore show how one study dealt with the difficult case of evaluating a project when consumer sovereignty is in question But, on the whole (the social discount rate issue will be a major exception), we will accept that individuals are the best judge of their welfare. This is due not to any enthusiasm with this postulate. It is because the alternative view, that someone other than the individual knows better than the individual, is even more problematical as it is basically undemocratic.

Pareto optimality   The final step is to ascertain when social welfare has actually improved given changes in individual welfare. Society is better off when a change (a project) makes one individual better off, and no one is made worse off. In this case a 'Pareto improvement' has resulted. If all possible Pareto improvements have been implemented, then 'Pareto optimality' has been achieved. In other words, there is Pareto optimality when there are no Pareto improving projects remaining.

The desirability of Pareto improvements is not often in dispute (outside the health-care field). The case where individuals are envious seems to be an exception. For if one is made better off, then someone else (the envious person) automatically is made worse off. But, as Ng (1983) points out, this is not really an exception. If people are envious, they are worse off, and thus a Pareto improvement did not exist. So this does not imply that, if one did exist, it would be undesirable.

The main problem is whether, in practice, Pareto-improving projects can be found. It is hard to think of any significant project where there would be no losers. As we shall see in the next sections, the literature tried to extend the fourth Pareto value judgement to cases where there were losers. It is in this context where most of the controversy arises.

2.1.2   Compensation tests

Compensation tests are concerned with ensuring that Pareto improvements can be derived from economic changes that generate positive net benefits. These tests focus on the requirement that for a Pareto improvement *ultimately* there should be no losers. When a project takes place, there will always be some costs. Those who incur the costs (and do not share the benefits) are the (initial) losers. By definition, if a project has positive net benefits, then the benefits are greater than the costs. This automatically means, therefore, that the size of the benefits is greater than the amount that the losers have to give up. If part of the benefits are used to compensate the project losers then, after the compensation, no one ultimately is made worse off by the project. Similarly, having positive net benefits automatically means that there is something positive left over after compensation. So someone can gain. We get the result that with positive net benefits, someone can gain and no one need lose. In other words, there will be a Pareto improvement.

A good way to understand this point is to recognize that the first efficiency theorem of welfare economics (that perfectly competitive markets are Pareto optimal) can be interpreted in compensation test terms. A competitive market is in equilibrium where demand (*D*) equals supply (*S*). A derivation of the demand curve will be given in the next chapter. Here we just point out that it shows how much consumers are willing to pay for each unit of output. (In this chapter we assume that what individuals are willing to pay for a project is what they are willing to accept to forgo the project. In general this will not be the case and this distinction is covered in full in the next chapter.) *S* is the marginal cost (*MC*) curve in perfect competition. It indicates the value of resources that have to be forgone in order to produce the extra unit of output. The theorem says that at the market equilibrium, Pareto optimality holds.

Why should this be the case? Consider an output Q_1 below the equilibrium quantity Q_e in diagram 2.1. At Q_1, the price that consumers are willing to pay (P_1 on the *D* curve) is greater than the marginal cost (MC_1 on the S curve). The gainers (the consumers) can compensate the losers (the owners of the resources given up) to produce more of the good and there is some positive gain left over (the amount P_1 minus MC_1). Output will increase. At Q_e, the marginal gain (the price P_e) equals the marginal cost and there are no more possibilities for the gainers to compensate the losers. That is, we have a Pareto optimum.

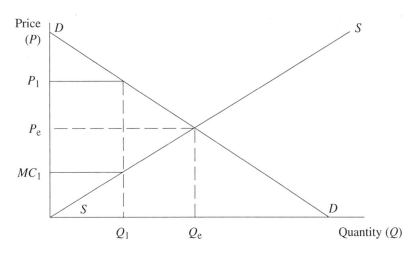

A market allocates resources according to demand and supply. At Q_1 the consumers are willing to pay P_1 on the demand curve, while costs are only MC_1. There is a positive difference P_1MC_1 whereby someone could be made better off and no one worse off. Only at the market equilibrium quantity Q_e will there be no possibilities for such a Pareto improvement.

Diagram 2.1

The conclusion, therefore, is that the competitive market mechanism, that determines output and price on the basis of demand and supply, operates basically as a compensation test. This explains why a lot of professional economists put their faith in the market as an instrument for determining public policy decisions. We will be using the competitive equilibrium as a starting point for our analysis in many chapters. But, as we shall see now (and throughout this book), there are social considerations not reflected in markets. So public policy needs to have a wider framework than that represented by competitive markets.

2.2   Compensation tests and the distribution of income

The Pareto test sanctions a change only where no one loses. In practice, there are virtually no policy changes where everybody gains and no one loses. It would be prohibitively costly in administrative terms to compensate everyone who might lose. How the CBA literature planned to deal with situations where losers may exist will now be discussed.

2.2.1   The Kaldor–Hicks compensation test

The new welfare economists tried to avoid making interpersonal comparisons (judgements that say that a gain of $1 to one person is worth more than a loss of $1 to someone else). They hoped to do this by extending the Pareto test. The Kaldor–Hicks test relied on a *potential* Pareto improvement. They argued that it would be sufficient that the size of the benefits be such that the gainers could compensate the losers, though the compensation did not actually have to be carried out. This test is also called the overcompensation test, because the gainers can compensate the losers and have something positive left over. The formal statement of the test is:

> an economic allocation of resources *x* is superior to an allocation *y* if, and only if, it is possible to reach an allocation *z* through redistribution from *x* such that *z* is preferred to *y* according to the Pareto test.

This new test can be explained in terms of Diagram 2.2. There is a fixed amount of income *Y* to be shared out between two individuals. (We use income rather than utility on the axes because compensation is to be given in income form. However, to use income we must assume that there is no interdependence between utility functions in terms of the income going to different individuals.) Y_a goes to individual A and Y_b goes to individual B. The budget line is given by I in the diagram, i.e., $Y_a + Y_b = Y$. Compare two points (two particular distributions of *Y*) *x* and *y*. For our purposes, *x* is the distribution with the public project, and *y* is the distribution without the project. At *x*, individual A gets more income than at *y*, so s/he is better off at point *x* than point *y*, and would therefore

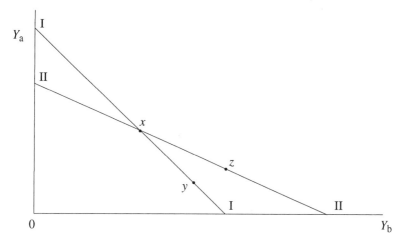

Budget line I is income before the project and II is income after the project. Allocations *x* and *y* are not comparable as there is more Y_a at *x*, but more Y_b at *y*. But, if one could redistribute income along II from *x* to *z*, one can have more Y_a and Y_b at *z* than at *y*. In this sense, *x* is potentially Pareto superior to *y*.

Diagram 2.2

prefer that the project be socially approved. On the other hand, B has more income at *y* than at *x* so s/he is better off at *y*, and would prefer that the project be rejected. Which point (distribution) should society choose? Should the project be approved? An interpersonal comparison would seem to be necessary. But, focus on point *z*. This can be obtained by using (for example) the tax-transfer system to redistribute income. This makes II the new budget line. It is drawn as going through *x* because redistribution is considered to be taking place from this point. If now one were to accept the project (that is, choose point *x*) and if one were then to redistribute income, one could obtain point *z*. At *z*, both A and B have more income than in the without-project state of the world, point *y*. *z* is therefore a potential Pareto improvement (both could be made better off), and the project should therefore be approved. (Note that an actual Pareto improvement would exist if *x* were to lie to the north-east of *y* on the original budget line I. The hypothetical redistribution then would not be necessary.)

2.2.2 Criticisms of compensation tests

There are four main criticisms of compensation tests, whether they be the original Pareto test or the extension:

i.   The Hicks–Kaldor test can lead to inconsistencies when prices change. The public project may be so large that it alters the relative prices of goods. So, the distribution of income (and hence individual willingness to pay and receive compensation) would be different with and without the project. It could happen that, at the old prices (without the project), the gainers could compensate the losers for the change and, at the new prices (with the project), it may be possible that the losers can also compensate the gainers to forgo the change. This is called the 'Scitovsky paradox', and is illustrated in Diagram 2.3. The analysis is the same as before, except that *x* and *y* are not now on the same budget line. (The slope of the budget line reflects the

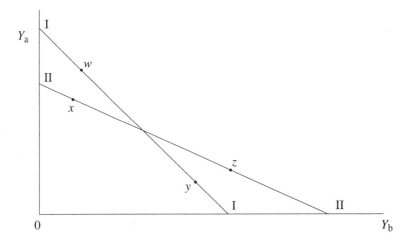

This diagram shows the Scitovsky paradox. The comparison is between allocations *x* and *y*. As before, budget line I exist without the project and budget line II is with the project. *y* is potentially Pareto superior to *x* as one can move along I to *w* and have more income for both individuals. But, *x* is potentially superior to *y* as well, as one can move along II to *z* and have more for both individuals. The paradox is that there is a potential improvement by moving from *x* to *y*, but there is also a potential improvement if one moves back from *y* to *x*.

Diagram 2.3

relative prices that determine the level of income *Y*. With different prices before and after the project, *x* and *y* must lie on different budget lines.) Again one is trying to compare *x* (with the project) with *y* (without the project). As before, we can redistribute *Y* to get to *z* which dominates (is Pareto superior to) *y*. This time, there is also a redistribution through *y* that leads to a point *w* that is superior to *x*. That is, if we reject the project (and hence start at *y*), and if we then redistribute income along II, we can reach the point *w* which is potentially Pareto superior to having the project (point *x*). The paradox is therefore that we can simultaneously have the outcome that the project should be accepted (because z dominates y) *and* the outcome that the project should be rejected (because w dominates x). (To remedy this problem, Scitovsky suggested an alternative test: the gainers must be able to compensate the losers, and the losers must not be able to compensate the gainers. But this can still lead to a paradox when there are more than two options to consider. See Ng, 1983.)

ii. The test can lead to inconsistencies when real income is greatly affected by the change. When the marginal utility of income is not constant, the project generated income alters the monetary expression of preferences, even though the preferences themselves are not altered. There are then two alternative measures of the gains and losses, with and without the large income change. The two measures may lead to different conclusions as to the desirability of the change. Once more, the gainers can compensate the losers to accept the project and the losers can compensate the gainers to forgo the project. (The two measures, the 'compensating' and the 'equilibriating variations', are explained fully in Chapter 3.)

iii. Assume that the inconsistencies given in (i) and (ii) do not apply. There remains a problem even if compensation actually takes place. The willingness to pay of the gainers, and the minimum compensation for the losers, is dependent not only on their preferences, but also their ability to pay. Therefore, the valuations reflect in part the original distribution of income. Since this distribution of income is not optimal, they reflect the status quo. Why should this be a problem for public policy? Obviously, if someone subsists on an income of only $300 per year, which is the per capita income in a number of less-developed countries (LDCs), the most one can be willing to pay for a project will be $300, even if it is a matter of life or death. Consequently, willingness to pay should be weighted, and this is reflected by:

$$a_2 B - a_1 C \qquad (2.1)$$

which is equation (1.2) from Chapter 1.

iv. Even with the distributional weights, the test still defines a hypothetical social improvement. Compensation will not be made and losers will actually exist. Given this, it seems necessary to incorporate formally in our benefit–cost calculation the existence of the number of uncompensated losers. This will now be explained.

2.3 Uncompensated losers and the numbers effect

The modern CBA literature, which requires that distribution weights be included, has focused on the possibility that when losers are poor, the distribution of income is made worse off. Incorporating distribution weights allows this to happen provided that there are sufficiently large efficiency gains to offset the distributional loss. But, what if the losers are not poor, or have the same weight as the losers? The CBA criterion $B - C$ would be indifferent to the number of losers. A third social objective needs to be included to recognize the number of losers.

2.3.1   A re-examination of compensation tests

Weighting benefits and costs as in equation (2.1) still means employing a *hypothetical* compensation test. It requires that weighted benefits must be greater than weighted cost. Compensation could be carried out in the sense that society in the aggregate is compensated in social utility terms. So one has allowed for the fact that losers may be poor, but not for the losers *per se*. What if the losers happen to be non-poor and thereby distribution is not an issue.

Consider a numerical illustration based on Londero (1987, ch. 1). The Kaldor–Hicks test would rank equally two projects, one with benefits of 300 and costs of 200, and a second with benefits of 100 and no costs. Both, would have net-benefits of 100. But, losers exist in the first project and this is given no special recognition.

Clearly, something is missing from the standard compensation tests. A Pareto improvement is fulfilled only if no one is made worse off. If in practice there will be losers, then one is in violation of this principle. This information about losers should be recorded and used to determine the social desirability of a project. Definitionally, losers are uncompensated losers (since if they are compensated they cease to be losers). One way of including the number of uncompensated losers N in our decision-making criterion will now be explained.

2.3.2   Allowing for uncompensated losers

The weighted benefit–cost test, allowing for distribution in-kind as well as cash, was given in Chapter 1 as:

$$a_{2.k}B - a_{2.m}R - a_{1.m}L \qquad (2.2)$$

This can also be interpreted as a compensation test, for if (2.2) is positive then society is potentially better off in terms of a joint consideration for efficiency (willingness to pay) and distribution. To include the third element into the CBA calculation, the numbers effect N can be factored out from (2.2), and separated from the two other objectives with its own weight a_n, to form (2.3):

$$a_{2.k}b - a_{2.m}r - a_{1.m}l - a_nN \qquad (2.3)$$

where the lower-case letters are the corresponding benefits, repayments and financial loss *per person who loses*, i.e., $b = B/N$, $r = R/N$, and $l = L/N$.

You may wonder why it is that, if (2.3) is based on (2.2), there are three objectives represented in (2.3) and not two as in (2.2). It is proved in Brent (1986) that no set of linear distribution weights, that give a higher weight to the low-income group, would produce a positive sign for the weight for the numbers effect a_n in any equation based on (2.1). In other words, if one wishes to use a criterion such as (2.1), and then add a concern for the numbers with low income (those in poverty) as an additional consideration, one ends up giving a perverse (i.e., negative) weight to the numbers in poverty. *Either* distribution is important (the weight on the low-income group is higher than the weight on the richer group) *or* the numbers removed from poverty is important (the weight on this reduction is positive). Both considerations cannot hold at the same time. Adding the numbers effect with the correct sign must therefore be based on a criterion with more than just efficiency and distribution (two objectives). A three-objectives welfare function is implied.

2.3.3   The CBA criterion with the numbers effect

What does it mean when the numbers effect is added to efficiency and distribution to form three social objectives? As we saw in the previous two sections of this chapter, there are two essential features of a two-objectives benefit–cost criterion. It is individualistic and governed by consumer sovereignty. But, these are the main ideas of Jeremy Bentham: 'That man should get what they want and the individual is the best judge of what he wants'. We can then proceed from this to consider Bentham's famous maxim: 'The best society is the one that provides the greatest good for the greatest number'. (Both these quotes are from Barkley and Seckler, 1972.)

One can now interpret the cost–benefit criterion (2.3) in two stages:

i.   The first part of Bentham's maxim relates to Pareto optimality, that is, 'good' occurs (society is better off) when there is a positive difference for equations (2.1) or (2.2). This information is reproduced in the first three components of equation (2.3). Good is then 'greatest' when this positive difference is largest. This is what maximizing net benefits means.

ii. Relaxing the Pareto principle requires adding the second part of his maxim – the greatest good must be for the 'greatest number'. The fourth component in equation (2.3) records this numbers effect in negative terms. That is, the greatest number of beneficiaries exist when the number of uncompensated losers is least. Together, the four components of equation (2.3) therefore represent a plausible, yet measurable, interpretation of Bentham's principle that projects should provide the greatest good for the greatest number.

The reason why the number of losers rather than the number of gainers appears in criterion (2.3) is because Pareto optimality emphasizes this aspect.

Not one individual must lose for a Pareto improvement. Given that losers will exist in practice, it seems necessary to record by how much (i.e., how many) one is departing from this ideal of no losers, and include this as a negative component of the particular project being proposed.

2.4 Applications

Compensation tests require that the social decision-maker accept all four of the Paretian value judgements. Most applications take these assumptions as axiomatic and therefore do not explicitly mention them. In the first application we present a case where the authors implicitly relaxed the value judgement related to consumer sovereignty. The rest of the applications deal with some of the important practical considerations involved with compensation tests in both actual and potential forms, that is, when compensation does and does not take place.

2.4.1 Consumer sovereignty and mental health

Benefits and costs are to reflect individual evaluations. When individuals are the best judge of their own welfare, we can ask what they are willing to pay, or willing to receive as compensation, for the project. But, what should be done if individuals are clearly not the best judge of their welfare, as is the case with patients in mental hospitals? Certainly the law in most countries does not treat them as responsible for their actions. So it would seem to be inappropriate for CBA to base project choices related to mental health options on patient preferences.

The particular choice we will be considering is whether to house a mental patient in a hospital, or allow the person out into the community under supervision. One advantage of permitting patients outside the hospital setting is that they can work and earn income. This consideration is, as we saw in section 1.4.4, central to the traditional (human capital) approach to health care evaluations, which measures economic benefits in terms of production effects (lifetime earnings of those affected). This approach does not attempt to measure the willingness to pay of those concerned. For most evaluations, this is a major drawback (even though under some conditions the willingness to pay for improved health of other people may be a function of the productivity improvement of the latter). But, in the context where one has ruled out the validity of the willingness to pay of those directly involved on competency grounds (as with mental patients), or ruled out willingness to pay on equity grounds because poor consumers are constrained by their ability to pay (as in the health-care field where evaluators are reluctant to use explicit distribution weights) the traditional approach may be useful.

This is especially true if one concentrates precisely on the justification given by Weisbrod et al. (1980, p. 404) for using earned income as a measure of the benefits of non-institutional care for mental patients. They argue that earnings can be thought of as an indicator of programme success, 'with higher earnings reflecting a greater ability to get along with people and to behave as a responsible person'. Thus if one of the objectives of mental health treatment is to help get a patient back into playing an active role in society, then earnings are a sign that progress has been made.

The size of earnings was the largest category of benefits valued in monetary terms in the study of alternative mental health treatments by Weisbrod et al. As we can see from Table 2.1, mental health patients had annual earnings of $2 364 if treated in a community-based programme (identified as the experimental programme E), and only $1 168 if treated in a hospital (the control programme C). There were therefore extra benefits of $1 196 per patient if treatment takes place outside the hospital setting. Earnings were not the only category of benefits that were valued. Patients in the E programme were (surprisingly) less likely to get involved with breaking the law. The lower law enforcement costs were registered as a cost saving of the E programme. In aggregate though, the costs (direct and indirect as defined in Chapter 1, law enforcement, maintenance and family burden) were higher in the E programme (by $797) as supervision costs were obviously greater.

Table 2.1   Costs and benefits of alternative mental health programmes

	Community programme E	Hospital programme C	Difference $(E-C)$
Benefits (earnings)	$2 364	$1 168	$1 196
Costs	$8 093	$7 296	$797
Net Benefits	–$5 729	–$6 128	$399

Source: Weisbrod (1968)

The figures in Table 2.1 relate to a period 12 months after admission. They are therefore on a recurring annual basis (as explained in Chapter 1). The net benefits for either programme were negative. This need not imply that no mental treatment should be provided, seeing that not all benefits (or cost savings) were valued in monetary terms (for example, burdens on neighbours, co-workers and family members). However, if these non-valued effects were the same for both programmes, then the preferred option would be programme E. Its negative net benefits were $399 lower than for programme C.

2.4.2   Actual compensation and trade readjustment
Economic theory tells us (via the principle of comparative advantage) that there will be more output available (greater efficiency) if a country specializes in producing certain goods (and engages in free trade) rather than trying to produce

everything for itself. The country exports goods where it has a comparative advantage and imports those goods where other countries have the advantage.

We can interpret the free-trade argument in the context of CBA in the following way. An export project and an import project are to be combined into a package. It is the combined package that is to be subject to the CBA test. Provided that the export project is one where the country has a comparative advantage (and the import is one where there is a comparative disadvantage) then the net benefits of the package should be positive.

Although the net benefits of the package are expected to be positive, this results from two effects that are opposite in sign. The net benefits of the export project are positive, while the net benefits from the import project are negative. The latter negative effect occurs because the import is replacing a domestic activity that will cease to exist. In short, engaging in free trade *will* necessitate there being losers.

To deal with these trade losers, the US government passed the 1962 Trade Expansion Act (which was later incorporated into the 1974 Trade Readjustment Act). According to Schriver et al. (1976), the act was intended to promote the movement towards free trade by authorizing the President to reduce tariffs by as much as 50 per cent. The sponsors of the legislation recognized the possible adverse effects on some parts of US industry and therefore included trade re-adjustment assistance (TRA). TRA was cash compensation to trade-displaced workers. How TRA worked is a good example of some of the complications that any actual compensation scheme must try to address.

One reason why any compensation scheme is not administratively costless, is due to the need to establish eligibility. It is not sufficient that there be losers. It has to be demonstrated that the losers result solely from the project in question. For TRA, a special Tariff Commission was set up to establish eligibility.

Given that eligibility has been decided, the next step is to set out the terms in which compensation is to take place. This involves: (i) stating what is being compensated, (ii) specifying the amount of the compensation, and (iii) fixing how long the compensation is to last. In TRA, compensation was given for the *temporary* loss of a job. TRA benefits therefore started off with a relocation allowance (equal to 2.5 times the weekly mean national manufacturing wage) to enable the worker to move to a place where jobs were available. Then special unemployment insurance was awarded (equal to 65 per cent of the worker's mean earnings for a period not exceeding 52 weeks) to compensate for the time necessary to conduct a job search. If the worker was undergoing job retraining, the insurance period was extended by a further 26 weeks. Finally, certain expenses involved with finding a new job were reimbursed, such as registration fees, testing, counselling and job placement.

So far we have been discussing compensation. The theory given in this chapter is more stringent than just requiring compensation. The compensation must be such that the person is not worse off by the project. It is this aspect of TRA that was explicitly tested for in Schriver et al.'s (1976) case study related to a major electronics firm in the period 1971–73.

The electronics firm's profits suffered from the recession of the late 1960s. When foreign firms increased their share of the market by using cheaper and more compact units, the firm decided to close in 1970. Six months later, the Tariff Commission ruled that the firm qualified for TRA benefits. Schriver et al. sampled the work experience of 272 firm employees to assess the effectiveness of TRA benefits in improving the welfare of the displaced workers.

Schriver et al. hypothesized that if the Act were to operate as intended, then: (i) workers would increase the amount of time that they spent looking for a job; (ii) workers would earn a higher wage from the new job because of the longer job search; and (iii) workers that are retrained because of TRA will earn more than those who were not retrained. They found support for the first hypothesis, but not the other two. The duration spent between jobs was larger for those receiving TRA benefits than a control group of 165 unemployed persons without the benefits. This longer period did not translate into higher earnings, whether this time was devoted to job retraining or not. Overall, their findings were consistent with the idea that the trade-displaced workers used the benefits to increase their leisure.

The fact that, in this case, compensation causes leisure to rise, and hence output to fall, is an illustration of a central concern of public policy decision-making in mixed economies. One must always allow for the possibility of adverse incentive effects on the private sector when the public sector tries to meet its goals. (This concern is highlighted further in Chapter 6.) The important point to note is that when one talks about the 'administrative costs' of transfer programmes, one is not costing a fixed mechanical procedure. Officials are transferring incomes in a situation where the contributors are trying to reduce their obligations, while simultaneously the beneficiaries are trying to increase their receipts. As we shall see in Chapter 10, the existence of administrative costs of redistribution schemes is an important reason why the income distributional effects of a project should be included as part of the CBA criterion. That is, one is trying to avoid incurring the administrative costs.

2.4.3 *Compensation and highway budget constraints*
Even if one ignores the administrative costs, there still may be output effects just from the size of the financial provisions of the compensation scheme. As pointed out by Cordes and Weisbrod (1979), this occurs whenever an agency has a budget constraint. The more compensation that must be paid out, the less is available to cover the costs of constructing new projects.

Cordes and Weisbrod considered the case of the Highway Relocation Assistance Act of 1968 and the 1971 Uniform Relocation Act in the United States. Both of these required compensation to be paid to those forced to relocate by the introduction of new state highways. For these highway projects, all reasonable moving expenses were refundable. Renters receive the difference between their old and new rents for four years up to $4000 in value; and home owners receive up to $15000 of the difference in price between the home they sold and their replacement home. Clearly, compensation was considerable. But there was no separate provision for funds (other than a federal matching provision). Compensation was to be treated like any other expense and come out of the total highway allocation. From this fact, Cordes and Weisbrod suggested:

Hypothesis 1   The greater is compensation, *Comp*, as a share of total costs, *C*, the less will be capital highway expenditures, *I*.

The matching provision ensured that the states were refunded 90 cents for each $1 of compensation given in connection with the federal interstate system, and 50 cents for other federal-aid programmes. Thus, there was scope for the federal-to-state share variable to also have an effect on the amount of highway expenditures. When the federal government provides a share of the damages (compensation), then the budget constraint is less binding. Consequently, Cordes and Weisbrod deduced:

Hypothesis 2   The greater are federal subsidies relative to what a state must pay for compensation, denoted by *S*, the greater will be capital highway expenditures.

To assess the effects of *Comp/C* and *S* on highway expenditures, one first needs to explain what would be the level of such expenditures in their absence. Many studies indicated to Cordes and Weisbrod that the demand for highways depended on fuel consumption, *F*. In addition, the existing stock of miles on highways, *H*, was thought important. A test was then set up that involved regressing the policy variables *Comp/C* and *S*, and the non-policy variables *F* and *H*, on capital expenditures on highways, *I*. The data related to the 50 US states and Washington, DC (51 observations) for the year 1972. A typical regression is given in Table 2.2.

Because we will be referring to regression results throughout the book, we will explain in detail the findings reported in Table 2.2. There are three main things to look at, namely, (i) the signs of coefficients, (ii) the statistical significance of the coefficients, and (iii) the overall explanatory powers of the regression. We examine each of these in turn.

Table 2.2   Determinants of US state highway capital expenditures in 1972

Variable	Coefficient	't' statistic
Constant	246.2	1.12
Fuel consumption (*F*)	56.2	10.60
Stock of highway miles (*H*)	1.5	1.77
Fed. subsidies/State compensation (*S*)	130.8	1.44
Compensation/Total costs (*comp/C*)	−3 286.8	2.16
Coefficient of determination	$R^2 = 0.82$	

Source: Cordes and Weisbrod (1979)

i.   The signs indicate whether practice corresponds to *a priori* expectations. These expectations can be derived from a formal economic model or from intuitive theorizing. Both non-policy variables were predicted to be factors that would lead to higher levels of highway capital expenditures *I*, which was the dependent variable in the study. Thus the positive signs on the coefficients *F* and *H* (column 2) were as expected: an increase in either of them would raise the level of *I*. Hypothesis 1 of Cordes and Weisbrod suggested that an increase in compensation would decrease the amount that was likely to be spent on highways. The negative sign on *Comp/C* confirmed this. Cordes and Weisbrod also expected that additional federal subsidies would increase highway construction expenditure. The positive sign on *S* therefore supported hypothesis 2. All four variables in Table 2.2 therefore had the theoretically 'correct' signs attached to their coefficients.

ii.   It is not sufficient that a variable's coefficient be of the correct sign. It is also necessary to know whether that coefficient's value could have been obtained by chance. The 't' value helps us determine this. The 't' value is the ratio of a coefficient to its standard error. The greater the standard error the less confidence we have in the value of the coefficient. So we would want the estimated coefficient to be large relative to this magnitude of uncertainty. As a rule of thumb, one can say that if the 't' value attached to a coefficient is close to 2, it is generally accepted that the coefficient is not zero, for such a 't' value would happen by chance only 5 per cent of the time if the experiment were repeated many times. It is then said to be 'statistically significant'.

Two of the variables in Table 2.2 are insignificant (see column 3). But, because the variable *Comp/C* had a 't' value greater than 2, and the correct sign, Cordes and Weisbrod considered that their main hypothesis had been supported by the data. Compensation did come at the expense of highway construction. Clearly, actual compensation may affect efficiency (the level of expenditures) as well as the distribution of income.

iii. Apart from having significant coefficients with correct signs, it is also necessary that the set of independent variables as a whole 'explain' a large share of the variation in the dependent variable. For if there are important variables excluded from the equation, it may be that when admitted, both the signs and significance of previously included variables could be reversed. The main statistical measure of the explanatory powers of a regression equation is the 'R^2' (the square of the correlation coefficient, also known as the 'coefficient of determination'). This has a maximum value of 1 and a minimum value of zero. In the Cordes and Weisbrod study the R^2 equalled 0.82. This means that 82 per cent of the variation in capital expenditure on highways by the States could be explained by the variables in the model. There are no firm rules of thumb as to how high the R^2 should be for a satisfactory model. But, a figure of 0.82 is usually found only in studies where the data consists of a time series where the variables (dependent and independent) all move together, thereby guaranteeing a strong statistical association (correlation). It is safe to conclude therefore that the highway expenditures regression had a high explanatory power.

2.4.4 Uncompensated losers and railway closures

We have just seen illustrations of why compensation is costly and how it can affect public expenditures decisions. To complete the picture, we need to consider a case where compensation is sometimes considered too costly. ('Too costly' means that the amount of resources taken up in administrating the transfer to the losers exceeds the amount to be transferred itself, that is, the positive net benefits.) Can the number of losers affect decisions even when compensation is not paid?

Two laws in the UK (in 1962 and 1968) governed the process by which the fate of unprofitable railway lines were to be decided. The government claimed it would subsidize lines that were in the 'social interest'. The Minister of Transport was to decide whether the social benefits of keeping any line open were greater than the social costs of closing it. But, this was only after a special committee (a Transport Users' Consultative Committee) had first to decide whether train users would experience 'hardship' if a line were closed and a replacement bus service provided. Compensation was therefore in-kind and the committee had to review the conditions (number and frequency) of the proposed replacement bus service. To help them with their deliberations, the committee would hold a public hearing to receive written and oral testimony considering the adequacy of the proposed alternative bus service. If, on the basis of the evidence, the committee considered that the replacement bus service would not meet all the needs of users, and an extension of the proposed bus service was too costly (or otherwise infeasible) they would inform the Minister that hardship would result from closure. The Minister would then decide whether the residual hardship did, or did not, justify the retention of the unprofitable line.

The numbers in hardship were the uncompensated losers from closing unre-munerative lines. They indicated the extent to which Pareto optimality was being violated in any particular decision. The appropriate cost–benefit framework was therefore that expressed by equation (2.3). The precise specification of N was the number of persons who contacted the TUCC and claimed hardship from rail closure (even with the proposed replacement bus service).

The complete closure model will be covered in other parts of the book (and appears in Brent, 1976 and 1984a). Here we need only report results that pertain to the numbers effect. For reference, the main regression equation (in which the numbers effect is just one component) is reported in full in the appendix. The dependent variable D was the decision whether to close or keep open the unprofitable line. D was set equal to zero if the Minister closed the line, and D equalled one when a closure application was refused. Our hypothesis was that the larger the number of uncompensated losers, the less socially worthwhile the project. The project in this case is a disinvestment (that is, closing the line and having $D = 0$). Thus, to test our hypothesis, one needs to find a *positive* relation between N and D. The hypothesis was tested by analysing 99 actual closure decisions in the UK for the period 1963–79.

Table 2.3   Determinants of UK railway closure decisions (1963–1970)

Variable	Coefficient	't' statistic
Constant	–4.2017	4.003
Time Savings (b_2)	0.0906	2.457
Congestion avoided (b_2)	0.0279	2.772
Fare differences (r)	0.0235	2.094
Financial loss per journey (l)	–3.0902	2.034
Number of uncompensated losers (N)	0.5629	3.154
Coefficient of determination	$R^2 = 0.41$	

Source: Brent (1984a)

No matter the regression technique used, the coefficient attached to N was positive and significant well within the 1 per cent level (see Brent, 1984a, Table 1). However, equally important was the fact that when N was included *in addition to* the variables in equation (2.2), it retained its sign and significance (see Brent, 1984a, Table 2). Note that all the variables in equation (2.2) include

N as a component. For example, $B = b.N$. Thus, on its own, N might appear to be merely a proxy for B (the higher the numbers affected, the greater the efficiency effect). But, since N was significant when included with B (and R and L) in the regression equation, its significance must record an influence in addition to efficiency (and distribution). Expressed alternatively, since equation (2.2) reflects a two-objectives social CBA criterion, this equation plus the numbers effect must reflect a three-objectives criterion.

2.5   Final comments

We conclude this chapter with a summary and a set of problems.

2.5.1   Summary

When Pareto optimality holds, the marginal rate of substitution between any two goods is equal to the marginal rate of transformation; or, price equals marginal cost. The price reflects the maximum amount that consumers are willing to pay for a good, and the marginal cost reflects the minimum compensation that factors must receive in order to provide the good. The Pareto conditions therefore imply a criterion for judging a change in economic conditions: there should be sufficient gains from the change (e.g., the public project) that what people are willing to pay can at least compensate those who have to sacrifice the resources for the change. Thus, no one need be worse off.

When the economy is at the optimum, it is impossible to make one person better off without making someone else worse off. That is, there is no scope to make any Pareto improvements. Underlying this Pareto test are four value judgements. The first two are relatively non-controversial, at least within economics. They are: first, society is better off only when individuals are better off, which is the individualistic postulate that is the main philosophical tradition in the West; and second, individuals are better off when they receive more goods and services. Non-economic causes of welfare are thereby ignored.

This chapter was mostly concerned with explaining and assessing the two other Paretian value judgements. The third value judgement involves the consumer sovereignty postulate. For individuals' preferences to count, they must be considered to be the best judge of their own welfare. On the whole, this will be accepted by default; it is too problematical to assume that other people (especially the government) are better judges than the individuals themselves. But, especially in the health-care field, this postulate is often questioned. This explains why the other techniques identified in Chapter 1 (cost minimization, cost-effectiveness and cost-utility analysis) are so popular in the health-care field. Evaluators there hope to avoid explicitly allowing for preferences on the benefit side. Of course, preferences are still relevant on the cost side, in terms of what compensation must be received by factor owners. But, often this seems to be impersonal. Input prices are set by markets and regarded as outside the sphere of influence of the health-care industry. In our case study on mental health, we saw how the two areas (inside and outside the health-care field) could be reconciled. Weisbrod et al. (1980) used as an index of mental health the ability to earn in the labour market. Monetary earnings are used to quantify the progress towards consumer sovereignty and in this sense are the benefits of treatment.

The fourth value judgement, is the most well known. It defines when any kind of change is to be viewed as an increase in social welfare. The test is that someone should be made better off, and no one else should be made worse off. The only real complaint with this test emphasized in the literature is that, in practice, it may be too costly to compensate everyone to ensure that there are actually no losers. Saying that compensation is too costly means that it costs more administratively than the amount of the net benefits. Thus, if the transfer were to proceed, there would be a bill in place of a positive transfer payment to those who incur the costs. We presented two case studies which illustrated the factors which make compensation costly. In the first, those who would lose their jobs from removing trade barriers were given financial assistance. The problems of establishing eligibility and work incentives were emphasized. Then we examined the implication of trying to compensate when a budget constraint for projects exists. The greater the compensation, the less funds that were available to be spent on capital expenditures for highways.

Since compensation could not always be carried out, a hypothetical test was suggested to replace the Pareto test. This test, associated with Kaldor and Hicks, required only that there be positive net benefits, for if this occurred, potentially there could be no losers. The argument goes as follows: if society decides not to compensate the losers (for example, because it is too costly) then this is a separate consideration from the desirability of the project itself. There are two main drawbacks of this hypothetical test. Firstly, it could lead to inconsistencies if prices and incomes change greatly due to the advent of the project. Gainers may be able to bribe losers to accept the project, but simultaneously, losers may be able to bribe gainers to forgo the project. Secondly, the losers could be low-income earners. Income distributional fairness (or, equity) would be at risk if the project proceeded.

The correct response to allow for equity considerations, is to include distributional weights. The social welfare test, based on both efficiency and distribution, is that weighted benefits should exceed weighted costs. While this does solve the distributional dilemma, this does nothing to deal with the issue of losers *per se*. Losers nearly always will exist when public projects are carried out, except when compensation measures are an explicit part of the programmes. This is a violation of the Pareto test, and this test is at the heart of CBA. It seemed necessary, therefore, to record the extent to which there would be losers. This effect serves to work against the desirability of the project in our social criterion. The existence of a numbers effect is not just a theory requisite. We showed that, in practice, railway closure decisions in the UK were significantly affected by the number of uncompensated losers. In this case study, compensation (in terms of a replacement bus service) was considered *together with* the number of losers. The Minister of Transport's behaviour revealed that social welfare included the numbers effect in addition to efficiency and distribution.

2.5.2   Problems

Many times public expenditure decisions have to be made with incomplete information. Often this occurs because there is not the time, or it is too costly, to find out what individuals are willing to pay and receive as compensation. However, sometimes (especially in the health-care field) one may not *want* to use what data there is available, if this means utilizing individual evaluations when consumer sovereignty is not accepted. No matter the cause of why certain effects are left unquantified, the issue is whether (or, more precisely, under what circumstances) the included effects alone can be used to decide social outcomes. In the problems we indicate three ways to proceed. One when unvalued effects are the same across alternatives, and two others when they differ.

Consider once more the evaluation of mental health treatments by Weisbrod et al. (1980) summarized in section 2.4.1. The net benefits of the valued effects were $399 per annum higher (less negative) with the *E* (community) programme than the *C* (hospital) programme. Left unvalued were (*inter alia*) the effects of the programmes on the number of mental patient suicides. The number of suicides was recorded, but no monetary value was assigned. In their results, Weisbrod et al. state that in both programmes the number of suicides that took place was 1.5 per annum on average. Assume that without either programme, the number of suicides would have been 2.5 per annum. Then in each case the programmes had the effect of reducing the number of suicides by 1 per annum.

Whether one should treat any reductions in the number of suicides as a benefit (or not) is a value judgement. Clearly, to treat them as benefits violates the assumption of consumer sovereignty. For the individuals themselves 'chose' to end their lives. The analysis that follows assumes that reductions in suicides should be counted as a benefit. But, to learn from the problems below, all one needs to accept is that it is difficult to put an explicit monetary value on these effects, and one would rather avoid this evaluation problem (if it were possible to make social decisions without knowing the monetary values).

1. Taking the facts as given (that the net measured benefits of *E* were $399 per annum higher and that both *E* and *C* saved one person from suicide) calculate the net benefits of the two programmes under three different valuation assumptions. In the first case, assume that a life saved from suicide is worth $300. In the second case, assume a value of $300 000 per life saved; and in the third case, assume a value of $300 million. Does the relative advantage of programme *E* over *C* depend on the valuation assumption?

Explain why, or why not. Is the decision (as to which programme society should choose) affected by which valuation assumption one adopts?

2. Now assume that programme E saved one more person from suicide than programme C. Repeat the three calculations of net benefits that correspond to the three cases listed in question 1. Does the relative advantage of programme E over C depend on the valuation assumption? Is the decision affected by which evaluation assumption one adopts?

3. Finally, assume that programme C saved one more person from suicide than programme E. Again, repeat the three calculations of net benefits that correspond to the three cases listed in question 1. Does the relative advantage of programme E over C depend on the valuation assumption? Is the decision affected by which evaluation assumption one adopts? What is the minimum value that needs to be placed on a life saved in order for programme C to be chosen rather than E? Would knowing this minimum value help you decide whether you would choose programme C rather than E?

2.6 Appendix

In section 2.4.4, results for the numbers effect were reported in isolation of all the other determinants of railway closures. For reference we list here one of the full regression equations (the LOGIT regression in Table 1 of Brent, 1984a).

The only departure from equation (2.3) was that there were two beneficiary groups to consider. Apart from the train users, road users (who would have faced increased congestion on the roads from replacement train journeys) also gain when the train service is retained. The rail-user benefits, which were denoted b, will now be b_2 as they go to group 2. The road users can then be called group 3, which enables the congestion-avoided benefits to be termed b_3. The extended version of equation (2.3) that applied to railway closure decisions was therefore:

$$a_{2.k}b_2 + a_{3.k}b_3 - a_{2.m}r - a_{1.m}l - a_nN \qquad (2.4)$$

where $a_{3.k}$ is the in-kind weight to road users. The specifications for the independent variables were (all on a recurrent annual basis):

b_2 = time savings of train journeys over bus journeys (in mins);
b_3 = congestion avoided by continuing the train service (a dummy variable) which takes the value equal to 0 when no additional congestion results, according to the Divisional Road Engineer, and equals 1 otherwise;
r = fare differences between train and bus services (in old pence);
l = financial loss per journey (in pounds);
N = number of persons complaining of residual hardship.

The rationale for these specifications is given in Brent (1979 and 1984a).

3 Consumer surplus

3.1 Introduction

We have just seen that for a public expenditure to be efficient, the sum of the amounts that the gainers are willing to pay (the benefits) must exceed the sum of the amounts that the losers are willing to receive as compensation (the costs). In this chapter we develop the theoretical underpinning of willingness to pay (WTP) and explain how it can be measured.

The first section covers the basic principles. It shows how demand curves can be used to estimate WTP. WTP will then be split into two parts: what the consumer pays, and the excess of what the individual is willing to pay over what is actually paid. This excess is called consumer surplus. This is one main reason why markets, even if they are competitive, fail to measure the full social benefits of projects which are large. The inclusion of consumer surplus is therefore a crucial difference between private and public decision-making. This efficiency framework then will be extended to include distributional concerns.

The second section develops the welfare economic analytics underlying efficiency. The last chapter showed how competitive markets function as a compensation test. These markets operate according to the forces of demand and supply. Because WTP is bound up with the demand part of this allocation process, a central part in explaining WTP is to show how one can move from utility functions to form individual demand curves. However, there is more than one way of making this transformation. This means that there will be more than one measure of demand. So although we will explain the basic principles as if the demand curve were unique, section 3.2 will cover the alternative measures and suggest a way to choose from among them.

From the practical policy-making point of view, we need explain only the basic principles and their analytical underpinning. We therefore exclude discussion of all the technical issues surrounding consumer surplus and proceed straight to the applications of these basic principles. (Any good welfare economics book, such as that by Ng (1983), can fill in the missing theory.)

We begin the applications section by highlighting some of the difficulties in trying to estimate a demand curve using survey data. From there we go to a study which shows how the existence of consumer surplus can indicate whether to increase both the price as well as the quantity of publicly provided services. Transport evaluations have long relied on the estimation of demand and consumer surplus and we cover two of these studies. The first shows how different segments of the demand curve correspond to separate categories of consumer behaviour. It thereby provides an important checklist of effects that need to be included in any transport study. The second application in this area shows what difference it makes to: (a) estimate the alternative demand measures, and (b) include distribution weights.

3.1.1   Willingness to pay

As explained in the previous chapter, the welfare base of CBA comes from the Paretian value judgements. The initial one was the individualistic postulate that society's welfare depends on the welfare (or utility) of all the individuals contained in that society. This can be represented symbolically in an additive form as:

$$W = U_1 + U_2 + \cdots + U_n \tag{3.1}$$

where W is social welfare, the Us are the individual utility functions, and there are n individuals in society. The objective of this chapter is to explain how one can measure in monetary terms the extent to which individual utilities are affected by public policy decisions. As we shall see, the role of WTP is exactly to make equation (3.1) operational.

As a first step in transforming equation (3.1), one can think of using individual incomes y to act as a proxy for their utilities.

$$W = y_1 + y_2 + \cdots + y_n \tag{3.2}$$

The problem with this approach, as pointed out by Marglin (1968), is that y is too much based on market values. On a market, it is possible (if demand is inelastic) to reduce output, yet for revenues (market income) to rise. This possibility is illustrated in Diagram 3.1 below. P_1 is the price that corresponds to the current output level Q_1. If the price is raised to P_2, quantity demanded falls to Q_2. Revenue is the product of price and quantity. The new revenue is $P_2.Q_2$. If the demand curve were unresponsive to price changes, then this new revenue could exceed the old revenue $P_1.Q_1$. The lower output Q_1 would then have generated a larger income than the output Q_2.

WTP is derived from the whole area under the demand curve. It shows the total satisfaction from consuming all the units at its disposal. At Q_1, the area under the demand curve is greater than at Q_2. It would therefore be impossible ever to reduce output and increase WTP, no matter the shape of the demand curve. As a result, using the concept of WTP to measure the benefits (and costs) expresses the idea of economic efficiency in a more effective way than to just say that one is trying to maximize national income. The measure of equation (3.1) is now:

$$W = WTP_1 + WTP_2 + \cdots + WTP_n \qquad (3.3)$$

To obtain the familiar efficiency CBA criterion, we just need to group the n individuals into two mutually exclusive groups. Group 1 consists of all those who gain, and group 2 is all those who lose. The two-group version of equation (3.3) is: $W = WTP_1 + WTP_2$. We call the WTP of the gainers 'benefits' B, and the *negative* WTP of the losers 'costs' C, to produce $W = B - C$, which is effectively equation (1.1) of Chapter 1. (Negative WTP corresponds to the concept of willingness to accept. We use the former term here because throughout most of the book we use the term WTP generically to represent consumer preferences expressed in monetary terms. This chapter, however, will examine differences in the WTP measures.)

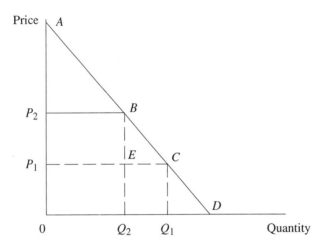

This demand curve shows that revenue rises from $P_1 \cdot Q_1$ to $P_2 \cdot Q_2$ (area $0Q_1CP_1$ becomes area $0Q_2BP_2$) even though output is reduced from Q_1 to Q_2.

Diagram 3.1

3.1.2 Consumer surplus

The fact that WTP may be different from actual market payments is given special recognition in welfare economics. The actual market price is what the individual has to pay for the product. The difference between what one is willing to pay and what one has to pay is called 'consumer surplus'. The relationship between the two concepts can be seen in Diagram 3.2 below. This diagram represents the market demand curve by road users for a bridge that has already been built.

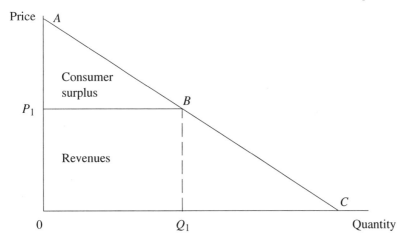

The area under the demand curve can be split into two parts; one showing the revenues that the consumer has to pay ($0Q_1BP_1$) and the other showing the consumer surplus (P_1BA).

Diagram 3.2

Assume that the price charged for using the bridge (the toll) is P_1. The number of cars willing to cross at this price is Q_1. The WTP that corresponds to the quantity Q_1 is the area $0Q_1BA$. What the consumers actually pay is the revenue amount $P_1.Q_1$, represented by the area $0Q_1BP_1$. The difference between these two areas is the consumer surplus triangle P_1BA.

Consumer surplus has a very important role to play in CBA. It can supply a social justification for providing goods that would otherwise be rejected by a private market. It was as long ago as 1844 that Dupuit (1952) introduced the idea of consumer surplus as a guide to public investment decision-making. He was the person who first suggested the bridge-pricing problem. We can use Diagram 3.2 to explain his argument.

Once a bridge has been built, there are very few operating expenses that need to be covered as people use the bridge. Assume that these operating expenses are zero. A private enterprise in control of the bridge would set a price that maximizes profits, that is, one where marginal revenue (*MR*) equals marginal costs (*MC*). With $MC = 0$, by assumption, the market determined output would be where $MR = 0$. If the demand curve is a straight line, the *MR* is always half the slope of the demand curve. This means that, on the quantity axis, the *MR* would be placed half-way between the demand curve and the vertical axis. Thus, if the price P_1 for the bridge in Diagram 3.2 had been set so as to maximize profits, Q_1 would be half-way between the origin and the number *C*, which denotes the quantity where the demand curve meets the horizontal axis.

The revenue collected at Q_1 by the private enterprise may, or may not, cover the costs of building the bridge. So, it is not clear whether a private market would have the financial incentive to provide the bridge. But even if the bridge were built by a private enterprise, the scale of operation would be wrong. By limiting the number of cars to Q_1 (by charging the price P_1) there is a potential consumer surplus that is being unnecessarily excluded. This excluded consumer surplus is the triangular area Q_1CB. What makes the exclusion unnecessary is the fact that there are no costs involved with allowing the extra cars to use the bridge. Benefits (WTP) can be obtained without costs and a Pareto improvement is possible. The socially correct output would therefore be C, which is twice the privately determined output level. As a zero-user charge should be applied, a private enterprise would never provide the socially optimal quantity (without a public subsidy).

The Dupuit analysis makes clear that by focusing on WTP, and not just on what consumers actually do pay, CBA in an efficiency context is aiming to maximize consumer surplus. How this analysis needs to be extended to allow for distributional considerations will now be explained.

3.1.3   Consumer surplus and distribution

As pointed out in Chapter 1, an efficiency calculation is a special kind of social evaluation; it is one that uses equal, unity weights. To see this in the current context, refer back to Diagram 3.1. The consumer surplus that is lost because quantity is being reduced from Q_1 to Q_2 is the triangle ECB. This area can be considered to have been accumulated in the following way. Benefits are reduced by Q_2Q_1CB by output being lowered from Q_1 to Q_2. This can be split into two parts, the area ECB and the rectangular area Q_2Q_1CE. If the quantity is produced at constant costs equal to the price P_1, then the rectangular area is the total cost savings from reducing the output to Q_2. The consumer surplus ECB has the interpretation of being what is left over after costs have been subtracted from benefits. It is the net benefits of the price change and is negative, as recognized earlier.

What is clear from this explanation is that the area Q_2Q_1CE appears twice. It is part of the benefits and it is all of the costs. By allowing the two to offset one another, an efficiency evaluation is treating them as of equal size and opposite in value. This ignores the fact that the benefits may go to a different income group from that which experiences the costs. With a_2 the social value of a unit of income to the beneficiaries, and a_1 the social value of a unit of income to those who incur the costs, as long as the two weights differ, area Q_2Q_1CE does not disappear. The magnitude $(a_2 - a_1)Q_2Q_1CE$ must be added to the consumer surplus triangle ECB to form a social evaluation. Since the consumer surplus goes to the beneficiaries, it should have the weight a_2. The complete summary of effects is therefore $a_2(ECB) + (a_2 - a_1)Q_2Q_1CE$. (It is shown in the appendix that this relation is equivalent to the social criterion given by equation (1.2) in Chapter 1.)

This analysis shows the difficulty in incorporating distribution weights into a consumer surplus evaluation at an aggregate level. It is not valid just to identify the income group receiving the consumer surplus and attach the appropriate distribution weight. For this would produce only the $a_2(ECB)$ term, which represents the difference between effects for gainers and losers. One needs also to disaggregate benefits to locate effects that are common to both groups affected by a project (for a complete analysis, see Londero, 1987).

3.2 Alternative measures of consumer surplus

The demand curve that is familiar to us from the analysis of competitive markets is known as the Marshallian demand curve. The starting point is the demand function D, which expresses the quantity purchased as a function of the main determinants:

$$D = D (\, Price; \, Other \, Prices; \, Income; \, Tastes; \, Population; \, \text{etc.)} \quad (3.4)$$

The demand curve is derived from this demand function by isolating the effect of changes in price on quantity demanded, holding all the other variables in the demand function constant. Different interpretations of what one is holding constant leads to different conceptions of demand. With different demand curves, there will be alternative measures of consumer surplus.

3.2.1 The three main measures

Consider one individual faced by a single price change. (When there is more than one individual, we need to apply distribution weights. When there is more than one product whose price change needs to be monitored, we need to assume that income elasticities of demand are equal.)

The Marshallian measure   The first case to consider is one where the price rise is so large as to cause the individual to cease consuming the product entirely. There is a current level of satisfaction with the product and a level of satisfaction without the product. The difference is the Marshallian measure. More precisely, Marshall (1924) defined consumer surplus as: 'The excess of the price which he would be willing to pay rather than go without the thing, over that which he actually does pay'. The Marshallian measure is an all-or-nothing comparison between not being able to buy any units and buying the desired number of units at the prevailing price. In terms of Diagram 3.2, the current consumption level is Q_1 and 0 is the consumption without the product. It is because one is aggregating the difference between what the individual is willing and has to pay *over the whole range 0 to* Q_1 that what we designated as the consumer surplus in the introductory section (the area P_1BA) was in fact the Marshallian measure.

The compensating variation   When one refrains from the all-or-nothing comparison, other measures of consumer surplus can be considered. These other measures are due to Hicks (1943). The compensating variation (*CV*) is: 'The amount of compensation that one can take away from individuals and leave them just as well off as before the change'. Again the change we are considering is a price reduction caused by an increase in the output from a public project. The *CV* works under the assumption that the price change will occur. For this reason it is called a 'forward test', that is, allowing the change to take place and trying to value the new situation. It asks what is the individual's WTP for that change such that the utility level is the same as before the price change took place. Although the concept is forward looking, the utility level after the WTP amount has been extracted returns the individual to the original utility level.

The *CV* is also a WTP concept, but it does not operate with the standard (Marshallian) demand curve. As always, one is changing price, holding income constant. But, the price change has an 'income effect' (the lower price means that the individual's purchasing power has increased, and so more can be spent on all goods) as well as a 'substitution effect' (the lower price for the public project means that other goods are relatively more expensive and their consumption will be reduced). The *CV* tries to isolate the substitution effect and eliminate the income effect. It tries to establish how much more the individual is willing to purchase of the public project assuming that the purchasing power effect can be negated. The resulting price and quantity relation, with the income effect excluded, is the *compensated* demand curve. The area under the compensated demand curve measures the *CV* of the price change.

The equilibriating variation   There is a second way of isolating the income effect which is called by Hicks the equilibriating variation (*EV*). This is defined as follows: 'The amount of compensation that has to be given in order that an individual forgo the change, yet be as well off as after the change'. For the *EV*, the price change does not take place. It is therefore called the 'backward test', that is, the individual is asked to value the forgoing of the change. The individual is to *receive* a sum of money to be as well off as if the change had taken place. It is, nonetheless, also a WTP concept, in the sense that it records what others have to be willing to pay to prevent the individual having the benefit of the change. The difference is that the *CV* measures the maximum WTP of the individual, while the *EV* measures the minimum that must be received by the individual.

There is an equilibrated demand curve to parallel the compensated one. The income effect involves giving the individual a sum of money to compensate for the purchasing power effect that is not being allowed to occur. The income effect is being neutralized, but at a higher level of purchasing power. In this way all that remains is the relative price effect, the substitution effect as before. The area under the equilibriated demand curve measures the *EV* of the price change.

All three measures will now be explained in terms of Diagram 3.3. We consider two goods, X and Y. The change that will be analysed is a fall in the price of good X. This can be thought to be caused by a public project, for example, say the government builds a hydro-electricity plant which lowers the cost of electricity to consumers. Good Y, on the vertical axis, will be the numeraire (the unit in which relative values will be expressed).

The top half of Diagram 3.3 presents the consumer's indifference map for X and Y, together with the budget constraint. An indifference curve shows all combinations of the two goods that give the individual a particular level of utility. Curves to the north-east show higher levels of satisfaction. The budget line shows all combinations of the two goods that can be purchased with a fixed income and a given set of consumer prices for X and Y. The individual's aim is to reach the highest indifference curve, subject to remaining on the budget line. For the specified budget line $Y_1.X_1$, the individual chooses point A which produces the level of satisfaction U_1. (A is the tangency point between the indifference curve U_1 and the budget line $Y_1.X_1$.)

The slope of the budget line is determined by the ratio of prices P_X/P_Y. Thus, when the price of X falls, the slope will flatten, causing the budget line to rotate outwards from Y_1. The new budget line is denoted by $Y_1.X_2$. With the new relative prices, the individual chooses point B on indifference curve U_2.

The bottom half of Diagram 3.3 traces the implications of the indifference curve analysis for the price and quantity relation (i.e., demand) for X. The original ratio of relative prices defines the price P_1. At this price Q_1 is purchased, being the X co-ordinate of A on the indifference curve diagram. The P_1 and Q_1 combination fixes the point a on the lower half of the diagram. In this way we move from point A on the indifference curve diagram to point a on the demand curve. With the lower ratio of relative prices, P_2 is defined. The individual by moving to point B on the top part of the diagram chooses Q_4 of X. The P_2 and Q_4 pairing locates point b on the lower part. Connecting points a and b (and all such points derived from tangency points between indifference curves and sets of relative price ratios) determines the traditional, Marshallian, demand curve.

The *CV* and *EV* both contain only substitution effects. They represent movements along indifference curves. For the *CV*, one is to be kept at the original level of satisfaction. The movement is along indifference curve U_1, from point A to point D. (D is where a budget line with the flatter slope is tangent to U_1.) In terms of the lower half of Diagram 3.3, this translates to the points a and d. Connecting these two points forms the compensated demand curve. Similarly,

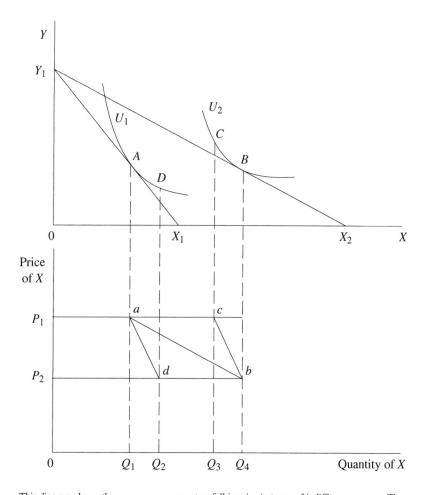

This diagram shows the consumer response to a fall in price in terms of indifference curves. The budget line swivels from Y_1X_1 to Y_1X_2. The three measures involve different adjustment paths:

Marshallian measure :   point A to point B.
Compensating variation :   point A to point D.
Equilibriating variation :   point C to point B.

The consumer response to a fall in price in terms of demand curves is also shown.
The change in consumer surplus is:

Marshallian :   in area P_2baP_1
Compensating :   in area P_2daP_1
Equilibriating :   in area P_2bcP_1.

Diagram 3.3

the *EV* keeps the individual at the higher level of satisfaction U_2 and traces the substitution effect movement from point *C* to point *B*. (*C* is where a budget line with the original slope would be tangent to U_2.) The corresponding points on the lower part of the diagram are *c* and *b*. Connecting points *c* and *b* forms the equilibriated demand curve.

The consumer surplus effect of the price change P_1 to P_2 is given as the area under a demand curve between these two prices. Since there are three demand curves, we have three separate measures. The Marshallian measure is the area P_2baP_1. The *CV* is the area P_2daP_1, and the *EV* is the area P_2bcP_1.

3.2.2 *Differences among the measures*

The relative sizes of the three measures is also shown in Diagram 3.3. The Marshallian measure is in-between the smallest measure, the *CV*, and the largest measure, the *EV*. This ordering always holds for beneficial changes (where people are better off after the change than they were before the change) as with the price reduction we were considering. The order is reversed for adverse changes. It is instructive to analyse further the relation between the *CV* and the *EV*.

The key to understanding the relative sizes of the measures lies in the concept of the marginal utility of income. It is usual to assume that the marginal utility of income diminishes as income rises. Thus, if one is at a higher level of income, one will value something higher in monetary terms just because money income is worth less. Diagram 3.4 illustrates this fact.

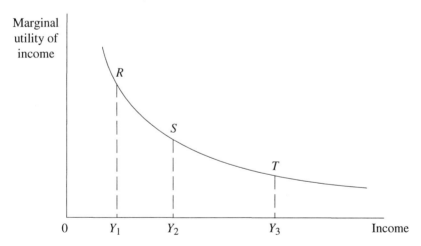

This marginal utility of income schedule depicts the marginal utility of income diminishing as income rises.

Diagram 3.4

Diagram 3.4 has the marginal utility of income on the vertical axis and income on the horizontal axis. The curve relating the two variables declines from right to left. Consider a given sized utility change, that is, an area of a particular magnitude. The income equivalent – measured along the horizontal axis – is larger the level of income (the more one is to the right on the diagram). Thus, even though the areas Y_1Y_2SR and Y_2Y_3TS indicate equal-sized utility changes, the income equivalents are different. The higher-income reference point would value the change as Y_2Y_3, while the lower-income reference point would value the utility change as Y_1Y_2, a considerably smaller amount. If the marginal utility of income were constant, the *CV* and the *EV* measures would indicate the same amount.

We have just seen that the higher the utility, or real income, the higher one evaluates a good in monetary terms. Thus, for a beneficial change one's money evaluation is greater after than before the change. Since the *EV* tries to make individuals as well off as they would have been with the change, it must involve a larger amount than the *CV*, which tries to make people as well off as before the change occurred.

3.2.3   Deciding which measure to use

Which measure one should use depends on the purpose one has in mind. The *CV* is the preferred measure in theoretical work. But often the legal system decides whom should compensate whom by its allocation of property rights. For example, if residents near a proposed airport have the right to peace and quiet, then the *CV* must be used. Residents are to be made as well off with the airport as they were previously. Builders of the airport must pay the residents to forgo their peace and quiet. Residents are not expected to have to pay the airport authority to refrain from building the airport.

At the practical level, the Marshallian measure is most often used. Apart from the obvious simplicity involved, there is a calculation by Willig (1976) that can be used to justify this.

Willig's calculation   Willig has developed a procedure for the *CV* which enables one to calculate the extent to which the Marshallian will differ from the *CV* measure. His approximation is:

$$\frac{C-A}{A} = \frac{\eta A}{2M(0)} \tag{3.5}$$

where:

C   = Hicks's *CV* measure;
A   = Marshallian measure;

η = income elasticity of demand; and

$M(0)$ = income level in the no-service (project) situation.

Thus, with $A/M_0 = 5$ per cent, and if η for a product has been calculated to be 1.2, the error $(C - A)$ is only 3 per cent of the Marshallian measure. Unless one considers the income elasticity of the product one is evaluating to be particularly high, one is safe to use the ordinary demand curve measure as a good approximation. Conversely, one can calculate A and then use the formula (3.5) to convert it to a measure of the *CV*.

3.3 Applications

WTP can be measured in three main ways:

i.   directly from estimating the demand curve; this is the best way, but it is not always possible, for example, if a market does not exist;
ii. indirectly, by asking people (this is illustrated by the water case studies below); or
iii. by inferring WTP from people's indirect market behaviour (this is the approach analysed in Chapter 8).

In many LDCs in the last two decades, the provision of water by planning agencies was considered a 'right'. That is, the benefits were assumed to be so obvious as not to be worth measuring. Consequently, water was provided at as low a cost as possible to as many people as possible. The problem with this approach was that many water systems were unused or fell into disrepair and abandoned. The crucial point was that community preferences (that is, demands) were ignored. The World Bank set up a water demand research team to estimate the WTP for water in a number of areas and in a wide range of social and economic circumstances. We report the findings of two of these studies that use survey methods.

The alternative estimation procedure, using actual behaviour, is illustrated by the applications related to the estimation of transport demand. There is no branch of public policy where demand and consumer surplus estimation have played a larger role in CBA than in transport evaluations. We present two case studies in this area. We start with the classic evaluation of the Victoria Line extension to the London underground system. Then we cover the more modern analysis of the net benefits of constructing an extra lane leading to the San Francisco Bay Bridge.

3.3.1 *The reliability of survey methods*

Survey methods for estimating demand curves are often termed 'contingent valuation methods'. This is because the respondent has to answer questions related to a hypothetical market situation. The obvious issue raised by the hypothetical nature of these surveys is whether one has managed to record the 'true' WTP of those questioned.

Whittington et al. (1990) set out to test whether the question format itself affected what people stated they were willing to pay for water in Laurent, Haiti. The population of Laurent (about 1 500 in 1986) were primarily illiterate, small farmers, with malnourishment widespread among the children. Fresh water was available in wells and springs which were on average a 3-kilometre round trip away. Individuals often had to wait an hour to draw water supplies.

Apart from questions on household characteristics (to establish the non-price demand determinants) and the location and quality of the water available, the main question asked was whether a respondent would bid specified monthly amounts for access to a public fountain. The question was of the form: 'would you be willing to pay $X per month for a public standpost near your house?'. A series of explicit values for X was specified in the questionnaires. The enumerators claimed that the bidding format of the questions was similar to the ordinary kind of bargaining that takes place in the local rural markets. The responses could be 'yes', 'no', or 'I don't know'. Of the approximately 225 households in the village, 170 completed the questionnaire. Fourteen per cent of the households answered 'I don't know' to the bid questions.

Whittington et al. identified three kinds of possible bias that could be present in the respondents' answers to their bidding questionnaire: strategic bias, starting-point bias, and hypothetical bias. What these biases entail, and how the researchers tried to measure them will be explained in turn.

i.   Strategic bias occurs when respondents think they can influence a policy decision by not answering truthfully. In the water context, this may lead to under- or over-bidding. Over-bidding would arise if the respondent thought that a donor was only going to pay for the public fountain provided they observe some positive WTP by beneficiaries. Under-bidding would arise if the respondent thought that a water agency had already decided to install the public fountain and was using the questionnaire to help decide how much beneficiaries should pay.

    To test for strategic bias, the sample was split into two, and different cover letters were sent to accompany the questionnaires. In the first, the cover letter stated it had already been decided to build the water system and no charge would be made for the public fountain. The stated purpose of the questionnaire was to help construct 'the best water system'. In the second, the commitment to install the system and provide the service free of charge was omitted. The purpose of the questionnaire was to establish how much people would be willing to pay to make the water project 'successful'. Since the first cover letter explicitly excluded charging and the second left this option open, it was hypothesized that it was more likely that the second group would behave strategically and offer lower bids than the first group (a lower bid by the second group would decrease the probability of having to pay for any water that might be supplied).

ii. Starting-point bias focuses on the possibility that the initial bid in the series of four questions could predetermine outcomes. Persons who are unsure of their answers might think that the interviewer was suggesting what an appropriate bid might entail, almost like the reservation price in an auction. The obvious test for this bias is to vary the initial bids and see if outcomes are affected. Three different questionnaires were distributed at random, each with a different starting value.

iii. The final category, hypothetical bias, can arise in two main ways. First, the respondent may not understand the characteristics of the commodity being priced. In Whittington et al.'s study this was thought unlikely to exist because many rural areas of Haiti had already been provided with water systems. Second, hypothetical bias may exist because the respondent is unlikely to take the questions seriously. What difference does it make to answer a hypothetical question? If the respondent thought this way then their answers would be random and unrelated to household characteristics and preferences.

The test for the second type of hypothetical bias involved trying to reject the hypothesis that answers were random. Economic theory specifies clearly how individual demand depends on price, income, the prices of other goods, tastes (household characteristics), and so on. If answers are random, then the demand determinants would not explain any of the variation in responses to the hypothetical bids.

The questionnaires were analysed using limited dependent-variable techniques. A simplified summary of the process is as follows. A 'yes' answer to a particular bid was coded as 1 and a 'no' coded as a 0. Since there is a zero–one interval for responses, it is natural to interpret them as probabilities. In which case one is using the demand determinants to try to explain the probability that the individual will accept a particular bid.

The results The main regression equation, with the probability that the individual is willing to pay a particular bid for the public fountain as the dependent variable and the demand determinants as the independent variables, is shown in Table 3.1.

Although the coefficients listed in Table 3.1 were estimated by non-standard estimation techniques (using Probit), their interpretation follows the same principles that were described in Chapter 2. That is, the signs and the size of individual coefficients are important, together with the overall explanatory powers of the regression equation.

Table 3.1   WTP bids for public fountains

Variable	Coefficient	't' statistic
Constant	0.841	1.35
Household wealth index	0.126	2.94
Household with foreign income (yes = 1)	0.064	0.23
Occupation index (farmer = 1)	−0.209	0.85
Household education level	0.157	2.11
Distance from existing source	0.001	5.72
Quality of existing source (satisfactory = 1)	−0.072	2.16
Sex of respondent (male = 1)	−0.104	5.41
Adjusted likelihood ratio	0.142	

Source: Whittington et al. (1990)

The results in Table 3.1 can be discussed in terms of testing for hypothetical bias. It will be recalled that if such a bias existed, one should expect that the demand determinants would play no role in explaining variations in WTP bids.

The coefficients for all the demand determinants were of the expected signs. That is: income (as proxied by wealth and remittances from abroad) had a positive effect; the price of (substitute) other goods (reflected by the distance, or time cost, of existing water sources) was negative; and taste proxies produced higher demand by females and those with more years of education. With limited dependent variables, the adjusted loglikelihood ratio is the counterpart to the usual coefficient of determination. Thus, around 14 per cent of the variation in responses (bids) were accounted for by the demand variables included. Overall, there was no support for the idea that respondents acted randomly. Hypothetical bias did not seem to be present.

Nor was there any need to adjust the WTP bids for strategic or starting-point bias. The mean bid for the public fountain was 5.7 gourdes per household per month (US$1.00 = 5 gourdes). As this represented about 1.7 per cent of household income, these bids were judged 'reasonable' (the old World Bank rule of thumb was that the maximum ability to pay for public fountains would be 5 per cent of household income). The average bid was higher from those with the cover letter omitting the exclusion of charging (5.4 gourdes as opposed to 6.0) which would support the existence of strategic bias; but this difference was not significant. The mean bids for alternative initial starting amounts were random. Those who started out with 2 gourdes offered a mean bid of 5.4 gourdes; those who started out with 5 gourdes offered a mean bid of 6.0; but those who started out with 7 gourdes offered a mean bid of (only) 5.7 gourdes. (Again note that none of these differences in mean bids were significant.)

Whittington et al. conclude: 'The results of this study suggest that it is possible to do a contingent valuation survey among a very poor, illiterate population and obtain reasonable, consistent answers'. They add that the contingent valuation approach has validity in a wide range of policy settings, especially for deriving the WTP for infrastructure projects.

3.3.2   *Consumer surplus and paying for water*

Now that we have seen that it is possible to have reliable estimates of WTP using survey methods, let us consider a case where a survey has been used to estimate the consumer surplus for water.

Singh et al. (1993) estimated the demand curve for yard taps (house connections) in the state of Kerala in India. In one part of the study, households were asked how they would respond to various prices for the monthly tariff, given the prevailing connection fee of 100 rupees (Rs). The current tariff was Rs 5 (approximately $0.36). A series of (up to four) contingent valuation questions were asked at prices above the current tariff (50, 30, 20 and 10 rupees).

Two sets of households were interviewed. The first (site A households) consisted of those living in an area where an improved water supply system had been in existence for a number of years and where house connections had been made. The second (site B households) were people currently without an improved system, but were targeted for an improved system within the near future. An *improved* water system can be defined as one where the quality and reliability of the water provided is enhanced, and/or one where household connections are possible (without reducing the pressure and reliability for the rest of the system). Most households in Kerala are served only by free public standposts.

The resulting demand curve is shown as the curve *ABCD* in Diagram 3.5 (their Figure 3). The monthly tariff is on the vertical axis and the number of connections is on the horizontal axis. At the current tariff of Rs 5, the number of connections that households were willing to pay for was 3 500. However, the water authorities connected only 250 (supply was constrained at this level). At this constrained level of connections, the WTP was Rs 25. Benefits were the area under the *AB* segment of the demand over the range of connections 0 to 250. This was estimated to be around Rs 6 725. Since what consumers actually paid was Rs 1 250 (that is, Rs 5 times 250), consumer surplus was calculated to be Rs 5 500 (per month).

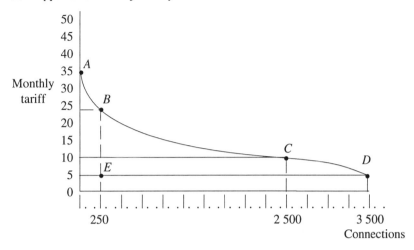

The demand for water connections in Kerala has point *E* as the existing price and quantity. This is a constrained quantity as 250 is provided, when 3 500 is demanded (point *D*). The 'project' involves charging a higher price in order to provide a greater quantity, i.e., move from point *E* to point *C*.

Diagram 3.5

Singh et al. considered that the unconstrained supply of connections would be 2 500. We see from the demand curve that, at this level of connections, the market would clear at a tariff of Rs 10. This suggested to the researchers a hypothetical water expansion 'project', which consisted of raising the level of connections to 2 500 while raising the tariff to Rs 10 (that is, moving from a price of Rs 5 and quantity of 250 to a price of Rs 10 and quantity 2500).

At the new (proposed) connection level, total revenues would be Rs 25 000 (i.e., Rs 10 times 2 500). These revenues could be used to cover Rs 10 000 for connecting the extra 2 250 households onto the system, and have a further Rs 15 000 available to meet recurrent costs of operation. The 'project' would therefore be self-financing. But would it be socially worthwhile? The test was to see what happened to consumer surplus. At the 2 500 connection level, total benefits (the area under the *ABC* segment of the demand curve over the range of connections 0 to 2 500) were estimated to be Rs 50 000. By subtracting from this amount what the consumers would have to pay (Rs 25 000), the new consumer surplus would be Rs 25 000, which is 450 per cent higher than the existing figure of Rs 5 500. The tariff hike and expansion project was clearly beneficial.

The Singh et al. study highlights a very important public policy issue. Often public services are provided with low user charges. Over time this leads to budget problems. With the constrained budget, quality levels deteriorate, and this reduces even further the willingness of people to pay for the service. Singh et al. call this problem a 'low-level equilibrium trap'. Their study shows how important it is to estimate user demand for these services. If WTP exists, users can be made better off if charges are raised somewhat and used to improve services.

3.3.3 *Different categories of transport demand*
A useful way of thinking about many transport investments is to regard them as cost-reducing activities. A journey that had a particular cost before is now cheaper. There are likely to be two effects of this cost reduction. First, existing traffic will receive additional consumer surplus. Then there will be new consumer surplus from the traffic attracted by the lower cost. One of the first studies to identify and incorporate these two categories of effect was the Foster and Beesley (1963) evaluation of the Victoria Line extension to the London Underground. Many of the general principles of applying CBA to the particular circumstances of transport appraisal are illustrated by this study.

One common problem faced by any comparison of transport modes is how to treat 'price', when the fare paid is just one element that determines the cost of making a journey. In particular, journey time differences and variations in travel comfort are also key ingredients.

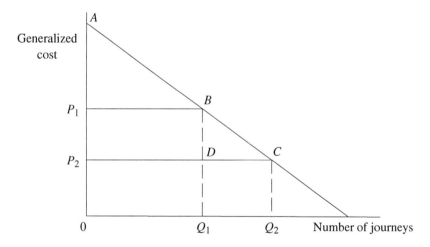

The transport project lowers costs from P_1 to P_2. The existing journeys Q_1 receive a consumer surplus gain of P_2DBP_1. In addition, new journeys are now being made, the difference Q_2Q_1. The new journeys are called 'generated traffic' and they also receive consumer surplus (the triangular area DCB).

Diagram 3.6

To deal with this problem, transport economists have come up with the idea of a 'generalized' price (or cost). This is a composite estimate of all the disparate elements that make up the cost. For example, if a train journey costs $1 more per journey than a bus journey and is 15 minutes slower, then by valuing the time difference at some multiple of the wage rate (say $8 per hour), the generalized cost would be $3 greater for the train journey.

We can use this idea of a generalized price to visualize the benefits of the Victoria Line, as shown in Diagram 3.6. The demand curve represents the benefits of making a journey independent of the particular travel mode chosen. The generalized cost prior to the introduction of the Victoria Line is P_1. The corresponding number of journeys is Q_1 (consisting of pedestrians, bus and train users, and journeys made on other lines of the underground). The effect of the Victoria Line is to lower the generalized cost to P_2. Q_2 are the new number of journeys. The impact of the Victoria Line can be expressed in terms of the change in consumer surplus P_2CBP_1. This area has two parts, the rectangular area P_2DBP_1 and the triangular area DCB.

i.   The rectangular area is the cost saving to existing users. For the Victoria Line study, this was split into two categories: *diverted* and *non-diverted* traffic. The former category consists of cost reductions (lower fares, time savings, lower vehicle operating costs and increased comfort) received by travellers switching from other modes. The latter category are travellers on the rest of the system, who do not transfer to the Victoria Line, but gain by the reduced congestion, time savings and increased comfort caused by there being fewer journeys made on the other modes.

ii. The triangular area comes from *generated* traffic. These are people who formerly did not make the journey because it was considered too expensive. Now with the cost reduction from the Victoria Line, they are induced to make the journey.

The full social benefits and costs of the Victoria Line are listed in Table 3.2. (based on Table 2 of Foster and Beesley). The useful life of the project was arbitrarily set to last for 50 years (and then sold for its scrap value). Six per cent was used as the discount rate (though they also tried 4 per cent and 8 per cent which did not materially affect the results). The table shows that the amount corresponding to the area P_2DBP_1 in Diagram 3.6 was £5.971 million per annum, being the sum of £2.055 million coming from diverted traffic and £3.916 million from traffic not diverted by the Victoria Line. The triangular area DCB, representing generated traffic was £0.822 million. Total benefits were therefore £6.793 million per annum.

Table 3.2   Benefits and costs of the Victoria Line

Category of effect	Annual amount £million	NPV at 6% £million
Operating costs	1.413	16.16
Recurring benefits		
Diverted traffic	2.055	29.34
Non-diverted traffic	3.916	44.79
Generated traffic	0.822	11.74
Total recurring benefits	6.793	85.87
Recurring net benefits	5.380	69.71
Capital expenditure	—	38.52
Total net benefits	—	31.19

Source: Foster and Beesley (1963)

An important feature of the benefits results was that traffic not diverted contributed 52 per cent of the total. This means that most of the benefits of the Victoria Line accrued to the system as a whole. They could not have been appropriated as revenues by a private enterprise if it were to have invested in the project. This shows clearly how using a CBA produces different results from a private profit–loss calculation and is more valid as a social criterion.

Another feature of the benefits results was that time savings from all sources had a present value of $40.68 million, nearly half of the total benefits. This highlights the importance of valuing time savings in transport studies.

When we include the costs with the benefits, we see that the NPV was positive at £31.19 million. (The NPV was £64.97 million using the 4 per cent discount rate and £12.57 million at the 8 per cent rate.) The Victoria Line was clearly worthwhile. Although the evaluation was made after the Victoria Line had already been built, it is important to check that projects that intuitively seem worthwhile can survive a systematic appraisal. At a minimum they can prevent the chance of making the same mistake twice. While it is best to carry out a CBA in advance, with an *ex post* evaluation one will usually have much more complete data available.

3.3.4   Consumer surplus measures with distribution weights

We know that the *CV* and the *EV* will differ from each other and the Marshallian measure, but how large will these differences be in practice? Also we would like to find out how using distribution weights alters actual outcomes. Both these aspects were covered in Hau's (1986) estimation of the net benefits of constructing an extra lane to the San Francisco Bay Bridge in California. We start with the efficiency analysis, and later supply the distributional dimension.

Consumer surplus measures in an efficiency context   The extra lane would, on average, reduce travel times 10 minutes per vehicle between Interstate 580/California 24 Interchange and the San Francisco Bay Bridge. This 25 per cent reduction in journey time translates into recurring net benefits of 5.38 cents per commuter per working day (there are assumed to be 260 working days per year). This was equal to 0.07 per cent of daily income ($76.70 on average). With such a small impact on income, it was not surprising that the three consumer surplus measures produced virtually identical results. The daily estimates were:

Compensating variation = $18 338;
Marshallian measure   = $18 347;
Equilibriating variation = $18 357.

Consistent with the theory provided in section 3.2.3, the *EV* was largest and the *CV* was smallest. But, the difference between the *EV* and *CV* was only $19.02 per day, or $4 945 per annum. Compared to the annual construction costs of $2.4 million per lane mile, this difference is very insignificant.

It is interesting to compare this result with another study by Hau on this stretch of highway. In Hau (1987), he also considered whether to introduce a price in order that commuters would bear the true costs of commuting (eliminating all subsidies). These charges would represent a 2 per cent reduction in income. For this change, the annual difference between the *EV* and the *CV* was $3.2 million. Compared to the $2.4 million construction costs, the difference was not now trivial.

Although the net benefits per person were small for the highway extension project, the aggregate effects were large. By assuming a 35-year lifespan for the project, Hau estimated that the NPV of the net benefits were $33 million, over ten times the capital costs of $3.1 million. On efficiency grounds, an increase in lane capacity was desirable.

Consumer surplus with distribution weights   Hau split his sample into three income groups with an equal number in each. Income inequality was therefore defined in relative terms. The bottom third had annual incomes below $15 000 and these were defined as 'low income'. The 'middle-income' group had annual incomes between $15 000 and $22 000, and 'high income' was the third of the sample above $22 000.

The methodology of using time savings to estimate demand benefits had an important implication for the distributional effects of the lane extension project. The higher a group's wage rate, the higher would be its benefits. Table 3.3 (based on Tables 2 and 6 of Hau) shows that the high-income group ended up with net benefits (cents per commuter per working day) that were over eight times that for the low-income group.

Table 3.3   Benefits and components by income group

Variable	All	Low income	Medium income	High income
No. of individuals	2 216	720	768	728
Wages ($ per hour)	8.44	5.31	7.73	12.27
Value of time ($ per hour)	4.38	2.08	4.01	7.04
Mean distance (in miles)	18.13	15.27	19.43	19.57
Drivers in household	1.98	1.69	2.02	2.22
Cars in household	1.57	1.12	1.65	1.92
Net benefits (in cents)	5.38	1.16	5.21	9.73

Source: Hau (1987)

The next step is to weight the net benefits according to the group involved. Define a_i as the social marginal utility of income group i and use Δ to denote a (nonmarginal) change:

$$a_i = \frac{\Delta\,Social\;Welfare}{\Delta\,Income\;of\;Group\;i} \tag{3.6}$$

This is the income distribution weight that we have used, and will use, throughout the book. However, in this chapter where we are starting with utility changes and then putting monetary values on them, it is useful to follow Hau and think of the weight as being formed in two steps. Divide top and bottom of the right-hand side of equation (3.6) by the 'change in utility of group i' and rearrange to form:

$$a_i = \left[\frac{\Delta\,Social\;Welfare}{\Delta\,Utility\;of\;Group\;i}\right] \cdot \left[\frac{\Delta\,Utility\;of\;Group\;i}{\Delta\,Income\;of\;Group\;i}\right] \tag{3.7}$$

Equation (3.7) makes clear that a unit of extra income affects social welfare in two stages. First the unit of income increases the utility of a particular group. This is the marginal utility of income that is the second bracketed term in the equation, called λ_i by Hau. Then, by making the utility of a group better off, society's welfare has improved. This is the first bracketed term in the equation, called w_i by Hau, which is just the group version of the individualistic postulate that we covered in the last chapter. Equation (3.7) can then be written in symbols as:

$$a_i = w_i.\lambda_i \tag{3.8}$$

Equation (3.8) enables us to decompose our value judgements as they relate to income distributional weights. That is, we can think in terms of having to fix both w_i and λ_i. Conversely, as pointed out by Hau (1986, p. 331), if we impose values for a_i, we are implicitly fixing values for w_i and λ_i. Thus, if we follow Harberger (1978) and Mishan (1976) and the other traditional CBA economists by using unitary income distribution weights and assume $a_i = 1$, then we are setting $w_i = 1/\lambda_i$. This is anti-egalitarian in the sense that a group's contribution to social welfare is determined by the *inverse* of the marginal utility of income. (Note that the lower one's income, the higher will be the marginal utility of income. Hence the smaller will be the inverse of the marginal utility of income.)

Hau's approach to using equation (3.8) is to express the welfare effect of an increase in utility w_i as a function of the marginal utility of income λ_i. This then makes the distribution weight a_i a function only of λ_i. The welfare effect takes the form $w_i = \lambda_i^\gamma$ (where γ is a parameter to be specified) which makes the distribution weights:

$$a_i = w_i.\lambda_i = \lambda_i^\gamma.\lambda_i = \lambda_i^{\gamma+1} \tag{3.9}$$

What makes this version interesting is that the main formulations in the literature can be derived as special cases of values for γ. Three of these will now be discussed.

i.   Consider equation (3.1) with which we started the chapter. This has social welfare as a sum of individual utilities. In the literature it is known as the utilitarian social welfare function. Since this is an unweighted sum, this is equivalent to using equal *utility* weights (that is, the coefficient attached to each individual's utility is effectively unity). To obtain $w_i = 1$ from λ_i^γ, one sets $\gamma = 0$. Thus utilitarianism is the special case where $\gamma = 0$. For this value, equation (3.9) produces $a_i = \lambda_i$. The first listing in Table 3.4 (which combines Tables 7–9 of Hau) shows the utilitarian distribution weights and the weighted change in consumer surplus.

Table 3.4 Distribution weights and changes in consumer surplus

Weighting system		All	Low income	Medium income	High income
Utilitarianism	Weight	1.26	2.83	0.62	0.38
($\gamma = 0$)	Change	2.93	1.68	3.54	3.52
Traditional CBA	Weight	1.00	1.00	1.00	1.00
($\gamma = -1$)	Change	5.88	1.50	5.84	10.24
Intermediate	Weight	0.89	1.29	0.78	0.61
($\gamma = -0.5$)	Change	4.03	1.55	4.54	5.94

Source: Hau (1986)

ii. Next, consider equation (3.2). This replaced utility levels with income levels. Social welfare was the sum of individual incomes. Again this is an unweighted sum. But, this time it is unitary *income* weights that is implied. As the efficiency CBA equation (3.3) was just an extended version of equation (3.2), we can also associate unitary income weights with aggregate WTP, which is the traditional CBA criterion. In terms of equation (3.9), we obtain $a_i = 1$ by setting $\gamma = -1$. The second listing in Table 3.4 shows the results using the traditional CBA weighting scheme.

iii. Finally, we have the intermediate cases, where γ lies in between the 0 value for utilitarianism and the -1 value for traditional CBA. Hau focuses on $\gamma = -0.5$, which he calls 'generalized utilitarianism', and we list in table 3.4 as the 'intermediate case'. The weights are the square root of λ_i (i.e., $a_i = \lambda_i^{0.5}$)

Table 3.4 shows that the (per commuter per working day) change in consumer surplus varies from a high of 5.88 cents under the traditional CBA weighting scheme to a low of 2.93 cents under utilitarianism (with the intermediate case in between). The reason for the difference is that under utilitarianism, the fact that the high income group gets most of the benefits is penalized. The weight to the high income group is low (0.38) because the marginal utility of income falls rapidly with income.

3.4 Final comments

3.4.1 Summary
The main objective of this chapter was to show that there was something important missing from a private evaluation that looked at just profits, that is,

revenues and costs. The missing element was 'consumer surplus'. A social evaluation that includes this element is better able to ensure that all relevant benefits are being included.

The revenue and consumer elements combined aggregate up to the market demand curve that plays a crucial role in microeconomic theory. In the process of explaining how the demand curve relates to individual utility functions, we made clear why market forces should play a role in public policy decisions. Underlying market demand curves are consumer preferences. If we wish to maximize individual utilities, then the demand curve is an important source of information and valuation for social decisions. In short, the demand curve measures the 'benefit' part of CBA. We just have to be careful that we include all parts of the demand curve. Willingness to pay was the all-inclusive concept that corresponds to each and every point on the demand curve.

The main conceptual problem was that there is more than one way to move from individual utility functions to form the individual demand curves. When a price changes, there is an income and a substitution effect. When we allow both effects to vary, we trace out the traditional, Marshallian demand curve. When we consider only the substitution effect, there are two other measures of demand, and hence two other measures of consumer surplus. One holds real income constant at the original level of utility. This produces the compensated variation. The other measure holds real income constant at the level of utility after the change. This leads to the equilibrating variation.

Although there are the three alternative measures, for most practical purposes one need only concentrate on trying to estimate the Marshallian measure. If one had reason to doubt that the difference between the Marshallian and the *CV* measures would be small in any particular case study, one could use the Willig approximation. This allows one to obtain the *CV* value that corresponds to the Marshallian estimate.

Little (1957) has called consumer surplus 'a theoretical toy'. Our response to this charge was to present case studies where the concept was usefully used in practice. In general, as we explained in section 3.1.2, consumer surplus supplies a social justification for providing goods that would otherwise be rejected by a private market. To quote Mishan (1976): 'Without this concept how does the economist justify the free use of roads, bridges, parks, etc., or the operation of industries at outputs for which prices are below marginal costs, or two-part tariffs? Without attempts to measure consumers' surpluses, and rents, cost–benefit analyses would be primitive indeed.'

The applications covered all the main issues raised in the chapter and highlighted some philosophical concerns surrounding CBA. WTP and consumer surplus are derived from the demand curve. It was important to examine some of the problems that can arise when estimating demand curves using questionnaires. Then we summarized a Dupuit-type case study where extra water could be financed by extracting the consumer surplus that existed. Many non-economists question whether CBA should be based on demand rather than *need*. By undertaking these water-demand studies, the World Bank provided a practical response to this debate. Providing water because outsiders believed a need existed was not helpful. Water connections were not used and not maintained because, in many cases, a demand did not exist. If one wants water to be used, demand must be considered. The third application showed how consumer surplus changes can be interpreted as 'cost savings' from transport projects. The applications closed with an illustration of how the alternative consumer surplus measures (with and without distributional weights) can impact on project outcomes.

3.4.2 Problems

We have argued that CBA is useful for analysing any public policy decision, not just those that are explicitly called 'projects'. In the first problem we show how consumer surplus analysis can be used to evaluate trade restrictions. The data comes from Tarr and Morkre (1984). We see that there is a loss of consumer surplus by one nation that does not have a positive counterpart for the other nation. In a nutshell, this is why most economists are against trade restrictions

In this chapter we explained why there were alternative measures of consumer surplus. Our main conclusion was that, since in practice the *best* we can usually hope for is knowledge of the Marshallian demand curve, the traditional (uncompensated) consumer surplus measure will have to suffice. However, we always have the option of converting this Marshallian measure to the *CV* equivalent if we have knowledge of the ingredients necessary to make the Willig approximation. The second problem therefore requires one to use the Willig formula to rework one of the case studies which analysed effects only in Marshallian terms.

1. In 1981, Japan imposed a quota on itself for car sales to the United States. The effects were: to restrict consumption from 2.69 million cars in 1981 to 1.91 million; and to raise the average price from $4 573 to $4 967.
   i.   Draw the demand curve for Japanese cars and record the pre- and post-quota prices and quantities. (Hint: assume that the demand curve is a straight line linking any two points on the curve.)
   ii. By how much did the welfare of American consumers fall by the introduction of the quota? Show this on the diagram.
   iii. Of the total reduction in welfare by Americans, how much was offset by a rise in the welfare ('economic rents') by Japanese producers obtained by their now earning a higher price? Show this on the diagram.

    iv. So how much of the loss in welfare by Americans was a 'deadweight loss' (that is, a reduction in welfare that was not matched by a gain by anyone else, whomever they may be)? Show this on the diagram.

2. Use the Willig (1976) approximation procedure, equation (3.5), to see what difference it would have made to the evaluation of the Victoria Line to have used the *CV* measure rather than the Marshallian measure of consumer surplus. In your calculation of the *CV*, use the same basic values as Willig used in his example, i.e., $A/M_0 = 5$ per cent and $\eta = 1.2$. (Hint: *A* is the Marshallian measure of the benefits of the Victoria Line, £69.71 million.)

3.5   Appendix

In section 3.1.3, we promised to prove that $a_2(ECB) + (a_2 - a_1)Q_2Q_1CE$ corresponds with the social criterion $a_2B - a_1C$, presented as equation (1.2) in Chapter 1. This we now do. $a_2(ECB) + (a_2 - a_1)Q_2Q_1CE$ can be written as $a_2CS + (a_2 - a_1)C$, where *ECB* is the consumer surplus *CS*, and Q_2Q_1CE is costs *C*. Collecting terms with the same weight, this simplifies to $a_2(CS + C) - a_1C$. Our assumption that the price P_1 covered the costs means that *R* (repayments) equals *C*. Substituting for *C* in the first term produces the criterion: $a_2(CS + R) - a_1C$. By definition, $B = CS + R$, so we end up with $a_2B - a_1C$.

PART III

4   Shadow prices

4.1   Introduction

Shadow price (social value) determination is at the heart of CBA and public policy. To encourage or discourage any activity one needs to know its social value. If the market price is below its shadow price, then the scale of the activity should be expanded. The encouragement may take many forms. One could build a project for this purpose, or one could place a subsidy on the activity. Similarly, if the current price is above its shadow price, the activity should be reduced in scale. Disinvestment may take place (as with the closing of unremunerative railway lines) or the activity can be taxed. The knowledge of shadow prices is therefore essential to guiding the direction of policy changes. Many policy issues, such as whether to provide a labour subsidy to promote employment, or whether physicians' salaries are to be considered 'too high', are not specialized topics. They simply require an estimation of shadow prices.

Although this chapter (which is the first in Part III) is entirely devoted to shadow pricing, shadow price determination is the underlying theme behind most chapters in the book. Thus, externalities and public goods (which are the next chapter titles) are just special cases where the (private) market prices differ from their shadow prices. Here we concentrate more on identifying the general, fundamental principles and indicate the wide range of alternative techniques available. Other chapters can be viewed as discussing shadow pricing in particular, identified situations. (The shadow pricing of labour is covered extensively in Brent (1990, ch. 5) so will not be discussed in this text.)

Distributional considerations can, and have been, incorporated into shadow price formulations (see, for example, Diamond, 1975, and Boadway, 1976). However, this chapter will focus more on efficiency rather than distributional issues. As mentioned in Chapter 1, our approach to distribution weights means that efficiency effects are incorporated in the measures of benefits and costs, and distributional considerations are then included in terms of the weights that will be attached to those benefits and costs.

The introduction section defines shadow prices and relates them to the analogous problem of trying to set optimal commodity taxes. Applications often express shadow prices as a ratio of market process and the advantages of doing this are explained. A simple way of thinking about how government involvement in the mixed economy impacts on private markets is then presented. Alternative candidates for shadow prices suggested in the literature are introduced. It is shown how these alternatives can be combined into a simple expression and this will be referred to when more advanced shadow price formulations are being discussed.

The next section deals with the three main methods for calculating shadow prices. The first, relying on Lagrange multipliers, is the most general and can be applied no matter the objective or the constraints, as long as both of these are made explicit. The second follows the types of objectives and constraints that are usually considered in welfare economics. The objective is the individualistic social welfare function and the constraint is the production function, or more generally, a financial budget constraint. The shadow prices follow from maximizing this particular objective and constraint. This process is explicitly modelled in Appendix 4.5.2, where the Ramsey (1927) rule is derived. The main body of the text takes this rule as given and discusses its basis in intuitive and graphical terms. The final method involves a short-cut procedure. Rather than specify a general formula, it relies on using a particular data source that is a direct and simple alternative to using market price data. That source is producer price data. There is a justification for this procedure based on an explicit maximization model, called the Diamond–Mirrlees theorem. We go behind this theorem to explain what makes shadow pricing different in a mixed economy.

We take the position that CBA is applied welfare economics. Thus selecting a method that is based on welfare maximization is central to our way of thinking about CBA. For the special case where the objective function is an individualistic welfare function, and the constraint is a public budget constraint, method one would give the same result as method two. Similarly, producer prices can be derived (and have been in the literature) from maximizing welfare subject to a production function and individual budget constraints. There is thus, *in theory*, a unity about all three techniques covered in this chapter. In practice, it all boils down to how much information one has at hand for the project that one is evaluating. When details of production and consumption data are available, method one can be used. With knowledge of consumer elasticities (and marginal costs) method two applies. With limited data, method three is most useful.

The applications illustrate the three main shadow price methods. For the Lagrange multiplier method we take a 'stylized' (ideal type) case study which enables the reader to check all the derivations using simple arithmetic. An appreciation of the general method can be gained without having to explore all the technical details. The second case study shows how to apply the Ramsey rule. The final two case studies deal with the determination of shadow prices for physician services. The first of these relates to the producer price method. Then we go back to the Ramsey pricing rule in order to compare and contrast findings using the second and third methods.

4.1.1   Definition of a shadow price

A shadow price, S, can be defined as the increase in social welfare resulting from any marginal change in the availability of commodities or factors of production. If public investment output of good g is denoted by Y_g, then:

$$S_g = \frac{\Delta\,Social\ Welfare}{\Delta\,Output\ of\ Good\ Y_g} \tag{4.1}$$

A shadow price reflects the social evaluation of the input or output. This value may or may not equal the market price. It is called a 'shadow' price as it does not have an existence apart from its use in the social evaluation. Because of their role in government accounts to value inputs and outputs, shadow prices are also known as *accounting prices*.

There are various methods of estimating shadow prices. The method one chooses depends on three main factors.

i.   The goals of society (the welfare function). If one is concerned about unemployment, then one is more likely to accept a low shadow price (wage) for labour, relative to the market wage.
ii.   The ability of the government to control the economy. If one cannot control the rate of saving (the country is underinvesting), then one gives a higher shadow price to investment funds rather than consumption funds.
iii. Durability of market imperfections. For example, if import controls exist, one must give a high shadow price to foreign exchange.

4.1.2   Shadow prices and optimal commodity taxation

In many countries (especially developing countries and the United States) public investment and production is limited. Public policy may then be more concerned with working with private sector market prices P rather than setting prices for public production. When these market prices reflect imperfections (externalities, monopolies, etc.), one may need to adjust them using commodity taxes T in order that they reflect their social value. Since a good's social value is its shadow price S, this means that the commodity tax must be set equal to the difference between the market price and its shadow price:

$$T = P - S \tag{4.2}$$

This relation explains why much of the literature concerned with shadow prices for mixed economies also deals with optimal taxation – see, for example, the title of the pioneering Diamond and Mirrlees (1971) article.

4.1.3   Shadow prices and accounting ratios

There are many circumstances where it is useful to calculate the shadow prices and then express them relative to the market price for that input or output. Such a ratio is called an 'accounting ratio' AR and is defined as:

$$Accounting\ Ratio = \frac{Shadow\ Price}{Market\ Price} \qquad (4.3)$$

If one then multiplies the market price with the AR one obtains the shadow price. For example, if the market price is 100 units and the AR is 0.5, then the shadow price is 50 units.

An AR seems to be adding an unnecessary step, as one needs to know the shadow price first in order to calculate the AR. But, it is used when either: (a) the past value of an AR is used to find a current shadow price, or (b) the AR for one good is used to calculate the shadow price of another good. These two cases will now be illustrated.

i.   Say one calculates the current shadow price for computers as 100 units when the market price is 200 units. One then obtains an AR of 0.5. If next year the market price of computers due to inflation has risen to 300 units, then one does not have to re-estimate the shadow price. One knows its value is 150 units using the AR of 0.5.

ii. One does not always have the time or resources to calculate the shadow price for everything that enters a CBA. Sometimes short-cuts need to be taken. It may be possible to argue that, when groups of products are being considered which are subject to common market conditions, an AR for one item in the group may be representative of all. Thus, if the AR for cars is 0.4, and one is considering how to value trucks produced by the same company (and subject to the same rates of tax), one may just multiply the truck market price by 0.4 to obtain a rough estimate of the shadow price for trucks.

4.1.4   Shadow prices and competitive markets

Consider a competitive market for computers, as in Diagram 4.1, where the price is determined by demand D and supply S. The equilibrium occurs at point A, where price is P_1 and quantity is Q_1. The social value of the quantity Q_1 is given by the market price P_1. This value can be derived in two ways. We can ask what consumers are WTP for this quantity (equal to the demand price AQ_1); or we can measure the value of resources used to produce Q_1 (which is the supply price AQ_1). With demand equal to supply at equilibrium, the two measures of social value are the same, both equal to P_1. We can therefore use either the consumer (demand) price or the producer (supply) price as the shadow price for computers.

Now assume that the government requires some of the computers for its own activities. Let Q_1Q_2 be the number that it wants to use. In a mixed economy, private agents can not just be commanded to give up their resources. They have to be induced by price incentives (or disincentives). Let the government impose a (revenue-raising) tax of $T = BC$ per unit. The tax acts as a wedge that both lowers the price (net of the tax) that producers receive and raises the price that consumers have to pay. The new equilibrium is at point B where P_C is the consumer price. (Think of the supply curve shifting to the left such that it intersects the demand curve at B.) Q_2 is the quantity that is consumed by the private sector. In order to obtain the quantity Q_1Q_2, the government must use the tax revenue to purchase the desired quantity at the price P_1. It is only at the price P_1 that firms will produce a total quantity Q_1, whereby the government gets Q_1Q_2 and the private sector consumes Q_2. That is, $0Q_2 + Q_1Q_2 = 0Q_1$.

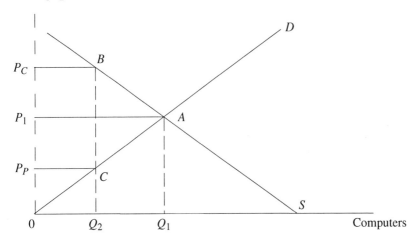

At the competitive equilibrium quantity Q_1, the demand price at A equals the supply price. Then the government removes Q_1Q_2 from the market for the project. A tax of BC is imposed. At Q_2, the demand price P_C is above the supply price P_P, and neither is equal to the market price.

Diagram 4.1

At first glance, nothing significant seems to have occurred. Quantity is still Q_1, supply is still S_1, and D_1 remains the total demand curve faced by private firms. Only the composition of this demand has altered. The government gets a share, when originally it had none. But this composition change has caused a difference between the consumer and producer prices. The producer price P_P (the supply price at point C) is below the consumer price P_C (the demand price at B). This difference is important when we consider a further expansion of demand by the government for private resources, that is, a public project which necessitates the use of more computers by the government.

When we ask what is the value to the private sector of the extra computers the government is requiring them to give up, we have two different valuations to consider. Should the shadow price be the producer price P_P or the larger consumer price P_C? The answer depends on the source of the additional resources. If consumers are to give up the extra computers, the consumer price is the correct shadow price. This is what they are willing to pay for those computers. While if the private sector responds by satisfying all the private demands as before, and meeting the additional government demand by producing more computers, then the producer price is the correct shadow price. The value of the forgone resources used to produce the extra computers is what P_P measures.

In general, we can expect the resources for the public project to come from both sources. Let α be the share of the public sector's extra resource requirements that comes at the expense of the private consumption. Hence $(1 - \alpha)$ is the share that comes from additional production by the private sector. The shadow price can then be expressed as a weighted average of the consumer and producer prices (similar to Tresch's (1981) equation (22.60)):

$$S = \alpha P_C + (1 - \alpha)P_P \qquad (4.4)$$

4.2   General ways of deriving shadow prices

In this section we show: (a) how to derive shadow prices in a setting where the objective and constraint are specified only in general terms; (b) how to derive shadow prices when we have an individualistic objective function and individuals maximize utility at market prices; and (c) how to derive shadow prices in a public sector which is competing for resources with the private sector.

4.2.1   Lagrange multipliers

A public project (or a policy change generally) can be thought to be associated with a vector x, which is a set of inputs and outputs. These inputs and outputs have value and we denote by $F(x)$ our objective function. At the optimum the vector is $\bar{x}$. The maximum value function V is the value that corresponds to the optimum vector level, i.e., $V = F(\bar{x})$. The constraint is written in implicit form as $G(\bar{x}) = c$, where c specifies the availability of resources. The allocation problem here is to maximize F subject to the constraint G. Shadow prices (the derivative of V with respect to c) are then simply equal to the Lagrange multipliers λ attached to the constraint (a proof of this is in appendix 4.5.1). From which we get:

$$\frac{dV}{dc} = \lambda \qquad (4.5)$$

Thus, the Lagrange multiplier tells us the rate of change of the maximum attainable value with respect to a change in a constraining parameter.

An example illustrates the approach. Say a policy-maker is concerned about two outputs, the proverbial guns (x_1) and butter (x_2). These goods are assigned values by a social decision-maker. For instance, one gun is worth two units of butter. The objective function F then appears as $2x_1 + x_2$. The constraint could be that there is a fixed labour force, $\bar{H}$, which can produce either guns or butter. If one worker can produce a quarter of a gun or a fifth of a unit of butter, then the constraint is: $\bar{H} = 4x_1 + 5x_2$. The problem involves maximizing: $2x_1 + x_2 + \lambda(\bar{H} - 4x_1 + 5x_2)$. When one feeds in a figure for the labour force, and solves this by the appropriate technique (i.e., linear programming), a value for λ is obtained (as well as for x_1 and x_2). A solution value such as $\lambda = 2$ implies that if the labour force were to expand by one extra worker, then the value to the social decision-maker would go up by 2 units.

What is important to understand about this approach is how general it is. The valuation function F can respect consumer sovereignty, or it can be dictatorial and undemocratic. F can take any form (be linear, quadratic, and so on). The constraint can be simple, to recognize only labour as a resource, or it can be multiple to include many different factors (as equalities or inequalities). The framework requires only the two ingredients for rational economic decision-making, namely, a statement of the objectives and the constraints. Different formulations of the problem require different solution techniques (for example, linear, non-linear, integer, and dynamic programming). But, once values for λ have been obtained (one for each constraint), they all have the same shadow price interpretation.

4.2.2 *The Ramsey rule*

We have previously referred to the result that, under perfect competition, a firm will set price equal to MC. MC would then seem to be a good candidate to use as the shadow price. This is the case under certain circumstances (*inter alia*, when there are no other distortions in the rest of the economy and we ignore distribution issues). But it may not apply if the sector doing the pricing has a budget constraint. To see how the existence of a budget constraint can become an issue, consider an enterprise (such as in the electricity or gas industries) that is usually publicly owned in Europe or regulated in the United States. Such an enterprise typically has falling average ACs, as illustrated in Diagram 4.2.

MC pricing means finding the intersection between the MC and the demand curve D and using this as the shadow price. Recall that the demand curve indicates the set of prices that individuals are WTP for each and every unit of the good or service. The intersection of the demand curve with the MC curve then indicates which point on D is to be the particular price that one is to use. In Diagram 4.2, this intersection takes place at point A. At A, P_M is the MC price and Q_M is the quantity.

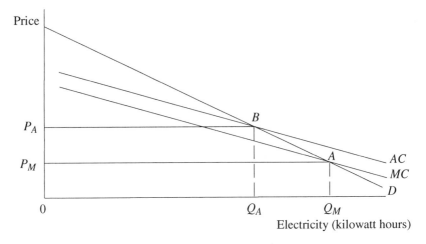

In a falling cost industry, $MC < AC$. Thus, $P = MC$ implies $P < AC$ and a loss will result at the competitive output level Q_M. At Q_A, where $P = AC$, there is no loss. But there is no welfare significance to this level of output. The Ramsey rule decides how to move in between the two price extremes P_A and P_M.

Diagram 4.2

With a falling AC curve, MC pricing has an inevitable result. Falling costs mean that the MC curve is always below the AC. With $P = MC$ and $MC < AC$, it implies that $P < AC$. A financial loss will occur from such a pricing rule. Some mechanism for dealing with this financial deficit must be specified whenever MC pricing is recommended for goods in declining cost industries.

MC pricing is the solution to a particular public policy problem, that is, how to obtain the largest amount of consumer surplus. This is the reason why 'demand equals supply' in competitive markets was the most efficient outcome. If consumer surplus is maximized at this point, clearly it would not be possible to move away from it and have gains large enough to compensate losers. With supply being derived from the MC curves of individual firms, demand equals supply was also $D = MC$, exactly the MC pricing strategy.

With the recognition of the need to cover the financial loss, a new problem can be identified. This is to maximize consumer surplus subject to a budget constraint. The budget constraint can be anything that the central government decides. For example, the loss could be capped at an upper limit, a break-even requirement could be set, or the sector doing the evaluation may need to generate a surplus to subsidize other activities. This new problem was first tackled by Ramsey (1927). His solution is known as the Ramsey rule:

$$\frac{S_i - MC_i}{S_i} = k \cdot \frac{1}{e_{p_i}} \tag{4.6}$$

Equation (4.6) is the inverse elasticity rule for any activity i. The percentage mark-up of social price over marginal cost should be inversely proportional to the price elasticity of demand e_p, where k is the proportionality factor. Thus, prices should be set most above MC when elasticities are the lowest. Our task now is to explain (i) how, and (ii) why, the Ramsey rule works.

i. Refer back to Diagram 4.2. If the budget constraint was that the enterprise must break even, then the rule is simply to set price equal to AC at point B. With price equal to P_A, there is no loss; but there is a considerable reduction in consumer surplus relative to price P_M. When there is a single-product enterprise, there is little room for manoeuvre. To break even, one *has* to charge P_A. But, when there are multiple products (cars, buses, trucks) or different categories of user (residential, commercial and industrial users of electricity) then there is scope for charging different prices. The Ramsey rule gives guidance in those situations. Prices can be closest to average costs (or even exceed AC) when elasticities are low; and prices can be closest to marginal costs when elasticities are high.

ii. Baumol and Bradford (1970) explain the rationale behind the Ramsey rule based on a diagram first devised by Vickrey, and reproduced as Diagram 4.3 below. This has two demand curves D_A and D_B (representing two products or two categories of user) going through a common point K, where P_0 is the price and Q_0 is the quantity. The analysis involves using the Marshallian measure of consumer surplus to compare the loss of utility from a price rise against the gain in extra revenue. First consider the less elastic demand curve $D_B K$. The rise in price to P_1 causes a loss of consumer surplus of $P_0 K E_B P_1$ and a change in revenue of $P_0 K_B E_B P_1$ minus $Q_B Q_0 K K_B$ (the revenue gain from charging the higher price P_1 less the revenue loss from selling the lower quantity Q_B). The positive part of the revenue change is offset by the rectangular part of the loss of consumer surplus, which makes the net loss of consumer surplus the triangular area $K_B K E_B$. The total loss of consumer surplus and revenue is $Q_B Q_0 K E_B$ ($K_B K E_B$ plus $Q_B Q_0 K K_B$). For the more elastic demand curve D_A, the total loss is the much larger area $Q_A Q_0 K E_A$. Hence, we get the result that the higher the elasticity, the greater the total loss of surplus and revenue.

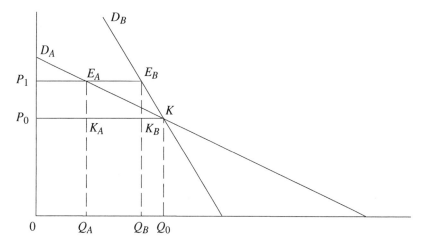

We are considering whether to raise the price from P_0 to P_1. With the inelastic demand curve D_B, the loss in consumer surplus and revenue is the area under the demand curve $Q_B Q_0 K E_B$. With the more elastic demand curve D_A, the loss is the larger area $Q_A Q_0 K E_A$. Thus, the more elastic the demand, the greater the loss of welfare from a price rise. Prices should be set lower in these cases. This is the Ramsey rule.

Diagram 4.3

4.2.3   Producer prices as shadow prices

As an alternative to using a formula to calculate the shadow prices, some economists use world prices as the generally correct shadow price. For example, the United States may import gasoline from Saudi Arabia. The consumer may pay $1.20 per gallon. But this may include taxes of 40 cents. So the import price would have been $0.80 per gallon. According to this way of thinking, the shadow price is the import (or world price) and not the market price. The theory behind this approach comes from the Diamond–Mirrlees (D–M) theorem. This theorem explains why (or when) producer prices are the correct shadow prices. For the foreign trade sector, the producer prices that the firms face are the world prices of the commodities. In this case, world prices are the shadow prices.

Consider two goods X and Y. The maximum amount of one good that is technically possible to produce, for a fixed amount of the other good (and with a given amount of inputs), is represented by the production possibilities curve FF in Diagram 4.4. Any point (combination of the two goods) within FF (including its boundary) is technically feasible to produce. This is the production constraint that any economy faces. It is constructed after the government has diverted some of the inputs to be transformed into outputs required for the public sector.

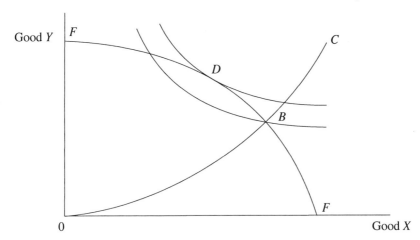

The Diamond–Mirrlees theorem relates to a mixed economy. Like any economy, it can only produce goods that are technically feasible. The economy must be on, or within, the production frontier *FF*. For a mixed economy, it also must have allocations that are on the price-offer curve *OBC*. The intersection of the two constraints is the line *OB*. The highest level of welfare that satisfies this joint constraint is at point *B*. This is the 'second-best optimum'. Note that equilibrium takes place on the production frontier *FF*. The economy is productively efficient. The slope of the production frontier at *B* defines the shadow prices. That is, producer prices are the correct shadow prices (provided that there is an optimum consumption tax that ensures that the consumer prices have a tangency point at *B*).

Diagram 4.4

In a mixed economy, there is an additional constraint. The private sector must choose to consume the output that remains. In the D–M world, only prices can be changed by the government (by consumption taxes) and income is assumed fixed (no income taxes are possible). This means that choices are determined by an individual's price-offer curve, which shows the optimum consumption path for each and every combination of prices. The price-offer curve for a representative individual is shown as the curve *OBC*. (*OBC* is the locus of tangency points of indifference curves with changing price ratios for the representative individual.) To satisfy both constraints, the economy must be somewhere on the *OBC* curve within the production possibility curve *FF*. This is shown by the path *OB*.

The representative individual's problem is to reach the highest indifference curve subject to being on *OB*. Point *B* will be chosen. Notice that *B* is not a tangency point. Point *D* would be the tangency point. But *D* does not satisfy the joint constraint and hence is not on *OB*. Point *D* is the 'first-best' combination, which would be the result if only production were the constraint. Since there is the additional budget constraint in the D–M framework, point *B* is referred to as a 'second-best' solution.

What is important about point *B*, the second-best solution, is that it is, like the first-best solution, on the boundary of the production possibility curve. This means that producing at *B* would be productively efficient. (By definition of *FF*, there is no way of obtaining more of one good without having less of the other good.) The prices that firms face at *B* (called 'producer prices') at which they are profit maximizing must therefore be the shadow prices as they guarantee that the second-best optimum will prevail.

To complete the analysis, we must recognize that since *B* is not a tangency point, the representative individual would not choose this combination if s/he faced the optimum producer prices. A flatter consumer price ratio at *B* would make this a tangency point. To achieve this, the government must set an optimal consumption tax equal to the difference between the slope of the production possibilities curve and the slope of the indifference curve.

The D–M theorem appeared in 1970. Throughout the 1970s and 1980s, many papers were written to see how robust was the result. For example, what happens for non-internationally traded goods, and what happens when taxes are not set optimally? It turns out that producer (world) prices are the correct shadow prices in a wide range of circumstances. (Atkinson and Stiglitz (1980, pp. 300–305) present a composite model that summarizes a number of the issues.) Here we wish to concentrate just on the intuition of the D–M theorem as it relates to the introductory statement of the shadow pricing problem given in section 4.1.3.

Refer back to the shadow pricing expression given by equation (4.4) and assume that $\alpha = 0$. The shadow price is then the producer price P_P. The D–M theorem can then be viewed as a sophisticated (general-equilibrium) statement of why it is that the resources for the public project will be at the expense of additional production by the private sector (rather than private consumption).

Diagram 4.1 can help us interpret the D–M requirement that consumption taxes must be optimally set. Producer prices are given by the supply curve. We need to know where one is going to be on this curve to specify the precise value for the producer price. Recall that the government wishes to take $Q_1 Q_2$ away from the market-determined equilibrium output Q_1. Hence, output Q_2 is the amount to be left for the private sector. This defines point *C* on the supply curve as the appropriate shadow price value. But, for consumers to purchase Q_1, and not Q_2, there must be a tax set at the rate *BC* per unit. Only this tax rate will ensure that private consumption is at the level to take up what is left over by the public sector.

4.3 Applications

All three methods for calculating shadow prices are represented in this applications section. A simple case of the general Lagrange multiplier method is when both the objectives and the constraints are linear. In this case the problem is one for linear programming. The solution can be represented graphically and all steps can be easily verified. The first application is such a problem based on Carrin (1984). The objective is to save lives, which illustrates the fact that the technique is very general and need not relate only to market-type economies. Whatever the social decision-maker is concerned about can be maximized subject to constraints.

The second application is Morrison's (1982) study of aircraft landing fees. Current fees in most airports are related to aircraft weight. The objective is to see whether Ramsey prices would differ from these weight-based prices.

Next we consider the 1992 introduction of resource-based pricing into the US system for compensating physicians supplying services for the elderly (the Medicare programme). We interpret this to be cases of producer pricing. The aim was to change the structure of compensation such that procedural services (e.g., surgery and invasive tests) would be paid less, and evaluation and management services (such as office visits) would be paid more. This was indeed what the new scale of payments for Medicare endorsed.

For purposes of comparison and contrast, the final case study used the Ramsey framework to estimate shadow prices for physician services. It questions whether the pre-existing Medicare pricing system did in fact underpay evaluation and management services.

4.3.1   Health-care planning

To implement the Lagrange multiplier method for deriving shadow prices, one needs two ingredients, namely, a statement of the objective and the constraints. One then maximizes the objective subject to the constraint. In the process, one obtains a value for the Lagrange multiplier, which is the shadow price for relaxing the constraint. We explain this method as it relates to Carrin's (1984) example applied to health-care planning in LDCs.

As stated in section 4.2.1, the objective function for the Lagrange multiplier method for deriving shadow prices was specified simply, and generally, as $F(x)$, where x was a set of inputs and outputs, and F was the decision-maker's valuation of those inputs and outputs. In the Carrin example, it was recognized that the ultimate goal of many interventions in the health-care field is to lead to a saving of lives L. Say there are two main ways of achieving this goal, by hiring health workers x_1 (measured in man-years), or by providing a nutritional supplement x_2 (tons of powdered milk). From medical research results one establishes that one health worker can save 163 lives per year, while a ton of powdered milk can prevent 100 people from dying. Then the objective function can be denoted as:

$$L = 163x_1 + 100x_2 \qquad (4.7)$$

L defines a family of isoquants, which shows all combinations of the two health-care interventions that can produce the same quantity of lives saved.

Note that the vector *x* here consists of the two variables x_1 and x_2 and they are linearly related by the coefficients 163 and 100. The coefficients reflect the decision-maker's preferences, that is, there is a linear specification of the *F* function. Since a life saved by one intervention is valued the same as a life saved by the other intervention, the only issue is how many lives each intervention saves. The coefficients are technically determined in this problem. A health-care worker is 1.63 times more productive than a ton of powdered milk. This is why a health worker has a higher weight than a ton of powdered milk.

The planning agency is assumed to face a budget constraint. There is only a fixed amount, 200 units, to spend on the two medical interventions. How much this 200 will purchase depends on the prices of health workers and milk. If the price of x_1 is 20 and the price of x_2 is 5, the budget constraint is:

$$20x_1 + 5x_2 \leq 200 \tag{4.8}$$

Equation (4.8) defines the constraint *G(x)* also as a linear function. With both the objective and constraint specified in linear terms, we are dealing with a linear programming problem.

In addition to the budget constraint, there are availability and other constraints. Say we know that the maximum number of workers available is 5, the maximum amount of powdered milk available is 30, and that both of the inputs cannot be negative. There is then another set of constraints expressed by

$$x_1 \leq 5; \, x_2 \leq 30; \, x_1 \geq 0; \, x_2 \geq 0. \tag{4.9}$$

The problem is to maximize (4.7) subject to (4.8) and (4.9). This is depicted in Diagram 4.5.

In Diagram 4.5, the number of health workers is on the horizontal axis, and tons of powdered milk are on the vertical axis. The set of possibilities that satisfy all the constraints (called the feasible region) is the area *ABCD*. This is the area:

i.   below 5 on the horizontal (satisfying the availability constraint);
ii.   below 30 on the vertical axis (satisfying the availability constraint);
iii. on or below line *EF* (satisfying the budget constraint *EF*);
iv.   in the first quadrant (satisfying the non-negativity constraints).

The highest isoquant that can be reached with *ABCD* as the feasible set is the *L* line *GH*. This can be obtained only if point *B* is chosen, that is, the solution is $x_1 = 2.5$ and $x_2 = 30$. It is easy to check that *B* is the solution. The solution to a linear programming problem is always at a corner (called a 'basic feasible solution'). Thus, any of the five points 0, *A*, *B*, *C*, *D* is a possible solution

Powdered milk x_2

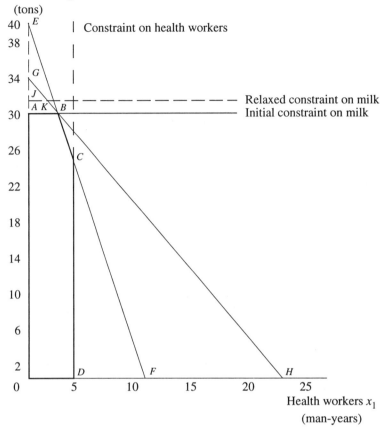

The aim is to choose the highest L line that satisfies all the constraints. EH is the budget line. Any point on or below EF is feasible. AB and CD are on the availability constraints, and BC is part of the budget line. This makes $ABCD$ the feasible set (this exists in the positive quadrant, thus satisfying the non-negativity constraints). Point B is the optimum because it reaches the highest L line (the isoquant GH). At B, 2.5 man-years would be hired, and 30 tons of milk would be bought.

Diagram 4.5

candidate. First take the origin 0. This uses zero of both interventions and will therefore produce no lives saved. Next choose point A. With $x_1 = 0$ and $x_2 = 30$ substituted in equation (4.7), we obtain $L = 163(0) + 100(30)$, which is 3 000 lives saved. The issue is whether any other corner point can save more lives than 3 000. Now choose point B. This has $x_1 = 2.5$ and $x_2 = 30$. With these values, $L = 163(2.5) + 100(30) = 407.5 + 3\,000$, and we save approximately 3 407 lines. This is the maximum value as no other corner point can match 3 407.

Now suppose that there were 31 units of powdered milk available, and not 30. The constraint $x_2 \leq 30$ in equation (4.9) would be replaced by $x_2 \leq 31$ (all other elements being the same as before). The new solution would be $x_1 = 2.2$, and $x_2 = 31$, corresponding to the point K in the new feasible region $JKBCD$. The quantity of lives saved would rise to 3 459 (i.e., 163 (2.2) + 100 (31)).

The Lagrange multiplier for this problem is $\lambda = 52$ (this is part of the solution output that comes from the linear programming problem solved by a computer). Hence, we can say that the shadow price of milk is 52. The definition of a shadow price in equation (4.1) tells us exactly why this is the case. The shadow price of powdered milk is the change in social welfare brought about by a change in the availability of powdered milk. If powdered milk were increased by 1 unit (from 30 to 31), social welfare (as proxied by the number of lives saved L) would increase by 52 units (from 3 407 to 3 459). Dividing $52L$ by 1 unit of powdered milk produces the rate of exchange of lives saved from having one extra unit of milk. The shadow price tells us what is the opportunity lost from not being able to employ additional units of this resource (because of a strict resource constraint).

4.3.2   Landing fees at uncongested airports

Morrison's (1982) study of landing fees at airports was careful to ensure that the preconditions for the Ramsey rule were present. If an airport is congested, then the activity is at the capacity level. Any extra output would require building a new facility. As a consequence, MC pricing would approximate AC pricing (strictly, *long-run MC* pricing) and there would be no financial loss with which to be concerned. Thus, by concentrating on uncongested airports, Morrison is dealing with situations where MC would be below AC and MC pricing would lead to a financial loss (as depicted in Diagram 4.2).

Morrison's objective was to compare shadow prices that would come from the Ramsey rule, using equation (4.6), with current landing fees to test the efficiency of the current system. The existing basis for fees in most countries was to charge according to aircraft weight. For example, in the United States maximum landing weight was the basis, while in Canada it was the maximum take-off weight. MC does vary by weight, but this is more a value-of-service pricing system.

Equation (4.6) determines the shadow price S_i in terms of the marginal cost MC_i, the price elasticity of demand e_{pi}, and the proportionality factor k. We discuss each component in turn, starting with an explanation of what are the activities i in this case.

i.   The Ramsey rule is specified with respect to different activities. In the airport landing situation, the activities are different planes that travel different distances. Morrison deals with five types (sizes) of aircraft (DC9–30,

B727–200, DC8–61, DC10–10 and B747) and five flight distances (500, 1 000, 1 500, 2 000 and 2 500 miles). There are thus 25 activities to shadow price. The activities are costed and shadow priced for a 'hypothetical representative airport'.

ii. MC was assumed invariant to weight (an assumption which did not affect the main findings concerning the structure of landing fees). In a prior survey of US airports by Morrison, the MC of an air carrier landing (and subsequent take-off) was approximately $25. Since this was for 1976, and 1979 was the year taken for valuation, the MC figure was raised by the rate of inflation to obtain a value of $30 in 1979 prices.

iii. The price elasticity for landing fees could be derived from the elasticity of demand for passenger trips, as there is a one-for-one correspondence between flights and landings. The elasticities of passenger demand rose with the length of the trip, varying from 1.04 for 500-mile trips to 1.16 for the 2 500-mile trips.

iv. The value of k depends on the extent to which the budget constraint is binding. k can vary between 0 and 1, where the upper value reflects a fully binding constraint, and the zero value is when the constraint is non-binding. (See problem set 2 in section 4.4.2 for an interpretation of these extreme values.) Morrison chose $k = 0.025$ because this is the value that produces an overall level of revenue from the shadow prices that is comparable to current fees. Existing fees are being set to cover overall costs. The aim is to see if these fees correspond at all with the efficient level of Ramsey fees, which is an alternative way of covering costs. By using $k = 0.025$, Morrison can focus on the *structure* of fees separate from their level.

The resulting shadow/Ramsey prices are shown in Table 4.1. As explained earlier, they vary by distance and aircraft type.

Table 4.1   Shadow prices for aircraft landings (in dollars)

Distance	Aircraft type				
	DC9–30	B727–200	DC8–61	DC10–10	B747
500	102	132	202	261	321
1 000	147	195	283	370	458
1 500	191	258	365	481	597
2 000	236	321	449	592	738
2 500	281	385	532	705	879

Source: Morrison (1982)

To facilitate comparison with the existing prices, Morrison expressed the shadow prices as ratios of the current prices. In other words, as explained in section 4.1.3, he formed accounting ratios for the activities. Two sets of comparisons were made, one with landing weight as the basis for current prices, and one with take-off weight as the basis. In either case, the *AR* for the DC9–30 plane was made the numeraire and set to 1.00. All other activities could then be compared to that starting value. As the landing weight *AR*s were similar to the take-off weight *AR*s, we report in Table 4.2 the *AR* results only for the landing weight basis for the current prices.

Table 4.2   Accounting ratios based on landing weights

Distance	Aircraft type				
	DC9–30	B727–200	DC8–61	DC10–10	B747
500	1.00	0.92	0.91	0.77	0.61
1 000	1.44	1.36	1.27	1.09	0.87
1 500	1.87	1.80	1.64	1.42	1.14
2 000	2.31	2.24	2.01	1.75	1.41
2 500	2.75	2.68	2.39	2.09	1.68

Source: Morrison (1982)

The pattern of results exhibited in Table 4.2 are easy to interpret once one realizes that the aircraft types are listed in increasing size order. For any given distance, the shadow prices relative to the current prices decrease with aircraft size (the *AR*s fall as we travel across any row). Also, for any given aircraft size, the shadow prices relative to the current price increase with distance (the *AR*s rise as we go down any column). The conclusion is that current aircraft landing fees: (a) do not, as they should, increase with distance, and (b) increase too rapidly with aircraft size.

4.3.3   *Resource-based relative values for Medicare*

There are many reasons to believe that markets are not appropriate for providing health-care services (see, for example, Arrow's (1963) classic discussion and a recent statement by Hsiao et al. (1988b, p. 835)). Market deficiencies are on both the demand and supply sides. Consumer demand is unpredictable and information is lacking as to the quality of the service given. Often physicians have the power to restrict entry to the profession causing earnings to be higher than otherwise. In these circumstances, governments often intervene in health-care markets and set fees for services and procedures.

In the United States, the main programme for providing health insurance for the elderly is Medicare. Since the early 1980s, what Medicare has considered to be the appropriate fee for a physician's services is the 'customary, prevailing and reasonable charge' (the CPR). Doctors were concerned that under this system the structure of fees seemed unfair. The claim was that physicians were heavily rewarded for procedural services (e.g., invasive surgery), and not much was given for office evaluation and management services (e.g., routine office visits). In order to remedy this perceived injustice, a number of Harvard economists and physicians under the leadership of William Hsiao devised an alternative compensation scheme for doctors, the resource-based relative values system (RBRVS). This alternative scheme was outlined in a series of papers by Hsiao and adopted by the US government for implementation in 1992.

Hsiao identified four categories of service, namely, evaluation/management, invasive, laboratory and imaging. According to Hsiao et al. (1988b) compensation to physicians for these services should be based on the cost of resources used in the production of the service. Resource cost has four elements, the first two of these being:

i. the time devoted to the service or procedure. The total time involved, including both before and after treating the patient, is recorded; and
ii. the intensity of the work done (that is, the mental effort, judgement, technical skill, physical effort and stress). The intensity was measured by the perceptions of physicians who were surveyed.

These two elements are combined into a total work input (work per unit of time). Table 4.3 (based on Table 3 of Hsiao, et al. (1988a)) shows how these two elements individually and combined differed among the four categories of service.

Table 4.3 Time and work per unit by category of service

Category	Number	Total work Mean	Total work Range	Time (in mins) Mean	Time (in mins) Range	Work/Time (in mins) Mean	Work/Time (in mins) Range
Evaluation	145	108	16–378	35	5–145	3.2	1.6–6.1
Invasive	136	497	19–2445	67	4–328	7.1	1.9–19.4
Laboratory	32	48	9–195	13	3–63	3.7	2.1–6.3
Imaging	34	78	14–463	17	3–92	4.7	3.0–7.0

Source: Hsiao et al. (1988a)

The work intensity figures in Table 4.3 (the last pair of columns showing work per unit of time) are relative to a typical (benchline) service in that category. The benchline category is fixed at 100. Services that are judged easier than this are ascribed a score less than 100, and those that are viewed harder are measured greater than 100. The time taken per service (the middle pair of columns) differs among the categories to a slightly greater degree than work intensity. When the total work units are formed in the first pair of columns (by multiplying work intensity by the time per service) the means and ranges are compounded by the differences in both the time and intensity elements. Total work is most in evaluation (and management) services, as Hsiao had anticipated.

The total work per unit of service is denoted by *TW*. This has to be scaled up by the third and fourth elements (expressed as indices in relative terms across services) that determine resource costs:

iii. Relative practice costs (*RPC*). Practice costs relative to gross earnings for each speciality was the index. Information on this was obtained from physicians' tax returns and from national surveys.
iv. Amortized value for the opportunity cost of specialized training (*AST*). These costs (training and forgone earnings) are spread over the career lifetimes of physicians.

The resource-based relative value (*RBRV*) combines the four elements by multiplying total work units by added practice and training costs:

$$RBRV = TW(1 + RPC)(1 + AST) \qquad (4.10)$$

It is important to recognize that the figures that are produced by equation (4.10) are in quantity units. They need to be converted into value terms in order to specify a fee scale for physicians. The conversion method used by Hsiao was based on the target that the new scale would produce a total payment by Medicare for physicians equal to the prior system.

Using equation (4.10) for 7 000 separate services, and the derived conversion factor which requires budget neutrality, Hsiao et al. (1988a, Table 6) produced an estimate of the difference that the RBRVS would make relative to the prior CPR system. Table 4.4 (with Medicare revenues in millions of dollars) shows the results.

Given that there is much more work (time and intensity) involved with evaluation services, it is not surprising then that, under an RBRVS, Medicare would have to pay more (by 56 per cent) for evaluation services, and less for invasive, laboratory and imaging services (by 42 per cent, 5 per cent and 90 per cent respectively).

Table 4.4   Comparison between RBRVS and prior Medicare charges

Category	Medicare revenue under CPR system	Medicare revenue under RBRVS	Percentage difference
Evaluation	3 244	5 072	56
Invasive	3 591	2 077	–42
Laboratory	159	150	–5
Imaging	995	689	–90

Source: Hsiao et al. (1988a)

Interpreting the RBRVS   Hsiao (1987) writes: 'In economic terms, what we are trying to do here is measure the average production cost of specific procedures and services that would have emerged from a reasonably competitive marketplace'. This focus on production costs helps define the RBRVS as an example of producer prices being used as shadow prices.

Moffit (1992), complains that the RBRVS fee schedule is fixed with 'no reference to market forces'. It is the absence of demand as a factor that is of most concern. One is thereby ignoring the 'quality' or 'benefit' of a service. In addition, (a) the skill of a physician is not taken into account, and (b) by using *average* time one is not measuring the efficiency of an actual physician's performance or the severity of the cases.

There is much that is valid about Moffit's critique. But, one point needs to be clarified. There is nothing inherently conceptually wrong about fixing social values independent of demand. As the Diamond–Mirrlees theorem proves, producer prices can be appropriate shadow prices in certain circumstances. If one finds the Diamond–Mirrlees theorem too esoteric, one can fall back on first principles identified in section 4.1.3. If a unit of resources that is taken up by a physician's service is offset by producing more resources, rather than cutting back consumption, then producer prices are the relevant shadow prices. There are thousands of examples in the shadow pricing of non-traded goods in LDCs where the values of the product are derived from the values of the inputs. (Reference here is to the Little and Mirrlees decomposition procedure used in project appraisal, see Brent, 1990.)

The most telling criticism of the RBRVS made by Moffit involves the absence of market forces on the supply side. The fact that a typical physician had a work time and intensity of a particular amount on average does not say anything about the efficiency of the work provided. If a part of the work is unnecessary, then it should not be included in the shadow price. Thus, while it has been conceded that the RBRVS is a producer price regime, not just any producer price qualifies as the shadow price. It must be the *cost-minimizing* producer price. There is no evidence that Hsiao's values correspond to this particular concept.

4.3.4   Shadow prices for a physician's services

The Hsiao work assumed budget neutrality between the amount paid for physicians under the old Medicare system and under the RBRVS. It cannot deal with the issue of whether overall physicians' salaries can be judged 'too high' or not. In the Brent (1994) study of the shadow prices of a physician's services, he used the Ramsey rule to try to estimate the correct values for these services. This study therefore enables us to see one answer to this most fundamental of health-care issues. Also, because it covered evaluative (office visits) and invasive (surgery) services, we can provide some independent check of whether Hsiao and others were right to consider evaluative services as undervalued.

The model used was the Ramsey rule as specified by equation (4.6), except that Brent distinguished the consumer (insurance group) paying the price. Most of the finance for paying for health care in the United States comes from third-party payers (private insurance companies and the government). It was thought appropriate to check the extent to which there was price discrimination by physicians according to the different payers. The Ramsey rule sets the price above marginal costs according to the inverse elasticity of demand. If different payers have different elasticities, the physician would charge higher prices than those with the lower elasticities.

As data on the elasticities were not readily available, a method was developed to impute the elasticities from past firm pricing behaviour. The *actual* prices charged (as opposed to the shadow prices we are dealing with in the model) are related to price elasticities assuming that the physician maximizes profits. Recall from microeconomic theory that $MR = P(1 - 1/e_p)$. So equating $MR = MC$ means $MC = P(1 - 1/e_p)$, which when rearranged produces $(P - MC)/P = 1/e_p$. Thus, if one has data on P and MC one can estimate (using regression analysis) the elasticities. P was the bill to the third party for a particular service. The (heroic) assumption was made that what the physician received from the insurance company was the MC.

The physician whose services are being shadow priced was a plastic surgeon who operates in a New York teaching hospital. The 'individual' consumers are the third-party insurers who pay the patients' bills, namely, Medicare, GHI, HIP, Blue Cross, Empire and Union. Since these represented large groups of individuals, rich and poor alike, distribution was not thought to be an issue. The shadow price of public funds λ was given as 1.33 in another study. The sample consisted of 766 bills by the plastic surgeon to third parties (what they charge is P and what they actually receive from the third parties is MC) over the period 1986–88. The main results are summarized in Table 4.5 below. The elasticities determined the shadow prices under the assumption that k in equation (4.6) was equal to 0.2481. (Values of 0.0909 and 0.3590 were also tried without materially affecting the conclusions.) For ease of interpretation, the shadow prices are presented in the form of accounting ratios.

Table 4.5 Estimates of the elasticities and shadow prices

Variable	e_{pi}	Shadow price / Market price
Medicare	1.5246	0.4110
GHI	1.6090	0.4475
HIP	2.0173	0.5750
Blue Cross	1.8598	0.5335
Empire	1.6892	0.4782
Union	2.0325	0.5786

The results shown in the table indicate that the plastic surgeon's services were price elastic for all third-party payers. The e_p were all significantly different from unity within the 1 per cent level. The fact that the elasticities were greater than unity is consistent with the assumption that the physician tried to maximize profits. That is, with elasticities above unity, the marginal revenues are positive. So the marginal revenue equals marginal cost condition for each physician takes place at a positive output level. The estimates therefore support the underlying theory behind the implicit elasticity method.

The estimates for the *AR*s are also in line with most people's *a priori* expectations, given the imperfections in the market for physicians. They are less than unity, signifying that the social value of the services are less than the prices actually charged. Furthermore, they do vary by category of user. On the basis of the estimates in the table, we see that the ratios vary from 41 cents for every dollar charged to Medicare, to 58 cents for every dollar charged to Union. So, roughly, one-half (between 42 and 59 cents) of every dollar charged was *not* relevant for social valuation purposes.

The other interesting finding relates to the differential between consultation fees and the prices charged for surgery. In the period of Brent's study, it was not just Medicare that used the CPR fee schedule, but most third-party payers. Thus, it was the system prior to RBRVS that was being analysed. In the regressions Brent found that consultations were paid at a statistically significant higher rate than surgery. That is, per dollar that was billed to the third parties, they gave a larger share to evaluative services than to invasive procedures. Consequently the shadow price equations required a negative adjustment for consultations. This questions whether Hsiao's starting assumption, that evaluative services were under-rewarded, was justified. It could be that RBRVS attempted to fix something that was not broken!

4.4   Final comments

We close the chapter with the summary and problems sections.

4.4.1   Summary

A shadow price is the change in social value by producing one unit more (or less) of a good or input. It critically depends on one's objectives (how one defines social value) and the specification of the constraints. In this chapter we presented three main methods for calculating shadow prices. Each method had its own way of dealing with objectives and constraints.

The first method was based on determining Lagrange multipliers. The objective and the constraints could be anything that is relevant to the particular decision-making context one finds oneself in. In the application, we used the most general way of looking at health-care interventions in terms of saving lives. The constraint was a budget constraint and a fixed availability of health workers and powdered milk. As part of the maximization process, one obtains values for the Lagrange multiplier. In the health-care planning study, the Lagrange multiplier, and hence the shadow price, for powdered milk was 52. This meant that an extra ton of powdered milk had the value of saving 52 lives.

The second method used the Ramsey rule. The objective is the individualistic social welfare function outlined in Chapter 2. The constraint was a budget constraint. Maximizing this objective subject to this constraint produced shadow prices that were inversely related to the elasticity of demand for the particular good or service being evaluated. We supplied two applications of this rule. The first related to airport landing fees, where the tradition was to use prices based on the weight of an aircraft (either landing or taking off). Ramsey prices differed greatly from these prices. The second application related to the services provided by a plastic surgeon. In most market-based economies (and many others), physicians' salaries are amongst the highest in the society. Many people suspect that physicians' fees in the United States are too high. We found confirmation for these suspicions using the Ramsey rule. Around a half of what the plastic surgeon charged was not socially justified.

The third method is a variation of the second. The maximization problem is basically the same, except that there is an additional constraint. The consumer must be left on his/her budget line after the government has taken resources away from the private sector. Rather than provide a formula that varies with the circumstances of the good or service being evaluated, a short-cut is taken. A 'second-best' equilibrium is invoked, where the shadow price is given as the producer price. This should be interpreted as a general approximation. Just as many economists use market prices as a rough approximation to shadow prices in CBA, using producer prices is an alternative approximation that is applicable in situations where market imperfections are considered to be so pervasive that market prices cannot possibly be correct. The health-care field in the United States is thought to be such a situation. Hence the RBRVS, a particular way of producer-pricing physician services, was chosen as the application. However, as we noted, not any producer price can act as the shadow price. It must be the cost-minimizing producer price.

Under RBRVS, the shadow prices for evaluative services were higher than for invasive procedures, such as surgery. Using the Ramsey rule, the reverse was the case. This highlights the important conclusion that shadow price determination very much depends on the method used to make one's estimates.

4.4.2 Problems

The main advantage of using the linear in objectives and constraints version of the Lagrange multiplier method was that one could (using simple arithmetic) easily find the solution values. The first problem exploits this advantage, and asks that one confirm the solution for the new optimum in the health-care planning application. The second problem set returns to the issue of how to interpret the proportionality factor k that appears in the Ramsey rule equation.

1. In section 4.3.1, the new solution when the number of units of powdered milk available was increased to 31 was at point K in Diagram 4.5. Show that this is the 'basic feasible solution'. (Take the bases (corner points 0, J, K, B, C and D) and confirm that they are all feasible (satisfy the constraints). Then calculate the number of lives saved at each point and verify that point K is the optimum (produces the maximum value).)
2. The objective is to define k and interpret the extreme values 0 and 1.
   i. Express in words the definition of k. (Look at the derivation of the Ramsey rule in Appendix 4.5.2 and compare equations (4.6) and (4.29). What two terms determine the value of k and what do they mean?)
   ii. In the non-binding case, $k = 0$. Substitute this value in equation (4.6) and interpret the resulting pricing rule.
   iii. In the binding case, $k = 1$. Substitute this value in equation (4.6) and interpret the resulting pricing rule. (Hint: compare the result just obtained with the result from the following manipulation: take the relation between MR and elasticities given in microeconomic theory, $MR = P(1 - 1/e_p)$, and then assume $MR = MC$. The two should be the same. See also application 4.3.4 where this binding case is used.)

4.5 Appendix

We now derive the two main results that this chapter has been built around, namely, the equivalence of Lagrange multipliers as shadow prices, and the Ramsey rule.

4.5.1   Lagrange multipliers as shadow prices

We prove this result for the case where there are just two resources, i.e., $x = (x_1, x_2)$.

We start with the maximum value function:

$$V = F(\bar{x}) \tag{4.11}$$

Consider a change in V due to the project affecting x. That is, take the total differential of equation (4.11):

$$dV = \frac{\delta F(\bar{x})}{\delta x_1} dx_1 + \frac{\delta F(\bar{x})}{\delta x_2} dx_2 \tag{4.12}$$

The Lagrangian is:

$$L = F(x) + \lambda[c - G(\bar{x})] \tag{4.13}$$

The first-order conditions are:

$$\frac{\delta L}{\delta x_1} = \frac{\delta F}{\delta x_1} - \lambda \frac{\delta G}{\delta x_1} = 0; \quad \text{or,} \quad \frac{\delta F}{\delta x_1} = \lambda \frac{\delta G}{\delta x_1} \tag{4.14}$$

$$\frac{\delta L}{\delta x_2} = \frac{\delta F}{\delta x_2} - \lambda \frac{\delta G}{\delta x_2} = 0; \quad \text{or,} \quad \frac{\delta F}{\delta x_2} = \lambda \frac{\delta G}{\delta x_2} \tag{4.15}$$

Substitute for $\delta F/\delta \bar{x}$ from (4.14) and (4.15) into (4.12) to obtain:

$$dV = \left(\lambda \frac{\delta G}{\delta x_1}\right) dx_1 + \left(\lambda \frac{\delta G}{\delta x_2}\right) dx_2 = \lambda \left[\frac{\delta G}{\delta x_1} dx_1 + \frac{\delta G}{\delta x_2} dx_2\right] \tag{4.16}$$

But, by definition, the term in brackets is dc. Thus equation (4.16) becomes:

$$dV = \lambda dc \tag{4.17}$$

From which we get equation (4.5) in the text:

$$\frac{dV}{dc} = \lambda \qquad (4.18)$$

Thus, the Lagrange multiplier tells us rate of change of the maximum attainable value with respect to a change in a constraining parameter.

4.5.2   Deriving the Ramsey rule

We consider here a publicly owned/controlled firm that produces two products Z_1 and Z_2 with prices S_1 and S_2. The government can affect the profits of the public firm by providing a transfer T (i.e., a subsidy or tax). There exists also a private sector that produces a good that has a price q. The indirect social utility function V has the form:

$$V = V(q, S_1, S_2, T) \qquad (4.19)$$

The firm faces the budget constraint

$$S_1 Z_1 + S_2 Z_2 - C(Z_1, Z_1) + T = \Pi_0 \qquad (4.20)$$

where C is the total cost function and Π_0 is the target profit set by the government for the public firm.

The problem is to set optimally the public sector's prices S_1 and S_2. That is, one must choose the S's such that one maximizes equation (4.19) subject to equation (4.20). The Lagrangian is:

$$L = V(q, S_1, S_2, T) + \lambda[S_1 Z_1 + S_2 Z_2 - C(Z_1, Z_1) + T - \Pi_0] \qquad (4.21)$$

The first-order condition for Z_1 (assuming independent demands) is

$$\frac{\delta V}{\delta S_1} + \lambda \left[S_1 \frac{\delta Z_1}{\delta S_1} + Z_1 - C' \frac{\delta Z_1}{\delta S_1} \right] = 0 \qquad (4.22)$$

Note that by Roy's identity, the partial derivative of the indirect utility function with respect to price is equal to (minus) the quantity consumed times the marginal utility of income a_i.

That is:

$$\frac{\delta V}{\delta S_1} = -a_i Z_1 \qquad (4.23)$$

Substituting this into equation (4.22) produces:

$$-a_i Z_1 + \lambda \left[Z_1 + (S_1 - C')\frac{\delta Z_1}{\delta S_1} \right] = 0 \tag{4.24}$$

Divide both sides by Z_1:

$$-a_i + \lambda \left[1 + \frac{(S_1 - C')}{Z_1}\frac{\delta Z_1}{\delta S_1} \right] = 0 \tag{4.25}$$

and multiply both sides by S_1 to get:

$$-a_i S_1 + \lambda \left[S_1 + (S_1 - C')\frac{\delta Z_1}{\delta S_1}\frac{S_1}{Z_1} \right] = 0 \tag{4.26}$$

But in equation (4.26):

$$\frac{\delta Z_1}{\delta S_1}\frac{S_1}{Z_1} = -e_{P_1} \tag{4.27}$$

where e_{P_1} is the price elasticity of demand. So this can be rewritten as:

$$-a_i S_1 + \lambda[S_1 - (S_1 - C')e_{P_1}] = 0 \tag{4.28}$$

Finally, by rearranging equation (4.28) we obtain:

$$\frac{(S_1 - C')}{S_1} = \left(\frac{\lambda - a_i}{\lambda} \right)\frac{1}{e_{P_1}} \tag{4.29}$$

Thus, prices are above marginal cost in proportion to the inverse of the price elasticity of demand. This is the 'Ramsey rule' given as equation (4.6) in the text.

5 External effects

5.1 Introduction

The last chapter indicated what alternatives to market price valuation can be used in a social CBA. For the rest of Part III we will explain why these alternatives to market prices are necessary. In fact, we began this avenue of enquiry earlier in Chapter 3 when we saw that market revenues exclude consumer surplus. Consumer surplus is more important the larger the project involved, seeing that large projects involve benefits that occur away from the margin where market prices operate. In this chapter, we use the consumer surplus metric to demonstrate that markets may under- or over-produce even for small, marginal levels of private market activity. External benefits and costs need to be measured in order to possibly adjust the market equilibrium. In effect then, we have a choice of how we adjust for market imperfections or other omissions. We can use shadow pricing to revalue the physical inputs and outputs; or else we can add to the list of monetary benefits and costs for the distorted or excluded factors.

We start by presenting a complete set of definitions related to externalities. The theory and applications are structured around these definitions. Most of the discussion is in terms of external costs. The analysis is symmetrical for the case of external benefits. Externalities may exist, yet not require government intervention. The circumstances underlying this result, the so-called Coase (1960) theorem, are identified. When these conditions do not exist, corrective taxes and subsidies may be optimal (policies attributed to Pigou, 1920). As the data requirements for these policies are too demanding, alternative instruments are examined. In particular, we cover policies that deal with both the quantity and the price sides of the market.

The first application puts externalities in the framework of making a CBA expenditure decision. Then insights into the workings of the Coase theorem are provided by the study of externalities caused by blood transfusions. Next, the classic externality problem of road congestion is placed in a CBA setting where the 'project' consists of devoting resources to allow for the charging of a price for a target reduction in road congestion. The applications section closes with an optimal excise taxation exercise. The situation is a very general one where it is not possible to tax separately those who cause externalities and those who do not. Pigovian taxes are shown to be a special case of the optimal tax formula.

5.1.1 Definitions of externality

Buchanan and Stubblebine (1962) provided a battery of definitions of externality that are very useful for public policy purposes. They define when an externality exists, and when there is, and there is not, an externality problem.

When an externality exists   An externality is said to exist when there is an *inter-dependence* between the utility (or production) function of individuals. Say individual *B*'s consumption (or production) affects another person *A*. An externality exists when:

$$U^A = U^A[X_1, X_2, ..., X_m; Y_1] \tag{5.1}$$

This states that the utility of individual *A* is dependent on the activities (X_1, X_2, ..., X_m) that are under his/her control, but also on another Y_1, which is by definition under the control of a second individual *B*. This outside activity Y_1 can enhance *A*'s utility (for example, if *B* is a gardener who grows beautiful flowers that decorate *A*'s neighbourhood) or can detract from *A*'s utility (for example, if *B* is a smoker who indirectly causes the non-smoking *A* to get cancer).

When an externality is potentially relevant   Two aspects of the above specification are important:

i.   The marginal utility to *A* from Y_1 should not be zero. For example, I may not care whether another person smokes or not. In this case the smoking does not cause an externality to me.
ii. If *A* is not affected when *B* is in his/her best position, then this would not be an important external effect. For example, I may care whether another person smokes. But, if that person chooses not to smoke, then again we do not have an externality.

These two considerations lead to a more precise formulation. Let *B*'s equilibrium value of Y_1 be denoted by Y_1^*, and denote *A*'s marginal utility (*MU*) from Y_1 by $MU_{Y_1}^A$. A *potentially relevant externality* is when: 'the activity actually performed generates any desire on the part of the affected party, *A*, to modify the behaviour of the party empowered to take action, *B*, through trade, persuasion, compromise, agreement, convention, collective action, etc.'

$$MU_{Y_1}^A \neq 0 \text{ (and } Y_1 = Y_1*) \tag{5.2}$$

As long as (5.2) holds, an externality remains (utility functions are interdependent). It is called potentially relevant because *A* would like *B*'s behaviour to adjust (produce more or less) and there is the potential for someone to gain.

An external economy is when (5.2) is positive, and an external diseconomy is when (5.2) is negative. When (5.2) is equal to zero, the externality is irrelevant (for public policy purposes).

When an externality is Pareto relevant   The removal of an externality will promote losses as well as gains. *B* will no longer be in his/her best position. So, not all potentially relevant losses are necessarily to be modified. That is, it may not be efficient to change the existing externality. The mere existence of an externality does not necessarily imply inefficiency, and hence government intervention. This leads to a final refinement in the definition of an externality.

A *Pareto-relevant externality* is when: 'the extent of the activity may be modified in such a way that the externality affected party *A* can be made better off without the acting party *B* being made worse off'. To formalize this definition, we need some statement of what optimizing behaviour *B* will be engaged in, in the absence of considerations about *A*.

Let *B*'s marginal cost of engaging in Y_1 be denoted by $MC_{Y_1}^B$. In equilibrium, any additional satisfaction will just equal the additional cost and hence:

$$MU_{Y_1}^B = MC_{Y_1}^B \tag{5.3}$$

The externality will be Pareto relevant when the gain to *A* (from a change in the level of Y_1) is greater than the loss to *B* (who has to move away from his/her

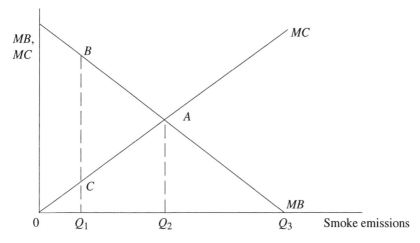

The optimal amount of smoke emissions is Q_2. Between Q_2 and Q_3, the laundry can bribe the factory to reduce emissions. This is because over this range $MC > MB$. Between 0 and Q_2, the factory can bribe the laundry to put up with the smoke, as $MB > MC$. At Q_2, neither party can bribe the other to change the scale of activities. This is the social equilibrium.

Diagram 5.1

equilibrium level of Y_1, thus making the left-side of (5.3) smaller than the right). That is, a Pareto-relevant externality is where:

$$MU_{Y_1}^A > [MC_{Y_1}^B - MU_{Y_1}^B] \tag{5.4}$$

The externality is irrelevant when both sides of the expression in (5.4) are equal.

All the externality definitions are illustrated in Diagram 5.1 (see Turvey, 1963). Say there is a shoe factory that produces marginal profits (benefits) given by the *MB* curve. The factory causes smoke which leads to external costs to an adjacent laundry – given by the *MC* curve.

A profit-maximizing factory would produce up to the point where marginal profits are zero. Equilibrium for the factory would therefore be at Q_3. For any scale of output between 0 and Q_3, an externality exists (the laundry has the interdependence). Between 0 and Q_2, e.g., at Q_1, there is a Pareto-relevant externality (the *MB* is greater than the *MC*). The social optimum is at Q_2, where the *MB* is equal to the *MC*. There is an externality at Q_2, but it is Pareto irrelevant (it is not possible to make the laundry better off without making the factory worse off).

5.1.2 The Coase theorem

When property rights exist, and there are a small number of individuals involved, the parties can get together to internalize the externality. Depending on who has the property rights, either the polluter will pay compensation to the pollutee to produce more, or the pollutee will bribe the polluter to produce less. In these circumstances, government involvement of any sort is not required to obtain the socially efficient outcome. Only a concern with fairness (the distribution of income) may necessitate government action over externalities. These statements specify what is known as the 'Coase theorem'.

The main implication of the Coase theorem is that the presence of externalities may not always imply market failure. The affected parties could come together and negotiate an optimal level of the externality generating activity.

a. If the factory has the right to pollute the atmosphere, then the starting point would be at level Q_3. The laundry, however, would not allow the factory to remain there. Between Q_3 and Q_2, the laundry would obtain gains (avoided *MC*) that exceed the sum (*MB*) to compensate the factory. It would therefore bribe the factory to cut back its scale of activities. Only at Q_2 would the laundry not be able to bribe the factory to reduce output.

b. If the laundry has the right to a clean atmosphere, then output would start at the origin. But, again, this is not an equilibrium position. Between 0 and Q_2, the gain to the factory of increasing its scale of operations exceeds the costs to the laundry. It could therefore compensate (bribe) the laundry the value of its costs, and have some positive amounts left over. Only at Q_2 would the factory be unable to bribe the laundry to put up with the smoke.

In either case, whether we start at zero or start at Q_3, we end up at the social optimum Q_2. The legal issue of who should pay the compensation is irrelevant to the final outcome. If the laundry were a small family business and the factory were a giant multinational corporation, then one might care about the process by which the optimum is reached. It is only in terms of equity or distributional fairness that the legal system has a role to play.

The Coase theorem is very important for public policy purposes. When the conditions are right, it is unnecessary for the government to get involved with correcting externalities. These conditions are that property rights must exist and the numbers involved must be small. For some goods, property rights do not exist. Who owns the blue whale? And how many people are involved with the problem of having a hole in the ozone layer? How can so many people meet with polluters to bribe them to restrict their activities? In the circumstances where property rights do not exist, and the numbers affected are large, governments may need to devise policies to try to obtain socially optimal levels.

5.1.3 *Pigovian taxes and subsidies*

The recommended public policy instrument for bringing about the social optimum when an externality exists (and the conditions of the Coase theorem do not hold) is to use Pigovian taxes or subsidies. Pigou suggested that when there is an external diseconomy, a tax should be introduced according to the value of the damage done. The agent causing the externality treats the tax like an increase in its marginal costs and reduces its scale accordingly. Diagram 5.2 illustrates the workings of a Pigovian tax as it applies to road congestion.

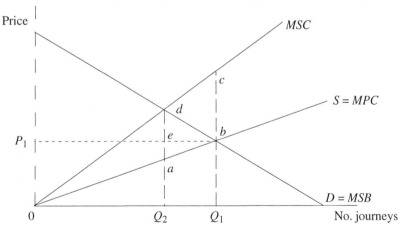

The market equilibrium is at Q_1 where $D = S$. The social optimum is at Q_2 where $MSB = MSC$. A tax of ad would raise the supply price from Q_2a to Q_2d at Q_2 and ensure that the market produces the correct quantity Q_2.

Diagram 5.2

The demand curve for travel measures the marginal social benefits (*MSB*). The time and operating costs define the marginal private costs (*MPC*) of making a journey. The *MPC* is the supply curve in a competitive market. Equilibrium is where demand equals supply, leading to a price P_1 and a quantity Q_1. The market equilibrium ignores the existence of the external costs that road congestion creates. Every car on the road during peak periods causes other vehicles to slow down their travel speeds. Time losses and extra vehicle fuel costs are incurred by others making the journey. The external costs when added to the marginal private costs form the *MSC* curve. The social optimum requires *MSB* = *MSC*, in which case Q_2 would be the desired number of journeys. The private equilibrium would therefore correspond to an excessive quantity. To remedy this, a tax of *ad* per vehicle should be imposed. With a tax of *ad* and a private cost of Q_2a, the aggregate cost for a marginal journey at Q_2 would be Q_2d. With Q_2d also the *MSB*, individuals would now choose to make the socially optimal number of journeys Q_2. The tax *internalizes* the externality.

A consumer surplus analysis of the Pigovian tax makes clear why it leads to a social improvement. Q_2Q_1 is the decrease in the number of journeys. Over this range, the reduction in benefits is the area under the demand curve Q_2Q_1bd, and the reduction in costs is the area under the *MSC* curve Q_2Q_1cd. The cost reduction is greater than the benefit reduction by the area *bcd*. This is the net benefit of the tax.

Although there is an overall social improvement with the tax, Hau (1992a) explains why this tax is not popular among those directly involved on the roads. There are two groups affected. The people who pay the tax (the 'tolled') and those who no longer make the journey because of the tax (the 'tolled off'). Both categories of road user are made worse off by the tax. The tolled off (the Q_2Q_1 journeys) are clearly worse off. Their lost consumer surplus is area *ebd* (*adb* is the total surplus lost). The tolled would seem to be better off as they have cost savings of *ae* per unit for the $0Q_2$ journeys that they make (Q_1b, equal to Q_2e, is the cost per unit before the tax and Q_2a is the cost per unit after the tax, making *ae* the difference). However, this ignores the fact that they are now paying a toll. Total revenues of $0Q_2$ times the tax *ad* go to the government and this always exceeds the cost savings (as *ad* is greater than *ae*). In efficiency terms, the toll revenues are a transfer from the beneficiaries to the government, and do not have any allocative significance. But the toll is still a loss to remaining users and they will not voluntarily vote to pay it.

Subsidies in the Pigovian scheme of things should be applied to industries which have external economies (like education). The subsidy is added to the private marginal benefits (demand) to provide an incentive for the producer to supply more of the underprovided good. The analysis is just the reverse of the external diseconomy case just discussed (provided that we can ignore income effects and the different distributional consequences).

5.2   Non-Pigovian taxes and quantity restriction
In the introductory section we covered government interventions that dealt with the over-, or under-, provision effects of externalities by changing the prices that agents face. Next we analyse interventions that operate on the output side directly. We concentrate exclusively on external diseconomies, that is, trying to deal with environmental pollution.

5.2.1   Common quantity restrictions
Government policy in the United States towards pollution has not followed the Pigovian prescriptions. The Environmental Protection Agency (EPA) concerning air and water pollution has often imposed common quantity restrictions. Consider the case of automobile emission control equipment. Since 1970, all cars are legally required to be equipped with particular antipollution devices. All cars are forced to reduce emissions by the same amount even though benefits may be different. This common quantity restriction thus causes inefficiency. The general nature of this inefficiency can be explained with reference to diagram 5.3.

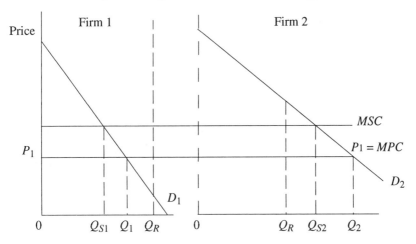

Prior to regulation, firm 1 produces Q_1 and firm 2 produces Q_2. The common restriction Q_R is then imposed on both firms. This causes 2 to reduce its output greatly, while 1's output is unchanged. The inefficiency can be seen by 2's *MB* (demand D_2) being greater than *MSC*, while 1's *MB* (D_1) is less than *MSC*. The socially optimal levels would be Q_{S1} and Q_{S2}.

Diagram 5.3

Consider two firms 1 and 2. Let the firms have the same *MPC* and *MSC* curves which are assumed constant. Competition exists and firms face a price P_1 equal to *MPC*. The external pollution costs when added to the *MPC* forms the *MSC* curve. If firm 2 gets more marginal benefits (*MB*) than firm 1, then the regulation imposing equal fixed quantities means that 1 produces too much and 2 produces too little.

This result follows because the *MB*s are reflected in the demand curves. By having a larger demand, firm 2 produces (without the regulation) a larger quantity, Q_2, as opposed to firm 1's Q_1. When both firms are required to produce the same amount Q_R, this means a greater reduction for firm 2. In fact, firm 1 produces at the same level as before, because the regulation quantity exceeds what it wishes to produce anyway. Firm 2 bears all the burden of the regulation. Its output is reduced from Q_2 to Q_R. The socially optimal quantities are Q_{S1} for firm 1 and Q_{S2} for firm 2. Thus, we obtain $Q_R > Q_{S1}$ for firm 1 and $Q_R < Q_{S2}$ for firm 2.

5.2.2   Standards and pricing approach

Baumol and Oates (1971) recognize the weaknesses of imposing common quantity restrictions, but they do not advocate using Pigovian taxes. A number of theoretical problems exist with such taxes. The setting of the tax is no easy matter. One cannot just tax the output of the polluting industry, because that may cause the firm to use more of the input that is causing the pollution (e.g., coal). Also, technology may be variable. The level of pollution may be reduced by changing the methods of production. (Turvey (1963) discussed the possibility of requiring that a larger chimney be used by the factory to help reduce the external costs on the laundry.)

Separate from these difficulties, Baumol and Oates emphasize that the Pigovian tax solution has two insurmountable practical (information) problems:

i.   One needs to be able to measure the marginal damage caused by pollution. Even with technology fixed, the number of persons affected is large, and the effects are intangible (for example, damage to health). So, measurement is extremely difficult.
ii. The marginal damage that one needs to measure is not the existing level, but the damage that would occur at the optimum. In terms of diagram 5.2, the relevant external cost is *ad* per unit at the *hypothetical* level of output Q_2, rather than the *bc* per unit at the actual level of output Q_1.

Baumol and Oates recommend a hybrid approach, relying on both taxes and quantity restrictions. The aim is to set an arbitrary standard for the pollution, and set taxes in an iterative process to achieve the standard. The tax (equivalent to a price) is set on the existing level of pollution and reduces the marginal damage. If the targeted reduction is not achieved, the tax is raised. If the reduction is too large, the rate is lowered. In this way the tax rate is adjusted until the desired quantity is reached.

Diagram 5.4 shows how this 'standards and pricing approach' works. The set-up is similar to the common quantity restriction case that we analysed in the previous section. The main difference is that, unlike Diagram 5.3, the *MSC* is unknown and therefore not drawn. Instead of having equal quantity targets set, each firm faces a tax that is added to the market price P_1. The tax reduces the output of firm 1 by ΔQ_1 (the difference between Q_1 and Q_1a) and reduces the output of firm 2 by ΔQ_2 (the difference between Q_2 and Q_2a). The tax is not the optimal tax, but simply the rate at which the sum of the reductions $\Delta Q_1 + \Delta Q_2$ equals the preassigned target reduction total.

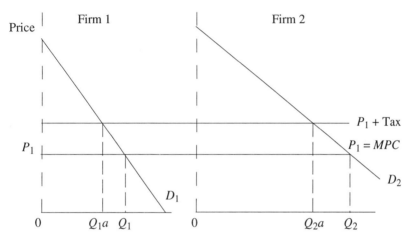

The private equilibrium is where demand equals *MPC*. Firm 1 produces Q_1 and firm 2 produces Q_2. When a tax is introduced, the firm adds it to the *MPC* and equates demand to this sum. Firm 1 now produces Q_1a and 2 produces Q_2a. If the tax is set at the right level, the reductions in output by 1 $(Q_1 - Q_1a)$ and by 2 $(Q_2 - Q_2a)$ equal the target output reduction.

Diagram 5.4

The major advantage of the Baumol and Oates approach is that the taxes are the least-cost method to realize the pollution standard. Here we simply note how the common quantity restriction problem has been avoided. In Diagram 5.3, the reductions were set independent of market conditions. The fact that firm 2 had a higher demand was ignored. In Diagram 5.4, the reductions are basically determined by market forces. The sum of the marginal private cost and the tax are equated with the demand curves to produce the new levels of output.

The obvious disadvantage of the approach is that the standards are set arbitrarily. One does not know whether the social benefits of achieving the target reduction are greater than the social costs. In this respect, the pricing and standards approach shares the drawback of the cost-effectiveness and cost-minimization techniques outlined in Chapter 1. It is the least-cost method of obtaining the policy goal under the crucial assumption that the policy goal is socially worthwhile.

5.2.3   Taxes causing externalities

It is a paradox that, in trying to deal with external diseconomies, government tax policies have often been the *cause* of negative external effects. Pogue and Sgontz (1989) have analysed this with respect to taxing alcohol abusers. But, the problem is a general one that appears whenever the government must use public policy tools that operate only indirectly on the externality. The result of using blunt instruments is that some agents who were not causing externalities are being forced to reduce their scale of activity by policies that were intended to apply only to those who do cause externalities. The loss of output by the innocent third party is the negative externality that the government is causing. Because most countries of the world impose excise taxes on gasoline, it is informative to apply the Pogue and Sgontz analysis to examine the extent to which gas taxes are inadequate instruments for limiting road congestion.

Road congestion is a problem mainly in urban and not rural areas (see Diagram 5.5). The rural roads (on the left-hand side of the diagram) thus have no external costs, while the urban roads (on the right-hand side of the diagram)

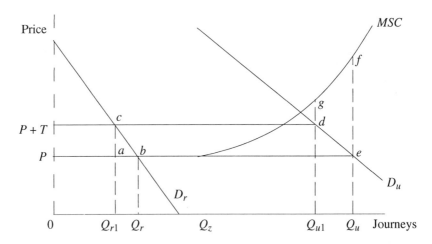

Prior to a tax, urban road users make Q_u journeys and rural road users make Q_r journeys. There are no external costs for the rural road users. The tax at a rate T reduces journeys in both areas. The fall in the urban area is to Q_{u1}, and to Q_{r1} in the rural area. The gain in surplus by urban users (*defg*) must exceed the loss to rural users (*abc*) for the tax to be worthwhile. An optimal tax is where the net gain is greatest.

Diagram 5.5

have external effects causing the *MSC* to diverge from the *MPC* (which is assumed constant and equal to the market price). The divergence starts at the Q_z level of road usage, which only the urban road users exceed. In the absence of the excise tax, the generalized price per journey is *P*. At this price, rural roads users make Q_r journeys and urban road users make Q_u journeys. A gasoline tax is now initiated at a rate *T*. The price for all users goes up to $P + T$, hence both sets of users reduce the number of journeys they make.

For urban road users, the reduction in journeys is a social improvement. Forgone benefits are given by the area $Q_{u1}Q_u ed$ and cost savings are $Q_{u1}Q_u fg$, making a positive difference equal to the area *defg*. But, for the rural road users, the tax causes a welfare loss equal to the consumer surplus triangle *abc*. In this framework, an optimal tax is one where the difference is greatest between the net gain coming from the urban side and the loss coming from the rural side.

It is because the gasoline tax does not distinguish between users who do, and those who do not, cause road congestion that it is a blunt instrument for dealing with road externalities. It can still be beneficial relative to doing nothing, if the rate is such that the net gain exceeds the loss. But it is clearly inferior to a system of road congestion pricing that follows the Pigovian principle of only taxing journeys that cause external damage.

5.3 Applications

If one wishes to tax the marginal external damage of an activity, one must be able to value it in monetary terms. The first case study presents an estimate of the social costs of alcohol treatment programmes. This estimate is then placed in the context of the CBA framework introduced in Chapter 1. It will be seen how difficult it is to measure externalities directly, thus limiting the general usefulness of the Pigovian tax solution.

The Coase theorem seems straightforward. Fix liability and the two parties will (if the numbers are small) negotiate the socially optimal outcome. The case study of the external costs involved with blood transfusions explains why fixing liability will not automatically take place. Fixing liability for consumers is not always feasible; fixing liability for producers is sometimes resisted. Government intervention can cause markets to fail as well as remedy market failure when externalities exist.

Rather than trying to quantify in monetary terms the external effects, the standards and pricing approach assumes a particular level of activity is desirable and uses taxes/prices to realize this quantity. The Singapore road congestion pricing scheme illustrates this approach. The final case study covers the determination of the optimal rate of excise tax on alcohol.

5.3.1 A CBA of alcohol treatment programmes

As explained in Chapter 1, most health-care applications of CBA rely on the human capital approach to benefit estimation. A treatment is valuable if it increases the lifetime earnings of individuals. The Swint and Nelson (1977) study of alcohol rehabilitation programmes uses this methodology. External benefits are the social costs of alcohol that are avoided by having treatment. These social costs are measured as the difference between the present value of the expected future income of non-alcoholics over alcoholics.

It is appropriate to discuss the human capital approach in the context of externalities because the external perspective is the *only* one that is being used in this approach to health benefit estimation. The individual's willingness to pay is not considered. It is the effect on income available to the rest of society that is of sole concern. One way of seeing this is to place external benefits squarely in the context of the CBA framework of Chapter 1. (This was also done in the appendix to Chapter 2, see equation (2.5).)

In expression (1.1), the aim was to maximize the net benefits, $B - C$. B is the total benefits of the project. These can be split into two categories, B_1 for the direct benefits, and B_2 for the external benefits. With $B = B_1 + B_2$, the efficiency criterion becomes:

$$B_1 + B_2 - C \tag{5.5}$$

It is very important to include B_2 in our social calculations, even though private decision-makers would exclude it. This does not mean that measures of B_1 should now be ignored. But, this is exactly what occurs in most evaluations of alcohol treatment programmes (apart from Swint and Nelson, 1977, see also Holtman, 1964 and Rundell et al., 1981). The Swint and Nelson study must be viewed as working with the partial criterion: $B_2 - C$. The omission of B_1 is contrary to the theory of rational addiction developed by Becker and Murphy (1988). This shows that an individual can have an addiction and still be a utility maximizer.

The analysis involved an 'ideal type' rather than an actual treatment programme. In this way the authors hoped to provide a model that can guide other evaluations. Middle-income working males are to be provided with an outpatient treatment programme consisting of: (i) 2 psychiatric social workers for daytime sessions, each meeting 30 patients in groups of 6, for 1 day per week; (ii) 2 psychiatric social workers for night-time sessions with the same work load; (iii) 1 full-time psychiatrist for individual therapy as needed; and (iv) 1 programme administrator with 2 000 square feet of office space and supplies.

The programme unit to be evaluated is the successful rehabilitation of 30 alcoholics. There is to be an all-or-nothing comparison between cure versus no cure. There are two aspects of this type of comparison that warrant discussion because this is a feature of many health-care evaluations (see Drummond et al., 1987). First we consider the 'cure' aspect, then the 'all-or-nothing' basis.

Before any treatment or health intervention begins, evidence of its effectiveness should be demonstrated (preferably on the basis of a random clinical trial).

However, in the case of alcohol treatment programmes this is rarely done. Nor is it clear that one can demonstrate effectiveness in this area. Fingarette (1988) argues that there is a natural recovery rate from alcoholism. Once one controls for the fact that certain groups have a better recovery rate than others (for example, those with high income who have a work-related incentive to rehabilitate) most programmes do not have a success rate much better than the natural recovery rate. Swint and Nelson merely assumed that when treating 120 patients, there would be 25 per cent rehabilitation, which produces the result that 30 people would be successfully treated.

Even if it were possible to obtain a complete cure, it is not clear that, from the public policy perspective, an all-or-nothing comparison is the most useful. Section 5.1 showed that there is an optimum amount of externality. Rarely would the optimum correspond to a zero output level. Whether one is dealing with alcoholism, or any other illness, complete eradication may entail more costs than benefits (and may not be medically or financially feasible).

The total costs of the treatment programme envisaged by Swint and Nelson are listed in Table 5.1. They correspond to the base case where the costs are spread out over 7 years and discounted at a rate of 10 per cent. These costs are the sum of direct and indirect costs. The main direct costs involved labour, and the indirect costs were the forgone income of those patients receiving treatment.

Table 5.1 Benefits and costs of alcohol rehabilitation programmes

Category	Present value
Increased life expectancy	$3 045 398
Lower unemployment rate	$548 305
Higher work efficiency	$2 863 299
Total benefits	$6 457 002
Total costs	$1 157 146
Net benefits	$5 299 856

Source: Swint and Nelson (1979)

Benefit estimation was built around the value of lifetime earnings. This was calculated from the year of treatment until the age of 65. Most of the individuals treated nationally are males in the age range 35 to 44. So, 12 patients for each age in this range were considered to exist in the hypothetical programme. The median annual income of working males in 1973 of $10 039 was aggregated over the remaining working life, compounded by a 3 per cent productivity growth, and discounted at 10 per cent.

Swint and Nelson used lifetime earnings to capture three categories of external benefit from alcohol rehabilitation (see Table 5.1).

i.   Alcoholism reduces one's life expectancy. Successful treatment therefore provides more years of lifetime income.
ii. An alcoholic was thought to be about 6 per cent more likely to be unemployed than a non-alcoholic. As with (i), there are more years of lifetime income to include on this account.
iii. Even when an alcoholic does not lose his job, there will be a greater amount of inefficiency involved at the workplace and higher rates of absenteeism. Swint and Nelson judge that 20 per cent of a person's lifetime earnings would be lost because of this inefficiency.

The three categories of benefit amount to a present value of $6 457 002. Subtracting the costs of $1 157 146, produced a positive $5 299 856 outcome for the programme. When a pessimistic scenario was used to replace the base case (with median annual working income assumed to be $7 500, inefficiency 10 per cent and extra unemployment 4 per cent, all the other parameters remaining the same), the net present value was still positive at $174 373.

The biggest problem with the Swint and Nelson study is the extent to which benefits are underestimated. It is not just the fact that B_1 is excluded completely; it is also in terms of the external benefits B_2, which is the category that is emphasized in their study, that omissions have been made.

Rundell et al. (1981), following Berry and Boland (1977), used four categories to capture the tangible external costs from alcoholism. They were productivity costs (forgone earnings), health costs, automobile accidents costs, and arrest and criminal justice costs. Swint and Nelson present a more complete version of the productivity costs. But, the other three kinds of costs are ignored. These non-productivity costs contributed almost 40 per cent of the benefits per person in the Rundell et al. study, and around two-thirds in the Berry and Boland analysis.

Apart from the tangible external costs, there are all the intangible external costs that are ignored. The pain and suffering of the rest of the family and friends are significant effects. Swint and Nelson (1977, p. 69) are correct to argue that since the net benefits are positive without these other external effects, the programme outcome would be even more strongly positive if these effects were included. But that is not helpful if one is comparing an alcohol treatment programme with some other project, possibly outside the health-care field, and one needs to establish which one has the higher net benefits in total.

That Swint and Nelson did not measure the benefits to the alcoholic him/herself is an omission that is not easily remedied. In principle, one would estimate B_1 by reference to the willingness to pay of the patient. The problem is that willingness to pay and the human capital approach do not provide complementary procedures. If a person is willing to pay $10 000 to be free of alcohol problems, this may in part be due to the fact that otherwise hospital bills and forgone earnings are involved. The danger then is that 'double counting' would take place.

Avoiding double counting is one of the most difficult issues of applied CBA. When explicit markets for activities do not exist, one often is forced to appeal to implicit markets. With an implicit market used for each characteristic of the project, there is a large probability that values are put on the same element from more than one source. This probability is especially large when using forgone earnings to measure health benefits, as we now illustrate.

It is well known that alcoholics suffer from low self-esteem. This effect is never explicitly included in a conventional CBA of rehabilitation programmes. But it is not obvious that it should be included once forgone lifetime earnings have been used. The greater chance of being unemployed, and lower efficiency when employed (two factors included in the Swint and Nelson study) are proxies for this low esteem. The point is that if one is not sure what precisely one is measuring, then there is a good chance that double-counting will take place.

5.3.2 Blood transfusions and the Coase theorem

The Coase theorem tells us that, if the interested parties were able to negotiate, the social optimum for an externality would prevail without the government having to undertake an expenditure project or imposing a tax. Kessel (1974) applied this logic to the market for blood and found a contradiction. The actual outcome was a quantity of blood that corresponded closer to the producer's private optimum (refer to quantity $0Q_3$ in Diagram 5.1). At this outcome too much of the externality was generated.

The externality in question was contacting serum hepatitis as a result of blood transfusions. The incidence of this occurring in the United States was about four times as frequent as in the UK, a country that relied more on voluntary blood donations. The expected cost of contracting hepatitis was put at \$23 225 by Kessel. This was made up of costs for: (i) hospitalization and inpatient treatment, \$1 875; (ii) death and permanent disability, \$20 000; (iii) home nursing, \$425; (iv) absence from the labour market, \$675; and (v) outpatient medical treatment, \$250.

In section 5.2.2, we pointed out that the level of an externality may be reduced by changing the methods of production. Thus, the costs that are relevant for policy purposes may not be the actual external costs, but those after the effect of externalities have been minimized. (In Coase's example, the cost of having cattle graze on the crop of a neighbouring farmer was not the value of the crop, but the cost of building a fence to keep the cattle off the arable land.) Kessel's evaluation of the benefits of switching from low quality to high-quality sources is effectively such a calculation.

In the United States, some of the hepatitis-contaminated blood came from low-status donors (drug addicts, alcoholics and prisoners). Other sources, such as donors from the populations of small towns in Minnesota to the Mayo clinic, provide a low incidence of hepatitis. The difference in probability in contracting hepatitis from a blood transfusion was 6.8 per thousand units of blood transferred as between the best (2.0) and worst (8.8) sources. A reduction in probability of one in a thousand would produce a reduction of $23 (as $23 000 is the expected cost of certain hepatitis). On this basis, a switch from the worst to the best source would produce benefits of $156 per unit ($23 times 6.8).

The issue to be resolved then was, why did not parties in the United States blood transfusion system negotiate a shift to reduce the amount of the externality (by switching to safer sources)? Coase's theorem predicts that if either side had liability, Pareto improvements would be implemented.

Kessel points out that, in the market for blood, liability on the buyers' side would not be effective. The full knowledge and transactions-cost free requirements of the Coase theorem are violated, especially as some of the patients are unconscious at the time blood is being transfused. This means that the cause of the absence of an optimal solution must be sought on the supply side. If product liability existed for physicians and hospitals involved with blood transfusions, there would be an incentive to seek out the low-cost donors. But, the medical profession had sought, and achieved, exemptions from strict liability in tort for blood. Most states have this exemption. Kessel therefore concludes that it is the unnecessary absence of liability by the medical profession that explains why the Coase theorem predictions did not apply in the United States market for blood. It was not because the profit motive would necessarily produce suboptimal outcomes.

There are numerous pieces of information and analysis in the Kessel study that pertain to the theory outlined in section 5.1. However, there are two main conclusions of wide applicability.

i. It is well understood (and clear from the definitions given in 5.1.1 which involve a party *A* and a party *B*) that it takes two individuals or groups to cause an externality. One should always check that an externality is marginally relevant. In the blood transfusion case, there exists one group of users who incur no costs even from low-quality sources. A substantial number of haemophiliacs have had so many blood transfusions that they are likely to have contracted serum hepatitis in the past and have now become immune. Here the externality exists, but is not potentially relevant (and therefore cannot be Pareto relevant).

ii. The optimum amount of an externality is not usually zero, but it also may not correspond to low levels either. The fact that the United States had four times as much serum hepatitis from blood transfusions than the UK does not, *in itself*, indicate greater market failure in the United States. Kessel refers to studies that conclude that, in the UK and unlike the United States, over one-third of the surgeons surveyed reported that they sometimes postpone operations due to insufficient blood. The benefits of having more blood, even if it were contaminated, may therefore exceed the costs. The real test of whether low levels of externality are optimal for the UK is therefore whether the net benefits of the operations that are being forgone are below the hepatitis external costs.

5.3.3   Singapore's road-licensing system

Over 70 per cent of the world's largest agglomerations are projected to be in LDCs by the year 2000 (see Bahl and Lin, 1992). It is very unlikely that road capacity can keep pace. This means that trying to restrict car use, rather than catering for car use, is a priority for many countries. It is in this context that Singapore's introduction of a road area licensing system to reduce road congestion generates a lot of interest. This is the world's foremost example of road pricing. Although not portrayed as such, it is also a very clear example of the pricing and standards approach. A target reduction in peak traffic was set and a licence fee fixed to achieve that target.

Seventy per cent of the 2.2 million inhabitants of Singapore live within a radius of 8 kilometres of the central business district of Singapore. In 1974, there were a quarter of a million registered vehicles and this number was projected to rise to three-quarters of a million by 1982. Congestion was therefore a serious problem in Singapore, one that was expected to increase over time.

The government's goal was to reduce traffic by 25–30 per cent during the peak periods. To achieve this, an area licensing scheme (ALS) was introduced in 1975. The original scheme was labour intensive and is to be upgraded into a capital intensive, electronic pricing system to be fully operational in the mid-1990s. Major revisions to the ALS occurred in 1989. We explain the system as it operated between 1975–78, based on Watson and Holland (1976). Data for evaluations come from Hau (1992b). They relate to 1975 and the period 1975–89.

The Singapore ALS required that a special, supplementary licence be obtained and displayed in order that a vehicle can enter a designated congestion area during the peak hours. The restricted, congested area covered 62 hectares and had 22 entry points that were monitored. The visibility of the date-coloured stickers allowed traffic wardens to check the vehicles while they were moving. This non-stop feature produces large time-savings benefits relative to manually operated toll booths. The licence fee of 3 Singapore (S) dollars a day (S\$3 = US\$1.30 in 1976) applied to all vehicles except buses, commercial vehicles, motorcycles and car pools (cars that carry at least four persons). The licence numbers of cars not displaying an area licence were recorded and a fine issued (equal to S\$50). The peak hours were defined as 7.30–10.15 a.m.

There were two other elements in the Singapore road congestion alleviating package apart from the ALS.

a. Parking fees were raised 100 per cent at public car parks in the restricted zone. A surcharge was levied on private car parks to restore pricing balance in the two car-parking sectors.
b. A 'park-and-ride' alternative mode of transport to the ALS was provided for those motorists who had become accustomed to driving into the central area. For half the price of the supplementary licence, spaces in car parks on the periphery of the restricted zone were provided, with a fast, limited-stop bus shuttle running to the central areas.

One of the important features of a road pricing scheme is the flexibility it provides to fine-tune the system as more information is collected. This is unlike the standard expenditure project, where it is not possible to build half a bridge and see what happens! In the Singapore road licensing case, there were a number of 'mid-stream' corrections. Here are some examples that illustrate the reiterative possibilities.

i. At first, taxis were exempt. When the number of taxis increased by about a quarter within the first three weeks, the exemption was removed.
ii. The peak period initially ended at 9.30 a.m. This had the effect of postponing the congestion till after the time-restriction period was over. As a consequence, the peak period was extended by three-quarters of an hour to 10.15 a.m. and this eliminated most of the congestion.
iii. The immediate reaction of some motorists, who formerly drove through the restricted zone, was to drive around it and cause congestion on bypass routes. In response to this problem, the timing of traffic lights was adjusted (to give priority to circumferential movements rather than radial in-bound traffic).
iv. When it became clear that the park-and-ride alternative was not being used, the authorities responded by converting the empty parking lots into hawkers' markets and cooked food stores. The shuttle buses were then integrated back into the regular bus system.

Watson and Holland (1976) made an evaluation of the ALS as of the first year when *net* traffic in the peak period fell by 40 per cent The big issue was how to deal with the capital expenditures involved with the park-and-ride part of the policy package which was unsuccessful (only 4 per cent of car-park spaces provided were taken up). Since the success of the ALS was independent of the park-and-ride part, one could make calculations with and without this component. The capital cost for the total package was S$6.6 million. As over 90 per cent of these costs were for the construction of car parks, bus shelters, provision of utilities and landscaping, the capital cost of the ALS itself was only S$316 000.

Revenues net of operating expenses were S\$420 000 per month, or S\$5.04 million per annum. The net financial rate of return was 76 per cent with the park-and-ride scheme and 1 590 per cent without, corresponding to a revenue–cost ratio of 16.9. Only a crude efficiency calculation was made. Watson and Holland came up with an efficiency rate of return of 15 per cent for the first year. Hau points out that this includes only time savings and not savings in operating costs and fuel. The time savings were valued at a single rate, rather than by varying the value of time according to the wage rate of the individual. When Hau excluded the park-and-ride component, he found that the economic efficiency rate of return would have been 60 per cent.

The Singapore ALS scheme provides a good illustration of the strengths and weaknesses of the pricing and standards approach. It will be recalled that the objective was to reduce traffic during the peak hours by 25–30 per cent and the effect of the ALS was to reduce the flow by 40 per cent. Since the reduction was greater than targeted, one could conclude that the licence fee was set at too high a rate. Over time the fee had risen from the initial value of S\$3 a day to S\$5 day. Beginning 1 June 1989, the daily licence fee was reduced to S\$3 a day.

However, it is worth reiterating the main reservation with this process. It had not been demonstrated that a 25–30 per cent reduction in traffic is socially optimal. Thus, 40 per cent could be the correct outcome and the price charged would then not need to change.

5.3.4 Taxing to control alcohol social costs
Just like the road congestion situation in section 5.2.3, there are some alcohol drinkers who cause external costs and others who do not. Pogue and Sgontz (1989) call the former group 'abusers' (group A), and the others 'non-abusers' (group B). An excise tax that reduces consumption will therefore produce net gains for the abusers and losses for the non-abusers. In terms of Diagram 5.5, abusers correspond to the urban group, non-abusers to the rural group, and Q_z is the consumption quantity at which heavy drinking imposes external costs on others.

The tax rate t is expressed in *ad valorem* terms. This means the tax T is set as a percentage of the price P, i.e., $t = T/P$. The tax rate that maximizes the difference between the net gain to abusers (area *defg* in Diagram 5.5) and the losses to the non-abusers (area *abc*) is given by (see the appendix for the derivation):

$$t = \frac{T}{P} = \frac{E}{P} \cdot \frac{1}{\left[1 + \dfrac{\eta_B X_B}{\eta_A X_A} \right]} \tag{5.6}$$

where:

E = average external costs (from Q_{u1} to Q_u in Diagram 5.5);
η_A = elasticity of demand for abusers (group A);
η_A = elasticity of demand for non-abusers (group B);
X_A = total consumption of alcohol by abusers; and
X_B = total consumption of alcohol by non-abusers.

Before examining all the ingredients of equation (5.6) in detail, it is useful to see that the expression is a very general one that includes the Pigovian tax as a special case. If there are no non-abusers, $X_B = 0$. The bracketed term would then become equal to unity. Equation (5.6) becomes $T/P = E/P$, or $T = E$. Thus, the tax would equal the external damage caused, which is exactly the basis of the Pigovian tax.

More generally, equation (5.6) expresses the optimal tax as a function of three main factors:

i.   the relative size of the consumption levels of the two groups X_B/X_A;
ii. the size of the external costs relative to the consumer price E/P; and
iii. the relative size of the price elasticities η_B/η_A.

We explain the Pogue and Sgontz estimates of these three factors in turn, as they relate to the United States for 1983.

An abuser is classified as a person who reported at least one alcohol-related problem in the 1979 survey of adult alcohol use (by Clark and Midanik, 1982). Abusers are only 10 per cent of the adult population, but account for around 38 per cent of total consumption. Adding a further 3 per cent by adolescent abusers, abuser consumption was set at 41 per cent. Non-abuser consumption was therefore 59 per cent. This made the ratio of non-abuser to abuser consumption approximately 1.42 (i.e., 0.59/0.41).

A report by Harwood et al. (1984) identified the main types of abuse costs as alcohol-related treatment and support, deaths, reduced productivity, motor vehicle crashes and crime. Total abuse costs were put at $116.7 billion, or $127 per gallon of alcohol (ethanol) on average. Pogue and Sgontz then assumed that these average abuse costs were equivalent to the required marginal external costs, E. The average pretax price per gallon of alcohol for 1983 was $102.65. This made the ratio $E/P = \$127/\$102.65 = 1.24$.

There was no information available that could indicate whether the price elasticities of demand for the two groups differed or not. One could say that Pogue and Sgontz were using the applied economist's old standby: 'the law of equal ignorance'. This states that if one does not know that factors are different, one might as well assume that they are the same. In any case, the 'best guess' estimate was to set $\eta_A = \eta_B$.

The best-guess estimate for the optimal tax rate involves inserting $X_B/X_A = 1.42$, $E/P = 1.24$ and $\eta_B/\eta_A = 1$ into equation (5.6). The optimal tax rate was therefore calculated to be 51 per cent:

$$t = 1.24 \cdot \frac{1}{[1+1.42]} = 0.51$$

The best-guess estimate also provided the highest value for the optimal tax rate. All other combinations of values for the three factors tried by Pogue and Sgontz resulted in values lower than 51 per cent. When $\eta_B/\eta_A = 4$ was used, the lowest value for t of 19 per cent was obtained.

The existing average tax rate on alcohol from all levels of government in the United States for 1983 was 24 per cent. The 1955 tax rate was 54 per cent, much closer to the optimal rate. Pogue and Sgontz then considered the following policy alternative, which we can call a 'project'. What would be the increase in social welfare if the actual rate of 24 per cent was nearly doubled, that is, raised 27 percentage points to the optimal or (roughly) past 1955 value?

As explained in Diagram 5.5, raising the tax rate on alcohol consumption would have two effects that are opposite in direction. The increase in net benefits to abusers (corresponding to the *change* in the area *defg*) was $1.398 billion. The increased loss of consumer surplus by the non-abusers (representing the change in the area *abc*) was $0.863 billion. The overall effect of the tax increase project would be to raise social welfare by $0.535 billion (i.e., $1.398 billion minus $0.863 billion).

An important feature of the Pogue and Sgontz analysis is that they present an alternative set of results for those who do not accept the assumption of consumer sovereignty as being appropriate for certain alcohol consumers – those who are 'alcoholics'. Such consumers are addicted or believed to have imperfect information. Thus, *all* of the consumption of alcoholic abusers can be thought to decrease their welfare, if one rejects consumer sovereignty for this group. The loss of welfare has two components. (a) The expenditure by alcoholics on alcohol that could have been spent on something which does contribute to their welfare. In addition, (b) alcohol consumption produces 'internal' abuse costs to the alcoholic.

When treating alcoholics as a group who always lose utility by consuming alcohol, one must adjust equation (5.6) to include the two negative components of their consumption (see equation (9) of Pogue and Sgontz, 1989). It will be recalled that in the original formulation, a tax increase had a negative effect for abusers related to the area $Q_{u1}Q_u ed$ which acted to offset (in part) the positive effect of the reduction in external costs. When one rejects consumer sovereignty for the alcoholics (who consume about 73.5 per cent of abusive consumption) this negative effect is eliminated completely. So it is not surprising that the optimal tax rate is higher when the consumption by alcoholics is treated as disutility rather than utility. The best-guess estimate of t rises to 306 per cent and the minimum value is 87 per cent, well above the maximum value obtained earlier. In the new calculation of the optimal tax, internal abuse costs were put at almost four times the size of the external abuse costs (that is, $441 million as opposed to $127 million).

5.4   Final comments

As usual, we conclude the chapter with a summary and a set of problems.

5.4.1   Summary

Externalities exist when an agent cannot adjust optimally to a variable because it is within the control of someone else. Just because an externality exists in a private market, it does not necessarily mean that the equilibrium output is not socially optimal. Externalities are Pareto relevant for public policy purposes only when the gains are greater than the losses from movements away from the market outcome.

On the other hand, one cannot automatically assume that, because a market exists, an externality will be internalized. The Coase theorem requires the existence of property rights and groups small enough to be able to negotiate the optimal solution.

The main issue is what to do with externalities that are Pareto relevant. Pigou has suggested that we tax (or subsidize) the externality according to the marginal damage (or gain) incurred. Consumer surplus will be maximized at such a solution. But, the informational requirements for such a solution are formidable. Alternative policy options must therefore be considered.

Non-Pigovian strategies can be implemented on the price and/or quantity sides of the market mechanism. Environmental policy has often focused on common quantity standards. This has the problem of causing interfirm inefficiencies. Baumol and Oates's prices and standards approach removes this problem, because reductions in the externality are undertaken in the lowest cost way. They recommend using a tax to achieve the quantity reduction. This tax is not a Pigovian tax. It is set at a rate to achieve the target rate of externality reduction; it is not equal to the marginal damage caused. The quantity reduction is arbitrarily fixed. This is appropriate when externality damage is obviously excessive (e.g., causes a large loss of lives). But, eventually the standard itself will have to be put to a CBA test, to see if the benefits of imposing the standard exceed the costs.

Policy instruments cannot always be directed solely at the externality-generating agent. When abusers and non-abusers are taxed at the same rate, the tax must be lower than otherwise to allow for the lost consumer surplus of the non-abuser. In this way the tax itself causes an externality. The lower tax means that the socially optimal level of output is greater (to accommodate the consumption of the non-abusers).

The applications covered all the main themes presented in the theory sections. We highlighted the problems in measuring the external costs of alcohol abuse to show that the Pigovian remedy could not yet be applied in this area. It is useful to show that underestimated external costs are sufficient to justify resources for an alcohol treatment programme. But the underestimation means that one could not fix a tax that equals the marginal external damage caused by alcohol excesses.

There is a grave danger in practice of over-emphasizing the external costs at the expense of the direct effects. In the alcohol treatment case study we saw that the direct effects on alcoholics were excluded completely. Similarly, in the blood transfusion case, focusing only on the hepatitis side-effects ignores the fact that even contaminated blood can be worthwhile, if it means that necessary operations can take place.

The Singapore road-congestion application showed how any tax policy can be considered in the CBA framework. Resources are entailed in administering the tax (or price) system. It is worthwhile to invest those resources only if the net benefits of the tax exceed those resource costs. This study also illustrated the Baumol and Oates pricing and standards approach. What was readily apparent was the flexibility that this approach provides. Price changes and price discrimination (by varying the groups who are exempt) are features that any country can utilize.

The final case study considered setting an optimal tax rate on alcohol consumption. This affected abusers and non-abusers alike. It does not operate like the common quantity restriction because those who value alcohol the most will restrict their consumption the least. The Pigovian tax is a special case of this optimal tax formula. Questioning the relevance of consumer sovereignty is a major issue in dealing with certain kinds of externalities (in such areas as smoking and the drinking of alcohol). It is useful to be familiar with a framework that allows the analyst to vary the viewpoint in this regard.

5.4.2 Problems
The following problems are based on Newbery's (1988) study of road pricing principles, focusing on road damage costs. These costs falls into two types: the road damage externality (the increased operating costs by subsequent vehicles travelling on the rougher road) and pavement costs (which involve repairing the road and are paid for by the highway authority). The questions relate to each type of road damage cost.

1. The damage to a road by a vehicle does not just depend on its overall weight. The damage is more precisely measured by the number of equivalent standard axles (ESAs), where one ESA is the damaging power of an 18 000-pound single axle. Road engineers have estimated the following relation:

$$Damage = [ESA/8.2]^4.$$

   i.   By what exponential power is the damage caused by ESAs?
   ii. If a passenger car has an ESA of 1 and a truck has an ESA of 10, by what multiple does the truck do damage to the road relative to the passenger car?
   iii. On the basis of your answer to part (ii), would it be fair to say that almost all road damage is caused by heavy vehicles?
   iv. If you were devising a tax (or licence fee) to charge heavy vehicles, what else would you need to know apart from the ESA of the vehicle?

2. Newbery has a theorem that relates to road damage externalities. The purpose of the questions is to develop some intuition concerning the theorem and help identify the crucial assumptions. There are two effects of having more cars on the roads. First, the road surface (measured by its roughness) deteriorates each year the extra vehicles are on the roads. Vehicle operating costs are positively related to the roughness of the road surface and therefore these costs increase. If the transport authority replaces the surface whenever the roughness exceeds a target level, roads will have to be replaced earlier. Road maintenance costs (the pavement costs) therefore also rise. Second, because the road surface is replaced earlier, the roughness of the surface is lower than it otherwise would have been. Vehicle operating costs are lower because of this reduction in roughness.

   i.   Do maintenance costs rise by extra road usage by cars?
   ii. Do vehicle operating costs have to rise by extra road usage by cars? Under what circumstances would these costs (and hence road damage externalities) remain unaltered?

5.5   Appendix

Here we derive equation (5.6). As can be seen in Diagram 5.5, the tax T generates a cost saving to A of area *defg*, but simultaneously causes a loss of consumer surplus to A and B. The cost saving is treated as a rectangle, with a width equal to the average external costs E, and a length given by the change in output by A of ΔX_A. The cost saving area is therefore the product: $E.\Delta X_A$. By defining the total change in quantity ΔX_A as the per person quantity change Δx_A times the number of A-type users N_A, the cost saving area can be rewritten as: $E.\Delta x_A.N_A$. The consumer surplus areas are both triangles, whose areas are half base times height. The height in both cases is the tax T. The base for A is the change in quantity ΔX_A (equal to $\Delta x_A.N_A$) and the base for B is the change in quantity ΔX_B (equal to $\Delta x_B.N_A$). Since welfare W is positively related to the consumer surplus areas and negatively related to the cost area, it can be written as:

$$W = 1/2.\Delta x_A.N_A.T + 1/2.\Delta x_B.N_B.T - E.\Delta x_A.N_A \qquad (5.7)$$

The Δx's can be expressed in price elasticity terms by the definitions: $\eta_A = (\Delta x_A/x_A)/(\Delta P/P)$ and $\eta_B = (\Delta x_B/x_B)/(\Delta P/P)$. As the change in price ΔP denotes the tax T in both definitions, we obtain:

$$\Delta x_A = \frac{T.\eta_A.x_A}{P}; \text{ and } \Delta x_B = \frac{T.\eta_B.x_B}{P} \qquad (5.8)$$

Substituting for the Δx's of equation (5.8) into (5.7) produces:

$$W = 1/2.\frac{T.\eta_A.x_A}{P}.N_A.T + 1/2.\frac{T.\eta_B.x_B}{P}.N_B.T - E.\frac{T.\eta_A.x_A}{P}.N_A \qquad (5.9)$$

This can be simplified by collecting terms in T and switching back to aggregate rather than per person quantities to form:

$$W = 1/2.T^2\frac{\eta_A.X_A}{P} + 1/2.T^2\frac{\eta_B.X_B}{P} - E.\frac{T.\eta_A.X_A}{P} \qquad (5.10)$$

To maximize W, we take the partial derivative of W with respect to T and set it equal to zero:

$$\frac{\delta W}{\delta T} = T\frac{\eta_A.X_A}{P} + T\frac{\eta_B.X_B}{P} - E.\frac{\eta_A.X_A}{P} = 0 \qquad (5.11)$$

Collecting terms in T/P and isolating them on the left-hand side results in:

$$\frac{T}{P} = \frac{E}{P}.\left[\frac{\eta_A X_A}{\eta_A X_A + \eta_B X_B}\right] \qquad (5.12)$$

Dividing top and bottom of the bracketed term on the right-hand side of equation (5.12) by $\eta_A X_A$ reduces to (5.6).

6 Public goods

6.1 Introduction

The last chapter explained why markets sometimes fail to produce socially optimal levels of output. In this chapter, we analyse the case where private markets are alleged to fail *completely*. No output would be forthcoming if public goods are involved.

The modern theory of public goods originated with Samuelson (1954, 1955). The theory section begins with his definitions and identification of the distinguishing characteristics of such goods. The optimal conditions are presented and contrasted with those for private goods. It is because a free-rider problem is believed to exist that private markets would fail to implement the optimal conditions for public goods.

Orr (1976) uses the theory of public goods to explain why government expenditures which transfer cash to the poor take place. We use this extension of public good theory to explain in detail how a compulsory (government) setting could be preferable to individual initiatives working through a market. We end the theory section by using the Orr model to interpret the existence of distribution weights in CBA.

There are three main methods for trying to estimate the WTP for public goods. The contingent valuation (CV) method asks WTP in a hypothetical setting. The other two approaches are termed 'experimental'. A simulated market ties the WTP bids to the cost of providing the public goods. Respondents therefore make their bids conditional on others and the provision that total WTP must match the total costs. The third method is an actual market which requires that the WTP bids offered be put into effect such that the collective outcome is implemented. All three methods are covered in the applications.

The first application provides an introduction to the three methods and tests the existence of the free-rider problem. Then the contingent evaluation method is illustrated. The third application highlights more the other two methods. To close the applications, we explain how the theory of public goods can be used in a positive sense ('what projects will be done') as well as a normative sense ('what project should be done').

6.1.1 Public production and public provision

The theory to be developed here is geared to explaining public provision, and not public production. Public goods lead to complete market failure. This is why the government provides finance for these goods (usually out of general taxation).

Whether the production of the goods will be supplied by a privately-owned, or a publicly-owned firm, is a separate matter. For instance, the United States is a country which mainly prefers private production. Thus, in 1981, 12.1 per cent of total production was by the public sector. But public provision was much larger. Twenty point one per cent of output was provided through the Budget (see Musgrave and Musgrave, 1989). It is public provision only that concerns us here. (For the ownership issue see Jones et al. (1990), where CBA has been applied to assessing the merits of privatization.)

6.1.2 Definition and characteristics
Samuelson has defined a *pure* public good as one which is consumed in equal quantities by all. It is not the case that everyone places the same value on the commodity. It is only that each unit of output of the public good enters everyone's utility function simultaneously. When a country's resources are devoted to defence that provides greater security, everyone in that country can feel more secure. This is in contrast to a private good, where the more one person consumes a good, the less is available for others. A loaf of bread that is consumed by one hungry person, cannot make others less hungry.

This distinction can be formalized as follows. Consider two individuals, A and B. G is the total quantity available of the public good and X is the total quantity available of the private good. For the public good: $G_A = G_B = G$. Individual consumptions are related to the total via an equality. While for the private good: $X_A + X_B = X$. Individual consumptions are related to the total via a summation.

For a good to be equally consumed by all, it must have two characteristics.

i. Non-excludability: private markets exclude by price. If you do not pay, you do not receive the benefits. Certain goods, such as local street use, cannot charge prices (tolls) because there are too many access points. Similarly, with whale and seal fishing. The open seas are too vast to try to monitor and enforce pricing for commercial activities.
ii. Joint supply: provision to one can lead to provision to all at zero additional cost. If one person sees a movie, others can see it at no extra cost.

Pure public goods have both characteristics, while pure private goods have neither. It is true that there are very few examples of pure public goods. But instances of pure private goods are also rare. Most goods have a mixture of the two characteristics. The mixed case examples are movies and fishing in Table 6.1. Movies are in joint supply, but exclusion is relatively easy. Exclusion is virtually impossible with fishing. The more fish that one person catches, the fewer are left for others to catch; separate supply therefore characterizes fishing. Even though the mixed cases are the norm, it is important to explain the analysis of pure public goods. It is then a practical matter as to the extent that (a) the problems identified actually exist in any given situation, and (b) the recommended solutions are appropriate.

Table 6.1   Public goods, private goods and mixed cases

Characteristic:	Joint supply	Separate supply
Excludable	Movies (mixed case)	Bread (private good)
Non-excludable	Defence (public good)	Fishing (mixed case)

6.1.3   Optimal provision of public goods

The key to understanding the optimal conditions for public goods is the fact that a unit of output simultaneously gives satisfaction to all individuals. Thus, for a given marginal cost (*MC*) there is a *sum* of individual utility effects to aggregate. This is in contrast to the conditions for a private good where, as we saw in the earlier chapters, the requirement is that the marginal utility (for the individual consuming the last unit) must equal the *MC*. Samuelson was the first to derive these two sets of conditions, and the appendix goes through this analysis. Here we will just exploit one of the externality conditions of the last chapter to derive the main public good result.

Recall that a Pareto-relevant externality was given by expression (5.4). This stated that the gain to *A* must exceed the loss to *B* from moving away from his/her private optimum. The externality was irrelevant when both sides of (5.4) were equal. That is, the optimal output for a good generating an externality is where:

$$MU^A_{Y_1} = [MC^B_{Y_1} - MU^B_{Y_1}] \qquad (6.1)$$

If we add $MU_{Y_1}^B$ to both sides of equation (6.1) we obtain the Samuelson result that, for a public good, the sum of the marginal utilities must equal the marginal cost:

$$MU^A_{Y_1} + MU^B_{Y_1} = MC^B_{Y_1} \qquad (6.2)$$

All public goods have the externality relation. It is valid then to base the optimal condition for a public good on the Pareto-relevant externality condition. (The addition of joint supply will, as we shall see, add significantly to the public policy problems.) The only real difference in the interpretation of (5.4) and (6.2) is that, in the externality case, people are consuming different commodities (for example, *A* receives smoke, while *B*'s profits are derived from consumers of the output produced by the factory); while for public goods, individuals are consuming the same commodity. Though even this difference disappears when we consider some public goods. A dam provides flood protection, electricity and water for recreation use, services which may involve different groups of consumers.

The optimal condition for a public good is illustrated graphically in Diagram 6.1. Depicted is the demand by two individuals A and B for flood protection, as reflected by the height of a dam being built. As before, MU's (the prices that consumers are willing to pay) are captured by the individual demand curves. In Diagram 6.1, we start at the origin and unit by unit see what marginal utility is derived from each individual and sum them, thereby obtaining $MU^A + MU^B$, which is the social demand curve D_S. D_S corresponds with individual B's demand curve after quantity Q_1. After that point (i.e., dam height), individual A receives no benefits. So there is nothing to add on to B's demand curve. The intersection of the social demand curve with the MC curve, produces the social optimum Q_*. At this point, equation (6.2) is satisfied.

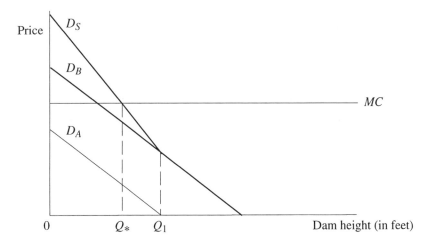

The social demand curve D_S For the public good (flood protection) is derived as the vertical sum of the individual demand curves D_A and D_B. Where the social demand curve intersects the MC curve is the social optimum level of output Q_*. At Q_*, the Samuelson condition holds: $MU^A + MU^B = MC$.

Diagram 6.1

The difference between a public and a private good is that, for the private good, the industry demand curve is derived by summing horizontally the individual demand curves; while for the public good, social demand is obtained by summing *vertically* the individual demand curves. With private goods, we ask at every price, how many each individual demands and sum them in the quantity (i.e., horizontal) direction. For public goods, we ask for every unit of quantity how much each individual is willing to pay and sum them in the price (i.e., vertical) direction. The reason for the difference is that if *A* wants 1 unit and *B* wants 1 unit, the private goods market must supply 2 units. For public goods, if each wants 1 unit, the total demand is only 1 unit.

The WTP methodology underlying CBA relies on measuring benefits by the area under the demand curve. The introduction of public goods into the analysis requires the modification that it is the area under the social demand curve, and not the market demand curve, that is needed for valuation purposes. However, as we shall now see, trying to get to know the social demand curve for public goods poses many practical difficulties.

6.1.4   The free-rider problem

Samuelson has called the individual demand curves in Diagram 6.1 'pseudo' demand curves. These curves exist, but are not knowable by the social decision-maker. Individuals have an incentive to under-reveal their preferences for public goods. If no one reveals what they are willing to pay, private producers cannot make a profit. The optimal solutions just outlined in section 6.1.3 will not materialize in private markets. Let us see what is the problem.

By the characteristic of joint supply, an individual receives benefits automatically if anyone receives benefits. No extra costs are involved. Thus, he/she *can* receive benefits at no charge. From the non-excludability characteristic, it is impossible to prevent those who do not pay for the good receiving them. So a person *will* receive the benefits at no charge. If a person has no incentive to reveal his preferences (by paying for the good) a private market will fail to produce the good. This is known as the 'free rider' problem.

In the more recent literature, the free-rider problem has been viewed as a hypothesis to be tested rather than an incontrovertible behavioural fact (see, for example, Smith, 1980). Even when it has been assumed to exist, there has been a lot of research into how to minimize its effect.

The standard solution to the free rider problem is to recommend use of the political process. If individuals fail to reveal their preferences voluntarily, it may be necessary to force people to pay for the goods by compulsory taxation. The individual now knows in advance what the tax price will be. With a known tax price, individuals may as well try to ensure that the quantities they prefer are provided. There is no incentive to under-reveal preferences. This does solve the problem. But, as the public choice literature has emphasized, one could be just replacing notions of market failure with that of political failure (for example, politicians may have their own objectives separate from that of the electorate). The social optimum may still not be achieved.

6.2 Income redistribution as a pure public good

The theory of pure public goods was extended and placed in an explicit democratic social decision-making framework by Orr (1976). This model was used to explain why rich individuals would voluntarily tax themselves to make cash transfers to the poor. Having shown that income redistribution can be treated as a public good, we then use the analysis to interpret income distribution weights in CBA.

6.2.1 Orr model

In the Orr model, the 'good' that generates the externality is a transfer of a unit of income from the rich A to the poor B. A's income Y_A declines by -1 and B'S income Y_B increases by $+1$. The transfer generates two effects for A and one for B. A loses marginal utility from the Y_A sacrificed, represented by $MU_{Y_A}^A$; but receives an external (psychic) benefit (marginal utility) from knowing that Y_B has been increased, denoted by $MU_{Y_B}^A$. B simply cares only about the fact that his/her income Y_B has increased, which produces additional utility represented by $MU_{Y_B}^B$. The transfer will generate a positive net gain (be Pareto relevant) provided that this version of expression (5.4) is satisfied:

$$MU_{Y_B}^A + MU_{Y_B}^B > MU_{Y_A}^A \qquad (6.3)$$

This states that the psychic satisfaction to A (from B receiving the transfer Y_B) plus the direct satisfaction to B should exceed the MC to A, in terms of the forgone satisfaction from the transfer Y_A given up by A. For example, if a 1 unit transfer from A to B gives A psychic satisfaction of 0.01, then $1.01 > 1$ and the transfer is worthwhile.

Although the transfer would be a potential Pareto improvement, it need not be an actual Pareto improvement. For an actual improvement, A would be better off only if:

$$MU_{Y_B}^A > MU_{Y_A}^A \qquad (6.4)$$

This condition is unlikely to be satisfied. It requires that A get more psychic satisfaction from a unit of his/her income going to the poor rather than retaining the unit for own consumption. Private charities do function, but not on the scale needed to reduce significantly the number of the poor. In the above numerical example, A would definitely not vote for the transfer as 0.01 is much less than 1.

When it is stated that condition (6.4) is unlikely to be satisfied, this relates to a single individual acting privately. In a social setting, this condition can hold much more readily. Redefine A to be a typical individual of a rich group with N members and B to be a typical individual of a poor group with P members.

Consider a public transfer scheme which provides that every poor person receive a unit of income. The amount to be transferred to the poor is then P units. These units transferred constitute a pure public good. Each unit transferred gives all rich persons psychic satisfaction. The converse is also true. All the units transferred gives each rich person psychic satisfaction. Thus from a typical rich person's perspective, the total satisfaction gained from all the units transferred to the poor is: $\Sigma_{B=1}^{P} MU_{Y_B}^{A}$. This sum replaces the single entry on the left-hand side of expression (6.4) and represents the vertical addition of marginal utilities in the Samuelson condition for a public good.

So far we have dealt only with the benefits part of A's involvement in the public transfer scheme. Taxes are required to pay for B's transfers. We have seen that P units are to be transferred. Assume that the rich pay equal tax shares. As there are N taxpayers, the tax to each A for the unit transfer per poor person is P/N. The MC (utility loss) of the tax is then $(P/N) \cdot MU_{Y_A}^{A}$ (that is, the tax times the marginal utility lost per unit of tax). This MC is to replace the private transfer utility loss that is on the right-hand side of expression (6.4).

When we combine the benefits and costs of the public transfer scheme (i.e., replace both sides of expression (6.4)) the condition for A to be better off is:

$$\sum_{B=1}^{P} MU_{Y_B}^{A} > \frac{P}{N} \cdot MU_{Y_A}^{A} \tag{6.5}$$

To help see what difference it makes to move from a public to a private setting, assume that there are as many rich persons as poor persons. In which case, with $P/N = 1$, the right-hand sides of (6.4) and (6.5) would be equal. The only remaining difference then would be that in (6.5) one is summing over all units transferred to the poor, while in (6.4) there is just a single psychic benefit term. This means for example, if each member of A gets 0.01 extra utility from a unit transfer, and there are P units transferred, approximately P times 0.01 is the total satisfaction per member of A. Hence, if there were 101 poor people receiving transfers, total satisfaction would be 1.01 per 1 unit transferred. The typical A would be better off with the public transfer scheme.

Orr's analysis is summarized in Diagram 6.2. Income transfers from the rich to the poor (denoted by Y_B on the horizontal axis) are examples of pure public goods. MBs are the sum of marginal utilities from the transfers. This is a declining relation. The more that is being transferred, the lower is extra psychic satisfaction. The MC is the forgone utility from paying the taxes to finance the transfers. This is a rising relation. The more income that A is sacrificing, the less is available to satisfy A's own consumption needs. The assumption of diminishing marginal utility of income for A therefore implies that transferring more entails a greater sacrifice of utility. Where the sum of the MBs equal MC (at Y_B*) is the optimum amount of transfers. This is the Samuelson condition placed in the setting of a public transfer scheme relying on equal tax shares. If the typical rich tax payer A is the median voter, and majority rule operates, Y_* would be the politically chosen amount of transfers.

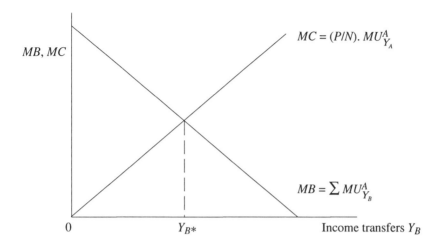

A typical rich person gets satisfaction from a unit transfer to each and every poor person. The sum of these satisfactions over the entire poor population forms the *MB* curve. The forgone utility to the rich of the income they pay in taxes defines the *MC* curve. The social optimum is Y_*, where $MB = MC$.

Diagram 6.2

The conclusion is therefore that income redistribution is an activity that a private market (charity) would fail to provide. The free-rider problem would prevent individuals from voluntarily making contributions to the poor. Rich taxpayers might vote for (be better off with) a public scheme that provides transfers to the poor and finances them with compulsory taxes .

It is important to understand that the Orr model is concerned only with income transfer programmes that the rich would *voluntarily* support. Note that the difference between expressions (6.3) and (6.4) is that, in the latter case, the preferences of the recipient group B are totally ignored. The donors' interests are the only ones considered. This is because an actual Pareto improvement is being sought. If we consider the more general case, where the gains by the poor may offset any losses by the rich, as reflected in criterion (6.3), the scope for redistribution programmes is much wider.

6.2.2   *Orr model and distribution weights*
There are two main implications of the Orr model for CBA. The first follows directly from the analysis presented. Governments may need to spend on income

transfer programmes to satisfy individual preferences for redistribution. CBA should then not only cover expenditures on goods and services, but also include the evaluation of cash transfer programmes. The second implication is that it supplies a justification for giving a premium to the weight given to the benefits that go to the poor in the CBA criterion. This second implication will now be explained.

It will be recalled from Chapter 1 (section 1.2.2) that, if society is concerned with how income is distributed, it should use the criterion (1.2). Society would be better off if weighted benefits exceeded weighted costs:

$$a_2 B > a_1 C \qquad (6.6)$$

In this criterion, the weight a_2 is to be set greater than a_1. Using the Orr model, it is now possible to interpret 'society' as the rich group who receive psychic satisfaction from income received by the poor. The issue to be resolved is the determination of the relative sizes of the distribution weight.

Whether in the context of an actual Pareto improvement or a potential Pareto improvement, there are administrative and disincentive costs of any redistribution scheme. This means that transfers will not be at the social optimal level. Transfers will then be Pareto relevant and Orr's expression (6.5) applies. Using the notation of Chapter 1 (where group 1 was the rich group, 2 was the poor group, and hence one is substituting 1 for A and 2 for B), condition (6.5) becomes:

$$\sum_{1}^{P} MU_{Y_2}^1 > \frac{P}{N} \cdot MU_{Y_1}^1 \qquad (6.7)$$

This relation can now be compared to the CBA criterion (6.6) element by element. The Orr analysis is in terms of a unit transfer. Thus B and $C = 1$ in (6.6). Equating left-hand sides of (6.6) and (6.7) identifies a_2 as $\Sigma\, MU_{Y_2}^1$. This states that the weight on the poor group reflects the sum of psychic satisfactions to the rich of a unit transfer to the poor. If we take the special case where the number of poor equals the number of rich $P/N = 1$, then equating right-hand sides of (6.6) and (6.7) identifies a_1 as $MU_{Y_1}^1$. The weight to the rich group represents the forgone utility by the rich attached to the unit that they are transferring to the poor. Immediately then we have that Orr's Pareto-relevant condition implies $a_2 > a_1$ as anticipated.

More generally, $P \neq N$. But, this does not affect the relative size of the weights provided $P < N$. Multiplying a_1 by a fraction less than 1, lowers its value, and makes the inequality even stronger. In most societies, there are more taxpayers N than people in poverty P. Therefore $P < N$ is to be expected.

6.3   Applications

The main issue raised by the theory of public goods was whether, in practice, methods could be devised to make individuals reveal their preferences, and thereby estimate the WTP for these goods. The first three applications address this issue. The first covers the classic test of the free-rider problem as it relates to estimating the benefits of TV programmes. This study is used as an introduction to the whole range of methodological/empirical attempts that have occurred in the last two decades to measure environmental benefits.

The next two applications are representative of this recent literature. The study of the WTP of the preservation of whooping cranes illustrates the contingent valuation approach that we first outlined in Chapter 3 to deal with private good demand. The CV approach is the only technique that can estimate environmental goods that have benefits that are unrelated to use. The approach is therefore the best one for dealing with *pure* public goods. Then the case study of the WTP for tree densities will be used to highlight a well-documented result in this field. Estimates of valuations to *keep* environmental goods have greatly diverged from estimates to *give up* the same environmental goods. The tree density study tests whether the choice of approach for valuation can account for this divergence.

Most of the analysis of CBA covered in the book so far has emphasized the normative aspects. Welfare theory has been used and applied to help identify socially worthwhile projects. The final case study shows that this framework is also capable of being reversed and used to generate positive explanations of social behaviour. That is, assuming that the decision-maker does try to maximize social welfare along the lines of the CBA models developed, the CBA determinants can be used to predict what decisions actually will be made. The study of Aid to Families with Dependent Children (AFDC) uses the Orr model of public goods to account for differences in transfer expenditures by the states in the United States.

6.3.1   WTP for closed-circuit TV broadcasting

Bohm (1972) was one of the first to use the experimental approach to valuing public goods. The 'good' in question was the creation of access to viewers of a new, half-hour, comedy programme to be seen by closed-circuit TV in Sweden. He wanted to check which of five approaches gave evidence of free-rider behaviour. These five approaches were to be compared with two versions of a sixth one in which such behaviour was thought to be irrelevant.

A one-hour interview was arranged for 605 persons in 1969. At the interview, one of six sets of questions was asked concerning the WTP for the programme. Each person had an incentive to answer the questions as 50 kroner (US$10 = Kr 50) was to be paid. Two hundred and eleven responses were actually used in the analysis. The approaches involved asking a person's WTP based on specified (and different) statements about the price system that is to apply.

The five approaches with an expected revelation problem asked one's WTP if the total cost was Kr 500 (and the programme would be shown if these costs were covered) and:

I.   The price to be charged was the maximum WTP for the programme.
II. The price was some *proportion* of the maximum WTP. For example, if the aggregate WTP was twice the cost, then each person would pay half their specified WTP.
III. The price has not yet been determined.
IV. The price is Kr 5 for everyone.
V.   The price is zero (paid for by the general taxpayer).

The sixth approach simply asked for the WTP and made no mention at all of prices. Two rounds of questions were asked:

VI:1.   What is your maximum WTP?
VI:2.   What is your maximum WTP if only the 10 highest bidders (out of 100) were to pay the amount that they bid and see the programme.

The logic behind these approaches needs to be explained. I is the extreme case where the free-rider problem is expected to appear in its strongest form. One has to pay what one bids, so one bids as low as possible. V is the other extreme. One is definitely not going to be charged at all, no matter what one bids. If anything, one may over-bid in order to try to convince the policy-maker that the provision that is going to take place anyway is worthwhile. Approaches II–IV were intermediate cases between the two extremes. Some would give underestimates, while others would give overestimates. For example, under IV, those who value the programme at least Kr 5 would inflate their WTP to ensure that provision takes place. Those who do not value the programme at Kr 5 would deflate their WTP to ensure that provision does not take place.

VI was (originally) thought to extract the truest set of WTP evaluations. If there is no mention of costs, why engage in strategic behaviour to avoid costs? Bohm thought that there would be some tendency for VI:2 to give lower values. One may just give a bid to get in the top 10 and thus may not have to offer one's highest bid.

The mean and median WTPs for each approach are shown in Table 6.2. The results in the table can be looked at in two stages. The first involves a comparison of the WTP bids among the first five approaches. The second is to compare the first five with the sixth approach. The first stage is non-controversial. The second stage is subject to dispute and we give two different perspectives, before presenting a summary of the general significance of Bohm's study.

Table 6.2 WTP for TV broadcasting by approach (in Kronor)

Approach		Mean WTP	Standard deviation	Median WTP
I	(Pay maximum WTP)	7.61	6.11	5
II	(Pay proportion of WTP)	8.84	5.84	7
III	(Payment undecided)	7.29	4.11	5
IV	(Equal payment, 5 Kr)	7.73	4.68	6.50
V	(Pay nothing)	8.78	6.24	7
VI:1	(No mention of payment)	10.19	7.79	10
VI:2	(No mention of payment)	10.33	6.84	10

Source: Bohm (1972)

The mean WTP values for approaches I to V are all in the Kr 7–8 range, and there is no statistically significant difference (at the 5 per cent level) between any of them. Approach III was supposed to be neutral (give unbiased results), yet the WTP was the same as either of the extreme cases I and V where bias was expected. This is a very important finding as it casts considerable doubt on whether strategic behaviour really will cause private markets to completely fail to produce public goods. Bias could still exist, but was unlikely to be large.

Bohm's interpretation of his approach VI The mean WTP for approach VI was higher than for all other approaches. Approach VI:1 or VI:2 had a WTP that was significantly different from III; but none of the pairwise differences between any of the other five approaches were significant. From this result, Bohm concluded that hypothetical studies of WTP, such as approach VI, are unreliable. It will be recalled that Bohm assumed that III would be neutral. So any significant difference by an approach from III's WTP would indicate bias. He argued that approach VI is like many public opinion polls that do not involve payments or formal decisions and therefore the results cannot be taken seriously. In addition, by mentioning that only 10 would get to see the showing, approach VI:2 was considering the possibility of exclusion and making the evaluation much more like a private than a public good.

A reinterpretation of Bohm's approach VI results Mitchell and Carson (1989, pp. 193–5) emphasize that the hypothetical approach VI:1 is a contingent valuation study. They take exception over Bohm's rejection of this approach as unreliable, and make two valid points. Approach VI:1 is not significantly higher than I, II, IV or V, which are considered *reliable* by Bohm. It is too strong then for Bohm to conclude that respondents treat only CV studies in an 'irresponsible fashion'. Also, approach VI:1 had an outlier, that is, an extreme value that greatly affected the results. The WTP range for 210 of the respondents was Kr 0.50–32.5. Only one person was outside this range and his/her valuation was Kr 50. If this outlier were removed from the sample for VI:1, the mean WTP bid would be 9.43 and 'barely significant'.

Mitchell and Carson go on to argue that approach VI:2 is the most valid as it resembles a 'real auction'. An *actual* screening was to take place for the 10 highest bidders. Auctions have been the centrepiece of experimental approaches since Bohm's study (see, for example, Smith, 1980). They capture the interactive behaviour that is part of the theoretical preference revelation mechanisms mentioned in section 6.1.5. As the hypothetical approach VI:1 gave a WTP bid that was not significantly different from the actual bidding mechanism VI:2, they concluded that the CV method has not been shown to be unreliable by Bohm's study.

General issues raised by Bohm's study   Bohm's study was very influential. As Mitchell and Carson point out, on the basis of it, a major advanced text-book on public sector economics (by Atkinson and Stiglitz, 1980) doubted the practical validity of the free-rider problem. This is when most of the intermediate texts, such as Musgrave and Musgrave (1989), treat the free-rider problem as all-pervasive. In addition, much of the applied literature, either directly or indirectly, was guided by its approaches. It is therefore useful to summarize some of the substantive issues arising from Bohm's work.

i.   The fairest way to interpret Bohm's findings is not to conclude that free-rider behaviour does not exist, but to recognize that, with the right set of questions, such behaviour can be minimized when evaluating public goods. Bohm was very careful to point out to the respondent what biases have to be faced. For example, the instructions for approach I stated: 'By stating a small amount, smaller than you are actually willing to pay, you stand the chance of being able to watch the program without paying so much. In other words, it could pay for you to give an under-statement of your maximum willingness to pay. But, if *all* or *many* of you behave this way, the sum won't reach Kr 500 and the program won't be shown to you'. It is likely that any reader of this would have second thoughts about whether it is sensible (or morally correct) to try to free ride.

ii.   When testing for free-rider behaviour, the size of the net benefits from such strategic behaviour needs to be noted. One is likely to see more free-rider behaviour the larger the gains to be had. In the Bohm study the cost was Kr 5 (with III) and benefit was Kr 7 per person. How much self-interest would be suppressed in order to gain Kr 2?

iii. When presenting results, one must always check for the presence of outliers and present a sensitivity analysis with and without those observations. Just one observation out of the 54 used by Bohm for approach VI:1 raised the mean value by 10 per cent and made an otherwise marginal difference statistically significant. (Note that the median value would have been Kr 10 in either case.)

iv. Lastly, one must be aware that varying the setting for questions (some of which may appear small) can imply totally different methodological approaches. Because Bohm's I, II and VI:1 did not state that the programme would not be shown unless the cost were fully covered by WTP bids, they are examples of the contingent valuation approach. When such a stipulation is made, the questions become part of the 'experimental' (simulated market) approach to the revelation of preferences. When the respondent really will be provided with the good according to the reported WTP bid (as with Bohm's VI:2), the questions correspond to an actual rather than a hypothetical market situation.

6.3.2   *WTP for preservation of the whooping crane*

If there were some ambiguity whether the Bohm TV programme was a pure public good or not, there is no doubt with the preservation of the whooping crane studied by Bowker and Stoll (1988). There is virtually no private, consumption value of the whooping crane (e.g., for hunting, eating or keeping it as a pet) which is an endangered species. The benefits come from preserving access to the birds for existing and all future generations. Non-use value dominates and contingent valuation then becomes the only way to value this public good.

A survey was conducted in 1983 of valuations for the whooping crane. Two groups were involved: on-site visitors at the Arkansas National Wildlife Refuge where whooping cranes were present; and mail-in non-users of the refuge in Texas, and four metropolitan areas (Los Angeles, Chicago, Atlanta and New York). Individuals were asked to make a dichotomous (yes–no) response to a specified WTP amount (set randomly) to contribute to a trust to support the continued existence of the whooping crane. It was declared that a policy change was being considered to cease public funds for this purpose and a replacement source was being sought. Four hundred and seventy-one responses were included in the sample used to make the estimates.

Because variations in the testing procedure made a big difference to the outcomes, it is necessary to explain in some detail how the WTP estimates were obtained. The dichotomous CV technique asks the individual to choose between a sum of money A to be offered as a contribution to a fund and the existence of the endangered species W (the whooping crane). If $W = 0$, the species is not preserved and the individual has an income M. If the species is preserved, $W = 1$, and the individual is left with $M - A$. All one knows for sure is the sum A

that was offered (that is, the WTP stipulated in the questionnaire to which the individual is to respond yes or no) and the response. On this basis one has to try to find the true WTP, E. If the individual says yes to A then we know that $E \geq A$, while a no response implies $E < A$. The probability P that the individual will say yes is therefore linked to the probability that $E \geq A$. This probability P is a function of the difference in utility U between the two situations: having the species and $M - A$, or not having the species and having M.

The two aspects that are crucial to how the dichotomous choice technique is to be carried out in practice are: (i) how to obtain the probability estimates, and (ii) how to specify the difference in the utility function. (It is only the *difference* in utility that is important because if some utility determinants are the same in two situations, then the choice between the situations cannot depend on the common determinants.) We address these two aspects in turn.

i.   The first thing to be decided in forming estimates of the probability is which probability density function to use. The two main options are the normal distribution, on which the technique Probit is based, and the logistic distribution, on which the technique Logit is based. In the Bowker and Stoll study, the two techniques gave very similar estimates. We therefore only deal with the Logit results.

Then one has to decide how to truncate the probability distribution that one is using. Distributions usually vary from zero to infinity. Since the upper value for a WTP for something as non-personal as a whooping crane is hardly likely to be infinite, much lower values must be chosen. It will be recalled that the WTP offers were generated randomly. Since estimation depends on the value of the highest offer chosen, Bowker and Stoll tried three different rules (upper limits), namely, $130, $260 and $390.

Finally, even with a given probability distribution and an upper value, one needs to decide which measure of central tendency to use to make the probability estimates. Does one use the estimates that correspond to the expected (or mean) value of the distribution, or those estimates that correspond to the median of the distribution. With a normal distribution the mean equals the median. But, as the distribution we are considering is being truncated, the two measures give different values even with this distribution. Bowker and Stoll use both the mean and median to see what difference this makes to the WTP estimates.

ii. Utility differences are expressed by Bowker and Stoll as a function of the amount of the offer A (all other prices constant), income M, and socio-economic conditioning factors S. In the whooping crane context, the S factors were represented by two dummy variables defined as follows: $D_1 = 1$ when the respondent was a member of a wildlife organization ($D_1 = 0$

otherwise); and $D_2 = 1$ if the respondent was an on-site respondent ($D_2 = 0$ if the respondent was a mail-in). The expectation was that both D_1 and D_2 would be positive (a WTP bid would be larger for these respondents). Members of wildlife organizations should have stronger feelings about preserving species, and on-site respondents would have had exposure to the whooping cranes.

The difficult issue was how to specify the relation between the three sets of determinants and the utility difference. Following work by Hanemann (1984), Bowker and Stoll (1988) tried these two specifications of the determinants of changes in U:

Hanemann 1: $a_0 + B_1A + a_1D_1 + a_2D_2$.
Hanemann 2: $a_0 + B_1log(1 - A/M) + a_1D_1 + a_2D_2$.

Hanemann 1 has a linear relation between changes in V and A, D_1, D_2, while Hanemann 2 replaces A with the log of the proportion of income left after paying for A. In addition, a third specification was added that entered all variables (except the dummies) in a log form:

Logarithmic: $a_0 + B_1log(A) + B_2logM + a_1D_1 + a_2D_2$.

Logit was applied to the three specifications to obtain estimates of the parameters a_0, a_1, a_2, B_1 and B_2. On the basis of these estimates, the WTP values shown in Table 6.3 were derived. Each of these estimates is for an individual on an annual basis.

Table 6.3 lists the WTP for the whooping crane according to: the three specifications for the utility difference; whether a respondent was on-site or a part of the mail-in group; and whether a respondent was a member of a wildlife group or not. As expected the WTP bids are higher for respondents who were on-site and members of a wildlife group. The mean WTP amounts vary between $21 and $95 (Bowker and Stoll cite the range $21–149). This large range forces Bowker and Stoll to conclude that, 'professional judgment plays a major role in making use of the dichotomous choice survey models'. There are three main reasons for this.

i.   Differences in the specification of utility differences. Hanemann 2 produced higher values than Hanemann 1, while the logarithmic form had no systematic relation to either Hanemann specification. The coefficient of determination (the R^2) was 40 per cent higher with the logarithmic than either of the Hanemann specifications. Most reliance can therefore be placed on the logarithmic estimates. Unfortunately, this does not reduce the range of values, as the logarithmic specification gave the highest as well as the lowest values.

ii. Differences in the truncation rule. The higher the upper limit for the truncation, the higher the mean WTP. Since there is no accepted method for setting the upper limit, no truncation rule is necessarily the best.
iii. Differences in the estimation approach. The mean estimator gave WTP values much higher than those based on the median estimator. Hanemann suggested that the median would be less sensitive to the truncated rule, and this was borne out in the results. But the median results turned out to be more sensitive to the specification of utility differences. With Hanemann 1 and 2, the yes–no probability was less than 0.5 which meant that they underestimated the median values. Hence, *negative* median WTP values were produced. (This, of course, makes no sense. As Bowker and Stoll point out, the whooping crane is not like a poisonous snake or certain viruses, where preservation leads to disutility for some persons. Zero should be the lower bound.)

Bowker and Stoll conclude that a WTP of $21 is the 'most credible' (corresponding to the mean WTP, with a logarithmic specification, and a $130 truncation rule). Only if the cost of preserving whooping cranes is less than $21 per person will 'professional judgement' of their contingent valuation study not be an issue.

Table 6.3   WTP for the whooping crane

Model specification	On-site	Club membership	Median WTP	Mean WTP $130	$260	$390
Hanemann 1	No	No	−13.00	21.21	22.38	22.43
Hanemann 2	No	No	−39.44	23.95	28.10	28.69
Logarithmic	No	No	5.17	21.00	27.35	31.50
Hanemann 1	No	Yes	23.99	39.13	42.00	42.12
Hanemann 2	No	Yes	22.14	45.92	55.92	57.43
Logarithmic	No	Yes	15.05	37.95	52.31	61.97
Hanemann 1	Yes	No	13.09	33.16	35.37	35.47
Hanemann 2	Yes	No	−3.82	35.68	42.65	43.67
Logarithmic	Yes	No	10.92	32.11	43.43	50.97
Hanemann 1	Yes	Yes	50.08	55.14	60.39	60.63
Hanemann 2	Yes	Yes	58.17	61.78	77.90	80.47
Logarithmic	Yes	Yes	31.82	53.84	78.14	94.96

Source: Bowker and Stoll (1988)

We close our discussion with a comparison of the Bowker and Stoll study with two other CV studies that we have covered. In Chapter 3 we first mentioned this approach in connection with estimating the WTP for water. Starting-point bias was one difficulty that was identified. In the dichotomous choice framework this bias is eliminated, as the values are chosen completely at random. On the other hand, this technique provides much less information. One yes–no answer provides one observation. While in the Singh et al. (1993) study, each respondent answered a series of WTP questions and generated four separate observations.

The finding that the choice of estimator can affect one's WTP results was anticipated by the Bohm study covered earlier in this chapter. We see in Table 6.2 that the median WTP values vary from their mean WTP counterparts. It will be recalled that we noted that the median value would have been Kr 10 in either case VI:1 or VI:2. Thus the problem of the outlier raised by Mitchell and Carson in connection with approach VI:1 would not have arisen if the median rather than the mean had been the estimator used to make conclusions about WTP.

6.3.3   *WTP versus WTA for tree densities*
We know that the optimum condition for public goods requires that the sum of marginal benefits be equal to marginal costs. This feature is precisely what the experimental methods of public good estimation try to reproduce. The respondent is first informed that the good will be supplied only if the sum of the WTP of all respondents covers the costs, and then asked for the individual's WTP bid.

Important experimental work has been carried out by Vernon Smith (see, for example, Smith, 1991). He set up a 'Smith auction' with the following three characteristics (outlined in Smith, 1980): collective excludability, unanimity and budget balance. While there is no individual excludability, the group as a whole will be excluded from consuming the good unless aggregate WTP covers the costs of its provision. Unanimity is important because everyone must willingly contribute or else no one gets to consume the good. If the aggregate WTP exceeds the costs, the offers would be proportionally scaled back so that costs are just covered (the balanced budget requirement). Clearly these three characteristics of the Smith auction combine to play the role of the planner in preference revelation theory.

Brookshire and Coursey (1987) included a hypothetical and an actual Smith auction to contrast with the contingent valuation method in their study of tree densities. The aim was to estimate the value of retaining, or adding to, the number of trees in a new public recreational area, Trautman Park in Colorado. The planned number of trees were to rise or fall by 25 and 50 (from a base level of 200 trees) and individuals were asked their evaluations of these increases and decreases.

A main concern of the study was to see whether differences in what people are willing to pay for having increases in the number of trees, and what they are willing to accept for allowing decreases in the number of trees, can be accounted for by the use of different approaches to estimate the evaluations. In particular, would these differences (asymmetries) disappear if an actual market (the Smith auction) were one of the methods used.

The CV questionnaire asked two sets of questions. One on the maximum WTP for 200 becoming 225 trees, and 200 becoming 250 trees; and one on the minimum WTA for 200 becoming 175 trees, and 200 becoming 150 trees.

The hypothetical Smith auction, called the 'Field Smith Auction Process' (SAF) by Brookshire and Coursey, has the same two sets of questions just stated and adds two other elements. Respondent are made aware that the evaluation must be made in the context of: (a) what other people are bidding, and (b) the cost of the alternate tree densities. Six hundred and sixty-seven households in the immediate Trautman area were to be contacted. It is the total WTP and WTA of all these households that is to decide the tree densities under this scheme.

The actual Smith auction, called the 'laboratory Smith auction' (SAL), sets up a fund into which contributions will be paid and from which compensation will be made. Apart from no longer being hypothetical, the SAL differs from the SAF by having five possible iterations of bids. In this way it provided a repetitive market-like environment.

Table 6.4 shows the WTP and WTA amounts that were estimated with the three valuation techniques. The anticipated result, that compensation required to accept a tree decrease far exceeds what they are willing to pay for a tree increase, is very much in evidence. The average mean WTA across the three techniques (using the final bid for SAL) is about 40 times larger than the average mean WTP for the 25 tree change, and 69 times larger for the 50 tree change. The Willig approximation outlined in Chapter 3 seems to break down for public goods. The income elasticity would have to be very large indeed to explain these differences.

Just as clear is the fact that this difference does vary with the approach used. The ratio of the mean WTA to the mean WTP for the 25 tree change is 61 to 1 for CV, 56 to 1 for SAF, and 2 to 1 for SAL (final bids). The ratios are even higher, with greater absolute differences by approach used, for the 50 tree change, that is, 89 to 1 for CV, 112 to 1 for SAF, and 7 to 1 for SAL. The difference between the WTA and WTP amounts are much reduced by the Smith actual auction approach.

The differences between initial and final bids for the SAL approach are revealing. Typically, WTP bids increase and WTA decrease as the number of trials proceed (see especially Table 2 of Brookshire and Coursey, 1987). These modifications occur due to the 'incentives, feedback, interactions and other experiences associated with the repetitive auction environment'. The marketplace appears to act as a 'strong disciplinarian' limiting the WTA–WTP differences that are estimated for public goods.

Table 6.4   WTP and WTA for tree densities (in dollars)

	Field surveys							
	CV–WTP		CV–WTA		SAF–WTP		SAF–WTA	
	25	50	25	50	25	50	25	50
Mean	14.00	19.40	855.50	1 734.40	14.40	15.40	807.20	1 735.00
Median	9.60	9.30	199.80	399.30	11.80	13.80	30.30	100.40
Standard deviation	18.40	28.20	1 893.20	3 775.80	12.40	15.30	2 308.00	4 391.10

	Laboratory experiments							
	Initial bids SAL–WTP		Final bids SAL–WTP		Initial bids SAL–WTA		Final bids SAL–WTA	
	25	50	25	50	25	50	25	50
Mean	7.31	8.33	7.31	12.92	28.63	67.27	17.68	95.52
Median	9.33	2.50	5.09	7.50	15.00	20.00	7.25	18.66
Standard deviation	6.39	10.08	6.52	14.38	26.48	132.02	23.85	272.08

Source: Brookshire and Coursey (1987)

The other conclusion drawn by Brookshire and Coursey is that the contingency valuation method is more reliable for WTP than for WTA valuation purposes. That is, the WTP values are much closer than the WTA values to the SAL amounts (which are presumably the most correct estimates). Not all CV studies should be dismissed as being unreliable.

6.3.4   State AFDC transfers

The theory of public goods can be used to predict government decisions as well as to guide policy decisions. The theory indicates that for a social optimum for public goods, relation (6.5) should hold:

$$\sum_{B=1}^{P} MU_{Y_B}^A > \frac{P}{N} \cdot MU_{Y_A}^A$$

That is, the sum of the marginal benefits should equal the marginal costs. If we now assume that governments actually do what they should do (i.e., maximize social welfare), relation (6.5) provides a theory of how governments will behave. Refer back to Diagram 6.2. Anything that will increase the marginal benefits, on the left-hand side of (6.5), will be predicted to increase public expenditures; while anything that will increase the marginal costs, on the right-hand side, will be predicted to decrease public expenditures.

The implications of the requirement given by (6.5) have been tested empirically for the allocation of AFDC among states in the United States by Orr (1976). This is a cash transfer programme to mothers in single-parent households whereby the states make their allocations and the federal government has a matching provision. In terms of the theory, A are the taxpaying group in a state, and B are AFDC recipients in the same state. The variable the theory is trying to predict is Y_B, the amount each state spends on AFDC transfers in a year.

The four main implications will now be examined in detail. The first concerns the benefits side, and the other three relate to the cost side.

i.   There is a summation sign on the left-hand side of relation (6.5). The rich get utility from every poor person who receives a dollar. This is the public good characteristic of cash transfers. Thus, as the number of poor P goes up (holding the price of transfers P/N constant), the rich get more benefits and the amount of transfers will increase. This leads to the prediction that transfers will be higher in those states that have more poor persons. That is, P will have a positive sign when regressed on AFDC transfers.

ii. Diminishing marginal utility of income is a fundamental principle of economic theory. The more one has of any good (including income), the less is the additional satisfaction. If this applies to the rich group A, one should then expect that $MU_{Y_A}^A$ will decline as Y_A increases. This term is on the right-hand, cost, side of (6.5). A reduction in costs will imply that the rich will give more. This is because the higher is the income of taxpayers, the less satisfaction they give up per dollar that is transferred from them. This implies that the higher is the income of taxpayers in any state, the higher will be AFDC transfers. Hence Y_A will have a positive sign when regressed on AFDC transfers.

iii. The second implication related to the satisfaction to the rich per dollar that they transfer. Also of interest to them is the number of dollars they are to give up. This is indicated by the 'price' variable P/N. When this goes up, taxpayers incur a higher cost. This will cause a cut-back in their willingness to transfer funds to the poor. One can predict that P/N will have a negative sign when regressed on AFDC transfers.

iv. Lastly, as AFDC is a federally matched programme, the higher is the share contributed by the state government, the higher is the marginal price (MP) to the state taxpayer. A rise in price increases the cost and will be expected to reduce transfers. There should then be a negative sign between MP and AFDC transfers.

The result of regressing AFDC transfers on Y_A, P, P/N and MP is shown in Table 6.5. (This is Orr's column (4)). Y_A was proxied by state per capita income. P was the number of AFDC recipients (lagged one year), and P/N was this number as a ratio of the civilian population (also lagged one year). MP was the marginal state share of total AFDC payments. Also included in the equation were dummy variables for race and regions of the United States. There were 255 observations related to the years 1968–72.

Table 6.5   Determinants of AFDC transfers by states (1968–1972)

Variable	Coefficient	't' statistic
Constant	663	—
Income (*Y*)	0.640	11.47
Recipients/Taxpayers (*P/N*)	–6905	3.81
Recipients (*P*)	0.250	2.34
Federal share (*MP*)	–672	9.20
Non-white households	–419	3.52
North east	148	2.32
West	–102	1.81
Old south	–690	8.22
Border states	–248	3.19
Coefficient of determination	$R^2 = 0.78$	

Source: Orr (1976)

Table 6.5 suggests that there was considerable support for the view that state income transfers in the United States could be explained by the theory of pure public goods. All four implications of the theory were confirmed. The variables were all highly significant (at above the 99 per cent level) and had the correct signs. In addition, the equation estimated had high explanatory powers. Seventy-eight per cent of the variation in the AFDC state payments could be explained by the key determinants identified by the theory (and other 'taste' variables).

6.4   Final comments
As usual, we complete the chapter with a summary and a problem set.

6.4.1   Summary
Public goods are those that are consumed equally by all. They have the characteristics of joint supply and non-excludability. For a social optimum one needs to add demands vertically. However, this is unlikely to take place in a free market. Individuals have an incentive to under-reveal their preferences in order to obtain a free ride. Public provision is indicated for such goods. This involves

the government using its general revenue sources to finance firms to produce the goods. These firms may be either privately or publicly owned.

The main theme of the chapter was how to extract preferences in order to estimate the social demand curve that differs from the usual market demand curve. This task is made especially difficult with the incentive of individuals to act strategically. While theoretical preference revelation mechanisms do exist, the emphasis has been more on the applied work in this area. Questionnaires have been derived to test and overcome the free-rider problem.

Three main interview techniques have been used in connection with public goods evaluations: the contingency valuation method, and the hypothetical and actual market-like auctions. The applications covered all three approaches. Bohm's study indicated that the free-rider problem can be overcome if the 'right' set of questions are asked. Bowker and Stoll showed that, even in situations where only one estimation approach could be employed, wide variations in valuations can be obtained. Technical features are still open to professional judgement. However, Brookshire and Coursey did argue that the choice of method was still very important in explaining why studies come up with such wide variations in valuations for environmental goods.

The theory of public goods was made fully operational by being used to explain why income transfers from the rich to the poor would take place in a government and not a private market setting. This theory was then used to uncover the determinants of AFDC transfer by the states in the United States. In the process we showed that the theory of public goods, and welfare economics generally, can be employed in a positive economics context to predict and explain actual social decision-making behaviour. With distributional issues highlighted, the opportunity was taken to explain the basis for how differences in distribution weights come about in CBA. The weights represent the interpersonal preferences of the rich in a public goods-type framework.

6.4.2 Problems

In the third application by Brookshire and Coursey, we highlighted the fact that, in many environmental studies, WTA and WTP have diverged much greater than can be explained by the Willig approximation. It will be recalled that equation (3.5) expressed the difference between the compensating and the Marshallian measure as a function of the income elasticity of demand for that good (η). In the following problems, instead of the Willig approximation, we use one based on Hanemann (1991). We see that the elasticity of substitution is also important in explaining differences in measures and not just the income elasticity. For the purpose of these problems, take the WTA–WTP difference of \$793 found by Brookshire and Coursey (for the 25 tree change using the SAF approach) as the difference to be explained.

1. Randall and Stoll reworked the Willig approximation for price changes to apply to quantity changes (which is what takes place with the provision of public goods)). They derived the following relation for the difference between the WTA and the WTP:

$$WTP - WTA = \xi \frac{M^2}{\overline{Y}} \tag{6.8}$$

where:

M = Marshallian measure;
$\overline{Y}$ = average income; and
ξ = 'price flexibility of income'.

ξ is defined as the income elasticity of price changes (the percentage change in price divided by the percentage change in income).

If $\overline{Y}$ is \$5 000 and M is \$100, how large does the price flexibility of income have to be in order to produce the difference found by Brookshire and Coursey for tree densities?

2. The concept of the price flexibility of income is not a familiar one to economists and is difficult to estimate. Hanemann (1991) derived a decomposition that is more tractable. He produced the result that:

$$\xi = \frac{\eta}{\sigma_0} \tag{6.9}$$

where:

η = income elasticity of demand (as in the Willig approximation);
σ_0 = elasticity of substitution between the public good and all other goods.

i. What combination of values for the components can produce large values for ξ?
ii. If a reasonable value for σ_0 is 0.1, how large must η be in order to explain the difference found by Brookshire and Coursey? Do η values of this magnitude ever appear in economics texts covering empirical measures of income elasticities?
iii. Thus what is the most plausible way to explain large differences between WTA and WTP values? Try to give a descriptive explanation of how this could come about. (Hint: consider someone in an apartment with no

windows and contrast this situation to a person in a private house who has trees in their back yard.)

6.5 Appendix
Here we derive the optimal conditions for private and public goods referred to in section 6.1.3.

6.5.1 The optimal condition for private goods
Assume there are two private goods X_1 and X_2 and one public good G. There are H individuals and h is any one individual, i.e., $h = 1, ..., H$. The social welfare function is individualistic and takes the form:

$$W = W(U_1, U_2, ..., U_h, ..., U_H) \tag{6.10}$$

The individual utility functions are given by:

$$U^h = U^h(X_1^h, X_2^h, G) \tag{6.11}$$

The production function can be written in implicit form as:

$$F(X_1, X_2, G) = 0 \tag{6.12}$$

The objective is to maximize social welfare subject to the production constraint. Writing this as a Lagrange multiplier problem:

$$L = (U_1, U_2, ..., U_h, ..., U_H) - \lambda[F(X_1, X_2, G)] \tag{6.13}$$

Taking the partial derivative with respect to X_1 and setting it equal to zero:

$$\frac{dL}{dX_1} = \frac{dW}{dU_h} \cdot \frac{dU^h}{dX_1} - \lambda \frac{dF}{dX_1} = 0, \ (\forall h) \tag{6.14}$$

or:

$$\frac{dW}{dU^h} \cdot \frac{dU^h}{dX_1} = \lambda \frac{dF}{dX_1} \tag{6.15}$$

Similarly, for X_2:

$$\frac{dW}{dU^h} \cdot \frac{dU^h}{dX_2} = \lambda \frac{dF}{dX_2} \qquad (6.16)$$

Dividing (6.15) by (6.16), we obtain the optimal condition for a private good:

$$\frac{dU^h / dX_1}{dU^h / dX_2} = \frac{dF / dX_1}{dF / dX_2} \qquad (6.17)$$

Equation (6.17) implies that, for a private good X_2, each individual's *MU* (relative to that for the numeraire good X_1) must equal to the *MC* (i.e., the marginal rate of transformation of X_2 for X_1).

6.5.2 *The optimal condition for public goods*
Remember that for the public good, when one person has more, everyone has more. So everybody's utility function is affected when we change G. This means:

$$\frac{dL}{dG} = \frac{dW}{dU^1} \cdot \frac{dU^1}{dG} + \cdots + \frac{dW}{dU^h} \cdot \frac{dU^h}{dG} + \cdots + \frac{dW}{dU^H} \cdot \frac{dU^H}{dG} - \lambda dF dG = 0 \quad (6.18)$$

or:

$$\frac{dW}{dU^1} \cdot \frac{dU^1}{dG} + \cdots + \frac{dW}{dU^h} \cdot \frac{dU^h}{dG} + \cdots + \frac{dW}{dU^H} \cdot \frac{dU^H}{dG} = \lambda dF dG \quad (6.19)$$

Divide the left-hand side of (6.19) by the left-hand side of (6.15), and the right-hand side of (6.19) by the right-hand side of (6.15) to obtain:

$$\frac{dU^1 / dG}{dU^1 / dX_1} + \cdots + \frac{dU^h / dG}{dU^h / dX_1} + \cdots + \frac{dU^H / dG}{dU^G / dX_1} = \frac{dF / dG}{dF / dX_1} \qquad (6.20)$$

Condition (6.20) implies that, for a public good, it is the sum of *MU*s (relative to the numeraire) that must be set equal to the *MC*.

7 Risk and uncertainty

7.1 Introduction

Uncertainty is one of the most technically difficult parts of CBA. To help simplify matters, we start off defining the key concepts. Next we give numerical or graphical illustrations, and then finally we explain how these key elements fit together to help determine decisions under uncertainty. In the process, section 7.1 introduces the ideas, and 7.2 builds on and otherwise develops the concepts. With this base we can then in section 7.3 analyse an important special case of uncertainty, whereby future benefits are more uncertain than current costs. Whenever one is comparing the future with the present, one must inevitably examine the role of the discount rate. Discussion of the determination of the discount rate will take place in Chapter II. In section 7.3 we assume that this rate is given and consider whether an adjustment to this rate should be made due to the existence of uncertainty.

The first pair of applications relate to the health-care field. It is shown how an allowance for risk makes a radical difference to the standard protocol that doctors have been following. They would routinely operate for lung cancer when patient preferences for risk avoidance suggested otherwise. Then we deal with the situation where the surgeon deciding whether to treat a patient has only a vague idea of the probability that the person has a particular disease.

The second pair of applications provide empirical support for the existence of a risk premium in the estimation of the discount rate. The first deals explicitly with different types of risk and shows that the discount rate varies with the risk type. The second uncovers a discount rate difference due to the time horizon of the decision being specified. Since the more distant time horizons are interpreted as being more uncertain by respondents, there is evidence of a risk premium simply according to the timing of benefits or costs.

7.1.1 Uncertainty and sensitivity analysis

There are two aspects of an evaluation about which the analyst may be uncertain.

i.   The first is what values to set for the value parameters, such as the distribution weights or the discount rate. For this type of uncertainty, one should use a sensitivity analysis. This involves trying higher and lower values, and seeing whether the decision is altered by (sensitive to) the different values. If the outcome is unaffected, then it does not matter that the value parameter chosen for the study is problematical. But, if the results are sensitive to the alternative values tried, then a much more detailed defence of the chosen value must be presented in the study. To help find the upper and lower values that one is to try, one can use values used in other research studies, or the judgements by those who actually will be making the decisions.

ii. The second type of uncertainty concerns the measures of the outcomes or the costs. This requires that one consider a probabilistic framework for the decisions. The theory sections of this chapter are concerned with presenting such a framework.

7.1.2 *Basic definitions and concepts*
There are a number of interdependent concepts that need to be defined (see Layard and Walters, 1978), namely, risk and uncertainty, expected value, expected utility, the certainty equivalent and the cost of risk, risk neutrality and risk aversion. Diagram 7.1 below illustrates these concepts and depicts the basic interrelationships involved. The figures in this diagram use Dorfman's (1972) example of a reservoir that is used for both irrigation and flood protection, presented as Tables 7.1 and 7.2 below (Dorfman's Tables 6 and 10).

Risk and uncertainty According to Dorfman, risk is present when the evaluation requires us to take into account the possibility of a number of alternative outcomes. These alternative outcomes will be accommodated by placing probability estimates on them. Then by some specified rule these probability-weighted outcomes are aggregated to obtain the decision result.

The classical distinction between risk and uncertainty was developed by Knight (1921). He defined risk as measurable uncertainty. This means that under risk one knows the probabilities, while under uncertainty the probabilities are completely unknown. Much of the modern literature, and the Dorfman approach just explained, must be regarded as cases of risk. What has happened is that situations of uncertainty were converted to situations of risk by introducing probabilities subjectively when they were not available objectively. Thus, if past rainfall levels are unknown when deciding whether to build a dam or not, the decision-maker can use his or her experience of other situations to help ascribe probabilities. This type of assessment is called a 'risk analysis'. The method was introduced into CBA by Pouliquen (1970) and explained fully in Brent (1990, ch. 8). In this chapter we assume that the probabilities are known and discuss how to use this information. (On techniques for dealing with uncertainty proper, see Dasgupta, 1972, ch. 5 and Reutlinger, 1970.)

Consider the probabilistic outcomes represented by Dorfman's reservoir example presented in Table 7.1 below. What generates alternative outcomes (incomes) in this case is whether a flood will occur. The decision choices involve the extent to which one spills the reservoir. If a flood does come, the outcome would be greater if one spills more (two-thirds rather than one-third);

while if there is no flood, net benefits are greater if one spills less. If one spills all, there is no flood protection left and the net benefits are the same whether there is a flood or not. The probability of the flood occurring is judged to be 0.4, which means that 1 minus 0.4 (or 0.6) is the no-flood probability.

Table 7.1   Reservoir outcomes (in dollars)

Decision	Flood	No flood	*EV* of returns
Spill one-third	$130	$400	$292
Spill two-thirds	$140	$260	$212
Spill all	$80	$80	$80
Probabilities	0.4	0.6	

Source: Dorfman (1972)

Expected value   The expected value *EV* is defined as the sum of possible outcomes weighted by their probabilities. It has the meaning of an average outcome, that is, the value one would observe as the outcome on the average if the project were to be carried out a large number of times. Consider the option to spill one-third in the reservoir example. The *EV* is: (0.4)$130 + (0.6)$400 = $292. In Diagram 7.1, *EV* appears on the horizontal income axis and is denoted by $\bar{Y}$. If the probability of the flood occurring were 1, the *EV* would be $130; and if the flood had a zero probability, the *EV* would be $400. As the flood occurrence is not known with certainty, $\bar{Y}$ is located between the $130 and $400 values. The $\bar{Y}$ of $292 is nearer to $400 because the relative probability is greater that the flood will not occur.

Using expected values is one way of deciding among uncertain outcomes. The decision rule would be to choose the option with the highest *EV*. The *EV* is $292 for the one-third spill. This is higher than either of the other two options (i.e., $212 and $80). Thus, the one-third spill option would be chosen if the objective were to maximize the *EV*.

Expected utility   An alternative way of considering outcomes is in terms of the utility values of the dollar figures. Table 7.2 shows the corresponding utility values that Dorfman assigned to each dollar outcome.

The expected utility *EU* is defined in an analogous way to the *EV*. It is the sum of possible utility outcomes weighted by their probabilities. Thus, for the one-third spill option the *EU* is: (0.4)0.30 + (0.6)1.15 = 0.81. The *EU* appears on the vertical axis of Diagram 7.1 and is denoted by *U*. Using expected utilities is an alternative way of deciding among alternatives. As the one-third spill option has an expected utility greater than the other two (0.81 is larger than 0.61 and –0.23), this would be the most preferred option when one tries to maximize the *EU*.

Table 7.2 Reservoir outcomes (in utility units)

Decision	Flood	No flood	*EV* of utility
Spill one-third	0.30	1.15	0.81
Spill two-thirds	0.37	0.90	0.68
Spill all	–0.23	–0.23	–0.23
Probabilities	0.4	0.6	

Source: Dorfman (1972)

If an outcome is to be socially optimal, the aim must be to maximize utility (or satisfaction) not to maximize income. There would be no difference in the two criteria if there were a simple, proportional relationship between income and utility. The straight-line *ABC* in Diagram 7.1 depicts such a linear relationship. But, usually one assumes that there is diminishing marginal utility of income (that is, the more income one has, the less the *additional* satisfaction). The utility curve *ADC* in Diagram 7.1 is drawn with this diminishing marginal utility of income property (it is concave from above or convex from below). All the other concepts that are to follow help to clarify the essential difference between the linear and the nonlinear cases drawn in Diagram 7.1.

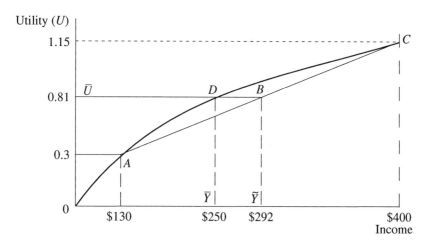

The relation between utility and income is drawn as the curve *ADC*. This shows risk aversion. Risk neutrality is depicted by the straight line *ABC*. The cost of risk is the horizontal distance *DB* between these two relations at the expected utility level 0.81, being the difference between the *EV* level of income $292 and the certainty equivalent income $250.

Diagram 7.1

The certainty equivalent and the cost of risk   The certainty equivalent income is that level of sure income that gives an individual the same level of satisfaction as a lottery with the same expected utility. One can view the reservoir project as a lottery, in the sense that there are a number of outcomes, each with its own probability. For the one-third spill option, one 'wins' the lottery if the flood does not occur and the utility value 1.15 is obtained; the lottery is lost if the flood does occur and the utility value 0.3 results. The certainty equivalent tries to convert the set of uncertain outcomes to a figure known with certainty.

The lottery is represented in Diagram 7.1 by the linear relation *ABC*. This is the expected utility relation. The line *ABC* shows all combinations of the utility outcomes 0.3 and 1.15 that correspond to each probability value of the lottery (that is, for each probability of the flood occurring). When the probability of the flood occurring is 0.4 (which means that the value 1.15 occurs with a probability 0.6 and the value 0.3 occurs with a probability 0.4) we obtain the point *B* on the line, because this was how the *EU* value of 0.81 was calculated. Point *A* would be when the probability of the flood occurring was 1, and *C* would be when the probability was 0.

The nonlinear relation *ADB* has the interpretation of showing what the utility level is for any level of *certain* income. Typically, this curve will lie above the expected utility line *ABC*. This means that individuals will prefer to have, say, $292 with certainty than have a lottery with an expected value of $292. Because curve *ADB* lies above line *ABC*, the certainty equivalent of point *B* is a value less than the expected value. To obtain the same level of satisfaction as *B* (with the *EU* of 0.81) one must move in a leftward, horizontal direction to point *D* on the certain utility curve (with an *EU* of 0.81 and an income value of $250). By construction, point *D* shows the level of sure income with the same satisfaction as the lottery *B* with the expected utility 0.81. Thus, $250 is the certainty equivalent of the expected value $292, and this is denoted by point $\tilde{Y}$ in Diagram 7.1.

The cost of risk *K* quantifies the difference between the two relations *ADC* and *ABC* (in the horizontal direction). *K* is defined as the difference between a project's expected value and its certainty equivalent income. That is, $K = \bar{Y} - \tilde{Y}$. For the one-third spill option shown in Diagram 7.1, the cost of risk is $292 – $250 = $42. This means that one is willing to give up $42 if one could obtain $250 for certain rather than face the risky project with an expected value of $292.

Risk neutrality and risk aversion   The cost of risk helps us categorize different individual perceptions and valuations of risk. A person is risk neutral when a project's expected value is equal to its certainty equivalent income. For such people, where $\tilde{Y} = \bar{Y}$, the cost of risk is zero. There would then be no difference between the *ABD* curve and the *ABC* line in Diagram 7.1 (which is to say that the utility curve would be linear). However, most people are risk averse. They value a sure income higher than an uncertain one with the same expected value. Their cost of risk would be positive. They would be unwilling to play a fair game, where the entry price is equal to the expected value.

7.2 Uncertainty and economic theory

In this section we provide a little more of the background to the analysis included in section 7.1.2. We identify the four key ingredients in the general decision-making framework when outcomes are uncertain and show how they fit together to help determine decisions. Then we explain how the utilities that appeared in the previous tables and diagrams can be measured .

7.2.1 The four ingredients

The main ingredients of uncertainty theory can be identified by looking at the table (payoff matrix) below, based on Hirshleifer and Riley (1979). It will become apparent that the Dorfman example exhibited in Tables 7. 1 and 7.2 is in fact a payoff matrix. We make the Hirshleifer and Riley table less abstract in Table 7.3 by filling in the categories according to the choice whether to treat (or not treat) a patient who may (or may not) have a particular disease (see Pauker and Kassirer, 1975).

Table 7.3   Payoffs with and without treatment

		Consequences of acts and states		
		States		Utility of acts
		Disease	No disease	
Acts	Treat	$92.50	$99.99	U_1
	No treat	$75.00	$100.0	U_1
Beliefs		0.5	0.5	

Source: Adapted by the author from Hirshleifer and Riley (1979)

There are four main ingredients:

i.   Acts   These are the actions of the decision-maker, which is what one is trying to determine. The decision to act or not corresponds with the decision whether to approve or reject the 'project'. In Table 7.3, the acts are whether to treat, or not treat, a patient for a suspected disease.

ii.   Consequences   These are the outcomes (i.e., net benefits) that are conditional on the acts and the states of the world that exist. Since the consequences
depend on the states of the world, they are uncertain. The consequences
may be measured in income (dollar) terms, as in our example, or in increased
probabilities of survival, as in Pauker and Kassirer (1975), or in years of
additional life, as in McNeil et al. (1978). The highest-valued consequence
is arbitrarily set at $100, which corresponds with the situation where one
does not treat the disease and there is no disease that needs treating. All
other consequences produce lower-valued outcomes that are measured
relative to the $100 base.

iii.   Beliefs   These are the probabilities of the states occurring. The probabilities can be objectively or subjectively determined. Table 7.3 assumes that
the probability of the patient having the disease is the same as not having
the disease. Thus, the probabilities are set at 0.5 in both states. The beliefs
do not differ by acts, and therefore are outside the control of the decision-
maker.

iv.   Utilities   These are the satisfaction levels of the consequences. The utilities
are treated as unknowns in Table 7.3 (to be determined later). As the
choices relate to acts, we need to find some way of converting utilities of
consequences into utilities of acts. As we shall see, the expected utility rule
does this for us.

We now show how these ingredients can be assembled to help decide whether
to treat the patient or not.

7.2.2   Analysis of uncertainty

To choose an act (that is, to make a decision) is to choose a row in the payoff
matrix. This is equivalent to choosing a probability distribution, seeing that each
row has consequences and associated probabilities. The list of all the consequences and the probabilities is called a *prospect*. For example, the act of
deciding to treat the disease can be written as:

$$Prospect_{Treat} = (92.5, 99.99; 0.5, 0.5)$$

and the act of deciding not to treat the disease becomes:

$$Prospect_{No\ Treat} = (75.0, 100.0; 0.5, 0.5)$$

The analysis starts by summarizing the prospects in terms of their expected
values. This is obtained by taking the probability of each state times its prob-

ability and summing over both states. The expected values of the acts are therefore:

$$EV_{Treat} = (92.5)(0.5) + (99.99)(0.5) = 96.2$$

and

$$EV_{No\ Treat} = (75.0)(0.5) + (100.0)(0.5) = 87.5$$

If the person aims to maximize expected income, the recommended decision would be to choose the treatment, as this has the higher expected value.

However, making choices on the basis of expected values ignores the distribution of the outcomes, i.e., risk. To see how risk fits into the analysis, let us assume that the prospect not to treat was different from that given above. Let us assume it was instead:

$$Prospect_{No\ Treat} = (96.2, 96.2; 0.5, 0.5)$$

Then the $EV_{NoTreat}$ would be 96.2. In this case, the person would be indifferent between treating and not treating using the EV rule. But, most people would not be indifferent. The outcome of 96.2 would occur with certainty in the no-treat situation, as it would be the same amount in either state. In general, people would prefer an outcome with certainty to a gamble which has the same expected value (i.e., they are risk averse).

Assume the decision-maker considers that s/he would be indifferent between having 95 with certainty, and having a fifty–fifty probability of either 92.5 and 99.99 (which is the treat prospect). Then the certainty equivalent of the treat prospect would be 95.0, while the EV would be 96.2. Here the person is willing to take a cut of 1.2 in the EV to have the certainty equivalent. In other words, the cost of risk would be 1.2.

To measure the cost of risk, one must know how to estimate the decision-maker's utility function U related to acts. To obtain this, one first needs the utility function V defined over prospects. The utility of the treat prospect is:

$$V[Prospect_{Treat}] = V(92.5, 99.99; 0.5, 0.5)$$

The main way of forming the utility function V is to follow the 'expected utility hypothesis'. Using this criterion, people choose those options which have the highest expected utility. This allows us to write the utility of the treat prospect to be written as:

$$V[Prospect_{Treat}] = 0.5U(92.5) + 0.5U(99.99)$$

The expected utility (EU) hypothesis is valid only if certain axioms hold. If these axioms hold, they allow the utility function U to be calculated on a cardinal scale (where one can tell not only whether the utility of one income is higher than another, one can tell also by how much). In other words, the axioms justify not only the EU rule, but also the use of cardinal scales. The main method of constructing a cardinal utility scale is called the 'standard gamble technique' (first devised by Von Neumann and Mortgenstern).

7.2.3   The standard gamble technique

We illustrate the method for calculating utility by considering the treat prospect. The utility of the worst outcome is assigned a utility value of zero, and the best outcome is assigned a value of unity. That is, we set $U(92.5) = 0$ and $U(99.9) = 1$. They are the end points in Diagram 7.2 below and thereby the utility scale is predetermined to lie between 0 and 1. What we wish to calculate is the utilities for intermediate values. This is achieved by the standard gamble technique. For example, the person is asked: if you could have 96.2 for certain, what value for the probability P, in the gamble $P.U(99.5) + (1 - P).U(92.5)$, would make you indifferent to the certain income? If the person answers $P = 0.6$, then 0.6 is the utility value for 96.2. This is the case because U was constructed as a probability, a number between 0 and 1. To see this, one must understand that the question asked involved the equality:

$$U(96.2) = P.U(99.5) + (1 - P).U(92.5)$$

So, with $U(99.5) = 1$ and $U(99.5) = 0$, this is equivalent to setting: $U(96.2) = P$.

Once one has the utility of 96.2, one can find all the other utility values by asking people to combine this value with either of the end values in a standard gamble. Say one wants to find the utility of 95.0 and one has just calculated $U(96.2) = 0.6$. One can ask the individual to set the probability that would make him or her indifferent to having 95.0 with certainty or having the lottery $P.U(92.5) + (1 - P).U(96.2)$. An answer $P = 0.17$ means that $U(95.0) = P.U(92.5) + (1 - P).U(96.2) = 0.17(0) + 0.83(0.6) = 0.5$.

Finally, let us use Diagram 7.2 to confirm our understanding of: (i) risk aversion, and (ii) the cost of risk.

i.   The EV of the treat option was shown earlier to be 96.2. A person that was risk neutral would, by definition, give this a utility value of 0.5 (seeing that this is the probability value that would make him/her indifferent to having 96.2 with certainty, and having the gamble $P.U(99.5) + (1 - P).U(92.5)$). Therefore, when the person responds by setting a utility value equal to 0.6

of having 96.2 with certainty, the person must have been risk averse. As explained earlier, a risk-averse person's utility curve is always above the diagonal line shown in the diagram (which shows the *EV*s between any two incomes).

ii. We have just seen that the *EV* for the treat option was 96.2. The equivalent certain utility to the *EV* of 96.2 is obtained by reading horizontally from the point on the diagonal *EV* line, with a height of 0.5, to the utility curve. The horizontal difference represents the cost of risk. The utility curve is 1.2 to the left of the *EV* diagonal, so 1.2 is the cost of risk.

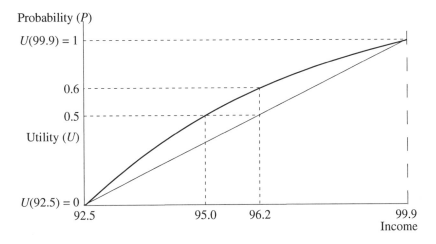

The diagram shows how the standard gamble technique works. The worst outcome, an income of 92.5 is given a value of zero; and the best outcome, an income of 99.9 is given a value of 1. All other points on the curve are found by seeking the probability *P* in a lottery which makes the individual indifferent between having a particular income and a lottery with higher and lower values. The *P* value is the utility value for that income. A *P* value of 0.6 means that the individual is indifferent between having 96.2 for sure rather than having a 0.6 chance of 99.9 and a 0.4 chance of 92.5.

Diagram 7.2

7.3 Risk and the social discount rate

This section will concentrate on the issue of whether the existence of variability justifies the use of a risk premium added to the discount rate. The issue can be set up in the following framework. It is assumed that current costs C_0 are known with certainty. Future benefits B have two characteristics. They are in the future, and therefore need to be discounted at the appropriate riskless discount rate i to make them comparable to the current costs. Future benefits are also uncertain. If ρ is a risk premium and future benefits occur only in the second period $t = 1$, the issue is the validity of the criterion:

$$NPV = -C_0 + \frac{B_1}{(1+i+\rho)} \qquad (7.1)$$

In equation (7.1), the risk premium is added to the discount rate to attempt to correct for the uncertainty characteristic of the benefits being in the future.

Our analysis proceeds in three stages. First, we will explain the correct way to allow for risk that relies on the certainty equivalent level of benefits. To do this one needs to estimate the cost of risk. Then, we examine the Arrow–Lind (1970) theorem which argues that this cost of risk can be dispensed with when making social decisions. In the final stage we summarize the issues.

7.3.1   The present certainty equivalent value

The correct method to allow for risk can be obtained by adapting the definition presented in section 7.1.2. The cost of risk K is the difference between the expected value of benefits $\bar{B}$ and the certainty equivalent level of benefits $\tilde{B}$. On rearranging terms we obtain: $\tilde{B} = \bar{B} - K$, which means that the certainty equivalent is the difference between the expected value for benefits minus the cost of risk. Thus, if one can obtain an estimate of K and subtract this from B, then one can obtain the certainty equivalent level of benefits. The criterion would then be the present certainty equivalent value (*PCEV*):

$$PCEV = -C_0 + \frac{\bar{B} - K}{(1+i)} \qquad (7.2)$$

We know how to obtain $\bar{B}$ (by weighting contingent benefits by their relevant probabilities and summing). What we also need is an estimate of K (which we have just shown how to derive in section 7.2.2). In this case, no risk adjustment to i is necessary.

On the other hand, instead of calculating K, one can obtain a numerical equivalent to equation (7.2) by including a risk adjustment ρ. That is, use equation (7.1) and treat B_1 as expected benefits $\tilde{B}$. Then one can obtain the same value by raising ρ on the denominator of (7.1) as one could obtain by subtracting K from the numerator of (7.2). For example, if $\bar{B} = 1.2$, $C_0 = 1$, $K = 0.1$ and $i = 0.1$, the *PCEV* would equal zero. Equation (7.1) would also produce zero with $B_1 = 1.2$, $C_0 = 1$, and $i = 0.1$ provided that $\rho = 0.1$.

7.3.2   The Arrow–Lind theorem

We have just seen that we can calculate the *PCEV* by either using a value K or an equivalent ρ. Hence if one can argue that K should be zero for public projects, then one is effectively implying that there should be no risk adjustment to the discount rate. This is exactly what the Arrow–Lind theorem states.

There are two main assumptions for the Arrow–Lind theorem to hold (see Layard and Walters, 1978):

i. The returns from the public project must be distributed independently of national income. The public project should not have any correlation with projects in the private sector. Note that: if (a) there were a positive correlation, then a positive value for ρ would be required; while if (b) there were a negative correlation, then a *negative* value for ρ would be indicated.

ii. The returns must be spread out over a large number of individuals. The larger the population affected, the more 'risk-pooling' takes place and the smaller would be the cost of risk. At the limit (if the public project affects the whole nation) K becomes zero, irrespective of the sign of the correlation.

The validity of the theorem depends on the two assumptions. The first assumption is particularly hard to justify. Even if the production function is such that the project itself gives a return unrelated to income in its absence, the fact that the government taxes income in the absence of the project ensures some correlation. For, in order to finance the public project, taxes will have to be adjusted. (The Foldes–Rees (1977) theorem says exactly this.)

The second assumption implies that the group variance will fall as the number increases. But when externalities and public goods exist (the non-rival characteristic is present) as they do with most public investments, the risk *per person* is not reduced when the number of individuals involved is increased. (This argument is due to James, 1975.)

From the point of view of this text, the key criticism of the theorem involves its neglect of distributional considerations. Projects should favour groups that would be poor in the absence of the project. A negative correlation would then exist, in violation of the first assumption. So, when distribution is important, a negative risk premium should be used to lower the discount rate.

7.3.3 Adjusting the discount rate for risk

The first question to ask is whether *any* adjustment needs to be made to the social discount rate because of risk. The answer is clear within an individualistic framework. For, if private individuals adjust for risk due to risk aversion, social decisions based on individual preferences must also adjust for risk. The conclusion would be otherwise if, when aggregating, individual risks cancel out (strictly, disappear in the limit). But the two conditions necessary for this result (Arrow–Lind theorem) are unlikely to exist. The expected value of benefits needs to be reduced by the cost of risk, which implies the use of a positive risk premium.

The next question is whether the public sector should make the same cost of risk adjustment as the private sector. The answer is that, in general, the public sector should not make the same risk adjustment. We saw that what was important in the formulation of risk was the covariance between a particular project and the state of the economy in the absence of the project. One should expect (for all the reasons explained in previous chapters) that the public sector would undertake different projects from the private sector. Hence the covariance would be different, and so would the risk adjustment.

Finally, what do the previous subsections say about the common practice of adding a risk premium to the discount rate in an *ad hoc* fashion. Firstly, especially when the public sector has distributional objectives, there may be a negative covariance between public projects and the economy in the absence of such projects. Here it is appropriate to *reduce* the discount rate rather than raise it. Secondly, there are precise ways of determining just how large the adjustment to the discount rate should be (see Zerbe and Dively, 1994, ch. 16). Not just *any* adjustment is appropriate. Thirdly, precise adjustments can be made only within the context of a two-period model. The common practice adds a risk premium to the discount rate for each and every period. This can be correct only if uncertainty increases over time. In general, this may not be a correct assumption.

7.4 Applications

The applications relate to the basic principles outlined in the first two sections and the special cause of uncertainty covered in section 7.3. All the applications come from the United States. We start with two health-care studies that look at benefits and costs in non-monetary terms. As long as benefits and costs are in comparable units, CBA can still be used. The first case study, by McNeil et al. (1978), illustrates how the standard gamble technique was applied. It highlights how the desirability to operate for lung cancer would be different if it recognized the risk preferences of patients. The application by Pauker and Kassirer (1975) assumes risk neutrality and explains a method for making social decisions when probabilities are not known with any great precision.

The final two case studies present estimates of individual discount rates adjusted for risk in social settings, that is, in the context of future environmental risks that threaten life safety. Horowitz and Carson (1990) provide evidence that different types of risk involved different values for the discount rate. Cropper et al.'s (1992) work supports this finding that individuals do add a risk premium to the discount rate. Future benefits are discounted not only because they occur in a different time period, but also because they are uncertain.

7.4.1 Lung cancer treatments

Lung cancer was chosen because the alternative treatments (operation and radiation) differ primarily in survival rates, and not in quality of life dimensions.

One could compare treatments only in terms of this one dimension, life now versus life later. That is, with surgery, one's life expectancy is higher than with radiation treatment, provided that one survives the operation (which is not certain). The choice was therefore between one treatment (operation) with an increased life expectancy and a risk of early death, and the other (radiation) with a lower life expectancy, but little risk of early death.

Most patients in 1978 were operated on, rather than given radiation, because physicians 'believed' this was better. The choice was made because the 5-year-life survival rate was higher with surgery. McNeil et al.'s study was geared to examining whether patients were, or were not, risk averse. If they were, then it would not be appropriate to make decisions only on the basis of expected values. The patients' risk preferences would then have to be considered, in order to use the expected utility criterion.

The sample used in the study was very small, 14 patients. The study should therefore be regarded as a prototype, and not one indicating general conclusions. The data collected was *after* treatment had taken place. Six were operated on, and 8 had radiation treatment. It was thought to be unfair to influence treatment choices until greater experience had been acquired with their methodology.

The first part of their analysis involved measuring the utility function, to see whether it lay above or below the expected value line. They used the standard gamble technique (strictly, the time trade-off version). All gambles were set with a 50:50 probability because this is best understood by most people (equivalent to tossing a coin). The outcomes considered were in survival years (rather than in income). For the younger patients in their sample, the maximum number of years of good health that they could experience was 25 years. Thus, 25 years was the upper bound for utility, which made $U(25) = 1$. For those who die immediately, $U(0) = 0$.

Three questions were asked, and the answers are plotted in Diagram 7.3 below.

i.   First, the patients were asked to specify the period of certain survival that would be equivalent to a 50:50 chance of either immediate death or survival for 25 years. The answer was 5 years, and this is plotted as point *A* in Diagram 7.3. This means $U(5) = 0.5$, because $0.5U(25) + 0.5U(0) = 0.5$.

ii.   Then, the patients were asked to specify the period of certain survival that would be equivalent to a 50:50 chance of either immediate death or survival for 5 years. The answer was 1 year, and this is plotted as point *B* in Diagram 7.3. From this, $U(1) = 0.25$, because $0.5U(5) + 0.5U(0) = 0.25$, and $U(5)$ was determined in (i).

iii. Finally, the patients were asked to specify the period of certain survival that would be equivalent to a 50:50 chance of either surviving 25 years or survival for 5 years. The answer was 14 years, and this is plotted as point

C in Diagram 7.3. We can deduce, $U(14) = 0.75$, because $0.5U(25) + 0.5U(5) = 0.75$.

All other points on the utility curve were obtained by interpolation (i.e., assuming straight lines can be drawn between consecutive points). As can be seen, the utility curve 0*BACD* lies above the expected value line 0*D*. Thus the patients were risk averse.

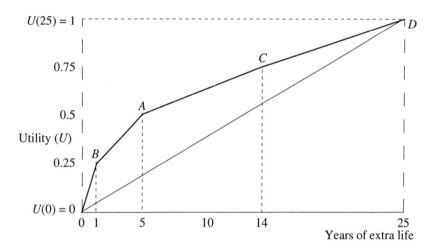

The diagram shows how the standard gamble technique came up with estimates of the utility of years of life for patients with possible lung cancer. A *P* value of 0.5 was used throughout. Point *A* records that a person would be indifferent between having 5 years of extra life for sure, rather than having a 0.5 chance of living 25 years and a 0.5 chance of dying now (living 0 years). Then, point *B* was the number of years where the person was indifferent between having 1 year for certain and a 0.5 chance of 5 years and 0.5 chance of 0 years; and point *C* was the number of years where the individual is indifferent between having 14 years for sure and a 0.5 chance of 5 years and a 0.5 chance of 25 years. Points 0*BACD* were connected by drawing straight lines. 0*BACD* lay above the diagonal expected utility line, signifying risk aversion.

Diagram 7.3

Given that patients were risk averse, the second part of their analysis involved forming the expected utilities for each treatment. This is obtained by multiplying the utilities just derived by their probabilities (the fraction of those patients with lung cancer dying in each year treated either by operation or radiation) and summing over all years. The results are presented in Table 7.4 below (which is Table 2 of McNeil et al.). They show, for different age groups, the decision outcomes that would be recommended using the existing 5 year survival rate as a guide, and those recommended by the expected utility criterion.

Table 7.4   Influence of the decision criterion on lung treatments

Criterion	% who should receive radiation with operative mortality rates of:			
	5%	10%	15%	20%
At age 60:				
5-year survival	0	0	100	100
Expected utility	64	71	100	100
At age 70:				
5-year survival	0	0	100	100
Expected utility	71	100	100	100

Source: McNeil et al. (1978)

The table shows that radiation treatment should be given in most cases. For example, at a 10 per cent operative mortality rate, 71 per cent of 60 year olds, and all 70 year olds, should receive radiation. At higher mortality rates, everyone over 60 years would find radiation preferable.

To conclude, lung treatment decisions should be based on the preferences of patients rather than the preferences of physicians, which is based on the 5-year survival rate. As McNeil et al. state (p. 1397): 'Doctors are generally more risk seeking than patients, perhaps because of age and perhaps because the consequences of the decisions may be felt less immediately by them than the patients'. They add: 'the patients' own attitudes should prevail because, after all, it is the patient who suffers the risks and achieves the gains'.

7.4.2   Diagnostic decisions

Many times doctors have to decide whether to give a treatment (administer a drug or undertake an operation) without being sure whether the patient has the particular disease one is trying to treat. Unfortunately, often doctors do not have a precise measure of how probable it is that the patient has the disease. In these circumstances, what is a physician to do? Pauker and Kassirer (1975) suggest a method that involves finding the threshold probability in an expected utility calculation.

Consider again the treatment (treat/no treat) decision represented by the payoff matrix given in Table 7.3. Construct the expected values as before, but this time assume that the probabilities are unknown. Let P be the probability of one state, which makes $1 - P$ the probability of the other state. There are two possible outcomes if one decides to treat a person who is suspected to have a particular disease. The person either has or does not have the disease (denoted by the subscript *Dis* or *No Dis*). The states of the world are the utility levels for each possibility, i.e., $U_{Treat/Dis}$ and $U_{Treat/No\,Dis}$. The expected value of the option to treat a disease, EV_{Treat}, is therefore now expressed as:

$$EV_{Treat} = PU_{Treat/Dis} + (1 - P)\,U_{Treat/No\,Dis} \qquad (7.3)$$

There are the same two possibilities if one does not treat a person, namely, the person either has or has not got the disease. If $U_{No\,Treat/Dis}$ is the utility in the disease state, and $U_{No\,Treat/No\,Dis}$ is the utility in the no-disease state, the expected value of the option not to treat a person, denoted by $EV_{No\,Treat}$, is:

$$EV_{No\,Treat} = PU_{No\,Treat/Dis} + (1 - P)\,U_{No\,Treat/No\,Dis} \qquad (7.4)$$

The threshold probability $P*$ is the value for P for which the expected utility if one treats the disease is equal to the expected utility if one does not treat the disease. That is, $EV_{Treat} = EV_{No\,Treat}$, or:

$$P * U_{Treat/Dis} + (1 - P*)\,U_{Treat/No\,Dis} = P * U_{No\,Treat/Dis}$$
$$+ (1 - P*)\,U_{No\,Treat/No\,Dis} \qquad (7.5)$$

(Note that Pauker and Kassirer wrongly call this equating expected values rather than equating expected utilities.)

Solving for $P*$ in equation (7.5), one obtains:

$$P* = \frac{U_{No\,Treat\,/\,No\,Dis} - U_{Treat\,/\,No\,Dis}}{U_{Treat\,/\,Dis} - U_{No\,Treat\,/\,Dis} + U_{No\,Treat\,/\,No\,Dis} - U_{Treat\,/\,No\,Dis}} \qquad (7.6)$$

Although one may not know P precisely, the issue is whether the range of likely values contains $P*$. To see how this works, let us look at Pauker and Kassirer's calculations for whether to treat someone for a suspected case of appendicitis. The utilities were measured by the probabilities of surviving (with or without treatment, and with or without having appendicitis). These utilities were:

$U_{Treat\,/Dis}$	0.999
$U_{No\,treat/Dis}$	0 990
$U_{No\,Treat/No\,Dis}$	1.000
$U_{Treat/No\,Dis}$	0.999

Substituting these values in the ratio for $P*$ produces:

$$P_* = \frac{0.001}{0.009 + 0.001} = 0.1 \qquad (7.7)$$

The doctor, on the basis of a physical examination, thinks that there is something like a 0.3 chance that the boy has appendicitis. Since this value is much larger than the P_* value of 0.1, the doctor can 'safely' decide to operate immediately. The doctor does not need to have any greater confidence level than 0.3 because (roughly speaking) the uncertainty over diagnosing the disease is small relative to the uncertainty of deciding not to operate.

Pauker and Kassirer's method is an example of an approach that has been utilized extensively outside the health-care field. UNIDO (1972) recommended the use of what they call the 'switching value' for finding unknown parameters. This is the value for the parameter that would make the net present value zero. In this case one would be indifferent between accepting or rejecting the decision. In this way, the switching value is the critical value that determines the outcome of the decision. If the best-guess value for the unknown parameter is less than the critical value, then one need not be concerned about obtaining more precise estimates. Pauker and Kassirer's P_* is exactly such a switching value, seeing that if the *EVs* are equal from treating or not treating, the NPV from treating the patient must be zero.

7.4.3   *Discount rates for types of mortality risk*

Horowitz and Carson (1990) have developed a version of the switching value technique just described to obtain values for the discount rate for situations with different types of risk. Specifically, the risk they are dealing with is the probability of dying conditional on various life-saving activities. The net benefits are therefore the expected lives that will be saved in different time periods. The risk types relate to life-saving activities, except that 'people view a particular risk class as a bundle of characteristics, such as how voluntary or how dreaded it is. In this light, the public's discount rate for a risk might be seen as one more of its characteristics'. This means that differences in estimated discount rates are interpreted as evidence that different risk classes are being considered. What is required is to estimate individual discount rates to see if the average (or median) values are different for varying life-saving activities. The three life-saving contexts were: air-travel safety improvements, worker safety improvements, and traffic safety improvements.

The essentials of their method can be explained in terms of a simple two-period model. The choice is whether to save 20 lives today or 24 lives next year. A life in any year is given an equal value. The only difference is the number of lives saved and when this life saving occurs. Let us view the problem from the point of view of the alternative of saving 20 lives next year. The cost *C* is the

20 lives that one does not save today. The benefit B is the 24 lives saved next year. Since B occurs next period, it must be discounted by the rate i. The NPV calculation is therefore:

$$NPV = -C + \frac{B}{1+i} = -20 + \frac{24}{1+i}$$

Define $i*$ as the value of the discount rate that makes the NPV equal to zero, i.e., $i*$ is the switching value. Horowitz and Carson call this value for i the 'equilibriating discount rate'. The condition $NPV = 0$ implies $B/(1 + i) = C$, i.e., $24/(1 + i*) = 20$. From which we deduce: $i* = 24/20 - 1 = 0.2$. The general solution for this problem is simply $i* = L_2/L_1 - 1$, where L_2 is the number of lives saved in the second period and L_1 is the number of lives saves in the current period.

If the number of lives saved in the second period were different from 24, then the equilibriating discount rate would be different. For example, if the number of lives saved next period were 22, $i* = 22/20 - 1 = 0.1$; and if L_2 were 26, $i*$ = 26/20 - 1 = 0.3. The important point to realize is that, for a given number of lives saved in the current period (fixed at 20 in our example), there is a unique value for $i*$. Horowitz and Carson exploit this uniqueness property by specifying different second-period values for lives saved in a questionnaire to obtain a distribution of values for $i*$.

The only difference between the simple method just explained and that used by Horowitz and Carson concerns the length of time that periods 1 and 2 are specified to last. We used one-year periods, this year and next. What we have called the current period is their 'present' policy period which saves 20 lives for the next 15 years. Their 'future' policy option saves L_2 lives over the 10-year period that starts in 5 years' time and ends in year 15. Chapter 1 explained how to discount over multi-year periods and so their method is a straightforward extension of our method.

The estimation technique used by Horowitz and Carson is similar to the contingent valuation method used by Whittington et al. (1990) to derive the demand for water (explained in Chapter 3). There the question was, will you pay $x for water, yes or no? Those that said 'yes' valued water at least $x, and those who said 'no' valued the water less than $x. Values for $x were randomly assigned. This time the question was, would you choose the L_2 number of future lives saved rather than the current 20 lives? This question was equivalent to asking would you accept the particular $i*$ implied by the particular L_2 lives specified. If the respondent accepted the future orientated option, s/he would be placing a value on i less than $i*$. While if the respondent rejected the future-orientated option, in favour of saving 20 lives today, s/he would be placing a value on i at least $i*$. The range of values for L_2 that were randomly assigned were between 29 and 54, which made the range of i^* (using their method) fall between −1 per cent and 20 per cent.

Horowitz and Carson (1988) gives the details of the three risk classes. The safety improvements were: in the design of airplanes or airports for the air travel scenario; in the ventilation system for the worker scenario; and in the layout of intersections for the traffic scenario. Other differences in the scenarios were in terms of the specified number of lives at stake today and in the future, when the future improvement would begin, and the length of planning period. An obvious further difference seems to be in the degree of generality of the experiences. Most people can relate to road traffic accidents. Hazards at work and in the air are likely to have been experienced by a smaller percentage of the population.

The estimated mean discount rates for the three risk classes in a sample of students are presented in Table 7.5. The mean rate for air travel safety was 4.54 per cent. It was 4.66 per cent for worker safety, and 12.8 per cent for traffic safety. All three estimated discount rates were significantly different from zero (at above the 95 per cent level).

Table 7.5   Discount rates for various safety improvements

Type of risk	Mean discount rate	Difference from market rate
Air travel safety	4.54	−0.62
Improvements	(2.91)	(0.40)
Worker safety	4.66	−0.50
Improvements	(2.54)	(0.26)
Traffic safety	12.8	7.64
Improvements	(5.09)	(3.04)

To help quantify the extent of any risk premium, the estimated mean discount rates for the three types of risk were compared with a measure of the riskless market rate of interest (for June 1987). The market rate of interest used was 5.16 per cent, being the difference between the nominal rate of return on 25-year treasury bonds (9.01 per cent) and the annual rate of inflation in the consumer price index (3.85 per cent). Table 7.5 shows that for traffic safety improvements there was a significantly different discount rate from the riskless market rate, indicating a risk premium of 7.64 percentage points (i.e., 12.8 minus 5.16). There were no significant premiums for the other risk types. There was therefore evidence that certain risk types may require a different social discount rate.

7.4.4   Discount rates for alternative time horizon lengths

Cropper et al. (1992) used a similar implicit procedure to Horowitz and Carson to reveal estimates of discount rates. This time the emphasis was not on different risk classes, but on different time horizons in which the life saving was to take place. The survey that they used had, in addition, a section allowing respondents to explain why they made their choices. This means that we can obtain some understanding of why any particular observed time pattern to discount rates occurs.

We can use again the basic method explained in section 7.4.2 to clarify the estimation process. It will be recalled that respondents were being asked to compare saving 20 lives today rather than 24 lives in the future. Rather than specify that 24 lives are being saved next year, Cropper et al. varied the time horizon for the future life saving. For example, say 24 lives are to be saved in 2 years' time. Then $i*$ is obtained by finding that value of i for which $24/(1 + i)^2$ = 20. The solution for $i*$ is $\sqrt{24/20 - 1}$, i.e., 0.1. If the 24 lives are to be saved in 3 years' time, the solution for $i*$ is 0.6 (i.e., $\sqrt[3]{24/20 - 1}$). (The general solution is $\sqrt[n]{24/20 - 1}$, where n is the number of years in the future when the life saving is to occur. Of course, 24/20 is L_n/L_1.) The time horizons specified were 5, 10, 25, 50 and 100 years. These time horizons were randomly assigned to a sample of 3 200 households.

Table 7.6 (Cropper et al.'s Table 1) presents the results for the discount rate for each of the five horizons specified. The median values for the discount rates in the raw data are listed first. Then the table gives the mean rates obtained by assuming that a normal distribution was used to obtain the estimates (with 't' values in brackets).

Table 7.6   Discount rates by time horizon

Time horizon	Median rate	Mean rate
5 years	0.168	0.274 (16.6)
10 years	0.112	0.179 (19.2)
25 years	0.074	0.086 (19.0)
50 years	0.048	0.068 (11.4)
100 years	0.038	0 034 (21.5)

Source: Cropper et al. (1992)

Table 7.6 shows (using either the median or the mean value) a clear trend for the discount rate to fall as the time horizon increases. However, the rate of decline is not constant, with the reduction coming most in the first 10 years, and flattening off thereafter. Cropper et al. interpret this as evidence that the discount rate is not a constant over time. But the reason why it is non-constant is instructive.

Cropper reports: 'About one-third of the consistently present-oriented respondents believe that society will figure out another way to save those whose lives would be lost in the future because of their choice. In other words, these respondents do not accept the trade-off with which we attempt to confront them.' Effectively, this means that a risk adjustment is being applied to the discount rate. This is because any modification that a respondent makes to the future number of lives being specified has a direct implication for the discount rate magnitude that is being revealed.

To see this point in its simplest form, assume that when a respondent is informed that 24 lives will *not* be saved next year (because resources will be devoted to saving 20 lives now), s/he believes that only 22 lives will in fact be lost (that is, a downward revision of 2 lives for risk is made). In terms of the basic method explained in the previous subsection, the researcher will be recording the response to $22/10 - 1$ (an i^* of 0.1) and not $24/10 - 1$ (an i^* of 0.2). Say the person's discount rate is exactly equal to the rate specified in the survey. The result will come out as a measured discount rate estimate of 0.1 and not 0.2 due to the downward adjustment for risk. In other words, the discount rate measured underestimates the rate specified. This explanation is consistent with the falling discount rate estimates in Table 7.6 as the time horizon increases (and future benefits become more uncertain).

A useful way of thinking about this process of adjusting for risk is in terms of a discount rate that was constant over time. Assume that over a 5-year horizon an individual does not adjust future benefits for risk (i.e., risk is not thought an issue). Then Cropper et al.'s estimate of 0.168 would be the riskless rate. It would also be the constant rate. Any deviations from this rate would be because of risk. For the 5-year horizon, the risk adjustment (premium) is zero. Line 1 of Table 7.7 records this information.

Table 7.7   Risk premium assuming a constant discount rate

Time horizon	Measured rate	Constant rate	Risk premium
5 years	0.168	0.168	0.000
10 years	0.112	0.168	0.056
25 years	0.074	0.168	0.094
50 years	0.048	0.168	0.120
100 years	0.038	0.168	0.130

Source: Constructed by the author from Cropper et al. (1992)

Risk begins to be a factor at the 10-year horizon point. The risk adjustment by an individual causes the measured rate to be below the constant rate. With 0.168 as the constant rate, and 0.122 as the measured rate, the risk adjustment is 0.056. The rest of the table is filled in assuming that risk increases with time, causing the measured rates to fall over time. Consequently, the risk premium (the difference between the constant and the declining measured rate) increases over time.

The suggestion is therefore that it is the existence of risk that causes the non-constancy in the measured rates. In sum, we return to the framework suggested at the beginning of section 7.3. Future benefits are distinct from current benefits not only because future benefits occur at a different point in time, but also because they are more uncertain than current benefits.

7.5   Final comments
The summary and problems sections now follow.

7.5.1   Summary
This chapter continues the list of reasons why private markets fail and why government intervention may be necessary. When there are a number of possible outcomes for a project (risk is present) a complete set of state contingent markets would ensure that prices would signal the best alternative. That is, with these prices, the certainty equivalent to the set of uncertain outcomes could be determined. In the absence of these state contingent markets, and consequently without the knowledge of the appropriate prices, the government must try to approximate the correct adjustment by measuring the cost of risk directly.

When there is diminishing marginal utility of income, risk aversion is present. The individual would turn down a fair game with a price equal to its expected value. The difference between the price that the individual would pay and the expected value is the cost of risk. Risk neutrality is the special case where the cost of risk is zero and decisions would be made on the basis of expected values. Allowing for the cost of risk on top of the expected value converts the decision-making process under uncertainty to one of maximizing expected utility. To implement the expected utility rule, the utility function must be measured. We explained how the standard gamble technique can be used for this purpose. The first application showed, using this technique, that the desirability of lung operations could be very different if one followed the expected utility rule rather than (as was standard practice) relying on expected values.

Given that usually there will be a lot of uncertainty over project estimates of subjective values or objective data, all CBA studies should contain a sensitivity analysis. This involves inserting alternative plausible values and testing whether the final outcome is affected by (i.e., sensitive to) the alternative estimates. A special type of sensitivity analysis involves finding the parameter estimate that renders the outcome indeterminate (the NPV would be zero). If the best estimate of a parameter is below this threshold level (the switching value) then the estimate can be accepted. When the best estimate exceeds the threshold value, the particular estimate is crucial to the determination of the decision. More research is then required to provide an estimate that can stand up to detailed scrutiny when the CBA outcome will be questioned by others. The second case study applied the switching value technique to the problem of how to find the probabilities that are needed when making diagnostic decisions under uncertainty.

A key issue for applied work is whether to adjust the discount rate for risk. Private investment decisions often make such an allowance and the issue was whether public investment decisions need to make the same, or a similar, adjustment. This depends on the validity of the two key assumptions of the Arrow–Lind theorem. With these assumptions, the government can avoid making any cost of risk adjustment. However, these assumptions are unlikely to hold. A cost of risk adjustment to expected benefits may be necessary for public investment decisions, which is equivalent to adjusting the discount rate.

While an adjustment to the discount rate may sometimes be in order, the necessary adjustment is not always to raise the discount rate, even for private decisions. Only if uncertainty increases over time is a positive risk premium required. Then when we recognize that public sector investments would most probably be in different industries from private investments, further grounds exist for doubting the wisdom of a positive risk premium. When there is a negative covariance between the public project and the course of the economy in the absence of the project, the discount rate should be lowered.

The final two applications focused on individual preferences concerning risk and the discount rate. They both found evidence that a risk adjustment is made to the discount rate. First, different discount rates were observed for different types of mortality risk. Then it was found that discount rates may not be constant over time because of the existence of risk.

7.5.2 Problems

In much of the theoretical literature on uncertainty, the cost of risk is not estimated directly, but is derived from a utility of income curve that is assumed to take a particular form. The problems specify two often-used functions for the utility of income and require that one derive the corresponding costs of risk. Use the cost of risk K as given by the formula (which is derived in the appendix):

$$K = -1/2 \frac{U''}{U'} Var\, Y \tag{7.8}$$

where U' is the marginal utility of income (the derivative of U), U'' is the second derivative, and *Var* is the variance of income Y.

1. Obtain the cost of risk when the utility of income U is given by: $U = A - e^{-Y}$, where Y is income as before and A is a constant. Draw the marginal utility of income curve U''. What property (shape) does it have?
2. Obtain the cost of risk when the utility of income is given by: $U = log\ Y$. Draw the marginal utility of income curve. What property does it have?
3. Which specification for U, in 1 or 2, is called 'absolute risk aversion' and which is called 'relative risk aversion'? Why?

7.6   Appendix

The certainty equivalent income, Y, is defined as that level of sure income that gives an individual the same level of satisfaction as the expected utility of income (the probability weighted sum of utility outcomes):

$$U(\tilde{Y}) = E[U(Y)] = \sum_i P_i U_i(Y) \tag{7.9}$$

The left-hand side of (7.9) can be approximated by a first-order Taylor series expansion expanded about the mean income value Y:

$$U(\tilde{Y}) = U(\bar{Y}) + U'(\bar{Y})(\tilde{Y} - \bar{Y}) \tag{7.10}$$

While the right-hand side of (7.9) can be approximated by a second-order Taylor series expansion about the mean income value:

$$\sum_i P_i\ U_i(Y) = \sum_i P_i[U(\bar{Y}) + U'(\bar{Y})(Y_i - \bar{Y}) + 1/2U''\ (Y_i - \bar{Y})^2] \tag{7.11}$$
$$= \sum_i U(\bar{Y})\ P_i + \sum_i U'(\bar{Y})\ P_i\ (Y_i - \bar{Y}) + \sum_i 1/2U''P_i(Y_i - \bar{Y})^2]$$

Because the probabilities sum to one, the sum of deviations of a variable from its mean is zero, and using the definition of the variance of Y, the above simplifies to:

$$\sum_i P_i U_i(Y) = U'(\bar{Y}) + 1/2U''\ Var\ Y \tag{7.12}$$

Substitute for (7.10) and (7.12) in (7.9) to get:

$$U'(\bar{Y})\ (\tilde{Y} - \bar{Y}) = 1/2\ U''\ Var\ Y \tag{7.13}$$

or,

$$\tilde{Y} - \bar{Y} = 1/2 \frac{U''}{U'(\bar{Y})} Var\, Y \qquad (7.14)$$

The cost of risk K has been defined as the difference between a project's expected value, given by its mean, and its certainty equivalence:

$$K = \bar{Y} - \tilde{Y} \qquad (7.15)$$

So the cost of risk is the negative of (7.14), which is equation (7.8) in the text.

8   Measurement of intangibles

8.1   Introduction

The measurement of intangibles (such as noise from airports and pain from medical treatments) is essentially a shadow pricing issue. Market prices for intangibles often are absent and this forces more indirect valuation methods to be used. The reason why markets do not exist is often a product of the pure public good properties (joint-supply and price non-excludability) of intangible items. But, a useful distinction is to consider the jointness involving the provision of *different products* (transport and noise) to the *same consumer* rather than the same product simultaneously to different consumers (as with the public good applications we discussed in Chapter 5). This explains why much of the analytics of this chapter concerns how best to deal with this composite commodity valuation problem. As we shall see, there are two main approaches. One, such as the travel cost method, tries to tackle the evaluation in an aggregate form and combine elements in one evaluation step. The second, as with the hedonic pricing method, tries to disaggregate effects, so that individual components can be valued separately.

In the first section we clarify many of the conceptual issues involved with evaluating intangibles. The principles behind the travel cost method are of general interest, and provide a useful background to the whole area. So an account is given here of the pioneering study by Clawson (1966) of the benefits of outdoor recreation. The second section covers the ultimate intangible problem, that is, how to value a human life. Given that this problem will always be a controversial one, many differing approaches are outlined.

The applications concentrate on the disaggregated techniques for valuing intangibles. Administering criminal sentences involves the use of resources as inputs which have a market price. Input prices substitute for the absence of output prices. A second approach is to use hedonic prices that attempt to identify the individual characteristics of a commodity. Intangible elements are combined with others and together they contribute to the value of a composite commodity that is priced. The problem then is one of allocating this known price to the contributing elements. Because there are these alternative evaluation techniques, the third case study compares and contrasts the hedonic approach with the contingent valuation method (outlined in earlier chapters) to measure the benefits of reductions to air pollution. A completely different approach to shadow pricing intangibles is to use the revealed preferences of social decision-makers. The final case study explains how this approach has been applied to uncover the implicit value of life behind Environmental Protection Agency (EPA) decisions.

8.1.1 Are we attempting the impossible?

People sometimes label intangible items 'unquantifiables'. By definition, these cannot be valued. An intangible effect, on the other hand, is merely one that cannot be touched. This does not imply that they cannot be valued. A painting by a Master, even though it constitutes an intangible item called 'Art', can be given a precise monetary evaluation (at an auction). People willingly pay for visits to museums to see historical artifacts and zoos to observe preserved endangered species. Measuring intangibles is not a problem that differs in kind from measuring tangible effects. The issue is one of degree. Evaluating intangibles is certainly more difficult, especially when there are no direct markets available, but not impossible.

The real danger in labelling an item 'priceless' is that in a project evaluation they will be ignored, that is, treated literally priceless, and given a zero price! It is better to provide one's best estimate of these intangible effects, rather than omit them completely.

Mishan (1976) has likened the inclusion of intangible effects in CBA to one of making a horse and rabbit stew. The rabbit is the 'scientific' part and the horse is the inclusion of the more problematic intangible ingredient. With a one-to-one share of horse to rabbit in the stew, the taste is bound to be dominated by the flavour of horse, no matter how carefully prepared is the rabbit. This analogy is often valid. However, sometimes the horse is the main course and then preparation of this needs to be carried out as precisely as possible. For large-scale dams, resettlement provision is not just an optional extra, as recent World Bank (1990) experience with these projects has found out. Current policy requires that resettlement plans be identified at the same time as the technical specifications of the dam is contemplated.

8.1.2 Defining the problem

There are two steps in valuing intangibles. First, a physical unit must be defined in a measurable form. For example, noise is expressed in decibels. Then a monetary value must be assigned to the physical unit. This usually involves using imputed market valuations (finding an actual market price for a good that is associated with the intangible unit, for example, lower housing prices near an airport reflect the cost of noise).

8.1.3 The travel cost method

How does one value an outdoor area (e.g., park with a lake) that allows one to walk, climb, swim, sail and fish? Clawson specified the physical unit as a *visit* to the area. This specification emphasizes that it is the total 'experience' of the trip that counts. The ingredients combine to form a composite good which can be valued as a whole. He recognized that people pay for a visit implicitly by the cost of travelling to the area. People at varying distances pay different 'prices', and from this data one can form the demand curve. This method is such a general one, that it is worthwhile to outline the approach from the outset.

Say there is something that is worth visiting at a particular location. It could be an outdoor site (park, mountain or lake) as in the original Clawson conception. Or it could be an indoor site, such as a museum or art gallery. Something that gives individuals satisfaction takes place at this location, and we wish to value the benefits of providing it. Currently, there is no charge for the activity and the objective is to discover the demand curve (the WTP) for the activity. Whether to charge an actual price is a separate issue from deciding first the size of any benefits involved with the activity. The Clawson approach estimates the demand curve in two stages.

The first stage begins with obtaining data on the visiting rates (e.g., visits per thousand of the population) from communities or residential areas at different distances from the site in question. Table 8.1 depicts four hypothetical visiting rates by communities according to distance from the location of the activity being valued. From the information on distances, one can obtain an estimate of the different travel costs that were incurred making the visits. Assuming a constant cost per mile of 50 cents, the travel costs of the four communities are listed in the last column of Table 8.1. These travel costs constitute the implicit prices paid by the communities to go to the site. The first stage is complete by relating the visiting rates to the travel costs incurred, as in Diagram 8.1.

Table 8.1   Community visiting rates and travel costs

Community	Visiting rate	Distance from site	Travel cost
A	10 000	1 mile	$0.50
B	8 000	3 miles	$1.50
C	5 000	6 miles	$3.50
D	3 000	9 miles	$4.50

Source: Clawson (1966)

The starting point for the second stage is the assumption that any explicit charge that is made is treated like an increased travel cost. This means that the visiting rate for a community facing a particular positive price is the one that corresponds to a community with higher travel costs of that amount. To see how this works, say one is considering to charge community A a price of $1 for a visit. The total cost would be $1.50, being the sum of the $0.50 travel cost and the $1 price.

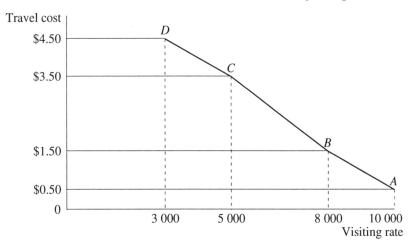

The first stage of the travel cost method involves relating the number of site visits (per thousand of the population) to the travel costs associated with making the visits.

Diagram 8.1

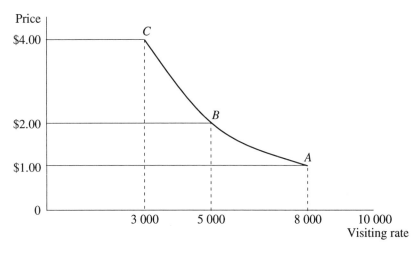

The second stage of the travel cost method involves relating the number of site visits to the prices to be charged. One takes the visiting rate of a community in Diagram 8.1 that has a travel cost that equals the sum of community *A*'s travel cost of $0.50 plus the price that is to be charged. Thus, point *C* is obtained by taking the price of $4, adding this to $0.50 to make a total charge of $4.50. In Diagram 8.1, the visiting rate for a cost of $4.50 is 3 000. So, the price of $4 is paired with the quantity 3 000.

Diagram 8.2

From Diagram 8.1, we see that for community *B* that had a travel cost of $1.50, the visiting rate was 8 000. This figure is then assigned to community *A* as the visiting rate for the price of $1. One now has the point *A* on the demand curve shown in Diagram 8.2.

The other two points in Diagram 8.2 continue the process used to derive point *A*. In both cases community *A* responds to a particular price increase by providing the visiting rate of the community with the equivalent travel cost. Point *B* has a price of $2 and a visiting rate of 5 000 (this being a total cost of $3.50 which community *C* faced and responded to with a 5 000 visiting rate). Similarly, Point *C* has a price of $4 and the visiting rate of 3 000. Joining up points *A*, *B* and *C* produces an estimate of the demand curve for that site activity.

8.2   Trying to value a life

In this section we survey some of the main methods used to value a life and indicate their strengths and weaknesses. All the various methods will be discussed in the context of the application by Forester et al. (1984), who made an evaluation of the legal 55 mph speed limit on highways in the United States. The details of this policy decision will be specified first and the basic data inputs indicated. Then we explain how this data can be assembled in different ways to produce evaluations of the speed limit decision.

8.2.1   The 55 mph speed limit decision

By lowering average road speeds by 4.8 miles per hour, the legal limit had two main effects. Firstly, it took longer to make a journey. The costs of the regulation would therefore be found by multiplying the number of extra hours by the value of time (the wage rate). Secondly, there would be fewer fatalities. The benefits of the regulation depend on the number of lives saved. Data on the number of hours spent on the road were available. The main problem was how to estimate the number of lives that would be saved. We present now the estimation method used by Forester et al.

A three-equation model was used to estimate the reduction in fatalities *F*. *F* was dependent on the legal limit *L*, average speed *S*, and speed variability or concentration *C*, as well as other variables *O*, such as income and age. Since *S* and *C* were also related to the speed limit, a recursive system was set up to reflect the indirect effects of *L* on *C* and *S*. The model therefore was:

$$
\begin{aligned}
F &= F(L, S, C, O) \\
C &= C(L, S, O) \\
S &= S(L, O)
\end{aligned}
\tag{8.1}
$$

Estimation was set up in this way because, although one would expect the overall effect of the speed limit would be to lower fatalities, there could be indirect effects that increase fatalities (because some people would drive less carefully and cause more accidents). The logic of the equations in (8.1) is that one starts off with knowledge of the speed limit L and the other factors O. First one determines the average speed S using these two variables (this is the third equation). Then with S determined, and with the knowledge of L and O, we can determine speed variability C (the second equation). Finally, as one has determined S and C, and one knows L and O, one can then determine the number of fatalities (the first equation).

Time-series data for the period 1952 to 1979 was used to make the estimates. L was measured by a dummy variable, which took a value of one in the years when the legal speed limit was in existence (from 1973 onwards). Ninety-nine per cent of the variation in fatalities was explained by the independent variables in the model.

The results showed that, surprisingly, the direct effect of the legal limit was to increase fatalities. That is, controlling for S and C, the longer journey time would induce fatigue and riskier driving practices leading to an increase in fatalities by 9 678. But the lower average speed and the lower concentration caused by the speed limit decreased fatalities by 17 124. Thus, the net reduction in fatalities due to the legal limit was 7 466.

To summarize: there were two main effects of the imposition of the speed limit. One was negative and involved an increase in the number of hours spent travelling on the road. Forester et al. estimated that individuals had to spend 456 300 extra years on the highways because of being forced to travel at slower speeds. The other effect was positive and entailed a decrease in the number of fatalities by 7 466. The 55 mph speed limit decision was therefore typical of many transport safety decisions where journey time was being traded in the expectation of saving lives.

8.2.2   The traditional methods

The two traditional methods of valuing a life are variants of the human capital approach. They measure the value of people's lives by their contribution to the economy. Method I looks at the economy in terms of national income. At the individual level, a person's contribution is the present discounted value of future earnings over one's expected lifetime. In the Forester et al. study, the average person was 33.5 years old, earning the 1981 national average of $15 496. With a retirement age of 65 years, these earnings could be expected to last 31.5 years. The total lifetime earnings ($15 496 times 31.5) when discounted at the rate of 0.5 per cent (which assumes that the expected growth in earnings will be 0.5 per cent greater than the opportunity rate of return on capital) equals $527 200. Multiplying this value of life by the 7 466 lives that were expected to be saved produced the money value of the benefits of the 55 mph speed limit.

The time spent on the road was valued by the wage rate. To allow for the fact that some leisure time may be involved, a number of alternate fractions of the wage rate were used. Multiplying these multiples of the wage rate by the 456 300 extra years on the highways due to travelling at slower speeds, provided different estimates of the costs of the speed limit.

Forester et al. used the benefit–cost ratio to summarize outcomes. The second column of Table 8.2 shows that, no matter which fraction of the wage rate was used, the benefit–cost ratio was less than one using human capital method I. The net benefits were therefore negative.

Table 8.2   Benefit–cost ratios for the 55 mph speed limit

	Life valued by		
Time valued at:	Human capital I	Human capital II	Schelling's method
Average hourly wage	0.24	0.17	0.25
Two-thirds of average	0.36	0.25	0.38
One-half of average	0.48	0.33	0.51
Thirty per cent of average	0.79	0.56	0.84

Source: Forester et al. (1984)

The second human capital method was similar to the first, except that it required deducting from earnings all the consumption that people make over their lifetime. The assumption is that it is earnings less consumption that the rest of society loses when a person dies. Forester et al. used a 30 per cent consumption rate derived from budget studies by the Department of Labor. This placed the value on a life equal to $369 040. With this value of life, and the cost figures as before, the results are shown in column three of Table 8.2.

8.2.3   A statistical life

The human capital approach has the advantage that it is simple to interpret and data are readily available on this basis. However, as stressed by Mishan (1976), neither of the traditional methods corresponds with the individualistic value judgement behind CBA. As we saw in Chapter 2, CBA is built on the assumption that individual preferences are to count. The human capital approach looks at the effect on society and *ignores* the preferences of the individual whose life is at issue.

It is often the case that only a small subset of the population are likely to lose their life due to the public project. Dividing this number by the total population produces the probability that a person will lose his/her life. It is preferences over risky outcomes that should therefore be the basis for making evaluations of the loss of life. Schelling (1968) consequently argued that it is a *statistical death* that one is contemplating, not a certain death (whose value could be thought to be infinite). By considering what individuals are willing to receive as compensation for putting up with the risk of death, Schelling provided an individualistic mechanism for measuring the value of life.

Schelling was careful to distinguish situations where actual lives were at stake from those where an anonymous person's life is at stake (which is the statistical life framework). When the individual's identity is known (as when donations are sought in the newspaper to help finance an expensive treatment that will save the life of a named person) valuations are likely to be much higher than when applying a small risk probability to a large, impersonal aggregate of people, to obtain a life that is predicted to be lost.

There have been two major studies that have used this willingness to pay approach. Thaler and Rosen (1975) analysed the risk premium included in the wage differentials of riskier forms of employment. Blomquist (1979) looked at people's trade-off of time used in using a seat belt (valued by the wage rate) against the extra risk of being fatally injured during an accident. In both cases they came up with an estimated value for a life of \$390 000. This valuation was remarkably close to the first human capital method. Hence, the cost–benefit ratios in the last column of Table 8.2 based on the Schelling approach are similar to those in column 2.

The conclusion that Forester et al. reached was that, using any one of the three methods covered so far, the 55 mph speed limit was not value for money (unless time is valued at much lower values than it has been in current applied work).

8.2.4   A life as a period of time

The Schelling approach is the mainstream approach and is clearly superior to the human capital approach. Nevertheless, many people (especially those in the medical profession) are still uncomfortable with the idea of putting a money value on a life. This will probably always be the case. The main response to these reservations is that, for most purposes, the CBA evaluator has no choice but to put a value on a life. If scarce resources measured in monetary units are to be allocated efficiently, one needs to be able to compare the net benefits of allocating them to competing ends. Resources used for health cannot be used for education, housing, transport, and so on. The relative values of these uses needs to be compared using a common metric to see which is the most worthwhile. The monetary unit is the most comprehensive and useful unit to employ in a CBA.

There is an exception to this general rule. As pointed out by Brent (1991a), for certain public policy decisions, especially those where safety regulations are at issue, one may be able to replace the monetary metric with *time* as the numeraire. Many public investment and regulation decisions involve forgoing some time in safety use to reduce the probability of losing one's life. For example, the 55 mph speed limit made journeys take longer in order to make them safer. Time must then be given up to save lives. But these lives themselves are simply periods of expected future time availability. When discounted, this expected future time is in comparable units to the time that must be given up to undertake the safety precaution. In consumer equilibrium, current time surrendered for time safety must have equal value to the present value of time expected to be gained in the future. This being the case, it is a simple matter to calculate the number of years expected to be gained and seeing whether it exceeds the years given up. The whole calculation can then be done in terms of units of time, rather than in monetary terms.

For example, let us again reconsider the 33.5 year old person in the Forester et al. study who is predicted to lose his/her life. S/he has a life expectancy of 42.4 years. If it is known that one such person in society would lose his/her life if a safety precaution were not undertaken, then all of the individuals in society in the aggregate should be willing to invest up to 42.4 years in preventive action. Using this logic, we can try to see whether the 55 mph speed limit decision provided more time in terms of lives saved than it used up time in making people travel more slowly.

The (undiscounted) benefits of the 55 mph speed limit were 316 558 years of life saved (7 466 lives times the 42.5 expected years of life in the future). The costs were the extra 456 279 years that travellers had to spend on the roads. The (undiscounted, and therefore maximum) benefit–cost ratio was 0.69. (For an analysis of the discount rate when time is the numeraire, see Brent, 1993.) Using time as the numeraire therefore supports the previous verdict. In the Forester et al. analysis, they found that the 55 mph speed limit was not 'cost-effective' (the monetary benefit–cost ratio was less than one). The outcome in the Brent analysis was that the 55 mph speed limit was not 'time-effective'. No matter the method of life valuation used, or the numeraire, the legal speed limit was *not* a social improvement .

From an individual's point of view, using time as the numeraire is equivalent to using money as the numeraire. But, from the social point of view, there are different implications of aggregating different individuals' time effects than aggregating their monetary effects. Many uses of time may not pass through the market process, in which case no direct monetary measure is available to value this time. People working at home are cases in point. With time as the numeraire, their time is given equal value as anybody else's time. Also, a retired person's life would still have a time value even though earnings have now ceased.

8.3   Applications

The first study by Gray and Olson (1989) is typical of many that try to value intangible benefits in the medical and criminal justice fields. The benefits are viewed as the costs that are avoided by having the social intervention, in this case, reducing the number of burglaries in the United States.

The use of hedonic pricing is covered in the second case study by Brown and Mendelsohn (1984). The aim was to measure the benefits of fishing sites. Building on the Clawson framework, it used travel costs in terms of both time and distance travelled to form proxies of the price for better quality sites. Next, for comparison purposes, the hedonic pricing method is contrasted with the CV approach. The Brookshire et al. (1982) study estimated the value of improving air quality in Los Angeles by looking at differences in property values in locations with different levels of clean air.

In the final application, we discuss Cropper et al.'s (1992) revealed preference approach to estimating the value of a statistical life. The EPA made decisions regarding the use of pesticides in the United States. These decisions indicated how much forgone output the EPA was willing to accept to reduce the risk of exposure to cancer.

8.3.1   A CBA of a criminal sentence

Criminals are given sentences because one expects to receive benefits in terms of crime control. This was the intangible effect that Gray and Olson were trying to value in their study of the costs and benefits of alternative types of sentences for burglars. The choices were whether to impose probation, jail or prison.

The analysis starts with the identification of the inputs and outputs that one is trying to value. We begin with the outputs and then cover the inputs.

The outputs of crime control   The outputs from a criminal being sentenced are: (i) rehabilitation (the modification of the convicted criminal's behaviour); (ii) incapacitation (the removal of an offender from society); and (iii) deterrence (the threat of punishment to would-be criminals). All three outputs produced reductions in the number of crimes that would take place. They were then valued by the cost that these crimes have avoided. In this way account was taken of the harm that a particular crime may cause.

i.   Rehabilitation   This was estimated by comparing the cost of the annual number of crimes before and after conviction. (The before and after comparison is often used in applied work as a proxy for the 'with and without project' comparison.) The convention prior to this study was just to look at the number of arrests before and after conviction. Gray and Olson refined this by finding out (using self-report data from those convicted) how many crimes were undertaken (even if an arrest had not taken place), and then multiplying these by the cost per crime. Note that, although the sample relates to convicted burglars who did not do a more serious crime, the crimes that they may do after conviction could be more serious.

ii. Incapacitation   This was measured in a similar fashion to the rehabilitation effects. The assumption was that criminals would have (if they were
free) convicted the same number (and types) of crimes as they did prior to
being caught.

iii. Deterrence   This category of output was also valued in terms of the number
of crimes deterred times the cost of those crimes. Table 8.3 shows Gray
and Olson's estimates of the number of crimes deterred and their cost. To
measure the number of crimes deterred, an elasticity estimate by Phillips
and Votey (1975) was used. They found that for all three sentences (prison,
jail and probation) the elasticity of crimes per capita with respect to the
certainty of punishment was –0.62. Given the population in Maricopa
County, Arizona, where the study was undertaken, this elasticity translated
into 6.59 crimes deterred per additional felony sentence imposed. The
number of crimes for each type were obtained by multiplying the aggregate
number of crimes by the share of Arizona crimes of that type in 1980. Haynes
and Larsen's (1984) estimates of the average cost of these crimes were used
(in 1981 dollars).

Table 8.3   Number and cost of crimes deterred per convict

Type of crime	Number of crimes	Cost of crimes
Grand larceny	3.94	$780
Burglary	1.74	$756
Murder	0.01	$349
Auto Theft	0.38	$223
Aggravated assault	0.32	$109
Robbery	0.16	$47
Rape	0.04	$10
Total	6.59	$2 274

Source: Gray and Olson (1989)

The inputs of crime control   To implement a sentence, society gives up scarce
resources involved with providing and operating the correctional facility and
with supervising parolees. These elements were measured by their average
costs, because marginal cost data were not available.

In addition, the convict produces less (legitimate) output. For inmates, this
is in terms of diminished social and job skills, lost contacts and stigma for ex-
convicts. For probationers, these lost output effects would be lower than for
inmates. Future forgone output effects were not estimated. Current lost output
due to confinement was measured on the basis of prior earnings (adjusted for
the value of output produced while in confinement).

The data for the study came from a random sample of 112 burglars taken from the 450 data set collected by Haynes and Larsen (1984) in the first half of 1980. The costs and benefits per convict for the three types of sentencing decision are listed in Table 8.4. The figures are for the 'benchmark case' which assumes (*et alia*): rehabilitation benefits last 27 months; deterrence benefits are attributed equally to each sentence; and the social discount rate was 7 per cent. Discounting was an issue because the timing of the different output types varied. The incapacitation benefit occurs during incarceration, while the rehabilitation and deterrence benefits occur afterwards. A sensitivity analysis was used to test all the main assumptions used in the study. The benchmark estimates shown in Table 8.4 were robust to a wide range of alternative assumptions. For example, the discount rate would have to be raised to 66 per cent to remove the difference between jail and probation, and raised to 186 per cent to eliminate the difference between prison and probation.

Table 8.4   Social costs and benefits per convict (1981 dollars)

Sentencing Decision	Incapacitation benefits	Rehabilitation benefits	Deterrence benefits	Social costs	Net benefits
Prison	$6 732	–$10 356	$6 113	$10 435	–$7 946
Jail	$774	–$5 410	$5 094	$2 772	–$2 315
Probation	0	–$2 874	$5 725	$1 675	$1 176

Source: Haynes and Larsen (1984)

Table 8.4 shows that only the probation sentence had positive net benefits. This is largely because prison costs the most and has the largest amount of *dehabilitation* (negative rehabilitation). For all types of sentence, rehabilitation benefits were negative. After sentencing, the number of crimes committed was larger than the number done previously. The intangible effect of having the stigma of being incarcerated was something that needed to be quantified. Gray and Olson concluded that the amount of resources devoted to the incarceration of burglars could be cut back. Some of the lesser offenders who are currently incarcerated could be put on probation and this would increase social net benefits.

One comment concerning the Gray and Olson methodology seems warranted. Even with competitive markets used to value inputs, there is a fundamental difficulty with using the value of inputs to measure the value of outputs. That difficulty is the exclusion of consumer surplus. As we saw in Chapter 3, only at the margin is the WTP of the consumer equal to the market price (and hence the marginal cost of the inputs). At levels below that quantity, what the individual is willing to pay exceeds the price that is actually paid.

8.3.2   Hedonic prices for recreation attributes

In section 8.1.3, we explained how the travel cost method could be used to value the total experience involved with visiting an outdoor recreation area. But, for the management of these outdoor areas, it is more useful to know how individuals value particular components of the trip, such as the trees on the slopes, game densities, or the fish in the streams. Resources can then be allocated efficiently to these competing ends. In the study of 5 500 licensed fishermen in Washington State in the United States by Brown and Mendelsohn, prices for the individual components were estimated by the hedonic pricing method. A site was defined as the river used for fishing.

The origins of hedonic pricing go back to the Lancaster theory of consumer choice. This says that people buy goods because of the characteristics or attributes that the goods possess. Hedonic prices are the implicit values that underlie each characteristic of a product that provides pleasure or satisfaction. The three prime characteristics of a fishing site were identified as: the scenic value, the crowdedness (lack of congestion) and the fish density in the rivers in the area. The scenic and crowdedness attributes were measured on a scale of 1 to 10, where 1 was the worst and 10 was the best. Fish density was the average number of fish caught per day by all those who fish at a particular river. For each characteristic, the mean values for all fishermen surveyed were used, rather than the individual judgements themselves. It was thought that the averages would be a more objective index of a site's quality. The average across all sites was 5 (per ten days) for fish density, 4.5 for scenery and 4 for lack of congestion. The difference between an average site and an excellent site was one unit for both the scenery and crowdedness characteristics and two units for fish density.

The value placed on the prime characteristics depended on how long was the trip. Brown and Mendelsohn distinguished three trip durations: 1 day, 2–3 days, and 4 days and over (4+). This meant that effectively there were nine characteristics of a trip, as there were three durations for each of the three prime characteristics.

A fishing trip involves two simultaneous choices. An individual must decide how much quality (quantity of attributes) to purchase on a given length trip, and also how many trips to take of each length. Estimation proceeded in two steps.

i.   The first step involved deriving the hedonic prices. This step can be thought of in terms of extending the Clawson travel cost model. Different costs of visiting sites define the travel cost implied with each characteristic. In the Clawson study, only the priced costs (e.g., for fuel) were included. Brown and Mendelsohn added to this the time spent travelling to a site. The idea (similar to using 'generic cost' in transport studies) was that a person would have to spend more time in addition to extra expenses when travelling to distant sites in order to enjoy greater amounts of the attributes. Different distanced sites, with alternative combinations of characteristics, thus reveal different characteristic prices.

ii. Then the hedonic prices from the first step were regressed on the characteristics. This second step involves finding the *inverse* demand function. For the regular demand function (as specified in Chapter 3), the quantity demanded of a particular characteristic is the dependent variable and price, income, and so on, would be the independent variables. For the inverse demand function, one has the price variable (i.e., the hedonic price) as the dependent variable and the independent variables are the quantities of the characteristics. The regression coefficient of the characteristics in the inverse demand function therefore indicate the contribution of each attribute to the hedonic price.

Because the number of visits to a site is determined simultaneously with the quality indicators, Brown and Mendelsohn included the number of visits in the inverse demand equations. This required estimation to be carried out allowing for this interdependence. But the regression coefficients and summary statistics can be interpreted in the usual manner. Table 8.5 reports the results for the 1-day trip category, which constituted 80 per cent of the sample. There are three equations because the price for each prime characteristic (the dependent variable in each regression) is determined separately.

The own price effects (the relations between the hedonic price and the quantity of the characteristic whose price is being determined) are all negative and significant as basic microeconomic theory would predict. In an inverse demand curve framework, these negative own price effects translate into the statement: the more a fisherman experiences any particular characteristic, the less s/he is willing to pay for additional units. When these coefficients are divided by their sample means, they produce price elasticity estimates. The demand for fish density was elastic (the price elasticity was -1.22). For longer trips the demand became insensitive to price. For example, the -1.22 own price elasticity figure for 1-day trips falls to -0.44 for 2–3-day trips.

The methodological contribution of hedonic prices to CBA is that it deals with the fixed quantity consumption property of public goods that makes them so hard to value. With pure public goods, each individual receives the same quantity. This makes it difficult to estimate what people are willing to pay for additional units. The way hedonic pricing tackles this problem is to replace the quantity dimension with one based on quality. For example, one makes a trip, but that trip can have variable amounts of specified characteristics. The Brown and Mendelsohn study makes clear that the intensity in which the fixed quantity is utilized is an important component of quality which can help to reveal the demand curve for public goods.

Table 8.5 Determinants of hedonic prices for 1-day trips

Variable	Scenery	Lack of congestion	Fish density
Constant term	–4.505	21.528	–55.779
	(1.22)	(4.89)	(2.39)
Income	–0.000	0.000	0.003
	(0.70)	(4.35)	(15.07)
Experience	0.170	0.119	–1.400
	(7.45)	(4.36)	(9.66)
Scenery	–3.049	1.370	–1.011
	(6.26)	(2.36)	(0.33)
Lack of congestion	–1.482	–4.621	7.270
	(4.06)	(10.61)	(3.14)
Fish density	–11.348	–2.540	–141.62
	(5 50)	(1.03)	(10.83)
No. 1-day trips	–0.400	0.636	5.380
	(6.12)	(8.16)	(12.99)
No. 2–3 day trips	–2.873	–0.251	20.582
	(8.17)	(0.59)	(9.23)
No. 4+ day trips	–4.752	–14.318	5.628
	(6.56)	(16.56)	(1.23)

Source: Brown and Mendelsohn (1984)

The fishing case study explains precisely how pricing can take place for public goods. One starts off by contemplating a particular outdoor recreation site which has joint supply and non-excludability. The possibility of travelling to a more distant site, enables one to transform the joint-supply property into separate supply. This transformation is bought at a price. The travel and time costs involved with the greater journey distance is the mechanism by which price exclusion now takes place. If one does not pay the travel cost, one does not get the separate supply.

8.3.3 Property values and the cost of air pollution
When populations around a site are very sparse, the hedonic pricing method cannot be used. One advantage of contingent valuation surveys is the flexibility it provides. Questions need not relate only to experiences or situations that have actually occurred. One can probe into hypothetical situations using 'thought experiments'. However, as we saw in Chapter 3 when we first discussed CV

methods, it was the hypothetical nature of the approach that also drew the most criticism. It is interesting then to see the extent to which CV and hedonic pricing are interchangeable as measurement techniques. The hedonic pricing situation under examination is one where differences in house prices (or rents) are being used to reflect differences in environmental quality (air pollution).

Brookshire et al. (1982) tested the extent to which CV and hedonic pricing can validate each other in the context of measuring the benefits of reduced air pollution in Los Angeles. What was important about this case study was that it presented a reason why hedonic prices would overstate the true WTP for clean air. We supply a simplified version of their analysis contained in Figure 1 of their paper.

Let clean (less polluted) air be represented by P. Assume that the only way that an individual can purchase any of it is by buying housing in locations subject to less pollution. The rent for this housing is denoted by R. With a fixed income, the more one spends on housing the less one has available to devote to other goods X. X is measured in dollars (its price is assumed equal to unity) and it is the numeraire in the analysis. The choice is then between P and X, and the budget constraint is adjusted to allow for the fact that as one purchases more clean air, one spends more on R and has less to spend on X. In Diagram 8.3, X is on the vertical axis, P is on the horizontal axis, and the budget constraint is (for simplicity) drawn as a straight line (has a constant slope).

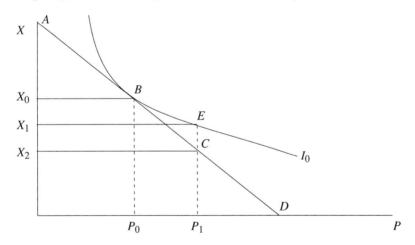

The choice is between clean air (P) and all other goods (X). The budget line is $ABCD$. Its slope is the 'rent gradient', the extra rent one is WTP for reductions in air pollution. The rental value of a reduction in pollution from P_0 to P_1 is the amount X_0X_2. This overstates the true value X_0X_1, which reflects the movement along the indifference curve I_0.

Diagram 8.3

Movements along the budget line indicate the implicit market for clean air. The slope (called the 'rent gradient') measures the higher housing costs paid for locations in areas with lower pollution. The hedonic price for an improvement in air quality from P_0 to P_1 corresponds to movement from B to C and amounts to $X_0 X_2$. If we ask the question how much of X is one willing to pay to move from P_0 to P_1, we obtain a much lower amount. The initial equilibrium is at B, where the indifference curve I_0 is tangential to the budget line. P_0 and X_0 is the initial consumption of the two goods. When we ask the question, how much X is a person willing to pay to obtain the higher level of clear air P_1, one is moving along the indifference curve I_0 from point B to point E. At E, consumption is P_1 and X_1. The amount $X_0 X_1$ is the true WTP for the change from P_0 to P_1. The rental price exceeds the true WTP by the amount $X_1 X_2$.

The hypothesis under test is this: an estimate of the value of a reduction in air pollution using hedonic pricing will be significantly higher than one using a survey approach. The hedonic and survey methods for measuring the value of reductions in air pollution in Los Angeles will now be explained. The levels of air pollution in metropolitan Los Angeles were measured by readings in terms of nitrogen dioxide (NO_2) and total suspended particulate matter (TSP). Three pollution regions were identified. A 'good' pollution region had $NO_2 < 9$ units and TSP < 90 units; 'fair' was $NO_2 = 9$–11 units and TSP $= 90$–110 units; and 'poor' was $NO_2 > 9$–11 units and TSP > 90–110 units. To correspond with the survey questionnaire, the sample was divided up into two groups. One group had households contemplating a move from a 'poor' to a 'fair' region, and the other from 'fair' to 'good'. Each of these changes corresponded roughly with a 30 per cent reduction in either of the two indices.

The property value method   To quantity the effect of changes in P on changes in property values, one needs to hold constant other characteristics of a house and its location. Nine communities that were considered to be homogeneous apart from their pollution levels were identified. The list of independent variables in the hedonic regression equation were: housing structure variables (sale date, age, living area, the number of bathrooms and fireplaces, existence of a pool); neighbourhood variables (crime, school quality, ethnic composition, housing density, public safety expenditures); accessibility variables (distance to beach and employment); and the air pollution variables (NO_2 and TSP). The dependent variable was the (log of the) home sale price. Ninety per cent of the variation in home sale prices were explained by the set of independent variables. The coefficient attached to the pollution variable in the equation with the NO_2 index for the various communities and for the two discrete pollution changes is reported in the second column of Table 8.6. The data came from a sample of 634 sales of single family houses between January 1977 and March 1978.

Table 8.6   The effect of pollution on rents and WTP

Community	Change in rent	Change in WTP	Difference
Poor–Fair			
El Monte	15.44	11.10	4.34
Montebello	30.62	11.42	19.20
La Canada	73.78	22.06	51.72
Sample Population	45.92	14.54	31.48
Fair–Good			
Canoga Park	33.17	16.08	17.09
Huntingdon Beach	47.26	24.34	22.92
Irvine	48.22	22.37	25.85
Culver City	54.44	28.18	26.26
.Encino	128.46	16.51	111.95
Newport Beach	77.02	5.55	71.47
Sample Population	59.09	20.31	38.78

We can see that the extra rents paid were $45.92 per month in the sample as a whole for an improvement in air quality from poor to fair. The corresponding figure for the movement from fair to good was $59.09 per month. Brookshire et al. report that the higher figures in both categories of improvement were in communities with higher incomes.

The survey (CV) method   A hypothetical market for clean air was posited and people were shown photographs depicting different levels of visibility to help appreciate the difference between poor, low and high pollution regions. Alternate price levels were specified and responses to these were recorded. The basis for the bids was an improvement from the existing pollution level in the area in which a person was residing. Two types of bids were presented: for improvements from poor to fair, and from fair to good. A total of 290 completed surveys were obtained over the period of March 1978.

The mean bids for both types of improvement, and for each of the nine communities, are listed in column 3 of Table 8.6. The mean bid in the sample as a whole was $14.54 for the improvement from poor to fair, and was $20.31 for the improvement from fair to good. In every case (shown in column 4) the differences are positive and statistically significant. This confirmed the main Brookshire et al. hypothesis that the rent figures exceed the survey estimates.

Discussion   The Brookshire et al. study has a number of important messages. There is a need to validate any method used to measure intangibles. When making comparisons one should also be aware that differences may sometimes be *expected*, rather than it being assumed that all methods will give the same result. The survey method should not automatically be assumed to be an inferior estimation technique. However, two points need clarification.

i.   The existence of a possible free-rider problem was tested as a separate hypothesis in the pollution study. Brookshire et al. considered the polar case. If there is to be a free rider problem in the survey method, then households would be expected to bid zero amounts for pollution improvements. As all the figures in column 4 of Table 8.6 are positive, (complete) free riding was not present in the study. They concluded that payments mechanisms suggested in the literature concerning the free-rider problem have 'been directed towards solving a problem not yet empirically observed'. Our judgement here is the same as in Chapter 5. The free rider problem may exist, but ways can be devised to circumvent it to reveal people's true preferences. Just like in the outdoor recreation study, where people had to incur costs to get more of what they want, the pollution study showed that clean air could be bought at a price. Note that in both cases, price exclusion *was* taking place. If one does not incur the travel cost, or pay the higher rent, benefits would be denied. The individual was not given the choice to obtain a free ride.

ii. Diagram 8.3 makes clear that one reason why the hedonic approach overstates the true value is that income effects are not being held constant in the measure involving the rental gradient. The true measure moves the individual along the indifference curve I_0. This is like responding to a change in price, holding income (that is, utility) constant. The property value approach moves one along a price–quantity equilibrium path, without holding income constant. So the rental gradient is clearly not a compensated variation. In the Brookshire et al. study, people in higher income regions bid higher amounts than those in poorer areas for a given type of improvement (poor to fair, or fair to good). Once more one has to recognize the importance of checking a study's income assumptions when it uses a WTP measure for a CBA.

8.3.4   The value of a statistical life behind EPA decisions

A special case of externalities is where the damage done by a product generates such severe side-effects that individual lives are being threatened. This occurs with many activities that affect the environment, for example, as with acid rain. One can still use the CBA framework to deal with these cases. But one does have to supply a monetary value for the value of life. In a study of pesticide use in the United States, which caused cancer to some of those affected, Cropper et al. (1992) obtained a revealed preference estimate of the value of life. The EPA made decisions which allowed or disallowed the use of certain pesticides. Since making these decisions involved trading off an increase in output benefits against additional expected cases of cancer, the EPA's decisions revealed the 'price' (in terms of output) that was placed on the additional risk.

Under the Federal Insecticide, Fungicide, and Rodenticide Act various pesticides were registered and thereby permitted. By 1972, approximately 40000 pesticides were approved for sale in the United States. Then Congress amended the act by requiring a reregistration of the 600 active ingredients used in the pesticides. In 1975, a special review process was set up to look at the risk–benefits of various active ingredients. Cropper et al. looked at a subset of 37 of these between 1975 and 1989. To be included in the sample the pesticides had to relate to food crops and also to have been found to cause cancer in laboratory animals. The cancer risk involved: (a) persons who mix and apply pesticides; and (b) consumers in the general population who ingest pesticide residues on food.

Prior to the creation of the EPA in 1970, all pesticides were regulated by the Department of Agriculture. One of the reasons for transferring was to lessen the influence of farmers and pesticide manufacturers and to increase the influence of environmental and consumer groups. There was now, therefore, more of a consumer sovereignty context to the decisions. Comments by environmental groups, grower organizations and academics did affect EPA decisions. Including these political influences increased the explanatory powers of the equations used to derive the revealed preference valuations. The estimates of the value of a life were thereby made more reliable, as there is less chance that the risk–benefit variables are proxies for excluded factors.

Before explaining the method used to derive the implicit value of life for pesticide applicators in the EPA decisions, we mention how the risks and benefits were measured. In the process, we indicate one of the strengths of the revealed preference approach. It has less stringent data requirements than the usual situation where one is trying to find the best measures of the benefits and risks.

The risks   From the study of animals, a relationship is produced between pesticide use and lifetime risk of cancer. This estimate is extracted to humans and multiplied by an estimate of human dosage (exposure) to estimate lifetime risk of cancer to a farm worker or consumer. Median lifetime cancer risks are much higher for pesticide applicators (1 in 100 thousand) than for consumers of food (2.3 in 100 million).

The correct measure of risk is the lifetime cancer risk associated with the particular pesticide minus the risk associated with the pesticide that will replace it. However, the EPA just used the lifetime risk of the particular pesticide on the assumption that the alternative was riskless. This illustrates the principle that, for a revealed preference estimate, all one needs to know is what the decision-maker *thought* was the value of a variable, not what was the true measure of the variable.

The benefits   The only measure of benefits that the EPA had available was the loss of firm income in the first year after cancellation of the pesticide. This loss comes from the forgone output that results from switching to an authorized, but less effective substitute pesticide.

When such output information was not available, Cropper et al. formed a dummy variable which simply recorded whether there would be *any* yield losses from the cancellation decision. In the standard CBA context, where a calculation is being made to guide future decisions, one must know the precise value for the benefits. But, as the revealed preference approach is an after-the-fact analysis, we can, by assuming that a rational decision was made, find out how influential was the qualitative variable in actuality.

The risk–benefit model   Risk–Benefit analysis is a particular type of cost–benefit analysis. A CBA requires that there be positive net benefits:

$$B - C \geq 0 \tag{8.2}$$

Note that because Cropper et al. make their analysis on a recurring annual basis (as explained in Chapter 1), B and C are constant benefits and costs per annum. A benefit–risk analysis, on the other hand, sets

$$\alpha_2 B - \alpha_1 R \geq 0 \tag{8.3}$$

where α_2 is the weight per unit of benefits and α_2 is the weight per unit of risk. The weights are necessary because B is in monetary units, while the risk R is the number of expected cancer cases, measured as a number of persons. If we divide through by α_2, equation (8.3) becomes:

$$B - \frac{\alpha_1}{\alpha_2} R \geq 0 \tag{8.4}$$

Clearly, for a risk–benefit analysis to equal a CBA, one must set $C = \alpha_1/\alpha_2 R$. In this context the ratio of the weights has a special meaning. It is the value of a case of cancer in terms of the value of benefits. Since B is measured in monetary units (dollars), the ratio of weights signify the dollar value of a life lost to (strictly, affected by) cancer. That is:

$$Value \ of \ a \ Statistical \ Life = \frac{\alpha_1}{\alpha_2} \ Dollars \qquad (8.4)$$

Equation (8.4) thus states that when R is multiplied by the dollar value of a life it is then in comparable monetary units to B.

Cropper et al. specified EPA decisions in terms of outcomes where pesticide use was *not* socially desirable. They postulated that the probability P of the EPA cancelling a registration was inversely related to the variables in a risk–benefit analysis:

$$P = -\alpha_2 B + \alpha_1 R \qquad (8.5)$$

This says that the higher the risk, the greater the probability of a cancellation; while the higher the benefits, the lower the likelihood of a cancellation. With data on B and R available, and P being proxied by a dummy variable (which takes a value of 1 when the EPA was observed to cancel a registration, and a value equal to 0 otherwise) estimates of the weights could be obtained by regressing B and R on the proxy for P.

The regression estimates of the coefficients in equation (8.5) produced, after adjustment (see the appendix): $\alpha_1 = 2.345$ and $\alpha_1 = 0.000000066$. The value of a statistical life revealed in the Cropper study was therefore $\alpha_1/\alpha_2 = 2.345/0.000000066$, i.e, \$35.53 million.

The revealed preference method There are a number of interesting features of the Cropper et al. study that highlight important characteristics of the revealed preference approach to valuing a statistical life.

i.   The assumption of linearity In most revealed preference studies in this area, a small risk of loss of life is being compared with a specified monetary gain. For example, in the EPA context, approximately a 1 in 167 risk of an applicator getting cancer was valued at \$213 180. The assumption is then made that each 1 in 167 chance of getting cancer has exactly the same value. The certainty of getting cancer corresponds to a probability value of unity (or 167/167). Thus, as a sure loss of life equates with a 167 times greater risk, a monetary value 167 times larger than the \$213 180 is required to compensate for the complete loss of life. Multiplying \$213 180 by 167 was effectively how the \$35.53 million figure was obtained. This linearity assumption is questionable. One would expect that a small risk might be acceptable, but that a large risk would require more than proportionally increasing amounts of compensation.

ii. Perceiving small risks   There is a second complication posed by the fact that most revealed preference studies of a statistical life work with small changes in risk. Consider the risk of getting cancer from eating food that was sprayed by pesticides. In the EPA study this had a 1 in 2 285 chance of occurring. This is clearly a small magnitude. But, if individuals cannot really perceive this risk and treat this as effectively zero, then the whole revealed preference approach breaks down. There is perceived to be no statistical life at stake and therefore no trade-off to record.

iii. Actual versus statistical lives   The value of an expected case of cancer imposed on applicators was estimated to be $35.53 million. Cropper et al. also provided an estimate of the value of a statistical life for consumers who get cancer from pesticide residues on food. This was revealed to be worth only $60 000. Such large divergencies in valuation (by a factor of 600) are not uncommon in this literature. Far from detracting from the approach, these divergencies justify its use. Divergencies indicate inefficiencies as, at the margin, the value of a statistical life should be equalized in all decision-making contexts.

But Cropper et al. remind us that not all divergencies imply inefficiencies. We need to be careful to check whether all risk situations fall into the same category. Recall the distinction between an actual life and a statistical life. One should expect that when the identities of particular individuals can be detected, valuations of their lives are much higher than when anonymous individuals are at risk. Thus, the fact that the applicators were more recognizable that the general public could explain the difference. (Note also the linearity problem pointed out in (i) above. The risk for applicators was around 15 times larger than for a typical consumer. The EPA may have scaled up their valuation by a much larger proportion than 15 because of this.)

8.4   Final comments
The chapter closes with the summary and problems sections.

8.4.1   *Summary*
This chapter continued the shadow pricing and public good themes discussed in earlier chapters. Many intangibles have public good characteristics and explicit markets do not therefore exist. The key element in trying to value an intangible commodity or service is to specify the *quantity unit* whose demand curve one is estimating. Four examples were presented: for outdoor recreation, the unit was the visit as a whole; for valuing a life, one could use (a) the probability of the loss of life, or (b) the expected future time that one was saving; for valuing pollution, clean air is one component that determines why a house has value.

One common way of measuring an intangible output is to value it by the sum of the values of its inputs. In the CBA of burglar-sentencing decisions there are costs of housing and otherwise incarcerating convicted criminals. The benefits of the sentencing decisions would then be the avoidance of these costs. This approach is consistent with our initial discussion in Chapter 1, where we defined a cost as a negative benefit. But, the major drawback of the approach is the exclusion of consumer surplus.

Many intangible commodities or services are public goods and in this chapter we explained how the literature has added to the general discussion of this subject. The main message from Chapter 5 was that CV (survey) methods could be used to value public goods, if they are designed to minimize the impact of the free rider problem. The second and third case studies showed how techniques are also available to treat the evaluation exercise 'as if' it were one of dealing with a private good. The hedonic pricing method applied to measuring the benefits of fishing and the value of clean air works precisely because it focuses on the exclusion possibilities with such goods. If we interpret 'more' of a commodity to mean enjoying higher quality of the good, then implicit pricing takes place in the real world. Fishing sites with higher densities of fish are excluded to those who are not willing to pay the higher travel costs involved with travelling to sites located at greater distances. Similarly, if one does not pay the higher rents of living in neighbourhoods with cleaner air, one does not receive the benefits of reduced pollution.

The final application illustrated the use of the revealed preference approach in the context of valuing a statistical life. In the study of EPA decisions, extra output was one of the main determinants and the extra risk of getting cancer was the other. Extra output was measured in dollars and risk in numbers of expected cancer cases. The regression coefficient showed that in past decisions concerning pesticide use, the EPA was willing to sacrifice $35.53 million dollars' worth of forgone output to avoid for sure one cancer case.

Apart from providing an estimate of a statistical life, Cropper et al.'s study is also important as it shows once again (like the Orr model in Chapter 5) that welfare-based CBA can provide a positive (predictive) as well as a normative basis for considering public policy decision-making. Benefits and costs were significant determinants of actual social decisions.

8.4.2 Problems
The Brent (1991a) model used time rather than money as the numeraire in a CBA. Since the approach is a very general one, the first problem seeks a simple extension to how it was used in that setting. The second problem aims to reinforce the understanding of the Cropper et al. revealed preference approach to valuing a statistical life.

1. In the Brent model, he treated time as equally valuable in all uses. Assuming that you wanted to allow for the fact that time spent travelling in a car was valued differently from time spent outside the car, how would you go about extending the Brent methodology. (Hint: re-read application 1.4.3.)
2. The Cropper et al. study used equation (8.5) to measure the risk to consumers of pesticide residues on food (called 'diet risk'). The coefficient attached to the benefits was 0.000000066 as before. But, this time the coefficient attached to the risk was 0.00396.
   i.   What was the implicit value of a statistical life in the context of diet risk?
   ii. How would you try to explain why the diet risk value of life was so different from the $35 million estimate for applicator risk. (Hint: three reasons were given in the text.)

8.5 Appendix

The data that the EPA received from the pesticide manufacturers for risk was in terms of N, the number of cancer cases per million of exposed persons, based on a lifetime of exposure. The actual equation that Cropper et al. used for estimation was therefore:

$$P = -\alpha_2 B + \alpha_3 N \qquad (8.6)$$

When Cropper et al. estimated equation (8.6), they found that $\alpha_2 = 0.00067$ and $\alpha_3 = 0.000000066$. (Cropper et al. report their α_3 coefficient as 0.066. But, as B was measured in millions, this is equivalent to 0.000000066 if B were measured in single units.) The only remaining problem that had to be overcome was how to convert the α_3 in (8.6) to the α_1 of equation (8.5). The required conversion follows from defining the relation between N and R.

N is the number of expected cancer cases *per million* of exposed persons, where a person is exposed over his/her working lifetime. If there were 1 million people who were applicators exposed to the risk of cancer due to the use of pesticides, then N would be the total number of persons at risk. But the number of exposed pesticide applicators was 10 thousand and not a million. So, dividing N by 100 (i.e., 10 thousand/1 million = 1/100) provides the absolute number of exposed persons for pesticides. Each person was assumed to be exposed over a working life of 35 years. Dividing the number of exposed persons by 35 thus produces the number of exposed persons in any one year. On a per-person, per-year basis therefore (which is how R was specified) there were $N/(100).(35)$ person years at risk. That is, N had to be divided by 3 500 (i.e., 100 times 35) to be comparable with R. (Cropper et al. in their equation (A.3) present the general relationship between N and R.)

A regression coefficient shows the effect on the dependent variable of a unit change in an independent variable. We have just seen that N in equation (8.6) is in units that are 1/3 500 of the R variable it represents. The end result is that if α_3 is multiplied by 3 500, it supplies the necessary estimate of α_1. This means that $\alpha_1 = (0.000667)(3500) = 2.345$. The ratio α_1/α_2 in dollars equals \$2.345/0.000000066. The value of a statistical life was therefore reported by Cropper et al. to be \$35.53 million.

To simplify matters, the process by which R is related to N can be ignored, and the text in section 8.3.4 states that for applicator risk $\alpha_1 = 2.345$ and $\alpha_1 = 0.000000066$. (Note: for the diet risk problem 2 in section 8.4.2, $\alpha_1 = 0.000000066$ was the same as for applicator risk. Cropper et al. report that the value of life for diet risk was \$60 000. From these two figures, the value of α_1 was deduced to be 0.00396, and this is the figure reported in the text.)

9 Marginal cost of public funds

9.1 Introduction

We saw in Chapter 3 that consumer surplus must be added to the money effects to obtain the benefits of public projects. The chances of the project being accepted are thereby enhanced. But now we need to consider a consumer surplus effect working on the opposite side. In order to pay for the public project, taxes may have to be raised. This causes a surplus loss called an 'excess burden'. The excess burden is added to the resource cost (assumed to be equal to the revenue costs of the project), to form the total loss of welfare from the increase in revenue. This total cost per unit of revenue raised is the 'marginal cost of public funds' (*MCF*). There is a traditional presumption that benefits have to be larger by the *MCF* to offset this extra cost element. Much of the analysis in this chapter is devoted to an examination of the conditions under which this presumption is valid.

The first section defines the concepts and shows how they are related. Then it examines how the basic cost–benefit criterion can be developed with the *MCF* in mind. This criterion is compared with a model developed by Atkinson and Stern (1974). As a result, the criterion presented is shown to be a special case of the Atkinson and Stern model. What is ignored is the effect on other revenue sources of raising taxes for the project.

The second section builds on the basics presented earlier to explain alternative views of the *MCF*. The traditional view requires that benefits exceed costs by the amount of the *MCF*. As we shall see, this is correct only if the *MCF* is greater than unity. If it is less than 1, then everything is reversed.

The applications begin with the traditional approach to estimating the *MCF* for labour taxes. The partial equilibrium framework is easy to understand and the underlying principles behind the *MCF* concept are clarified. Then, using the traditional approach, the role of the *MCF* is highlighted in the context of expenditures on higher education. The third case study, by contrast, uses the modern approach to estimate the *MCF* of capital taxes. The final case study extends the analysis to highlight the role of the *MCF* in designing tax reform.

9.1.1 Definitions and concepts

A central concept in traditional public finance theory is that of a *lump-sum tax*. This is a tax that does not give individuals any incentive whatsoever to change their behaviour when it is imposed. A poll (head) tax is a good example because, apart from suicide (or leaving the country) there is no way to avoid paying the tax. The modern approach does not focus on lump-sum taxes for two reasons. Firstly, there are very few examples of such taxes. Secondly, even if examples can be found, they are likely to be very inequitable. Such taxes cannot allow for the personal or family circumstances of the person paying the taxes.

In the traditional approach, lump-sum taxes were useful as a benchmark for comparison with other taxes. All taxes were thought to have a burden (a loss of utility incurred by the private sector from giving up resources to the public sector). Since there were no disincentive effects with lump-sum taxes, the utility loss from giving up the resources was the only burden involved. Taxes with disincentive effect would have an additional utility loss called an 'excess burden'. In general then, for any non-lump-sum tax change:

$$\Delta Welfare = \Delta Revenue + \Delta Excess\ Burden$$

The marginal welfare cost of public funds (*MCF*) expresses the welfare change from a tax as a ratio of the change in revenue collected:

$$MCF = \frac{\Delta Welfare}{\Delta Revenue} = \frac{\Delta Revenue + \Delta Excess\ Burden}{\Delta Revenue}$$

With the ratio of the change in excess burden to the change in revenue defined as the marginal excess burden (*MEB*), the result is:

$$MCF = \frac{\Delta Revenue}{\Delta Revenue} + \frac{\Delta Excess\ Burden}{\Delta Revenue} = 1 + MEB \qquad (9.1)$$

Lump-sum taxes act as the benchmark because, with *MEB* = 0, the *MCF* = 1. The magnitude of the distortions created by any other tax can be gauged by the departure of its *MCF* value from unity.

Two points need to be clarified before we proceed to analyse the role of the *MCF* in CBA.

i. Fullerton (1991) is right to point out that, although it is true that *MEB* = *MCF* – 1, *MEB* is really redundant because *MCF* is the relevant concept for CBA. That is, why bother to subtract 1 from the *MCF* when we are later just going to add 1 back in? Nonetheless, the literature does continue to emphasize the *MEB* (where it is sometimes called the 'marginal welfare cost') and we will cover this separately as well.

ii. The additional loss of consumer surplus *MEB* can be measured by either of the methods developed in Chapter 3, namely, by the compensating variation

(*CV*) or the equilibriating variation (*EV*). Note, however, that in the context of *marginal* changes, the two measures have been proved to be equal (by Mayshar, 1990). So, it does not matter for the *MCF* which measure is used.

9.1.2   *The* MCF *and the CBA criterion*

The starting point is the CBA criterion that requires that net benefits for marginal projects should be zero, i.e., B – C = 0. Now recognize that benefits go to the public sector and the costs are incurred by the private sector. Throughout this chapter we will assume that the costs borne by the private sector are captured by the loss of tax revenues necessary to pay for the resources given up. Let a_B be the social value of a unit of public benefits and a_C be the social value of a unit of tax revenues (i.e., costs). Then the CBA criterion becomes:

$$a_B B - a_C C = 0 \tag{9.2}$$

Divide both sides of equation (9.2) by a_B, and define $a_C/a_B = MCF$, to obtain the new CBA criterion:

$$B - (MCF)C = 0 \tag{9.3}$$

Assuming the traditional approach is correct, and the *MCF* > 1, the role of the *MCF* is to scale up the costs by the amount of the excess burden and require that benefits be larger by this amount.

9.1.3   *Atkinson and Stern's model*

The task in this subsection is to check the CBA criterion just derived with one that comes from a formal model of welfare maximization, as developed by Atkinson and Stern (1974).

Atkinson and Stern assume that the economy consists of identical households maximizing utility functions which depend on private goods and the supply of a (single) pure public good (which is the public project). Social welfare is the sum of the individual utility functions. α is the common marginal utility of income for any one individual. Individual budget constraints depend on consumer prices that have consumption taxes on them. The production constraint has the Lagrange multiplier λ attached to it, to signify the social value to the government of having an extra unit of resources available. Maximizing social welfare subject to the production constraint produces this relation as the first-order condition:

$$MRT = \left(\frac{\alpha}{\lambda}\right)\sum MRS - \frac{\Delta Total\, Tax\, Revenue}{\Delta Project\, Output} \tag{9.4}$$

In equation (9.4) *MRT* is the marginal rate of transformation of the public good with respect to a private good, and *MRS* is the individual marginal rates of substitution of the public good with respect to income. We will analyse equation (9.4) in two stages. First we focus on the second term on the right-hand side. Then we concentrate on the case where this term is equal to zero.

The effect of the project on the tax system as a whole   The second term records the effect on the revenue from the existing consumption taxes by having the change in the public good (i.e., the project). Its magnitude depends on whether the public project is a complement or a substitute for private goods. Say the project is a complement, as it would be if the project were a public TV channel which induced people to buy more TV sets which were subject to a sales tax. Then the project would cause revenue to rise and this would be a benefit of the project. The opposite would hold if the project were a substitute, for then the forgone revenue would have to be made up somewhere else. The additional benefit (or cost, in the opposite case) is not considered by those using the traditional approach (e.g., Browning's work). But the recent literature is aware of its existence and uses the assumption of a 'neutral' public project to ignore it. (See Mayshar (1990, p. 264) who defines a neutral project as one that has no feedback effect on tax revenue.)

The importance of this revenue feedback effect is clear when we consider the *MCF* definition given in equation (9.1). Say one actually could devise a way for financing the project in a lump-sum way. Then, in the traditional approach, it would seem that *MEB* = 0 and the *MCF* = 1. But, if there is an existing tax system prior to the project that is distortionary, then overall revenue could fall or rise which would make the *MCF* ≠ 1 even with the lump-sum tax.

The MCF *for a revenue-neutral project*   Assuming that the project is revenue neutral, what does the rest of equation (9.4) mean? With the second term zero, and multiplying both sides by λ/α, we obtain:

$$MRT\left(\frac{\lambda}{\alpha}\right) = \sum MRS \tag{9.5}$$

Atkinson and Stern do not state this, but if we define $\lambda/\alpha = MCF$, equation (9.5) becomes:

$$MRT(MCF) = \sum MRS \tag{9.6}$$

This is how Mayshar (1990, p. 269) summarizes their work. Equation (9.6) states how the well-known Samuelson condition for pure public goods needs to be amended when lump-sum taxes are not available. The Samuelson rule is $MRT = \sum MRS$. Now we see that MRT differs from $\sum MRS$ according to how MCF differs from 1.

We can compare the simple criterion expressed in equation (9.3) with that derived by Atkinson and Stern. It is clear that, when the simple criterion considers raising one particular tax to pay for the project, it ignores the effect on tax revenues in the system as a whole. Abstracting from this, that is, using equation (9.6) instead of (9.4), there is a strong correspondence between the two criteria. Consider the $\sum MRS$ to be the benefits of the public project (B), and the MRT to be the costs (C). Equation (9.6) then can be rewritten as:

$$C(MCF) = B \qquad (9.7)$$

This is exactly the simple criterion equation (9.3). From this identification with Atkinson and Stern's analysis we can confirm that:

$$MCF = \lambda/\alpha = a_C/a_B$$

The MCF is the marginal rate of substitution of units of tax revenue into units of utility (social welfare).

9.2   Alternative approaches to estimation of the MCF

In this section we will explain why the traditional approach always finds an MCF greater than unity, and why the modern approach can come up with numbers that are less than 1. We build on the basics presented in section 9.1 and also draw heavily on the crystal-clear synthesis provided by Ballard and Fullerton (1992).

9.2.1   The traditional method

The assumptions behind the traditional approach to estimating the MCF (and how these differ from the modern approach) can be best understood by working through a typical analysis of the MCF of a wage tax (similar to Ballard and Fullerton, 1992).

Consider the choice between leisure L (on the horizontal axis) and earned income Y (on the vertical axis) represented in Diagram 9.1. The price (opportunity cost) of leisure is the wage w that is forgone by not working. The budget line at the wage w is OY_1. The individual chooses a point such as A (where the budget line is tangential to the indifference curve I_1). At A, leisure is L_A. Now impose a wage tax at a rate t. The price of leisure falls to $(1 - t)w$ and the budget line becomes OY_2. The individual chooses a point B (where the new budget line is tangential to the lower indifference curve I_2). For simplicity of reading the diagram, B corresponds to the same number of hours of leisure as at A. Earned income at B, after tax, is $L_A B$. Tax collected is the vertical distance AB.

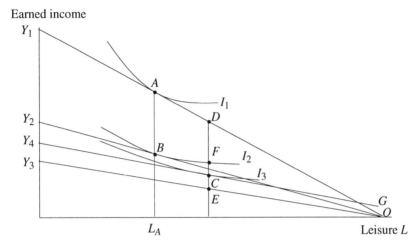

The initial equilibrium is at A. After a tax is imposed, the individual moves to B. The tax paid is AB. Then the tax is raised further still, but returned in a lump-sum way as a rebate. C is the new equilibrium after the tax and rebate (equal to CE). The marginal excess burden (MEB) is CF, the difference between the indifference curves at C and at F (which is the utility level if a lump-sum tax were used, and one would have had the same level of satisfaction as at B). The MCF is the sum of the revenue change and the MEB divided by the revenue change. As the revenue change is CE and the MEB is CF, the $MCF = (CE + CF)/CE$, which is clearly greater than 1. This is the MCF in the traditional approach.

Diagram 9.1

The concept of the MCF involves a consideration of *marginal increases* in taxes to finance increments in government expenditure for the public project. Let the higher wage tax be t'. This means that the price of leisure would fall even further to $(1 - t - t')w$ and this produces the new (flattest) budget line OY_3.

It is essential to grasp that, in the traditional approach, the new equilibrium will not take place anywhere on the new budget line OY_3. This is because the analysis assumes an *equal yield* framework. Effectively this means that the public project is an income transfer programme. Any additional tax revenue will be returned to the private sector in a lump-sum way. The budget line where the new equilibrium will take place will have two properties. (i) It will have the same slope as OY_3. This is because the incremental tax t' has been incurred and lump-sum income changes are to take place at these prices. (ii) It will be at a distance AB from the original budget line OY_1, in line with the equal yield assumption. Given the preferences of the individual, GY_4 is the relevant budget line. Equilibrium is at C (where indifference curve I_3 is tangential to GY_4) with the tax collected CD equal to AB. C is always to the right of B because there is a substitution effect, and no income effect.

We can now make the *MCF* calculation. The tax revenue collected (and returned to the individual) is distance CE. (E is on the budget line OY_3 vertically below C. DE is what the total tax revenue would have been if there were no rebate, and CD is the tax with the rebate, making the difference CE the tax rebated.) The excess burden is the distance CF. (F is on the indifference curve I_2, being vertically above C. If utility were held constant at the level prior to the incremental tax (i.e., at I_2) and the price of leisure would have been lowered by the tax rate t', then F would have been the equilibrium point.) The *MCF* is therefore $(CE + CF)/CE$, a value always greater than unity.

9.2.2   *The modern method*
The modern approach follows the traditional analysis up to the point where the new budget line OY_3 is introduced. Diagram 9.2 has the points A and B as before. But this time the revenue from the incremental tax t' is used to finance a public

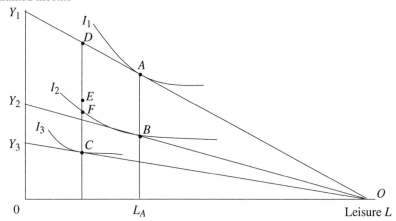

The initial equilibrium is at A. After a tax is imposed, the individual moves to B. The tax paid is AB. Then the tax is raised further still. C is the new equilibrium after the tax. DC is the total tax now paid. DE is the amount equal to the previous tax AB. Hence CE is the additional tax raised. The welfare change is the difference between indifference curves I_2 and I_3, equal to CF (F gives the same level of utility as prior to the additional tax increases). The *MCF* is the welfare change divided by the revenue change, i.e., $MCF = CF/CE$. As drawn (i.e., for the backward-bending supply of labour case), the *MCF* has a value less than 1. This is the modern approach.

Diagram 9.2

project that involves a transfer of resources to the government. There is no lump-sum rebate to accompany the tax. So equilibrium will take place somewhere on the budget line OY_3. Depending on the relative sizes of the income and substitution effects, the new equilibrium could be to the left or to the right of point B. We will consider the situation where the income effect outweighs the substitution effect and people work more due to the tax. This is the so-called 'backward-bending' supply curve case. With leisure reduced, equilibrium point C is drawn to the left of point B (where indifference curve I_3 is tangential to OY_3).

The equivalent amount of tax to AB that was collected before is given in Diagram 9.2 by DE. (D is the point on the original budget line OY_1 vertically above the new equilibrium C. E is also vertically above C, and positioned so that the distance DE equals AB.) DE is therefore the equivalent amount of revenue that would have been raised from tax rate t. The total tax collected at C (from t and t') is DC, which makes CE (the difference between DC and DE) the tax from the incremental tax increase t'. It is CE that is on the denominator of the MCF. On the numerator is the total change in welfare of CF (the difference between indifference curves I_3 and I_2). The resulting MCF is therefore CF/CE. As can be seen from Diagram 9.2, this is a ratio less than 1.

9.2.3 Reconciling the alternative approaches

It is clear from the previous two subsections that the traditional and modern approaches to estimating the MCF have very different kinds of public project in mind. The modern approach is more appropriate for the typical type of CBA analysis that relates to the building of bridges, highways, dams, and so on, while the traditional approach has particular relevance for transfer payments where resources are not moving from the private to the public sector. The domain of the traditional approach is wider if one interprets programmes such as the provision of public housing and food stamps as one-to-one substitutes for private expenditures.

There are two main ways of explaining the difference between the modern and traditional approaches. The first (as pointed out by Wildasin, 1984) involves the difference between the types of labour supply curve one is considering. In the traditional approach, the tax revenue collected is returned to the individual. This means that there is no *income effect* from the tax. The substitution effect is always negative, which leads to more leisure when its price has fallen (due to the tax increase). The MCF always exceeds unity. However, in the modern approach (where there is no lump-sum transfer back to the individual) there is an income as well as the substitution effect. Leisure may increase or decrease. When leisure decreases the MCF can be less than 1. The difference between the two approaches can therefore be understood in these terms: the modern approach uses the uncompensated labour supply curve, while the traditional approach uses the compensated supply curve.

The second way of understanding the difference between the two approaches is in terms of alternative specifications of the change in taxes that appears in the definition of the *MCF*. It will be recalled that the *MCF* is the ratio:

$$MCF = \frac{\Delta Revenue + \Delta Excess\ Burden}{\Delta Revenue}$$

In the traditional approach, the component '$\Delta Revenue$' is the same in the numerator and the denominator. One is considering the project in isolation of the rest of the tax system. When one divides through by $\Delta Revenue$, one *must* obtain 1 plus something (the *MEB*). On the other hand, when we presented the Atkinson and Stern model, we saw that the effect on the rest of the tax system was a part of the modern conception of the *MCF*. It is clear that in the backward-bending supply curve case of Diagram 9.2, because people work more, there is more tax revenue from the old tax *t*. The '$\Delta Revenue$' in the numerator and denominator are not now the same. On the denominator is the total change (from the new tax *t'* and the extra from the pre-existing tax rate *t*); while on the numerator is the change in revenue only from the incremental tax *t'*. The former is larger than the latter (in the backward-bending special case) and this could produce an *MCF* less than unity (if the *MEB* is not too large).

9.3 Applications

We begin the applications with the analysis of United States labour taxes by Browning (1987). This study provides estimates of the *MEB* using the traditional approach. The analysis is within a partial equilibrium model which is easiest to understand. In the process, the key elements in determining the *MEB* are uncovered. (For examples of the general equilibrium approach, see Stuart, 1984, and Ballard et al., 1985a, 1985b.) Then, still basically within the traditional approach, we present the Constantatos and West (1991) estimates of the social returns to expenditure on education in Canada. This study recognized that most CBAs in the education field have ignored the *MCF*. They attempted to see whether popular demands for expanding higher education in Canada could be justified if the *MCF* were included explicitly in the an analysis.

The third case study by Fullerton and Henderson (1989) illustrates the modern approach to estimating the *MCF*. In addition to this difference, it complements the Browning work by dealing with capital as well as labour taxes, and covering intertemporal as well as current distortions. It concludes that capital taxes are inherently a mixture of different instruments each with their own value for the *MCF*. The existence of variations in the *MCF* is itself the policy issue in the final case study by Ahmad and Stern (1987) of taxes in India. Tax reform requires replacing taxes with a high *MCF* with those taxes that have a lower value.

9.3.1   MEB and labour taxes

Because Browning (1987) wishes to focus on the percentage by which benefits must exceed costs due to the *MCF* being greater than 1, he concentrates on trying to estimate the MEB (which he calls the 'marginal welfare cost' per dollar of tax). His analysis is phrased in terms of the ratio of the change in welfare to the change in tax revenue. But it is clear that he is only dealing with the excess burden per unit of revenue. So we substitute the term *MEB* wherever Browning uses 'marginal welfare cost'.

Browning uses Diagram 9.3 (his Figure 2) to explain the basis for his calculation of the *MEB* of wages taxes in the United States. The demand for labour (by a firm) operates in the context of a perfectly competitive market, which makes the elasticity of demand infinite. w is the market wage in the absence of taxes and S is the compensated supply curve. The initial equilibrium has L_1 units of labour hired. The marginal wage tax rate is m and this makes the net wage $(1 - m)w$. Moving along the supply curve produces the with-tax equilibrium point A, with L_2 employed.

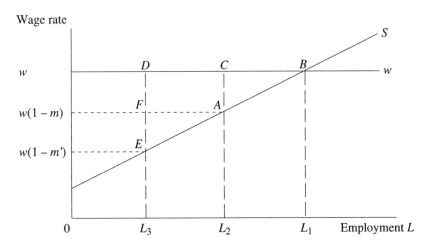

Prior to the wage tax, equilibrium is at B, with w the wage and L_1 the employment level. With the marginal wage tax m, equilibrium is at A. The net wage drops to $w(1 - m)$ and employment falls to L_2. The wage tax is raised still further to m', leading to the final equilibrium at E. The welfare loss is the area under the supply curve, given as *CDEA*. This is the marginal loss that Browning uses on the numerator in his calculation of the *MEB* of wages taxes in the United States.

Diagram 9.3

In order to finance the public project, the marginal tax rate must be raised to m'. The net of tax wage is $(1 - m')w$. The new equilibrium is at point E, with L_3 employed. There has been a reduction in employment of L_2L_3. Workers were receiving the wage rate w, so CL_2L_3D is forgone earnings. The disutility of working is given by the area under the supply curve, AL_2L_3E. The difference between these two areas, $CDEA$, measures the loss of utility from the reduction in employment. Area $CDEA$ thereby indicates the loss of welfare from the incremental tax for the project.

The area $CDEA$ determines the numerator of the *MEB* expression. The denominator ($\Delta Revenue$) depends on how the average tax rate t changes and the change in labour income. Browning considers two cases. We will just concentrate on the simpler case where revenue increases from fixed earnings (and hence revenue lost from reduced earnings is zero). This is like assuming that the incremental tax is revenue neutral. Browning calls this the 'earnings constant' assumption. For this case, the *MEB* of a wage tax is:

$$MEB = \left[\frac{(m + 0.5\Delta m)}{(1 - m)} \right] \eta \left[\frac{\Delta m}{\Delta t} \right] \qquad (9.8)$$

The derivation of equation (9.8) is given in appendix 9.5.2. Here we are only concerned with interpreting the equation and showing how it was used to provide estimates of the *MEB* for wages taxes in the United States. There are three main elements and these will now be discussed.

i.   The marginal tax rate (m)   The relevant concept is the weighted average marginal tax rate from all taxes and transfers that reduce the wage below the marginal product. In 1984, the income tax interacted with the social security payroll tax and means tested transfer programmes. Browning had, in an earlier study, produced a value for $m = 0.43$ and this was used as the benchmark estimate. Values 5 percentage points higher and lower than the benchmark figure were used in the sensitivity analysis.

ii. The elasticity of labour supply (η)   Diagram 9.1 made clear that the *MEB* was a function of the extent to which labour supply reacted to the tax. The greater the reaction, the greater the marginal excess burden. This is a general result related to elasticity and one that underlay the Ramsey rule covered in Chapter 4. Browning's formula expresses the labour supply reaction in terms of the (compensated) labour supply η. The literature on estimating supply elasticities was extensive. Most provided low elasticity estimates. Browning used the value of $\eta = 0.3$ as his benchmark, and tried values 0.1 higher and lower in the sensitivity analysis.

iii. The progressivity of the tax system   The ratio $\Delta m/\Delta t$ denotes how the progressivity of the tax system changes when the average tax rate changes. Browning recommended using the idea that the new project would follow the current rate of progressivity. Effectively, this means setting $\Delta m/\Delta t = m/t$, which in his study is 1.39 (i.e., $m = 0.43$ and $t = 0.31$). Browning suggested that for sales taxes this ratio would be about 0.8, and would be around 2.0 for the federal income tax. These values fixed the lower and upper values in the sensitivity analysis. A proportional tax system was also considered, where a 1.0 value was used.

The only other parameter to set was the scale of the tax change. Browning based his estimation on a one per cent rise in the marginal tax rate (i.e., $\Delta m = 0.01$). Table 9.1 presents the *MEB* estimates according to the assigned values used for m, η and the rate of progressivity for the case where earnings were assumed constant. The range of estimates for the *MEB* displayed in Table 9.1 is from a low of 9.9 per cent to a high of 74.6 per cent. Browning's personal preference is for values between 31.8 per cent and 46.9 per cent. But he admits that any of the other values could be just as accurate. Although there is a wide disparity in the estimates, none of the estimates are negative. This is what one would expect from the traditional approach. No combination of possible parameter values can produce an *MCF* estimate less than 1.

Table 9.1   The MEB *for wage taxes in the United States (in 1984)*

Pro-gress-ivity	$m = 0.38$			$m = 0.43$			$m = 0.48$		
	$\eta = 0.2$	$\eta = 0.3$	$\eta = 0.4$	$\eta = 0.2$	$\eta = 0.3$	$\eta = 0.4$	$\eta = 0.2$	$\eta = 0.3$	$\eta = 0.4$
0.80	9.9	14.9	19.9	12.2	18.3	24.4	14.9	22.4	29.8
1.00	12.4	18.6	24.8	15.3	22.9	30.5	18.7	28.0	37.3
1.39	17.3	25.9	34.5	21.2	31.8	42.4	25.9	38.9	51.9
2.00	24.8	37.3	49.6	30.5	45.8	61.1	37.3	56.0	74.6

Source: Browning (1987)

9.3.2   MCF *and education expenditures*
Most CBA's of education base estimation of the benefits and costs on the human capital approach. Education leads to a future income stream that would be higher than if the education had not taken place. Forgone earnings during schooling is what has to be given up to get the higher future income. The NPV of this stream before tax defines *social* benefits; *private* benefits correspond to the NPV of the income stream after tax. Costs are measured by market prices and are given by the expenditures on the education. Private expenditures are

usually supplemented with public expenditures. This means that the social (or total) costs of education are almost always greater than the private costs (tuition, books, and so on, and forgone earnings).

If public expenditures are financed out of taxes that have an excess burden, then an *MCF* should be applied to these funds. In many countries of the world, especially developing countries, higher education gets a disproportionate share of public expenditure education budgets (relative to the number of students involved). Constantatos and West (1991) were mainly concerned with ascertaining the extent to which allowing for the *MCF* would affect the social desirability of extensions to higher education in Canada.

The *MCF* figure used in the study was 1.50, derived from United States estimates by adjusting for the fact that the Canadian share of government expenditure in the economy was around 30 per cent higher than for the United States. An upper bound for the *MCF* of 1.80 was also used. This corresponds to the inclusion of tax evasion as an additional element in forgone output due to taxes, as recommended by Usher (1986).

Elementary education covered schooling between ages 7 and 14; high schooling occurred between ages 15 and 18; and university education related to ages 19–22. Differential income was calculated by comparing the predicted earnings of a person of any particular age with that predicted by someone of the same age who had education at the next lowest level. For example, someone who went to university would at the age of 23 (in the absence of this level of education) be expected to receive as income what a person who went to high school would have earned at the age of 23. Differential income was predicted to last till people reached the age of 65.

Most CBAs of education expenditures summarize outcomes in terms of the *internal rate of return* (IRR). This is the rate of discount when applied to the incremental income stream (minus costs) that produces a zero NPV. The CBA criterion here for a socially worthwhile project requires that the IRR be greater than the social discount rate (see, for example, Brent 1990). The discount rate in the Constantatos and West study was taken to be the opportunity cost of physical capital, a figure in the range of 6.5 per cent to 10 per cent. The issue then was whether, once one allows for the *MCF*, higher education rates of return were above the 6.5–10 per cent range.

Not all of any observed increases in income can be attributed to receiving more education. A part can be due to the fact that a student (especially in higher education) may have more ability than a non-student (and would have earned higher income anyway). Constantatos and West made an adjustment for this possibility. The social returns to education listed in Table 9.2 (their Table 4) present a number of alternatives, depending on: (a) the proportion of differential income due to ability and (b) values for the *MCF*.

Table 9.2   Social rates of return to Canadian education (1980)

MCF	Proportion of differential income due to ability					
	0.00	0.10	0.15	0.20	0.25	0.30
Elementary						
1.0	18.41	17.52	17.06	16.57	16.60	14.97
1.5	15.26	14.48	14.07	13.64	13.19	12.23
1.8	13.96	13.22	12.83	12.43	12.01	11.10
High school						
1.0	13.13	12.23	11.75	11.27	10.77	9.73
1.5	11.18	10.38	9.97	9.54	9.10	8.17
1.8	10.29	9.54	9.15	8.75	8.33	7.45
University						
1.0	9.89	9.24	8.94	8.63	8.29	7.58
1.5	8.77	8.23	7.94	7.63	7.32	6.63
1.8	8.25	7.72	7.43	7.14	6.83	6.15

Source: Constantatos and West (1991)

Typical of most studies in the education field, Table 9.2 shows that the IRR was highest for elementary education. In all but one case, the rate of return for any given level of education was lower the proportion of the differential to income due to ability, and was lower the higher the *MCF*. None of the rates of return for higher education would be acceptable if the 10 per cent cut-off criterion were considered relevant. Most emphasis in the study was placed on the results with the 0.25 adjustment for ability. In this case, even with a 6.5 per cent cut-off mark, the IRRs on higher education were only marginally socially worthwhile with an *MCF* above unity.

Constantatos and West conclude that there may be evidence of overinvestment in higher education in Canada, depending on one's assumptions concerning the cut-off level for the opportunity cost of public funds. With a low figure for the cut-off level, the desirability of devoting more funds to higher education is still questionable for a high *MCF* and a large adjustment for ability. Evidence of external benefits for higher education must be strong in order to ensure that public expenditure on higher education is clearly worthwhile.

This study is useful in explaining how the *MCF* can be used in a CBA in the traditional framework where all costs have to be tax financed and all benefits are unpriced. However, as we shall see in Chapter 12, once one allows for user charges, the role of the *MCF* is not so simple. The general principle that will be developed later can be stated now, and shown to be relevant even within the framework of analysis of Constantatos and West. The principle is that one must always be careful about being consistent with how one treats costs and benefits. If the part of the costs that are tax financed has an excess burden, then the part of the benefits that goes to the government as revenue has an 'excess gain' (it could be used to lower taxes and eliminate excess burdens). It will be recalled that social benefits in most education CBAs are incomes before taxes. In effect, through income taxes (and so on), part of the higher income from education goes to the government and this revenue should be given a premium. Such a premium is missing from the Constantatos and West study.

9.3.3 MEB *and capital taxes*
The excess burden discussed so far related to current choices. For capital taxes we need to recognize an intertemporal effect. Reductions in investment lead to future output reductions and thereby to utility losses. All the capital taxes covered by Fullerton and Henderson (1989) have this intertemporal excess burden. On the other hand, existing distortions are so great for some taxes that raising certain taxes can reduce these distortions and lead to utility gains that may or may not offset the intertemporal effects.

There are three kinds of existing distortion analysed by Fullerton and Henderson involving capital taxes.

i   Different assets are taxed at different rates. The investment tax credit favours equipment over other forms of capital. Also, depreciation allowances distinguish certain types of equipment and structures.
ii.   Different sectors are taxed at different rates. The corporate sector is taxed at higher rates than the noncorporate, and more than the owner-occupied housing sector (where imputed net rents are not taxed at all).
iii.   Old capital is taxed differently from new capital. Cut-backs in depreciation allowances or investment credits discourage new investment and leave the returns on past investment unaffected.

Fullerton and Henderson use a general equilibrium model to make their estimates. (They update and build upon previous work, e.g., Ballard et al., 1985a.) Selective capital taxes cause a substitution to less taxed capital or labour. The production function tells how much output will fall, and utility functions indicate the resulting loss of utility. Constant elasticity of substitution forms were assumed for both the production functions and the utility functions. Thirty-eight different assets were analysed and 12 separate household types.

Underlying their analysis is two main ingredients that appeared in Browning's partial equilibrium model outlined earlier, namely, the size of the marginal tax rates and magnitudes of elasticities of supply. We cover these in turn.

Marginal tax rates   The main reason that the size of the marginal tax rate helps to determine the magnitude of the excess burden can be understood from Diagram 9.3, where the *MEB* of a wage tax was being discussed. Note that when the tax rate *m* was introduced, the welfare loss was the triangle *BCA*. The loss from the incremental tax *m'* was *CDEA*. This can be decomposed into the triangle *AFE* plus the rectangle *CDFA*. The loss from *m'* was therefore greater than the triangular loss. There was no rectangular loss from the initial tax increase. This illustrates the principle that, when a new distortion (tax) is added to an existing distortion, the resulting loss is many times greater than if there were no existing distortion.

In the United States in 1984, the average marginal effective rate on capital income was 33.6 per cent. The average for the corporate sector was 37 per cent, and 35 per cent for the noncorporate sector; it was 23 per cent for owner-occupied housing. Within the corporate sector, the average rate for equipment ranged from –4 per cent (for office and computing machinery) to +3 per cent (for railroad equipment), and the average rate for structures varied between 32 per cent and 48 per cent. For labour taxes, the average effective tax rate was much lower (at 12.7 per cent) than the capital taxes. Personal income tax rates were (at 25.5 per cent) in between the labour and capital tax rate averages.

Elasticities of supply   The greater the elasticity of supply, the greater the excess burden. In line with the modern approach, the relevant labour supply elasticities are the uncompensated ones. Fullerton and Henderson use an elasticity value of 0.15 as their best estimate. They then use a sensitivity analysis using values of 0 and 0.3 as the alternates. Where the finance for investment comes from individual saving decisions, the elasticity of supply of saving also plays a part. A mean value of 0.4 was taken as the best estimate, with 0 and 0.8 as the extreme values used in the sensitivity analysis. A wide range for the asset and sector substitution elasticities were used, varying between 0.3 and 3.0.

The benchmark estimates of the *MEB* for the various categories of taxes are listed in Table 9.3. This corresponds to the set of assumptions: the labour supply elasticity is 0.14, the saving elasticity is 0.4, and unit elasticities for both assets and sectors. What is striking about these *MEB* estimates is the wide range of variation in values according to the particular tax involved. Interesting is the fact that the variation within the instruments of capital taxation is greater than the differences between categories of taxation (that is, capital, labour and personal income).

The variation of estimates displayed in Table 9.3 record differences *in kind* and not just degree. Some *MEB*s are actually negative. This means that *MCF*s < 1 are not only a theoretical possibility, they can exist in practice, contrary to the traditional expectation. It is instructive to understand why the negative *MEB* occurs, and we examine further the –0.376 estimate for the investment tax credit.

Table 9.3   MEBs *from specific portions of the tax system (1984)*

Capital tax instruments	
Investment tax credit	–0.376
Depreciation allowances:	
1. Lifetimes	–0.188
2. Declining balance rates	0.081
Corporate income tax rate	0.310
Corporate & noncorporate income tax rates	0.352
Personal income tax rates	
1. Capital gains	0.202
2. Dividends	0.036
3. Interest income	0.028
Noncapital tax instruments	
Labour tax rates at industry level	0.169
Personal income tax rates	0.247

Source: Fullerton and Henderson (1989)

Prior to contemplating an increase in revenue from the investment tax credit (i.e., by *removing* it), we saw that (because of the credit) the marginal rate of tax on equipment was the lowest. This meant that investment resources were larger in equipment than in other assets. The marginal product of capital was driven down for equipment and raised in other areas. This difference in marginal productivities was an efficiency loss which can be viewed as a reduction in output (over what it could have been without the credit). Then when the credit is removed, so is the output loss. In the United States context, the gain by removing the efficiency loss exceeded the intertemporal loss of output by discouraging investment. As a result the marginal excess burden was a negative 0.376. Adding –0.376 to the unit revenue effect produces a value for the *MCF* of 0.624 for the investment tax credit.

Apart from highlighting cases where the *MCF* is less than unity, the Fullerton and Henderson study is important in helping to identify cases where lump-sum taxes may exist in practice. As pointed out earlier, some of the capital tax instruments affect the relative desirability of new as opposed to past investments. Taxes that affect only old investment act like lump-sum taxes from an intertemporal point of view. This consideration was especially important in explaining why the excess burden for the tax on dividends was so low (the *MEB* was only 0.036). Taxes on dividends impact on the accumulated equity that investors have built up in a corporation in the past. These taxes can be raised without having a large impact on future investor decisions.

9.3.4 MCF and tax reform

Modern policy analysis typically distinguishes CBA from tax reform. CBA requires *an increase* in taxes to finance the project, while tax reform assumes a *constant* tax revenue and considers the effects of replacing one tax with another. But tax reform can be viewed from a CBA perspective. Both areas assume that we are not at the optimum and contemplate changes that are to be evaluated to see if they bring about a social improvement. Substituting one tax for another produces benefits as well as costs. The ingredients of a tax reform analysis are exactly those that make up the *MCF*. So this application will emphasize the commonality between the two types of policy change. The exposition will be in terms of commodity tax reform, where a tax on commodity *A* is being compared to a tax on commodity *B* (for a common yield of 1 unit of revenue).

Consider an increase in a tax rate on commodity *A* (i.e., Δt_A). This has two effects, one positive and one negative. The positive effect is that there is an increase in revenue to the government (which can be spent on socially valuable projects). This effect is represented by the ratio: $\Delta Revenue/\Delta t_A$. The negative effect of the tax change is that someone (some household) will experience a loss of utility by paying the tax. The rate of change in social welfare with respect to the tax change is defined as: $\Delta Welfare/\Delta t_A$. The full impact of the tax change can then be represented by the ratio of the negative to the positive effects, called the 'marginal social cost' of the tax on *A* (MSC_A):

$$MSC_A = \frac{\Delta Welfare / \Delta t_A}{\Delta Revenue / \Delta t_A} \tag{9.9}$$

The *MSC* is just a cost–benefit ratio of the tax change. One then needs to find the *MSC* of the tax one is considering to replace, say a tax on commodity *B*. The decision rule is that, if $MSC_A < MSC_B$, then one has a lower ratio of costs to benefits than from the existing tax. The tax on *A* can replace the tax on *B* in a socially beneficial tax reform.

This brief summary of the basic principles of tax reform is sufficient for our purposes. (There is, of course, a lot that needs to be explained to estimate *MCFs* in practice. For the details in the context of Indian tax reform, see Ahmad and Stern (1987).) Recall the definition of the *MCF* as:

$$MCF = \frac{\Delta Welfare}{\Delta Revenue}$$

If we divide top and bottom of this definition by Δt_A, we leave its value unaltered. The expression, which we can call MCF_A, becomes:

$$MCF_A = \frac{\Delta Welfare / \Delta t_A}{\Delta Revenue / \Delta t_A} \qquad (9.10)$$

Comparing equations (9.9) and (9.10), we can see that the *MSC* and *MCF* concepts are one and the same.

Ahmad and Stern applied the *MSC* framework to focus on commodity taxation reform in India. India has a fairly complicated federal system of taxation, with the central government controlling tariffs and excise duties on domestic production, and the state governments controlling sales taxes and excises on alcohol. The sales taxes basically combine taxes on domestic production with import duties. Comparisons were made of the *MSC* of individual commodity taxes (grouped into 9 categories), with a poll tax, an income tax, an export tax, an excise tax and a sales tax.

Table 9.4   Marginal social costs per rupee for a 1 per cent tax increase

Tax category	Equal weights	Proportional weights
Groups of taxes:		
Excise	1.1458	0.8497
Sales	1.1204	0.8509
Imports	1.1722	0.7729
Income	1.1431	0.2199
Individual goods:		
Cereals	1.0340	0.9862
Dairy	1.0037	0.7065
Edible oils	1.0672	0.8974
Meat, fish	1.0532	0.8538
Sugar, gur	1.0892	0.8812
Other foods	1.1352	0.9513
Clothing	1.2450	0.7966
Fuel, light	1.1632	1.0629
Other nonfood	1.1450	0.7173

Source: Ahmad and Stern (1987)

The *MSC*s for all the main groups of taxes in India are shown in Table 9.4. (This combines Tables (11–2), (11–4) and (11–5) of Ahmad and Stern.) The second column gives the results on the same basis as the rest of this chapter.

That is, distributional considerations have been ignored in the specification of the $\Delta Welfare$ on the numerator of MCF, implying that equal weights were employed. For contrast, we present also the results in column 3, which give (inverse) proportional weights (such weights are discussed in Chapter 10). There are three main results:

i. For the three broad groups of taxes, namely, excises, sales and imports, distributional values are very important in deciding which has the lower welfare cost. With equal weights, $MSC_{imports} > MSC_{excise} > MSC_{sales}$; and with proportional weights, it is the exact reverse. This is because sales taxes bear heavily on final consumption goods which are consumed by the lower income (expenditure) groups. Excises and import duties fall on intermediate goods and ultimately on manufactures. Excluding distribution weights from the MCF in CBA could therefore also distort outcomes.

ii. The across the board increase in all marginal rates of income tax had the lowest welfare cost of all the reforms, i.e., MSC_{income} was lowest. Incidently, a poll tax (the simplest lump-sum tax) had an MSC value of 1.1173. So, it was not the case that a poll tax was optimal. This result also follows from the inclusion of distributional considerations into the analysis. Indirect taxes relieve individuals of revenue in proportion to expenditure (if there is full shifting) while poll taxes charge equal amounts to all.

iii. For the individual commodity taxes, distributional judgements are again important. Fuel and light, and cereals, figure largely in the consumption expenditure of those with low expenditures. Thus, when distribution is ignored, these product groups have low welfare costs. But, when distribution is considered important, these two groups have MCFs much higher than the rest.

The main message from this study of tax reform in India is therefore the importance of including distributional considerations into the MCF. The other general issue posed by the Ahmad and Stern work relates to the fact that the MSC is not a fixed number independent of which tax instrument is being used to raise revenue for the public project. Even with distributional considerations included (as in column 3) the MCF could be greater than 1, or less than 1.

There are two obvious ways of proceeding in CBA. One can look at budget statements to try to uncover how increments of government expenditure are to be funded, and use the MCF for that source. Or, in the absence of detailed budget information, one can assume that new items of expenditure are going to be financed like past expenditures. In this case, one could use a weighted average of the MCFs, where the weights are the shares of the tax source in the overall government budget.

9.4   Final comments

We close with the summary and problems sections.

9.4.1   Summary

The *MCF* is just another shadow price. It is the shadow price of the public funds (obtained by raising taxes) used for the public project. In the traditional view this *must be* greater than 1; while in the modern approach it *can be* less than 1. This difference is very important for how CBA is to be practiced. Browning (1976) originally estimated the *MCF* to be 1.07. He argued: 'Thus, government expenditures would have to be 7 per cent more beneficial (at the margin) than private expenditures to constitute a net welfare gain'. *Only if* the *MCF* actually does exceed unity is Browning correct to require that the public sector outperform the private sector just to keep level.

Ballard and Fullerton's analysis showed that, in the traditional approach, the *MCF* would always be greater than 1 because the income effect of the tax increase was neutralized. At the same time as raising the tax, a lump-sum rebate was given of equal yield. The substitution effect was the only influence, and this necessarily caused private output to fall. In the modern approach, there is an income and a substitution effect to consider, and this can cause private output to increase or decrease. Because of the different ways that the two approaches treat the income effect of a tax, the traditional approach is more relevant for evaluating tax transfers, and the modern approach is appropriate for resource transfers to the public sector (which is the typical project in CBA).

The applications uncovered cases where the *MCF* was above 1, and others where the *MCF* was below 1. Browning's analysis regarding the marginal excess burden *MEB* (i.e., the *MCF* – 1) of the wage tax showed the fundamentals of the traditional approach. To combat the consumer surplus on the demand side for the output of the public project, there is a loss of consumer surplus on the supply side of the resource being taxed for the necessary revenues. The *MEB* is larger the marginal rate of tax and the elasticity of supply. Using the traditional approach, we saw that the *MCF* can make a difference in deciding intrasectoral choices. Higher education in Canada (and in many other countries) received a greater share of the financial subsidies. When this was properly shadow priced, the social return was very close to the opportunity cost of the capital.

The last two case studies emphasized that one should not assume that there is a single *MCF* such that *the MCF* exists. The *MCF* varies with the particular tax being considered. In the United States, differences within the class of capital taxes exceeded those between classes (capital versus labour or income taxes). Because there is this variation across taxes, it makes sense to consider replacing one tax with another that has a lower *MCF*. Tax reform theory is the counterpart to CBA that operates on the revenue side of government activities. However, true to the traditions of CBA, one should not always assume that policies in other areas are set optimally. If taxes were set optimally the *MCF* would be the same for all revenue sources. Since divergencies do exist in practice, one needs to try to establish which tax will be used; or else one can assume that future taxes will follow the pattern of past taxes.

9.4.2 Problems
The following two questions are based on the survey questions used by Ballard and Fullerton (1992). (For simplicity, the words 'with Cobb–Douglas utility of leisure' have been omitted from their question 1.) These questions were geared at eliciting what we can call the 'gut responses' of professors who teach graduate Public Finance at 'leading institutions' considering the *MCF*. The professors were told 'to take 60 seconds right now' and 'please do not ask for precise definitions, work out the whole model, or give long answers'. The survey questions were:

Q1: Consider a single aggregate individual facing a constant gross wage and a flat 50% tax, and a single consumption good such that the uncompensated labour supply elasticity is zero and the compensated labour supply elasticity is positive. Is this wage tax distortionary?
    Yes: No:
Q2: In the same model, with the same assumptions, suppose a public project with production costs (*MRT*) of $1, and benefits ($\Sigma MRS$) of slightly more than $1, could be funded by a 1% increase in the wage tax. Would this be desirable?
    Yes: No:

1. Answer Ballard and Fullerton's questions Q1 and Q2 without reviewing any material in this chapter.
2. Answer Ballard and Fullerton's questions Q1 and Q2 after reviewing the material in this chapter. As intermediate steps, provide answers to these questions:
   i. Is it the compensated or the uncompensated supply elasticities that cause the excess burdens?
   ii. Draw a diagram like Diagram 9.2, but this time let the income and substitution effects cancel out (which is what a zero uncompensated supply elasticity involves). What is the *MCF* in such a diagram?

9.5 Appendix
We derive in this section the two main analytical results presented in the chapter. The first is Atkinson and Stern's equation for the *MCF* that is used for comparison purposes in section 9.1.2. The second is Browning's expression for the *MCF* of labour taxes covered in section 9.3.1.

9.5.1   *Atkinson and Stern's cost–benefit criterion*

Atkinson and Stern (1974) assume that there are h identical households maximizing utility functions $U(x, e)$, where x denotes the consumption of n private goods, and e is the supply of a (single) pure public good (equally consumed by all). The prices faced by consumers are given by q, and the (fixed) producer prices are p. Taxes t are the difference between consumer and producer prices. The individual's budget constraint is $q.x = M$. We assume that there is no lump-sum income, and so $q.x = 0$ will apply in our case. Maximizing utility subject to the budget constraint leads to the indirect utility function $V(q, e)$.

The production constraint is $G(X,e) = 0$, where X is the total consumption of x, i.e., $h.x$. Let good 1 be the numeraire and assume it is untaxed, which means that $p_1 = q_1 = 1$. The firms are price takers and maximize profits. So $G_k/G_1 = p_k/p_1$ (where G_k is $\delta G/\delta x_k$). With $p_1 = 1$, and defining G in order that $G_1 = 1$, the profit maximization condition reduces to $G_k = P_k$

The objective is to maximize total utility $(h.V)$ subject to the production constraint. The Lagrangean is therefore:

$$L = h.V(q, e) + \lambda G[X(q, e), e] \qquad (9.11)$$

The first-order condition for e is (with $G_e = \delta G/\delta x_k$):

$$\frac{\delta L}{\delta e} = h.\frac{\delta V}{\delta e} - \lambda \left[\sum_{i=1}^{i=n} G_i \frac{\delta X_i}{\delta e} + G_e \right] = 0 \qquad (9.12)$$

Using the profit maximization condition (i.e., $P_i = G_i$) and using the fact that $G_1 = 1$, equation (9.12) reduces to:

$$h.\frac{\delta V}{\delta e} = \lambda \sum_{i=1}^{i=n} p_i \frac{\delta X_i}{\delta e} + \lambda \frac{G_e}{G_1} \qquad (9.13)$$

Multiplying and dividing the first term on the RHS by α (the individual marginal utility of income), and rearranging we get:

$$\frac{G_e}{G_1} = \frac{\alpha}{\lambda} \left[\frac{h.\frac{\delta V}{\delta e}}{\alpha} \right] - \sum_{i=1}^{i=n} p_i \frac{\delta X_i}{\delta e} \qquad (9.14)$$

Since $p_i = q_i - t_i$, equation (9.14) becomes:

$$\frac{G_e}{G_1} = \frac{\alpha}{\lambda} \left[\frac{h \cdot \frac{\delta V}{\delta e}}{\alpha} \right] - \sum_{i=1}^{i=n} (q_i - t_i) \frac{\delta X_i}{\delta e} \tag{9.15}$$

Note that if we differentiate the individual's budget constraint with respect to e this sets $\sum q_i \frac{\delta X_i}{\delta e} = 0$. Substituting this into equation (9.15) results in:

$$\frac{G_e}{G_1} = \frac{\alpha}{\lambda} \left[\frac{h \cdot \frac{\delta V}{\delta e}}{\alpha} \right] - \sum_{i=1}^{i=n} \frac{\delta t_i X_i}{\delta e} \tag{9.16}$$

The LHS of equation (9.16) expresses the marginal rate of transformation of the public good with respect to the numeraire, and can be labelled *MRT*. The term in brackets on the RHS is the sum of the individual marginal rates of substitution of the public good with respect to income and can be represented by ΣMRS (which is the benefit of producing a pure public good). Equation (9.16) can therefore appear as:

$$MRT = \left(\frac{\alpha}{\lambda} \right) \Sigma MRS - \sum_{i=1}^{i=n} \frac{\delta t_i X_i}{\delta e} \tag{9.17}$$

Equation (9.17) is equation (9.4) in the text.

9.5.2   *Browning's MCF for labour taxes*
Browning (1987) assumed that the funds to pay for the public project are to come from a tax on labour income (wages). The taxes include federal income taxes, state/local income taxes, sales taxes and payroll taxes. The welfare cost of the existing tax system is first estimated, and then an increment in taxes is considered (which is needed to finance the public project).

Total welfare cost   The welfare cost triangle (*W*) has an area equal to half base times height. With the change in base (*dL*), and the height given by *wm*, i.e., the change in the wage rate brought about by the taxes (where *w* is the average wage rate and *m* is the tax rate):

$$W = 1/2 \; dL \; wm \tag{9.18}$$

Since L is a function of the wage rate, the differential dL is given by:

$$dL = \frac{dL}{dw} \cdot dw = \frac{dL}{dw} \cdot wm \tag{9.19}$$

Substitute for dL from equation (13) into equation (12), and multiply top and bottom by $L_2(1-m)$, produces:

$$W = 1/2 \left[\frac{dL}{dw} \cdot wm \right] wm = 1/2 \left[\frac{dL}{dw} \cdot wm \right] wm \frac{L_2(1-m)}{L_2(1-m)} \tag{9.20}$$

On rearrangement this becomes:

$$W = 1/2 \left[\frac{dL}{dw} \cdot \frac{w(1-m)}{L_2} \right] \frac{m^2}{(1-m)} wL_2 \tag{9.21}$$

Since the elasticity of labour supply η defines the term in brackets in equation (15), we have as the final expression:

$$W = 1/2\eta \frac{m^2}{(1-m)} wL_2 \tag{9.22}$$

To estimate W we therefore need to know three things: (i) The supply elasticity η, the existing wage bill wL_2, and the marginal tax rate m. Browning's best estimates are $\eta = 0.3$, $wL_2 = \$2\,400b$, and $m = 0.43$ to obtain $W = \$116.78b$.

Marginal welfare cost   The marginal welfare cost of public funds is defined as dW/dR, where dR is the change in tax revenue. The numerator is again the 'half base times height' expression. With $wm + wm'$ the height and dL_2 as the base, we have:

$$dW = 1/2 \; (wm + wm') \; dL_2 \tag{9.23}$$

Since η is defined relative to labour supply in the presence of existing taxes L_2, this means:

$$\eta = \frac{dL_2}{dm} \frac{w(1-m)}{L_2}$$ (9.24)

Which on rearranging becomes:

$$dL_2 = \left[\eta \frac{L_2}{(1-m)} \right] dm$$ (9.25)

Note that dL_2 is the actual change in labour supply and not just the compensated effect. Also, by definition $m' = m + dm$. Using these two definitions (dL_2 and m') in equation (9.23) produces:

$$dW = 1/2 \ (wm + wm + wdm) \ \eta L_2 \ dm/(1-m)$$ (9.26)

This simplifies to:

$$dW = \left[\frac{(m+0.5dm)}{(1-m)} \right] \eta w L_2 dm$$ (9.27)

The denominator of *MCF* will now be derived. The change in revenue is the sum of (a) additional tax revenue if earnings do not change and (b) the revenue lost due to any reduction in earnings:

$$dR = d[t(wL_2)] = wd[tL_2] = wL_2 dt + wtdL_2$$ (9.28)

As $t = m + dm$, equation (9.28) is equivalent to:

$$dR = d[t(wL_2)] = wL_2 dt + wdL_2(m + dm)$$ (9.29)

Substituting equations (9.27) and (9.29) into the definition of *MCF* forms:

$$\frac{dW}{dR} = \frac{\left[\frac{(m+0.5dm)}{(1-m)} \right] \eta w L_2 dm}{wL_2 dt + wdL_2(m+dm)}$$ (9.30)

From this general expression, Browning considers two polar cases. The first case is the only one that we will focus on. Here the assumption is made that the government spends on a project that gives no benefits *per se*, but gives the individual an income effect. This is exactly what takes place with a transfer payment. What this implies is that the loss from paying the tax is offset by the income of the project, and so there is no net effect on the individual's income. As a result, *wdL* (the second term on the denominator of equation (9.30)) equals zero. With this value, equation (9.30) reduces to:

$$\frac{dW}{dt} = \left[\frac{(m+0.5dm)}{(1-m)}\right] \eta \frac{dm}{dt} \qquad (9.31)$$

Equation (9.31) is equation (9.8) in the text. Note that Browning is effectively defining the marginal welfare cost (*MEB*) as *dW/dt*.

PART IV

10   Distribution weights

10.1   Introduction

We have now completed Part III, where market prices were either inadequate or absent. The emphasis was on efficiency with income distribution aspects in the background. In Part IV distributional issues are brought centre stage. Weights are important in dealing with intragenerational distribution and this is the subject matter of the current chapter. As we shall see in the next chapter, weights also play a role in intergenerational distribution, which is the concern underlying the social discount rate.

Tresch (1981) writes: 'The distribution question is the single most important issue in all of cost–benefit analysis'. This probably explains why it is also the most controversial aspect of CBA. As was illustrated in the case study of Indian tax reform, it makes a big difference whether distributional weights are included into the evaluation. The end result is that one either does, or does not, include distributional considerations *explicitly* (implicitly, everyone uses weights). As this book takes the position that weights are essential, clearly we are taking sides over this issue. However, we will still attempt a balanced discussion by presenting the counter arguments and justifying rather than simply assuming our position.

The introduction sets out what are distribution weights and why they are needed in CBA. One of the reasons is to record the desirability of redistribution in-kind as opposed to cash transfers. This argument is then spelled out in detail in terms of the distributional externality argument first developed in Chapter 5. Once one decides to use them, weights can be included in CBA in two distinct ways. The main way is to attach them to the income changes (benefits and costs) of the groups (rich and poor) affected by the public project. The other way is to attach them to the good that is being provided by the government. In this second form, distribution weights become a part of the determination of shadow prices.

There are two methods that can be used to estimate the distribution weights. The 'a priori' approach is one method. This involves specifying a parameter that applies to the whole income distribution that reflects society's aversion to inequality. The first three applications use this method in one form or another. For natural gas price deregulation, the weighting function is made explicit. In the next case study, related to an evaluation of a hypothetical cure of arthritis, the weighting function is implicit. Both these applications use the framework whereby the distribution weights are applied to the benefit and cost categories. The alternative framework, including weights in the determination of shadow prices, is illustrated for the case of gasoline products.

The other method of estimating the distribution weights is to use the imputational or revealed preference approach covered in previous chapters. Because this method has the potential to be very useful in applied CBA, we have a separate section explaining the basic principles. The final case study uses the imputation approach. It provides a test of the redistribution in-kind reasoning presented in the introduction.

10.1.1 What are distribution weights?

Let us begin with a review of compensation tests as given in Chapter 2. When the benefits B are greater than the costs K, then there is sufficient for the gainers to compensate the losers. B is the willingness to pay for the programme, and K is what the losers must receive in compensation. It is important to note that the B and K used in this test are measured on the basis of the existing distribution of income. If this is not optimal, then one may question the validity of the test *even if compensation takes place* (that is, an actual Pareto improvement is effected). The notion of ability to pay needs to be incorporated into CBA as well as willingness to pay. The main way of allowing for ability to pay in CBA is to use distribution weights.

To understand the meaning of these weights, consider a society with just two individuals (or groups), person 1 who is rich and person 2 who is poor (or otherwise socially deserving). Assuming that social welfare W is individualistic, and measuring individual utilities by their income, we can write:

$$W = W(Y_1, Y_2)$$

A government expenditure decision has the effect of changing the individual incomes Y_1 and Y_2. The resulting change in W depends on both the size of the income changes and the importance of each income change on social welfare:

$$\Delta W = \left(\frac{\Delta W}{\Delta Y_1}\right)\Delta Y_1 + \left(\frac{\Delta W}{\Delta Y_2}\right)\Delta Y_2$$

This can be converted into cost–benefit terms as follows. Assign person 2 as the gainer and person 1 as the loser. In this case, the change in income by person 2 is positive and represents the benefits B, while the change in income by person 1 is negative and represents the costs $-C$. Finally, for notational convenience, define the terms in brackets as a_1 and a_2 (as we did in equation (3.6)). Then the criterion becomes:

$$\Delta W = a_2 B - a_1 C \qquad (10.1)$$

In equation (10.1), a_1 and a_2 are the distribution weights. The equation states that the extent of the change in social welfare is given by the difference between the weighted benefits and the weighted costs (and we want these to be positive). The weights reflect the social significance of a small change in the income of a person. As can be checked by reviewing equations (3.7) and (3.8), income makes the individual better off (this is the individual's marginal utility of income) and making individuals better off increases social welfare. From this we deduce that the weights register the 'social marginal utility of income' (society's valuation of the individual's marginal utility of income).

10.1.2   Why include distribution weights?

The traditional argument for *not* using distribution weights in expenditure decision-making is that the tax-transfer system can be used to bring about any desired income redistributional changes. That is, if a programme affects the poor more than the rich, one should use cash subsidies to ensure that the poor have sufficient income for their needs, rather than justify the programme simply on distributional grounds. Within this framework, one chooses the programmes that are the most efficient, and leaves to the tax-transfer system distributional objectives.

At heart, the traditional view follows the rule associated with the names of Thiel and Tinbergen. That is, the number of targets must match the number of instruments. There are two objectives, efficiency and distribution. Therefore there should be two instruments. Public expenditure is the instrument for efficiency. The tax-transfer system is the one for distribution.

It is well known that the targets and instruments view is correct only if: (a) objectives and instruments are linearly related; and (b) objectives are distinct (where satisfying one objective automatically fulfils the other) and not mutually exclusive (one objective is the opposite of the other) (see Fleming, 1968). In addition it requires a centralized policy setting whereby the system as a whole is set optimally. On the other hand, CBA works on the understanding that the policy-maker in one area cannot assume that policy in other areas will be set optimally. Specifically, one is aware that income distribution is not optimal. This needs to be recognized in the sectors making public expenditure decisions.

The qualifications to the target-instruments approach just mentioned give rise to two main reasons for questioning the traditional argument for excluding distribution issues. We now present these reasons.

The administrative cost argument   There are administrative costs involved with transferring income from the rich to the poor using the tax system. The existence of these administrative costs inherently requires that the weight to the rich be different from that of the poor. Since this argument is presented in full in Ray

(1984), and in outline in Brent (1990), we can give here a different version that follows immediately from the analysis of the *MCF* given in the previous chapter.

Assume that society wishes to transfer *T* units from the rich (group 1) to the poor (group 2) using the income tax system. The poor will gain by the amount *T* and the rich lose by the amount *T*. Thus, $B = C = T$. In line with the traditional view of the *MCF*, we assume that to raise taxes equal to *T*, there is an excess burden which leads to an $MCF > 1$. Applying the *MCF* term to equation (10.1) produces:

$$\Delta W = a_2 B - a_1 (MCF) C$$

If society uses the tax-transfer system optimally, transfers will take place until this equation is equal to zero. Using $B = C = T$, this implies: $a_2 T - a_1 (MCF)T = 0$, and:

$$\frac{a_2}{a_1} = MCF$$

With $MCF > 1$, we have $a_2 > a_1$. The weight on the benefits going to the poor should exceed that on the costs incurred by the rich. Let us be clear why unequal weights are optimal. In the absence of an excess burden, equation (10.1) is appropriate. Optimality would necessitate transfers taking place until $a_2 = a_1$. Because of the excess burden, transfers must stop short and be complete at an optimum with $a_2 > a_1$.

This administrative cost argument seems to have been accepted by traditional CBA economists. However, it is then applied in a particular form. Zerbe and Dively (1994), following Harberger (1984), interpret the argument to be saying that the *MCF* sets the upper bound to what can be the relative size of the distribution weights. Weights any higher than this are not justified because it would then be more efficient to transfer in cash. If, for instance, the excess burden estimate for the United States income tax is taken to be the average of Browning's most plausible estimates of 31.8 per cent and 46.9 per cent (making the *MCF* = 1.39), then a_2 should never be set more than 1.39 times a_1.

Even if one accepts the assumptions behind this latest interpretation, one still endorses the principle that equal weights are not optimal. If one then goes on to assume that the tax-transfer system has not *in fact* been set optimally, then one has a strong case for using relative weights greater than 1.39. Specifically, if political factors (of a non-welfare maximizing nature) limit the use of the tax-transfer system to below the optimal social level, then values greater than 1.39 may be acceptable.

The objective of redistribution in-kind   Another problem with using the tax-transfer system for redistributing incomes is that this operates using money/cash income. Often, society prefers to assist people in-kind, that is, providing particular goods and services rather than cash income. For example, health care is publicly provided in most countries of the world rather than giving people cash in order that they can purchase health services (or health insurance) for themselves. By providing these particular goods and services, society ensures that the needy receive these services, and not some other goods. If the needy are assisted in cash terms, a part would be spent on items for which the rich have no interest in seeing that the poor receive, such as cigarettes and alcohol. When the rich care about just a subset of the goods consumed by the poor, it is actually Pareto efficient for assistance to be given in-kind (see section 10.1.3 below).

Given that the way that income is redistributed is a separate social objective, the tax-transfer system cannot be used. Expenditure decisions need to be made considering both efficiency and distribution. One can see this in the targets-instruments framework in two ways. Firstly, one can think of redistribution in-kind as a third social objective (that is, redistribution is the second objective and the *way it is redistributed* is the third objective). Assigning an in-kind distribution instrument is required. But this is precisely what a public project entails. Dams, roads, schools and hospitals are all in-kind expenditures. If projects are also assigned to achieve efficiency, they must share this with the in-kind distributional objective. Secondly, as efficiency is being applied to the distributional objective, the two objectives are not distinct (Pareto efficient redistribution is the goal) and the one-objective, one-instrument rule breaks down.

This second reason for not relying on the cash tax-transfer system supports the idea that unequal distribution weights should be used. But, as it is redistribution in-kind that is being highlighted, it argues also for a two-tier system of distribution weights (cash and in-kind), as we now explain.

10.1.3   Weights for distribution in-kind

In-kind weights can be considered to be a special case of the public good explanation for assistance to the poor given in Chapter 5. In-kind weights are relevant when it is a subset of the poor's consumption expenditures that is the public good. The Orr model explains why cash transfers take place. However, many countries rely more on redistribution programmes that provide the poor with in-kind rather than cash assistance. The analysis behind in-kind transfers needs to be developed.

To a traditional economist, in-kind transfers are inefficient and therefore less worthwhile than cash transfers. The poor would prefer cash assistance as they can spend this as they wish. In-kind transfers restrict consumption to the particular good being provided.

In the Hochman and Rodgers (1971) analysis (and the Orr model discussed in Chapter 5), the preferences of the rich must be considered if transfers are to be voluntarily voted for by the rich. The weakness in the traditional approach to in-kind transfers is that it ignores the fact that the rich care about how income is redistributed. The rich may prefer that any assistance is given in-kind, since none of this will be spent on goods for which the rich do not have a positive externality.

There is therefore a conflict of interest to be resolved. The poor prefer assistance in cash and the rich prefer assistance in-kind. Brent (1980) resolved this conflict by giving priority to the rich. This was because if the rich do not vote for a transfer, it will not take place. Hence, the poor would be better off with an in-kind transfer than no transfer at all. Armed with the 'priority principle', we can now revise the Orr analysis.

The Buchanan and Stubblebine definition of externality used in the Orr analysis of cash transfers was based on utility functions for the rich (group 1) and the poor (group 2) of the form:

$$U^1 = U^1(Y_1, Y_2); \quad U^2 = U^2(Y_2)$$

where Y_1 is the income of the rich and Y_2 is the income of the poor. Hochman and Rodgers called this 'general interdependence'. The poor get satisfaction only from the goods they can buy with their income. The rich receive benefits from their income and also the total consumption by the poor (and cash transfers would positively affect all of this).

Alternatively, with in-kind considerations important, the externality would be specified as:

$$U^1 = U^1(Y_1, T_2); \quad U^2 = U^2(Y_2)$$

where T_2 is a subset of the total consumption by the poor (the subset that generates the positive externality to the rich). (T_2 can stand for train services used by the poor in rural areas, which is how it will be defined in the case study 10.3.4). This specification, called 'particular commodity interdependence', results in a Pareto-relevant version of condition (5.4) that takes the form:

$$MU^1_{T_2} > MU^1_{Y_1} \tag{10.2}$$

Relation (10.2) states that the satisfaction to the rich from the particular goods that are being transferred should exceed the cost to the rich. (Strictly, one needs to sum the MU^1 over all the poor members of society who receive in-kind assistance T_2 and apply P/N onto the cost side, as we did in Chapter 5. But, the logic comes out clearer if we stick to the simplified expression (10.2).) Brent formalized his priority principle as:

$$MU^1_{Y_1} > MU^1_{Y_2} \qquad (10.3)$$

This expression signifies that the rich would obtain greater utility from retaining their income rather than providing cash transfers to the poor. The rich give *priority* to their total consumption rather than that of the poor.

Together expressions (10.2) and (10.3) imply:

$$MU^1_{T_2} > MU^1_{Y_2} \qquad (10.4)$$

The inequalities (10.2) and (10.4) are important in explaining the relative size of weights in the CBA criterion (1.4). This defined positive net benefits as:

$$a_{2.k}B - a_{2.m}R - a_{1.m}L$$

where $a_{2.k}$ was the social value of benefits in-kind and $a_{2.m}$ the social value of benefits received in money income form. The financial loss term L was also in money income terms and it therefore had the weight $a_{1.m}$. Following the reasoning in section 5.2.2 (and the definitions given in section 10.1) we can identify the MU's as distribution weights. This means that we can identify in criterion (1.4):

$$a_{2.k} = MU^1_{T_2}; \quad a_{2.m} = MU^1_{Y_2} \quad a_{1.m} = MU^1_{Y_1}$$

Relations (10.2) and (10.4) therefore fix:

$$a_{2.k} > a_{2.m}; \quad a_{1.m} > a_{2.m} \qquad (10.5)$$

The weight to benefits in-kind exceeds the weight to benefits in cash; and the weight to a unit of income to the rich is higher than the weight to the poor (in opposition to the Orr model implication that $a_2 > a_1$). These inequalities in (10.5) have a straightforward interpretation. In order for redistribution in-kind to be worthwhile, redistribution in cash must *not* be beneficial.

10.1.4 Two ways of including weights in CBA

Even if one decides to employ explicit distribution weights, there is a choice as to how to incorporate them. Equation (10.1) attaches the weights to the benefits and costs. This is the way that distribution weights are applied in this book. There is though an alternative framework developed by Feldstein (1972a) that can be used. This attaches the weights to the project output. In this way the weights form part of shadow prices that combine efficiency and distribution. A simple way of seeing this will now be explained.

Let X be the output of the public project. This can be thought to be a single item, such as irrigation, education or transport. The inputs M can be represented by many different items (for example, concrete, electricity, labour, gasoline, and so on). The output can be valued by the shadow price S which is determined by efficiency and distribution. The social benefits are represented by $S.X$. The value of the costs, being spread over a large number of inputs, can be approximated by the market prices of the inputs P_m. The cost–benefit calculation appears as:

$$\Delta W = S.X - P_m.M \tag{10.6}$$

In this form, the weights that make up S are a mixture of the pure distribution weights a_i and the marginal propensity to consume on the particular public output by the various income groups. This mixture is called the 'distributional characteristic' of a product. It reflects the extent to which the good is consumed by people with a high social marginal utility of income (see case study 10.3.3).

The essential difference between equation (10.1) and (10.6) is that distribution and efficiency are distinct in the former and merged in the latter. In (10.1), benefits are solely the efficiency (WTP) effects, and the distribution weight is applied to this to produce $a_2.B$.

In equation (10.6), the benefits are the full social effects $B = S.X$, and distribution and efficiency are combined in S.

10.1.5   The 'a priori' school of distribution weights

(This section relies heavily on Brent, 1984a). The main way that the policy literature sets about determining the distribution weights is to specify in advance ('a priori') a set of reasonable assumptions and to derive the weights from these assumptions.

A good example of this approach can be seen in Squire and van der Tak (1975). They make three assumptions:

i.   Everyone has the same utility function. Thus, one need know only the utility function (U) for one individual to know the welfare function (W).
ii.   Let the one (representative) individual's utility function exhibit diminishing marginal utility with respect to income. The theoretical literature usually uses the constant elasticity marginal utility function as it is one of the most analytically convenient functions that satisfies this assumption. The social marginal utility of any group i is then given by:

$$a_i = Y_i^{-\eta} \tag{10.7}$$

where η is a positive constant signifying the elasticity of the social marginal utility function.

iii. The final step is to set a value for η, society's aversion to inequality. In general, there are no theoretically accepted procedures for deriving η, except for extreme cases. So let us examine first these extreme cases, and then in-between values.

Efficiency only: $\eta = 0$ At one extreme, set $\eta = 0$. Equation (10.7) produces the result that every group's weight must be the same, i.e., equal to 1. This is implicitly what traditional CBA assumes. With $a_2 = a_1 = 1$, we get the efficiency criterion $B - C$. Thus, when mainstream policy analysts claim to be 'ignoring' distribution weights, they are really simply advocating the use of a particular set of weights. If setting any weight is judged to be 'subjective', then the mainstream view is being subjective like everyone else. There is nothing scientific about using implicit weights rather than specifying them explicitly as we recommend.

Maximin: $\eta = \infty$ At the other extreme, one can set η equal to infinity, in which case only the effect on the worst-off individual in society matters. This in the Maximin principle associated with Rawls (1971). This position has serious difficulties as part of a social criterion for CBA. If a project benefits the worst-off individual, and makes *everyone else worse off*, then this weighting scheme would approve the project. This is the opposite of the 'numbers effect' introduced in Chapter 2. Numbers do not count at all. In addition, it ignores the fundamental policy dilemma that one should consider the trade-off between objectives when making social choices. The criterion $a_2B - a_1C$ acknowledges both efficiency (with B and C) and distribution (with the weights a_2B and a_1). By using this criterion one is furthering social welfare (not just efficiency, not just distribution).

Intermediate values: $0 < \eta < \infty$ Outside of the extremes, one has little guidance. Squire and van der Tak recommend that $\eta = 1$ should be assumed (though values between 0 and 2 are possible in a sensitivity analysis). In this case, the distribution weights are determined by the inverse of a group's income: $a_i = Y_i^{-1}$. This is the (inverse) proportionality version referred to in the last case study of Chapter 9. Often this version is expressed relative to a group at the average income level $\bar{Y}$ (one has 'constant relative inequality aversion'). This means that:

$$\frac{a_i}{\overline{a}} = \frac{Y_i^{-1}}{\overline{Y}^{-1}} = \frac{\overline{Y}}{Y_i} \tag{10.8}$$

Equation (10.8) states that if, for example, a person has an income one-fourth the size of average income, then a unit of his/her income would be given a weight four times as large as the average income person. Someone with above-average income would get a weight below one. This relation is depicted in Diagram 10.1. One can see that the relative weight $a_i/\overline{a}$ is a smoothly declining function of relative income $Y_i/\overline{Y}$.

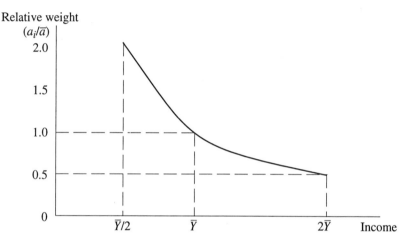

The inverse proportional weighting function is shown. When a group has an income equal to the average, its relative weight is 1. When its income is half the average, the relative weight is 2, and when its income is twice the average, the weight is 0.5.

Diagram 10.1

There are three main drawbacks with the 'a priori' approach just outlined.

i.   There is no clear basis for selecting a value for η.
ii. The weights are attached to income. Often a person is considered socially needy by a mixture of income and non-income criteria. For example, students have low incomes, but that is not of much social concern. Age is often a vital part of the specification of being needy. Thus, persons over the age of 65 that have low incomes are of prime social concern.
iii. The weighting function gives a complete specification of weights for all income groups. But not all income groups are of social concern. Does

society really care whether one middle-income person gets more than another? Surely it is the incomes of those that are below the poverty level which matters (and those at the upper-income ranges). Redistribution among the middle income ranges is usually of little social significance.

10.2 The revealed preference approach

We start with an outline of the basic principles of using the revealed preference/imputation approach and proceed to discuss the actual estimation of the weights. To illustrate the points being made, reference will be made to the results of trying to estimate the weights behind railway closure decisions in the UK. (The estimates come from a number of different models, see Brent, 1979, 1980, 1984b and 1991b.)

10.2.1 Basic principles

The imputation approach proceeds on the assumption that the decision-maker cannot without assistance make the necessary 'a priori' judgements concerning η. What is recommended is that one derive the implicit weights behind past society decisions. From these past weights one can understand the implications of using particular values. These past weights can then provide the basis for specifying new values for future social cost–benefit decisions.

This point needs developing because it not well understood. Musgrave (1969) presented an argument which seemed to question the internal logic of the imputational approach. He asked why, if past weights are going to be judged to be correct and used in the future, one needs them. If past decision-maker behaviour is to be interpreted as 'correct', we can just let them continue to be correct in the future and let them specify the weights they want.

The response to this argument is that the decision-maker is neither correct nor incorrect, but unclear. There is a great deal of uncertainty as to what 'fair' or 'equitable' means. The decision-maker needs assistance from the CBA analyst in order to articulate what precisely is intended. As has been said by Titchener, 'meaning is context'. In the context of past decisions one can firm up one's meaning of equity and thereby set the distribution weights.

To see how this method works, consider the study of past railroad closure decisions in the UK first referred to in Chapter 2. Railroads that were unprofitable were threatened by closure. The government claimed it would subsidize such railroad lines that were in the 'social interest'. It would use a cost–benefit framework, that is, make its decisions by a careful comparison of social benefits and costs. The beneficiaries, group 2, were the users of unremunerative branch lines in the rural areas. These areas were alleged to include a disproportionally large percentage of the 'economically weak'. Thus, distribution was an important consideration. The losers, group 1, were the taxpayers who had to pay for the railroad subsidies. From a statistical analysis of 99 past government closure decisions, a_2 in equation (10.1) was estimated to be 1.1, and a_1 was estimated to be 0.9.

The issue is: how useful is it to know these weights? We are *not* suggesting that these weights necessarily are the correct ones to use in making future social decisions. What is being advocated is this. Say one is asked to put a weight on the incomes of train users in remote areas relative to that for the general taxpayer. One can say with confidence that the weight should be greater. But how much greater? It is likely that one would not know how to go about answering this question (which is asked in the 'a priori' approach).

However, if one knew that the past weights were 1.1 relative to 0.9, one would have a basis, lodged in experience, for answering the question. The values a_2 = 1.1 and a_1 = 0.9 have a precise meaning. They are the values that one would use if one wanted to reproduce the past set of social closure outcomes; they are a vote for the status quo. If one thought that the past outcomes had the right mix of distributional fairness relative to efficiency, then one would use the same values in the future. If one thought that past outcomes were unfair to the poor, then one would want to give a higher weight to a_2. While if one thought that too many inefficient decisions had been made, one would want to give a lower value to a_2 (or a higher value to a_1). Regardless of one's values, one would understand the meaning of the numbers that one was assigning to the weights.

10.2.2   Estimating the distribution weights

We begin by defining the social welfare function in a way that is consistent with imputing the distributional weights. From this base we can discuss estimation issues.

A practical definition of the welfare function W is: the set of determinants, and their respective weights, behind government expenditure decisions. CBA assumes that one knows the objectives (basically, efficiency and income redistribution). Thus, the problem of estimating W reduces to one of estimating the weights.

Consider the case where there are three benefit and cost categories given by B_1, B_2 and B_3 (a cost is just a benefit with a negative sign). W (strictly, the *change* in social welfare) is usually assumed to be linear, in which case the weights, the as, are constants. W takes the form:

$$W = a_3B_3 + a_2B_2 + a_1B_1 \qquad (10.9)$$

Equation (10.9) assumes constancy in two senses, the social indifference curves over B_1, B_2 and B_3 are straight lines (hyperplanes), and the family of curves are parallel (a sort of constant income effect assumption).

In the imputational approach, W is revealed by decision-making behaviour. Let D be a past expenditure decision, where $D = 1$ means the project has been approved and $D = 0$ means that the project was rejected. If the decision-maker was motivated by social welfare maximization, $D = 1$ only if $W \geq 0$, and $D = 0$ only if $W < 0$. Thus D can stand as a proxy for W.

Modern estimation approaches proceed from equation (10.9) in two steps. First, an error term u is introduced to reflect all the random non-welfare determinants of government expenditure decisions. Then the framework is defined in probabilistic terms. The dependent variable is recast as the probability P that the decision-maker would approve a project:

$$P = a_3 B_3 + a_2 B_2 + a_1 B_1 + u \qquad (10.10)$$

The idea is that one finds the estimates of the a coefficients that make the observed, past values of D and B most likely. (This is the basis of the maximum likelihood technique for estimating coefficients (such as Probit and Logit) that was employed in earlier chapters.)

Equation (10.10) is now ready to be applied. We will assume throughout that B_2 is specified as the money-income effect of a low-income group, and B_1 is the money-income effect of the taxpayers (group 1). The coefficients a_1 and a_2 are the income distribution weights that we have been discussing in this chapter. A number of different specifications of B_3 will be considered.

i.   Assume $B_3 = 0$. This is the simple welfare maximization model of equation (10.1). The first thing to test is whether the regression coefficients are significantly different from zero. Assuming that the estimates are significant, one then needs to check that the overall explanatory powers of the regression are high. The lower the goodness of fit (or likelihood ratio) the more likely it is that other benefit and cost categories have been wrongfully omitted (the equation had been 'misspecified').

An important point to understand is that the estimation technique allows one to obtain only the relative values of the weights; the absolute values cannot be known. This is because the B values are themselves specified in only a relative and not an absolute scale. A simple way to see this is to consider altering the currency unit of the independent variables. Say that originally, all B amounts were expressed in British pounds and now we express them in United States dollars. At an exchange rate of 2 dollars to the pound, all the numbers representing the independent variables would be twice as large. Since behaviour is unaltered (the set of past decisions would remain unchanged) estimation adjusts by halving the values of all coefficients. The weights would therefore appear half the size. However, since all the coefficients are scaled down to the same extent, the relative size of the weights would be the same irrespective of which currency unit the B values are expressed.

ii.   Assume B_3 is a purported third social welfare objective. Say we wish to test whether there is a 'numbers effect' in addition to efficiency and distribution and we define B_3 in this way. A significant a_3 indicates that the decision-maker acted 'as if' the numbers effect was important. But one needs to be careful about what other social welfare B variables are to be included in the equation. There are two main considerations here. (a) When efficiency and distribution variables are included one has to ensure that variables are specified in a non-overlapping way. Thus, in the closure context, when the numbers effect was included, the other social objectives had to be included in per person units. (b) When not all three social objectives are included, one can have a problem of identifying what it is that has been estimated. There is no point in estimating a weight without knowing which social objective it is to be attached.

For instance, Brent (1991b) invoked the numbers effect to reflect a concern for employment (avoiding unemployment). Many macroeconomic studies try to uncover the relative weight of unemployment and inflation. But, if inflation is a proxy for inflation and the unemployment rate represents the numbers effect, where is the weight for the efficiency objective? In these circumstances, it is not surprising that Joyce (1989) found that the macro weights were not statistically significant and unstable (they varied over time).

iii. Assume B_3 is a purported non social welfare objective. It is to be expected that real-world public expenditure decisions are going to be a mixture of the social welfare objectives and what can be termed political self-interest or institutional variables. What these variables might be depends very much on the particular decision-making context. Almost always it is worth testing whether the personal identity of the decision-maker had an influence. A dummy variable is inserted which takes the value 1 when a given individual made the decisions, and is zero otherwise. In the UK rail closures context, there were six persons who were the Minister of Transport over the period covered. Only one of the six had a significant influence, and this raised the coefficient of determination by 1 per cent.

10.3   Applications

Most of the CBA literature that adopts explicit distribution weights relies on the 'a priori' approach. The first three applications are therefore within this weighting 'school'. The study by Loury (1983), considering natural gas price deregulation in the United States, emphasizes the role of distribution weights as being the mechanism for recording the trade-off between objectives (efficiency and distribution). Next comes Thompson et al.'s (1984) evaluation of the benefits of a potential cure for arthritis. They use weights, seemingly without knowing it. The third case study, by Hughes (1987), illustrates how weights can be used to form part of the shadow prices for gasoline products. The final case study by Brent (1979) obtains weights for redistribution in-kind using the alternative (imputational) estimation method.

10.3.1 *Natural gas deregulation*

Price controls, at some point in time, are observed in almost all economies. Interfering in the price mechanism can be expected to lead to inefficiency. The policy issue is whether any distributional gains exist to offset the efficiency losses. Price controls are therefore a good choice of application to highlight the role of distribution weights as a trade-off mechanism between efficiency and distribution. In the current case study we consider the reverse policy issue, i.e., the removal of price controls. This means the choice is between efficiency gains and distributional losses.

Loury (1983) analysed the effect of the removal of wellhead price controls in the natural gas industry in the United States. Under 1978 legislation (the Natural Gas Policy Act) there was a provision to decontrol (deregulate) existing restrictions. Natural gas was the single largest domestic source of energy in the United States. In 1979, undiscovered recoverable natural gas was estimated to be 16 per cent higher than undiscovered oil resources in equivalent energy units. Natural gas was an important component of federal energy policy.

To estimate the effects of any price control, one must have some idea of what the price would have been without the price control. The gas regulation in the United States applied only to interstate transactions, with intrastate production and sales largely unaffected. This enabled the intrastate activities to be used as a reference point. Prices in the interstate market were higher (by at least a third in 1977) than the regulated market. As a result, the intrastate market comprised an increasing share throughout the 1970s. There was therefore evidence of non-zero supply and demand elasticities.

The efficiency gain from deregulation was measured by a consumer surplus triangle as outlined in Chapter 3. Diagram 10.2 explains the basis of the calculation in terms of the demand and supply for natural gas. The 1981 regulated price $\bar{P}$ was set by legislation at \$1.90 per million cubic feet (mcf). The regulated quantity Q_S was estimated to be 20.2 trillion cubic feet (tcf). (A US trillion is 1 000 billion, and a billion is a thousand million.) At the regulated quantity Q_S, the consumer WTP (given by the demand curve) was $\tilde{P}$. $\tilde{P}$ was specified as a weighted average of industrial and residential/commercial prices for oil (which is assumed the main competitor for natural gas) and put at \$5.09 per mcf.

The consumer surplus for the marginal unit is the difference between the WTP and the regulated price, i.e., $\tilde{P} - \bar{P}$. This is shown as the distance AB in the diagram. Following deregulation, quantity will expand and the marginal consumer surplus will decline. At the market equilibrium quantity Q_e of 22.0 tcf, WTP will equal price and there is no marginal consumer surplus. The total consumer surplus

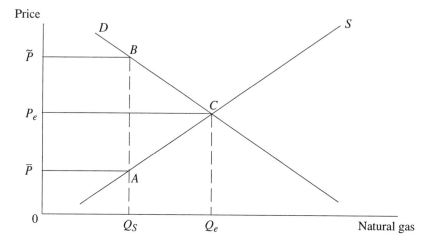

The regulated price is $\bar{P}$. At this price the WTP exceeds the marginal cost by AB. AB is the consumer surplus on this unit. If the price were deregulated, output would expand to the equilibrium quantity Q_e. The total consumer surplus from moving back to the market equilibrium is the triangle ABC.

Diagram 10.2

from the increase in quantity from Q_S to Q_e is the triangle ABC. The area of this triangle is: $1/2(\tilde{P} - \bar{P})(Q_e - Q_S)$ which is $1/2(\$3.19\text{tcf})(1.8\text{mcf})$, or \$2.87 billion.

This estimated efficiency gain can be viewed as a short-run estimate, say for 1981, just after the price decontrol. In the long run, one would expect that both the elasticity of demand and supply would increase. In terms of Diagram 10.2, one can think of the long-run demand curve starting at B and then swivelling to the right (to show the greater elasticity). Similarly, the long-run supply curve starts at A and swivels to the right. In the long run then the triangle ABC would be larger. Assuming elasticities of demand and supply of 0.3 in the long run (as opposed to 0.2 in the short run), Loury increased the estimate of the efficiency gain to \$5.23 billion. Column 2 of the evaluation summary in Table 10.1 (which combines Loury's Tables 13.3 and 13.4) shows the annual consumer surplus gain (after he made some adjustments). The rise in elasticity explains why all the gains, losses and transfers increase over time in Table 10.1.

Column 3 of Table 10.1 presents Loury's estimates of the gains from oil import reductions. His argument was that there was a higher monopoly price set by OPEC when gas was regulated. This was an external cost of gas price regulation. Removing the gas price regulation reversed the process. The lower expenditure by consumers on oil was then an external benefit of the gas price deregulation.

Table 10.1   Gains and losses from gas decontrol (billions dollars)

Year	Efficiency gains	Oil import gains	Net transfers	Equity loss
1981	4.15	2.56	4.11	1.30
1982	4.43	4.73	11.13	3.52
1983	4.70	6.57	15.14	4.79
1984	4.96	8.11	17.38	5.50

Source: Loury (1983)

Emphasis now switches to the distribution loss of price deregulation. Column 4 of Table 10.1 shows the size of the income transfer from the general population to private shareholders of natural gas. This estimate assumes that transfers to the government are neutral and only that going to the private sector significantly affects the distribution of income. Because of data limitations, it also had to be assumed that the ownership of natural gas by income class was in line with the overall US distribution of stockholdings. This distribution was heavily skewed in favour of higher-income groups. For example, the lowest-income class ($0–$4 999) constituted 22.0 per cent of the families in 1971 and owned 2.4 per cent of the stock, while the highest-income group (above $100 000) comprised 0.2 per cent of the families and owned 30.2 per cent of the stock.

The final step in the analysis is to apply weights to the transfers going to the natural gas stockholders. This was done in a relative way, using the form set out in equation (10.8), but using $\eta = 0.5$ as the inequality aversion parameter:

$$\frac{a_i}{a_m} = \frac{Y_i^{-0.5}}{Y_m^{-0.5}} = \left(\frac{Y_m}{Y_i}\right)^{-0.5} \tag{10.11}$$

Because group i (the stockholders) are an above-average income group in this case study, the relative weight should be less than one. Taking a weighted average (by number of families) Loury derived a social weight of 0.365. This was not applied to all of the transfer amounts given that pension funds owned 13.3 per cent of the stocks. The share owned by individuals was therefore 86.7 per cent. Applying this share to the social weight produced an adjusted weight of 0.316 (called an 'implied social cost'). Multiplying the transfers in column 4 by 0.316 produced the equity loss figures that appear in the final column of Table 10.1.

Discussion   There are two aspects of the analysis that require further elaboration.

i.   *The CBA Framework*   Loury's way of undertaking a CBA can be viewed as a special case of the general CBA framework introduced in Chapter 1 and developed in this chapter. Underlying equation (1.4) was the distribution and efficiency criterion ignoring the in-kind distinction: $a_2(B-R) - a_1(C-R)$. Collecting terms in R, we obtain:

$$a_2B - a_1C - R(a_2 - a_1) \tag{10.12}$$

R is the repayments term which is identical to Loury's transfer concept. The efficiency effects, B and C relate to the US economy as a whole and can therefore be judged to be distributionally neutral, i.e., $a_2 = a_1$. The transfer term can be interpreted to be a redistribution between stock owners (with a weight a_S) and the average-income group (with a weight $\bar{a}$). Effectively then, Loury's CBA criterion is this version of equation (10.12):

$$(B - C) - R(\bar{a} - a_S)$$

The first term is the efficiency gain and the second is the equity loss.

ii. *The inequality aversion parameter*   Loury's assumption of $\eta = 0.5$ is very interesting in the light of the controversy over using distribution weights in CBA. Most analysts who use non-unity distribution weights rely on the 'a priori' approach and adopt the constant elasticity form (10.7) with $\eta = 1$. The problem is that these analysts consider this as only *moderately pro-poor*. After all, they would seem to say, this leads to proportional weights. Using the analogy with taxation, they stress that proportional taxes are certainly not progressive taxes. What is ignored is that the case for progression (for either taxes or distribution weights) has never been conclusively proven to be 'fair'. What has much wider support is the much weaker axiom that the rich should pay more taxes than the poor, or that the weight for the rich be lower than the weight for the poor. In these circumstances, an inequality aversion parameter between 0 and 1 would seem to be in order, with $\eta = 1$ as the upper bound rather than the norm. For this reason Brent (1990) suggested that a value of $\eta = 0.5$ be adopted as the benchmark rather than 0 or 1.

Loury's study (by using $\eta = 0.5$) enables us to get some appreciation of what this compromise position implies. Even 'truly' moderate aversion to inequality can make a difference to the outcomes of public policy decisions. Note that the equity loss in 1983 and 1984 is larger than the efficiency gain.

The study shows that a necessary ingredient is that there be very large differences in the distribution of income (as there were among stockholders). Not everything was predetermined by the assigned value of η.

10.3.2 *Distribution weights and chronic arthritis*

Thompson et al.'s (1984) study of arthritis starts off as a standard attempt to test the validity and reliability of using WTP estimates to measure the benefits of health-care expenditures. Just like contingent valuation studies in the environmental field, the focus is on the usefulness (or otherwise) of using survey methods to extract preference evaluations. However, once a valuation for arthritis has been extracted, the authors express an unease with the concept of WTP. They feel the need to adjust it in order to be equitable as well as efficient. Although they do not seem to recognize the fact, Thompson et al. are simply applying distribution weights. In the process of making this weighting process explicit, we hope to show that one does not need to go 'outside' of CBA to incorporate equity. If one uses distribution weights explicitly, one can adjust WTP for ability to pay in a consistent fashion.

Arthritis was chosen as a good disease to assess WTP because it does not affect life expectancy. It was thought that people have severe difficulties assessing probabilities of the risk of losing one's life (which are required in the statistical life approach to measuring health benefits). By not being life threatening, the benefits of arthritis are more likely to be understood by those with the disease. WTP is more applicable than the human capital approach, seeing that the latter method is clearly inappropriate for dealing with this disease, as earnings are not an issue (people continue to work, albeit in pain).

Thompson et al. undertook a survey of 184 subjects with osteoarthritis (61) or rheumatoid arthritis (123). The subjects were asked their WTP for the elimination of arthritis in both dollar terms, and as a percentage of their income. The questions were asked twice, at entry and at exit from a one-year study of arthritis. The results are listed in Table 10.2 (their Table 6).

The main objective of the research was to see how many patients, if asked in uncoercing ways, could express their WTP for hypothetical cures in reasonable ways. The answer was 27 per cent. This compares unfavourably with the CV studies presented in earlier chapters. This is one study which supports the reluctance by those in the health-care field to use WTP as a measure of benefits and costs.

But what we are most interested in is Thompson et al.'s argument that using WTP as a percentage of income is a more equitable index of economic benefits than is the absolute amount of WTP (which is affected by ability to pay). They therefore gave most emphasis to the finding that patients were on average willing to pay 17 per cent of family income for arthritis cure. They explain (on p. 200) how WTP should be adjusted to 'avoid' the ability to pay problem. They

write: 'The problem might be avoided if WTP is calculated, if the mean proportional WTP is calculated, and if this proportion is multiplied by total income
to determine total, adjusted, societal WTP'.

Table 10.2   Response rates and stated WTP for arthritis

Annual income	Number	% Answering WTP question	Mean WTP ($ per week)
Less than $3 000	8	13	10
$ 3 000–$ 4 999	26	31	17
$ 5 000–$ 9 999	42	26	35
$10 000–$14 999	34	41	38
$15 000–$19 999	20	31	27
$20 000–$29 999	22	32	33
More than $30 000	15	47	54
No response	17	29	42
Total	184	32	35

Source: Thompson et al. (1984)

In the appendix, we show that this adjustment process implies for two groups
1 and 2:

$$Social\ WTP = W_1\left(\frac{\bar{Y}}{Y_1}\right) + W_2\left(\frac{\bar{Y}}{Y_2}\right)$$

If we regard the WTP of the poor patients (group 1) as the benefits and the WTP
of the rich patients (group 2) as the costs, then Thompson et al.'s criterion can
be restated as:

$$Social\ WTP = B\left(\frac{\bar{Y}}{Y_1}\right) - C\left(\frac{\bar{Y}}{Y_2}\right) \tag{10.13}$$

Now compare the terms in brackets in expression (10.13) with equation (10.8).
It is clear that the adjustment recommended by Thompson et al. is simply to
use $a_i/\bar{a}$ for each of the two groups. The benefits and costs are to be weighted
by an amount given by the ratio of average group income to a particular group's
income. This means that, although Thompson et al. do not recognize this, they
are advocating a particular set of distributional weights. The weights they

recommend are exactly those of Square and van der Tak based on the 'a priori' approach. Thompson et al.'s procedure therefore has all the strengths and weaknesses of that approach.

10.3.3   Gasoline shadow prices with distribution weights

In the first two applications we saw distributional weights being used when attached to the efficiency categories of benefits and costs. In this study of gasoline prices in Indonesia, Thailand and Tunisia by Hughes (1987), we see the second way that distribution weights can be used, namely, as a part of shadow prices. Hughes's study was a tax analysis. However, as pointed out in previous chapters, there is a very strong link between fixing shadow prices and setting tax rates. We exploit this similarity here.

To understand the case study, we need first to present the complete shadow pricing formula which combines distribution and efficiency. This is the so called 'many-person Ramsey Rule' derived by Diamond (1975). Then we isolate the distribution part of the formula and use Hughes's estimates as they relate to this component.

The many-person Ramsey rule (see Atkinson and Stiglitz (1980)'s equation (15–25)) determines the excess of the shadow price S over marginal cost MC by:

$$\frac{S_i - MC_i}{S_i} = \frac{\left(1 - \bar{a} \cdot r_i\right)}{e_{P_i}} \tag{10.14}$$

where:

$\bar{a}$ = average of the distribution weights a_h across households;
r_i = distributional characteristic of the good i; and
e_{P_i} = the price elasticity of demand.

If $\bar{a} = 0$, we return to the simple Ramsey rule given by equation (6.6). Thus we can interpret equation (10.14) as adjusting efficiency considerations on the denominator (reflected by price elasticities) by including distributional considerations on the numerator. The higher is r, the more the public project is consumed by low-income groups (those with a high distribution weight). This higher value is subtracted on the numerator. This means that the shadow prices will be lower (closer to marginal costs) for those project outputs consumed mainly by low-income groups (holding price elasticities constant).

Since it is only the distributional dimension that is different from what we have discussed before, we concentrate on this by assuming all price elasticities are equal to 1 in equation (10.14). Hughes implicitly sets $\bar{a} = 1$. The right-hand side of the shadow price equation reduces to $1 - r_i$. Shadow prices must be inversely related to the distributional characteristic of the good i. It is thus r_i that needs to be clarified and estimated.

The distributional characteristic is defined as:

$$r_i = \sum_h \left(\frac{x_i^h}{X_i} \right) a_h \qquad (10.15)$$

The term in brackets is the share of total consumption X (of good i) by household h. r_i uses these shares to find the weighted average of the distribution weights. It is this that constitutes the distributional characteristic of the good. The higher is r_i, the more the good is consumed by those with a high social marginal utility of income. Thus, because it is low-income groups that will have the high r_is, the shadow pricing rule is negatively related to r_i.

To obtain values for the a_h, Hughes used $W = \Sigma h \ log \ y_h$ as the welfare function. This is an additive individualistic social welfare function as discussed in Chapter 2, except that one is adding utilities in a logarithmic form. Note that it is the *marginal* utility that defines the distributional weights not the total utility (welfare). The marginal utility that comes from Hughes's W is $a_h = 1/y_h$. The ubiquitous constant elasticity form with $\eta = 1$ is being used, as in the Squire and van der Tak approach.

Using these weights, and data on the consumption shares by household, the calculated r values for petroleum and various other products in the countries in Hughes's study are presented in Table 10.3 (based on his Table 20–7).

The r values for petroleum products can be compared with the median characteristic value for all goods. In all countries, the more comprehensive category of petroleum products (i.e., gasoline) has a lower than median value. On distributional grounds, it is a product group where shadow prices can be set high relative to their MCs (or in Hughes's terms, it is a product group that can be more highly taxed).

The results for individual products in the petroleum group are not uniform. Kerosene is a product that has one of the highest r values, even higher (in 3 of 4 cases) than primary cereals, a product group typically thought to be consumed by the poor. On the other hand, diesel oil and liquid petroleum gas have low r values.

The variation found in the distributional characteristic values between countries, and between product groups, points to a major advantage of using shadow prices as the vehicle for distribution weights (rather than applying them to B and C categories). When weights are attached to the efficiency effects it has to be *assumed* that the weight one is attaching is applicable to all consumers of the public project. While if the weights are used in shadow pricing, one can *estimate* via the shares what the actual extent of distributional considerations are being furthered by promoting a product. However, it does mean that more data is required with the shadow pricing approach.

Table 10.3 Distribution characteristic (r) for various products

	Indonesia	Thailand (1975)	Thailand (1982)	Tunisia
Petroleum Products:				
Gasoline	0.236	0.379	0.406	0.253
Kerosene	0.754	1.035	1.136	0.871
Diesel oil	—	—	—	0.276
Liquid petroleum gas	0.245	0.395	0.397	0.461
Other items:				
Cereal (rice/wheat)	0.724	1.048	1.082	0.765
Fats and oils	0.685	0.747	0.765	0.549
Tobacco products	0.635	0.736	0.715	0.572
Clothing	0.522	0.717	0.737	0.468
Electrical goods	0.172	0.496	0.545	0.396
Electricity	0.359	0.454	0.457	0.465
Median characteristic value	0.501	0.673	0.625	0.461

Source: Hughes (1987)

10.3.4 Rail closures and in-kind distribution weights

The railway closure research area was first discussed in Chapter 2 when the numbers effect was introduced. Appendix 2.6 presented the regression results and section 10.3 of this chapter reported some additional results in the context of explaining the imputational approach. The main emphasis now is on the validity of including in-kind weights in CBA. In particular we wish to provide evidence in support of the weight inequalities set out in equation (10.5). It will be recalled that these were derived from the model which specified redistribution in-kind as a Pareto-relevant externality for the rich. Our test is in line with the imputational approach. That is, we wish to see whether decision-makers acted 'as if' redistribution in-kind was important.

To avoid constant rechecking of equations by the reader, we present a summary version of the closure model which is self-contained. (Basically we are retelling the story of Appendix 2.6 without the numbers effect.) Designate group 1 as rail users, group 2 as taxpayers and group 3 as road users who avoid congestion if the rail service is retained. There are two categories of benefits to the rail users, time saving B_1 and fare savings B_2. Time savings are in-kind and have the weight $a_{2.k}$. Fare savings are in cash and have the weight $a_{2.m}$. Road-users' benefits are given by B_3. These are in-kind and have the weight $a_{2.m}$. Finally, we have the financial losses borne by the taxpayers B_4, which being in cash form (and borne by group 1) has the weight $a_{1.m}$. The determinants of railway closures can therefore be expressed as:

$$a_{2.k}B_1 + a_{2.m}B_2 + a_{3.k}B_3 + a_{1.m}B_4 \qquad (10.16)$$

To test the theory behind in-kind redistribution, we wish to be able to estimate and compare coefficients. This is a problem in a regression context because the benefit and cost categories are not measured in the same units. To solve this, one can rescale the determinants by expressing them in 'standardized units'. That is, one divides the independent variables by their sample standard deviations. A 'large' or 'small' variation for a particular independent variable is therefore defined relative to the number of standard deviations it is away from its mean. If one observation for a B variable has a value that is one standard deviation above its mean, then this is comparable in size to a one standard deviation of some other B variable above its mean. The following estimates of the distributional weights were obtained from using these standardized units:

$$a_{2.k} = 1.1; \quad a_{2.m} = 0.7; \quad a_{1.m} = 0.9.$$

These findings were therefore consistent with the inequalities in equation (10.5). That is, $a_{2.k} > a_{2.m}$ and $a_{1.m} > a_{2.m}$.

In-kind benefits to car users (B_3) were not a part of the theory of section 10.1.3. Interestingly, the standardized weight for this category was the highest at 1.7. This probably reflects a policy inconsistency. One would assume that car users had higher incomes than train users and therefore would be less deserving on distributional grounds. Again we emphasize one of the main advantages of using the imputational approach. Once we uncover an inconsistency we know what weights *not* to use in future.

10.4   Final comments
The summary and problems sections follow.

10.4.1   Summary
Whether to include distributional weights in CBA is a very controversial subject. Although we come down in favour of using explicit distributional weights, it should be clear that we do so in a minimalist way. The only requirement we have is one of inequality, not of magnitude. The weight on the changes in income

for the poor should be greater than the weight for the rich. If redistribution in-kind is important, the weight on income in-kind should be greater than for cash income. How much greater this should be we do not state (or know).

Underlying our position was the realization that the existing distribution of income was not optimal. One reason for this was the existence of administrative costs involved in using the tax-transfer system. These costs mean that equal weights are not optimal. The corollary of this result is worth contemplating. If equal weights are optimal, how can it be that the *MCF* would be greater than unity? Excess burdens cannot exist as they would inhibit the use of taxes for redistributive purposes, and hence prevent the equalizing of the weights in the first place.

The other reason why we argued in favour of unequal distribution weights was due to the recognition of redistribution in-kind as a social objective. Public projects are in essence in-kind activities, not cash expenditures. To justify a premium on in-kind weights we invoked the 'redistribution as a public good' argument. Note that this argument is an individualistic case for setting distribution weights. Many are against distribution weights because they oppose values being imposed on individuals by governments. In our in-kind justification, we appeal to the possibility that the rich may be better off, according to *their* preferences, if unequal weights are used in CBA and redistribution in-kind takes place.

The real issue then is not whether to use distribution weights, but how to set them. We identified two estimation methods, the 'a priori' and the imputational.

From the case study on natural gas deregulation, we see the fundamental role of distribution weights in action. The weights show the trade-off between the efficiency and distribution objectives. It is true that using unequal weights means sacrificing some efficiency. But this is acceptable provided that there is a positive distribution gain to outweigh the loss of efficiency. If this is so, and this depends in part on the weights, then social welfare is being improved. This highlights the fact that modern CBA tries to maximize *W* not efficiency.

Because there are some who think that CBA is only about efficiency, they think that one needs to go outside of CBA to introduce notions of equity and fairness. The authors of the case study on arthritis seemed to hold such a view. They made an adjustment to WTP, which can be shown to be equivalent to using inverse proportional, distribution weights. Thus, CBA via distribution weights already provides a framework for incorporating efficiency and equity.

A central theme of the chapter was that analysts have a wide choice of options with regard to distribution weights. We contrasted 'a priori' and imputational approaches. We also explained that one can use weights to help determine shadow prices, as an alternative to attaching them to the efficiency effects. The case study on petroleum products was based on the shadow pricing approach. The main message was that one needs to use an incidence study to accompany the use of distribution weights. The weights are to be attached to income effects. But what the income effects will be is determined by the incidence of the public project (that is, the effects of the project on the distribution of income). In the shadow pricing approach, which relies on the distributional characteristic of a good, one is in fact undertaking a simplified incidence analysis. One is assuming that the gains of the project are allocated according to the past consumption shares by household income groups.

The imputational approach is a way of estimating the distribution weights. But it can also be used in a positive (predictive) way to explain actual expenditure decisions. In the study of past railway closure decisions in the UK, we saw that the decision-maker acted *as if* motivated by the reasoning behind the redistribution in-kind as a public good argument.

10.4.2   Problems

The following questions are based on Weisbrod's (1968) pioneering imputation study. They focus on his deterministic method for estimating the distribution weights. We simplify his method and the calculations.

Let there be two projects X and Y. In both cases assume that the benefits go to the poor (group 2) with a weight a_2, and the costs are incurred by the rich (group 1) with a weight a_1. The CBA criterion is: $W = a_2 B - a_1 C$. Project X has $B = 6$ and $C = 2$ and thus has a positive efficiency impact of 4. Project Y has more benefits going to the poor with $B = 12$, but the costs are also greater with $C = 10$. The efficiency impact of project Y is therefore only 2. Despite the lower efficiency impact of project Y, we find out that project Y was approved and project X was rejected.

1. If the decision-maker was rational, the distributional advantages of project Y must have compensated for the lower efficiency of project X. Set the welfare level of project X equal to its efficiency value of 4. Then assume that the welfare level of project Y must have been equal to this, or else the decision-maker would not have chosen it. Hence, deduce what the distributional weights must have been to have made the choice of project Y a rational decision. (Hint: there are two equations with two unknowns (the weights). The two equations correspond to the CBA criterion applied to the two projects.)

2. Weisbrod actually identified four groups, a white low- and high-income group and a non-white low- and high-income group. To use his technique to estimate the weights for the four groups, he had to consider four projects. His estimates of the weights were:

white, low income	=	−1.3
white, high income	=	+2.2
non-white, low income	=	+9.3
non-white, high income	=	−2.0

Do the relative sizes of the weights conform to the theory underlying distributional weights presented in this chapter? Are Weisbrod's estimates consistent with the assumptions identified as the welfare base to CBA (discussed in Chapter 2)?

3. What drawbacks do you see in Weisbrod's estimation technique? (Hint: can he include all the number of observations that are available, and can he allow for sampling error?)

10.5   Appendix

Here we derive the weighting scheme implied by Thompson et al.'s adjustment of WTP that was presented in section 10.3.2. We spell out step by step the calculations they recommend in order to adjust WTP for ability to pay.

Assume two individuals or groups: 1 the rich, and 2 the poor. Their WTP are WTP_1 and WTP_2. The traditional (efficiency) approach just adds the two to form the aggregate WTP. Thompson et al. recommend using a particular kind of weighted average. First express the two WTPs as percentages of the patient's income to obtain W_1/Y_1 and W_2/Y_2. The average of the two is:

$$Average\ WTP = \left(\frac{W_1}{Y_1} + \frac{W_2}{Y_2} \right) / 2 \qquad (10.17)$$

Thompson et al.'s 'social' WTP is the average WTP applied to the total income:

$$Social\ WTP = (Average\ WTP).(Y_1 + Y_2) \qquad (10.18)$$

By substituting (10.17) into (10.18), we obtain

$$Social\ WTP = \left[\left(\frac{W_1}{Y_1} + \frac{W_2}{Y_2} \right) / 2 \right].(Y_1 + Y_2) \qquad (10.19)$$

Taking 1/2 from the first bracket of (10.19) to the second produces:

$$Social\ WTP = \left[\left(\frac{W_1}{Y_1} + \frac{W_2}{Y_2} \right) \right].(Y_1 + Y_2) / 2$$

or,

$$\left[\left(\frac{W_1}{Y_1} + \frac{W_2}{Y_2}\right)\right].\bar{Y} \tag{10.20}$$

where $\bar{Y}$ is average income, i.e., $(Y_1 + Y_2)/2$. Finally, multiply out both terms in (10.20) by $\bar{Y}$ and rearrange to get the equation in the text:

$$Social\ WTP = W_1\left(\frac{\bar{Y}}{Y_1}\right) + W_2\left(\frac{\bar{Y}}{Y_2}\right)$$

11 Social discount rate

11.1 Introduction

Determining the social discount rate (SDR) is analogous to finding the distribution weights covered in the last chapter. Both distribution weights and the SDR involve attaching coefficients to the benefits and costs. For distribution weights, one values the benefits and costs that go to different individuals at the same point in time; while for the SDR, one values the benefits and costs that go to the same individuals at different points of time. In this chapter we concentrate only on intertemporal issues. We use the words income and consumption interchangeably to refer to project effects (benefits and costs). The subscripts 0 and 1 attached to variables and parameters are to be interpreted as time delineators. That is, 0 is the current period, 1 is the next period. We will often be distinguishing time periods in terms of generations, in which case, 0 is the current generation and 1 is the future (unborn) generation.

The mechanics of discounting was developed in Chapter 1. Here we explain how one can go about finding a value for i that appears in the NPV formula. The first section deals with the main themes. It defines the SDR and shows how setting i basically involves intertemporal weighting. It explains why the market rate of interest cannot be used to measure the SDR, and indicates the two main candidates, that is, the social opportunity cost rate (SOCR) and the social time preference rate (STPR). It will be argued that the STPR is the appropriate rate to use as the SDR. However, as we shall see, discounting practice is anything but homogeneous.

As the STPR is the recommended concept for the SDR, the theory section will focus on the two main alternative formulations of the STPR. The first is individualistic in nature and views the social SDR as correcting for an externality involved with individual savings decisions. The second formulation is outside the sphere of the Paretian value judgements which are normally assumed in CBA. It is thus authoritarian in nature and can represent the interests of unborn future generations relative to the existing generation.

The first application illustrates the primary function of the SDR as an instrument that focuses on the differential timing of effects. The second case study shows how the authoritarian approach goes about estimation of the SDR. One element in the authoritarian rate is the parameter which reflects the relative interests of current and future generations. This is called the *pure* STPR. The third case study explains how this parameter can be calculated and estimated for a large sample of countries. Given our interpretation of the determination of the SDR as a weight-setting exercise, the final application uses the imputational approach (highlighted in the last chapter) to reveal a social decision-maker's SDR.

11.1.1 Definition of the SDR

It is useful to go back to first principles to understand the concept of the SDR (see UNIDO, 1972). Investment, by its very nature, gives benefits over time. We take the simple two-period case where benefits today are negative (i.e., they are costs C_0) and there are positive benefits in the next period B_1. Total benefits B could then be expressed as:

$$B = -C_0 + B_1$$

Thus, CBA involves intertemporal choice. However, as pointed out in Chapter 1, the value of these benefits at different points of time are not the same. If C_0 is the basis for all the calculations (i.e., the numeraire), the benefits can be weighted relative to C_0 using the time-dependent weights a_t (a_t is the value of a unit of benefits in any year t):

$$B = -a_0 C_0 + a_1 B_1 \tag{11.1}$$

As a unit of benefits today is worth more than one in the future, the weights a_t will decline over time. If the rate of decline in the weights is a constant, i, then:

$$i = \frac{a_0 - a_1}{a_1} \tag{11.2}$$

The benefit stream can be expressed in *today-value* terms by dividing every term in equation (11.1) by a_0. Hence, the benefit stream B can be renamed the *NPV* and it can be represented by:

$$NPV = -C_0 + \left(\frac{a_1}{a_0}\right) B_1 \tag{11.3}$$

Equation (11.2) can be written equivalently as:

$$\frac{a_1}{a_0} = \frac{1}{1+i}$$

Substituting this value for the ratio of the weights into equation (11.3), we can produce the two-period CBA criterion:

$$NPV = -C_0 + \left(\frac{B_1}{(1+i)} \right) \qquad (11.4)$$

This derivation establishes the general definition of the SDR i as the rate of fall in the value of the numeraire over time. It also confirms our interpretation of the determination of the SDR as basically a weight-setting exercise.

11.1.2   The market rate of interest as the SDR

Consider the two-period CBA criterion given by equation (11.4). If we measure effects in terms of consumption, then the intertemporal choice is whether to consume output today or next period. This choice can be analysed using the standard Fisher diagram. Current consumption C_0 is on the horizontal axis and future consumption B_1 is on the vertical axis. The production possibilities curve PP' shows the maximum amount of future consumption that is technologically feasible by reducing current consumption (holding all inputs constant), see Diagram 11.1. The slope of the production possibilities curve is $1 + r$, where r is the marginal product of capital. r is also called the social opportunity cost rate (SOCR).

Society's preferences are given by the family of social indifference curves I, which has a slope $1 + i$, where i is the social time preference rate. The STPR is the rate at which society is willing to forgo consumption today for consumption in the future. At equilibrium, that is, for a social optimum, the slope of the social indifference curve I_1 equals the slope of the production possibilities curve. The optimum is shown as point E_1 in Diagram 11.1. Since at E_1 the two slopes are equal, $1 + i = 1 + r$, which implies that $i = r$.

If competitive financial markets exist, the market budget line MM' will go through point E_1. The budget line has the slope $1 + m$, where m is the market rate of interest. The fact that the slope of the budget line at E_1 equals the slopes of the other two curves produces the happy result:

$$i = m = r$$

This means that all three discount rates are equal. It is immaterial whether one bases discounting on the STPR, the SOCR or the market rate of interest. The market rate of interest is as convenient a rate to use as any other.

The situation just described is called a 'first-best' optimum, where the only constraint affecting welfare maximization is the production function (the PP'

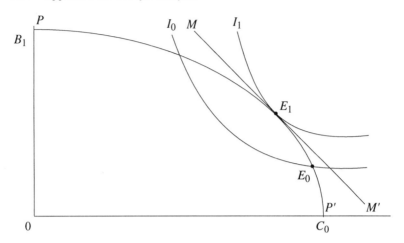

E_1 is the first-best optimum, where the production possibilities curve PP' is tangential to the social indifference curve I_1. At E_1, the time preference rate i is equal to the opportunity cost rate r. Both are also equal to the market rate of interest m. If there is an additional constraint, a second-best optimum takes place. The highest social indifference curve one can obtain is now I_0, at point E_0 on the production frontier. Here $r > i$.

Diagram 11.1

curve). If there exists some additional constraint, then one is in a 'second-best world'. In developing countries, the additional constraint is thought to be the absence of competitive financial and production markets. In developed countries, capital taxes are imposed that drive a wedge between what investors are willing to pay and savers are willing to receive. No matter the particular cause, as long as there is an additional constraint, one must now choose which rate to use as the SDR. Note that Feldstein (1977) estimated that, for the United States, the STPR was 4 per cent, while the SOCR was 12 per cent. So, there is a big difference in practice between the two rates.

A second-best optimum is depicted in Diagram 11.1 by point E_0. E_0 corresponds to the highest indifference curve I_0 that can be reached given the production and other constraints. I_0 is not a tangency point to PP' in the second-best world. At E_0 the slope of PP' is much greater than the slope of the indifference curve I_0. This means that $r > i$. This is typically the case, and is consistent with the Feldstein estimates for the United States.

One immediate implication of the second-best situation is that the market rate of interest m is no longer equal to *either* the STPR or the SOCR. The existence of additional constraints is therefore one reason why the market rate of interest should not be used as the SDR. The other reason, explored in greater depth in section 11.2, is that social indifference curves may not be the same as individual indifference curves. The *I* curves that are in Diagram 11.1 need not necessarily be based on the rate at which individuals are willing to save. Individual savings decisions may be distorted or judged too short-sighted.

11.1.3 *Alternative conceptions of the SDR*

Ignoring the unrealistic first-best world, in which case the market rate of interest is ruled out, the main choices for the SDR reduce to opting for the STPR or the SOCR, or some combination of the two. Of these alternatives, we will argue that the STPR is the most appropriate basis for the SDR. To justify our selection of the STPR, we need to explain what is wrong with the alternative approaches.

The SOCR as the SDR The basic weakness of the SOCR is that it is the wrong concept to use for the SDR. The idea behind the SOCR is that if the funds that are devoted to the public project could have earned, say, 10 per cent as a rate of return on investment in the private sector, then the government should not use a rate less than this. Anything less would be depriving society of funds that could be more productively used elsewhere. The weakness in the argument is that, essentially, it is assumed that a fixed budget constraint is in existence. Private funds are being squeezed out and these may be more valuable if devoted to investment than used for current consumption. While this may be a legitimate concern, it is not an SDR issue *per se*, which is inherently one of valuing consumption today rather than the future (i.e., an STPR issue). If investment is undervalued relative to consumption, then (strictly) this is a matter of determining the correct shadow price of capital, not the SDR. We have discussed the shadow price of public funds in detail in Chapter 9. The distortionary effect of a capital or income tax does not directly fix society's intertemporal consumption preferences.

In sum, if investment is undervalued for any reason, one should incorporate a shadow price of capital, denoted *MCF*. The appropriate two-period CBA criterion would be:

$$NPV = -(MCF)C_0 + \frac{B_1}{(1+i)} \tag{11.5}$$

The shadow price of capital *MCF* is a different concept from the SDR *i*.

The weighted-average formula In an indirect way, it may seem that the SOCR does fix the SDR. Bradford (1975) has devised a two-period model where, (a) all of current funds comes at the expense of investment, and (b) all of the returns from the government project (received next period) are in terms of consumption. In these circumstances, the rate of fall in the numeraire over time, i.e. i, is greater than the STPR and equals the SOCR. (This is Bradford's case C.) However, this is just a special case. Interestingly, when one considers a two-period model, one almost forces the above-mentioned special conditions to hold. There is no point in investing in the second period in a two-period model. Thus, necessarily, all of the resources available would be devoted to consumption in the second period. A two-period model almost prejudges the SOCR to be the appropriate SDR.

The more general case is where only a part of the funds for public projects comes at the expense of investment (the rest comes from consumption), and a part of the future return from the project is reinvested (thus enhancing rather than detracting from total investment). This has led some, especially Harberger (1968), to argue that a weighted-average formula r^* be used as the SDR:

$$r^* = wr + (1 - w)\, i \tag{11.6}$$

where w is the share of the funds for the public project coming at the expense of investment (or private saving).

The main weaknesses of the weighted-average formula have been identified by Feldstein (1972b). With r^* used to fix i, equation (11.4) would appear as:

$$NPV = -C_0 + \left(\frac{B_1}{(1 + r^*)} \right) \tag{11.7}$$

Feldstein compares this criterion (11.7) with the correct criterion equation (11.5) to show why the weighted average approach is invalid. A simple example proves the point. Say there are no future benefits, i.e., $B_1 = 0$ (which makes the CBA a cost-minimization evaluation). Equation (11.7) would produce the criterion, $-C_0$ while equation (11.5) requires $-(MCF)\, C_0$. We obtain the paradox that the weighted-average approach, which was devised to ensure that opportunity costs were incorporated, now actually ignores the MCF! As with the SOCR school, the problem with the weighted-average approach is to confuse the two issues (the SDR and the shadow price of capital) rather than treat both issues separately.

11.1.4   *Discount rates in practice*
Tresch (1981) writes: 'In our view, it would be difficult to mount a decisive case for or against any rate of discount governments might choose over a range of 3 percent to 20 or even 25 percent'. This verdict is understandable given the different schools of thought on what should determine the SDR. But it is

still fair to say that the lower part of the range would be associated with the STPR approach, and the higher values recommended by the SOCR advocates. In this connection, it is interesting to see where actual decision-makers lie in this continuum. Do they choose low values in the STPR range, or the higher ones associated with the SOCR?

The main study of discount rates actually used by US government agencies was carried out by Staats (1969). He extracted the SDRs that the agencies claimed that they used in 1969. Table 11.1 reports Staats's findings. Tresch, commenting on these rates, points out that inflation was low in 1969. Thus, these rates would be indicative of what were thought to be the real discount rates. He claims the rates 'are indicative of the variations that persist to this day'.

Table 11.1   Discount rates used in US government agencies

Agency	Rate of discount
Defense	10–12% (only on shipyard projects and air stations).
Agency for International Development	8–12% (this applies to investments in LDCs).
Department of the Interior	6–12% (energy programmes); 3–6% (all other projects).
Health, Education and Welfare	0–10%.
Tennessee Valley Authority Department of Agriculture Office of Economic Opportunity Department of Transportation	All < 5%.
All other agencies.	No discounting.

Source: Staats (1969)

The results show that of the 23 agencies covered, Defense used the highest rates of 10–12 per cent, 10 used values of 0–12 per cent, and 13 claimed not to use any discounting procedure at all. It would appear then, as suggested by Tresch, that these low rates indicate support by US government officials for the STPR approach rather than the SOCR school.

11.2   The social time preference rate
(A recent survey of theories of the STPR, which also incorporates the numbers effect, is provided by Brent, 1991e, 1992.) Individuals living today make

savings decisions concerning how they wish to allocate their lifetime resources between today and the future. The issue is to what extent social time preference rates should be based on these individual time preference rates. The complication is that as yet unborn individuals will exist in the future. The preferences of future generations need to be included in a social time preference function, as well as the preferences of those currently living.

Two approaches will be developed. The first is individualistic. The preferences of the existing generation is given priority, but these preferences depend on the consumption of future generations. The second approach is authoritarian. The existing generation is assumed to have what Pigou called 'a myopic telescopic faculty' in regard to looking into the future, in which case the government needs to intercede and replace individual time preferences with a distinct social perspective which explicitly includes the preferences of future generations.

11.2.1   An individualistic social time preference rate

Sen (1972) provided a model which explains why it is that individual saving decisions may not be optimal in the presence of an externality. The analysis covered in this section is based on Layard's (1972) summary. The externality arises because the current generation care about the consumption by the future generation. An individual's heir will be part of the future generation and clearly this would expect to give positive benefits (though possibly not as much as the individual values his/her own consumption). In addition, an individual living today may receive some (small) benefit from other people's heirs consuming in the future. As a consequence, we can assume that each individual in society makes the following valuation of one unit of consumption according to whom consumes it (see Table 11.2). That is, the individual values one unit of consumption that s/he receives as worth 1 unit, and values the consumption by others as some fraction f_i of a unit, depending on whether that other person is living today, an heir of a person living today, or the individual's own heir.

Table 11.2   Values of a unit of consumption to various groups

Person or group doing the consumption	Marginal value
Consumption by the individual now	1
Consumption by the individual's heir	f_1
Consumption by others now	f_2
Consumption by others' heirs	f_3

Source: Layard (1972)

Assume that one unit of consumption forgone (saved) by the present generation leads to m units extra of consumption by the next. m is the market return on saving. Let the individual's own heir receive $(1 - t)$ of the return, where t is the intergenerational tax rate (say, death duty or estate tax). This means that the individual's heir gets $(1 - t)m$ from the unit saved, and the heirs of other individuals obtain the tax (via a transfer) from the return equal to tm. An optimal saving plan requires that the individual save until the extra benefit equals the cost (the unit of consumption forgone). The value to the gain by the individual's own heir is $f_1(1 - t)m$ and the value to the gain by the heirs of others is $f_3 tm$. The extra benefit is the sum of the two gains, i.e., $f_1(1 - t)m + f_3 tm$. Equating this marginal benefit to 1 (the unit of cost) and solving for m produces:

$$m = \frac{1}{(1-t)f_1 + (t)f_3} \tag{11.8}$$

Equation (11.8) is the free market solution. Now we determine the return on saving if the individual were to be involved in a (voluntary) collective agreement, just as we did in Chapter 6 when considering redistribution as a public good. There we assumed that when one individual paid a unit of taxes to be transferred, everyone else was required to make the same contribution. This time we suppose that when an individual saves one unit, every other individual does the same. As before, the decision on whether everyone will save one more unit is to be decided on the basis of a referendum. The return from this collective saving plan is $m*$. Let there be n individuals in society, each with one heir. The extra benefit to each individual is the $m*$ that goes to the individual's heir (valued at f_1) and the $m*$ that goes to each of the $n - 1$ heirs of others (valued at f_3). In sum, the extra benefit is $m* f_1 + (n - 1) m* f_3$. The extra cost is the unit given up by the individual and the $(n - 1)$ units given up by others (with a value of f_2) making a total $1 + (n - 1)f_2$. Equating the extra benefit and cost, and solving for $m*$, we obtain:

$$m* = \frac{1 + (n + 1)f_2}{f_1 + (n - 1)f_3} \tag{11.9}$$

What has to be established is the relative size of the market-determined rate m and the socially optimal rate $m*$. That is, one has to compare equations (11.8) and (11.9). Only by chance will $m = m*$. The comparison can be facilitated by: (a) assuming that $t = 0$ in equation (11.8), which makes $m = 1/f_1$, and (b) considering a large population (n approaches infinity), which makes the limit of $m*$ equal to f_2/f_3. Under these conditions $m > m*$ if:

$$\frac{1}{f_1} > \frac{f_2}{f_3} \qquad\qquad (11.10)$$

Obviously, the inequality holds only for certain parameter values and not for others. So it is not inevitable that the market rate must overstate the social rate. But let us consider the following set of values: $f_1 = 0.4$; $f_2 = 0.2$; and $f_3 = 0.1$. This set has the property that the individual is very egoistic. While the consumption of others (including one's own heir) does have a positive value, all of them have low values relative to consumption by the individual, which is valued at the full amount of 1. As a consequence, the ratio of the values on the right-hand side of the relation (11.10) are closer together (being both external to the individual) than the ratio on the left-hand side (which has the ratio with the individual's own consumption being valued). With the specified particular values inserted in relation (11.5), we see that $2.5 > 2$. In this case, the market rate of interest would overestimate the social rate.

Layard points out that no one yet has tried to use this externality argument to produce an actual estimate of the STPR. But, we have just seen an argument which suggests that the market rate can be used as an upper limit as to what the social rate should be. This boundary value can then be used as the alternative value in a sensitivity analysis for the discount rate.

11.2.2   *An authoritarian social time preference rate*
The issue is how to allow for the preferences of unborn generations. One approach is to use the preferences of the existing generation to represent the future. Usually, one can assume that individuals are the best judge of their own welfare. But Pigou has argued that, for intertemporal choices, the individual suffers from myopia. That is, the individual has a 'defective telescopic faculty' causing future effects to be given little weight. There are three main reasons why the individual is claimed to be myopic.

i.   Individuals may be thought irrational. Irrationality in the context of savings decisions may occur because individuals might not have sufficient experience in making such choices. Unlike intratemporal choices (e.g., buying bread and milk), savings decisions are not made every day. Without making such choices repeatedly, it is difficult to learn from one's mistakes.
ii. Individuals do not have sufficient information. To make sensible intertemporal choices one needs to compare lifetime income with lifetime consumption. Most people are not able to predict with any precision what their lifetime incomes are going to be.

iii. Individuals die, even though societies do not. If an individual does not expect to live into the future, then saving for the future will not take place. The individual's survival probability would provide the lower bound for an indivualistic SDR (called the 'pure time preference rate'); but it may be ignored if society wishes that every generation's consumption be given equal value.

This myopia has caused many authors to consider an authoritarian SDR. The starting point is the value judgement that society should be responsible for future generations as well as those currently existing. Equal consideration does not, however, imply equal generational weights. There are two aspects to consider. Firstly, over time, economic growth takes place which means that future generations can be expected to be richer (consume more) than the current generation. Secondly, as assumed in Chapter 10 concerning income going to different groups at the same point in time, there is diminishing marginal social value of increases in consumption. The additional income going to those in the future should be valued less than the additional income going to the current generation.

These two aspects can be combined in the following manner. Equation (11.2) defines the SDR *i*. If we divide top and bottom of this expression by the percentage change in income over generations $(Y_1 - Y_0)/Y_0$, we obtain:

$$ i = \left[\frac{(a_0 - a_1)/a_1}{(Y_1 - Y_0)/Y_0}\right]\left[\frac{(Y_1 - Y_0)}{Y_0}\right] $$

The first bracketed term defines the elasticity of the social marginal utility of income (the percentage change in the weight divided by the percentage change in income), which we have denoted by η in previous chapters. The second bracketed term is the growth rate of income over generations. Call this growth rate *g*. The determination of *i* can therefore appear as:

$$ i = \eta\, g \tag{11.11} $$

Equation (11.11) shows that the two considerations can simply be multiplied to obtain the SDR. For example, if $\eta = 2$, then, with the growth rate of income of 2 per cent, the SDR is 4 per cent. This is how Feldstein's value of 4 per cent (stated earlier) was derived for the STPR for the United States.

Some authors, such as Eckstein (1961), add to the expression for *i* a term ρ to reflect the 'pure rate of time preference'. This is the rate that society discounts effects that are received by generations yet unborn. The STPR becomes:

$$i = \rho + \eta \, g \qquad\qquad (11.12)$$

Individuals living today (with their myopic view) would want to discount the future just because it was the future (and hence would not include them in it). So even if the future generation had the same income as today (implying that distribution was not an issue), they would still want a positive SDR. Including ρ in equation (11.12) ensures that i was positive even with $g = 0$. (The derivation of equation (11.12) is shown in the appendix.)

Equation (11.12) is the Squire and van der Tak (1975) formula for the STPR (which in the project appraisal literature is called the 'consumption rate of interest' CRI). A positive rate of pure time preference puts a premium on the current generation's consumption. Squire and van der Tak recommend for ρ, 'fairly low values – say, 0 to 5 per cent – on the grounds that most governments recognize their obligation to future generations as well as to the present'.

11.3   Applications

All the case studies covered here rely on the STPR as the underlying concept for the social discount rate. Cohn (1972) focuses on the implication of having a high discount rate for the choice between: (i) eradicating a disease completely, and (ii) allowing it to continue. Eradication ties up resources today. Allowing the disease to survive saves resources today, but requires resources for treatment in the future. The basic role of the SDR as the device for indicating intertemporal priorities is thereby illustrated.

The second and third case studies are based on the authoritarian STPR formula. Kula (1984) uses the formula to derive estimates of the SDR for the United States and Canada. One component of the formula is the rate of pure time preference. Brent (1993) shows how values for this rate can be derived from estimates of changes in life expectancies.

In section 11.1.1, the SDR was shown to be an intertemporal weighting scheme. The last chapter suggested that the imputational approach was a useful way of deriving weights. Thus, the last application by Brent (1989) uses the revealed preference approach to extract the implicit SDR behind past farming loan decisions.

11.3.1   Discounting and malaria eradication

The old saying related to the health-care field is that 'prevention is better than cure'. The article by Cohn questions this logic by recognizing that there is an intertemporal distinction between prevention and cure. If one waits till an illness occurs, rather than trying to prevent it today, one incurs the costs at a later date. The greater the discount rate, the less important will be the future costs, and the less beneficial will be a policy to devote all the resources today to obtain complete eradication of the disease. The disease with which Cohn was concerned was malaria.

Because no explicit measure of the benefits was made, Cohn's study should be interpreted as a cost-minimization analysis. The Government of India calculated that malaria eradication would cost 800 million rupees (US$100 million) over 10 years. The control programme that was in existence cost around 68 million rupees annually indefinitely, and would rise slowly with population growth. It was thought that, if one looked only 3 to 4 years beyond the 10 years, a break-even point would be reached. Thereafter eradication, by being free, would be much cheaper. But, Cohn stresses, this ignores discounting.

Cohn argued that for developing countries, those most likely to be engaged in anti-malaria programmes, the SDR would not be less than 10 per cent. A 30-year time horizon was chosen to make the comparison (any costs over 30 years in the future when discounted at 10 per cent would be negligible anyway). The discount rate was (for some unspecified reason) adjusted downwards for 2 per cent annual growth in population. (For an interpretation of this adjustment, see problem 2 in section 11.4.2.)

The cost streams for the two alternative anti-malaria schemes are summarized in Table 11.3 (the costs are in millions of rupees). The table shows that at low discount rates the eradication programme is preferable (cheaper); while the opposite is true at high rates. One cannot decide between eradication and control without knowing the SDR. At an (adjusted) rate of 14 per cent, one is indifferent between the two programmes. Thus, for SDR's above 14 per cent, prevention (i.e., eradication) is *not* better than cure (i.e., control). Only for SDR's below 14 per cent is the old health-care adage valid in the context of anti-malarial programmes in India.

Table 11.3   Cost comparison of control and eradication programmes

Discount rate	Discount rate minus 2%	30-year control NPV	Eradication NPV
8	6	930	654
10	8	761	613
12	10	636	574
14	12	545	542
16	14	473	508
18	16	417	479

Source: Cohn (1972)

11.3.2   The social time preference rate

Kula has made estimates of the STPR for Canada and the United States which essentially use the authoritarian formula (11.12). However, he gives an individualistic interpretation. There is a 'Mr Average' whose intertemporal indifference curves are miniature versions of the social indifference curves. The STPR is therefore the same as Mr Average's time preference rate.

There are three ingredients in equation (11.12), namely, the rate of growth of consumption per head g, the elasticity of the social marginal utility of income η, and the rate of pure time preference ρ. How Kula estimated these ingredients will be explained in turn.

The rate of growth of per capital income (g)   Kula used a time series for the period 1954–76 to estimate the growth rate. He ran a regression of time on per capita consumption, with both time and consumption measured in logarithmic terms. The coefficient in such a regression produced the value for g. (The slope of the regression equation is $\Delta log\ c/\Delta log\ t$, which in turn is equivalent to $(\Delta c/c)/(\Delta t/t)$, and this is the definition of the growth rate g.) Using this method, Kula found that the growth rate for Canada was 2.8 per cent, and it was 2.3 per cent for the United States.

The elasticity of the social marginal utility of income (η)   Kula uses the individual's (Mr Average's) marginal utility of income to measure the social marginal utility of income. We have stressed a number of times that one has to make value judgements in CBA. The only difference among practitioners is whether the value judgements are made explicit or are left implicit.

The value judgement implicit in Kula's approach has already been identified in Chapter 3. There, in equations (3.7) and (3.8), we used Hau's decomposition of the social marginal utility of income a into the product of w (the effect of the change in utility of an individual on social welfare) and λ (the individual marginal utility of income). To equate a with λ is therefore to assume that w can be set equal to 1. When this 'egalitarian' value judgement is made, the individual and social elasticities of the marginal utility of income are equal.

One of the practical advantages of using the concept of the individual's marginal utility of income is that this may be indirectly observable from market behaviour. Following Fellner (1967), one needs to assume a utility function that is additively separable in terms of two goods, food and non-food. This implies that there is no consumer substitution between food and non-food. The elasticity of the marginal utility of income in this case equals the ratio of the income elasticity of food to the (compensated) price elasticity of demand for food.

Kula used macro data to estimate the income and price elasticity for food. These elasticities were obtained from a regression equation for the demand for food which depended on income and relative prices expressed in logarithmic form (which means that the regression coefficients immediately give the elasticity estimates). The income elasticities for Canada and the United States were 0.50 and 0.51, and the corresponding price elasticities were (–) 0.32 and

(–) 0.27. As a result, η for Canada was 1.56 (0.50/0.32), and it was 1.89 (0.51/0.27) for the United States.

The pure time preference rate (ρ)   Kula has a very interesting interpretation of the pure time preference rate. He includes an adjustment for individual mortality; yet he rejects the idea that this adjustment implies bringing irrationality into the estimation of the STPR. In fact, he argues that it is illogical to admit any concept of irrationality into the SDR. The whole purpose of conducting a CBA is to introduce more rationality into public policy decision-making. Mortality is a fact of life for Mr Average and all individuals. It is therefore rational for individuals to allow for this mortality. If it is Mr Average's time preferences that are to represent social time preferences, his mortality must be acknowledged in the SDR. An immortal individual can not be representative of mortal individuals.

The way that mortality enters Mr Average's calculations is as a measure of the probability of surviving into the future. Over the period 1946–75, there was an average survival probability of 0.992 for Canada and 0.991 in the United States. The probability of not surviving into the future was therefore 0.8 per cent in Canada and 0.9 per cent in the United States. These then form the estimates for ρ for the two countries.

The values of the three ingredients for Canada and the United States, and the resulting estimates of the STPRs using equation (11.12), are shown in Table 11.4. The estimates of the SDR (i.e., 5.2 per cent for Canada and 5.3 per cent for the United States) using our formula are exactly those found by Kula. He remarks that the two countries have similar STPRs because they have similar economies.

Table 11.4   STPRs for Canada and the United States

Parameter	Canada	United States
g	2.80%	2.30%
η	1.56	1.89
ρ	0.80%	0.90%
$i = \rho + \eta g$	5.17%	5.25%

Source: Kula (1984)

The strength of the Kula approach is also its main weakness. Using the construct of a Mr Average enables one to use individual preferences to derive estimates η from market demand behaviour. However, there are problems with accepting these individual revealed preference estimates for η for social decision-making purposes. As pointed out in the last chapter, $\eta = 1$ should be regarded as the *upper bound* for the elasticity of the social marginal utility (the income inequality parameter) in most circumstances. Only if the poor have such a low income that actual starvation is taking place, would the unit upper bound not apply. Kula is using the isoelastic weighting scheme given by equation (10.7) for Mr Average, someone who is presumably not starving in either Canada or the United States.

Consider the implication of using the $\eta = 1.89$ figure for the United States. This says that, in the social intertemporal setting that we are intending to use the value for η, a unit of income given up by Mr Average today (with an income of 10) is worth 21 times a unit of income gained by Mr Average in the future (with an income of 50). It is hard to conceive of a CBA outcome ever being politically or socially acceptable in the United States if it involves a weighting scheme that values a dollar to a rich person as worth less than 5 cents.

11.3.3   The pure time preference rate

Brent (1993) provided an analysis of the STPR that was based on changes in life expectancies. This study will be utilized in two ways. First we will use it to establish an STPR that is an alternative to the consumption based SDR. Then we will go back to consumption as the numeraire to show how it can be used to estimate the pure time preference rate ρ.

The STPR with time as the numeraire   We saw in Chapter 8 that it was possible to construct a CBA with a numeraire based on time rather than money income. This could be used whenever (as when valuing a life) one has misgivings about the validity of the monetary approach. We now show how to determine the SDR when time is the numeraire. The analysis is virtually the same as for the construction of the STPR based on consumption. As with equation (11.11), there were two considerations. The future generation could be expected to be better off and we needed to weight this difference. The only new element is how we are to judge that a generation is 'better off'.

With time as the numeraire, a generation j's welfare can be thought to depend on the life expectancy of the individual's L_j. One generation is better off than another in terms of how much greater their life expectancy is projected to be. As with income/consumption as the base, we will assume that the marginal value V_j of the greater life expectancy has the property of diminishing marginal utility. It can then be presumed to have the iso-elastic form similar to equation (10.7):

$$V_j = L_j^{-\alpha} \quad (\alpha \geq 0) \tag{11.13}$$

where α is the elasticity of the social marginal utility of time (i.e., life expectancy), just as η was the elasticity with respect to income. Using the same reasoning as with the derivation of equation (11.11) (that is, define the time SDR as: $(V_1 - V_0)/V_0$, and then divide top and bottom by $(L_1 - L_0)/L_0$), the life expectancy SDR (called the LEDR) is expressed as:

$$LEDR = \alpha \lambda \qquad (11.14)$$

where λ is the growth rate in life expectancies.

Equation (11.14) has the same structure as equation (11.11). It depends on a value parameter (an elasticity) and an objectively measurable variable (a growth rate). We will compare the implications of using the two STPRs i and ρ, by assuming the elasticities are both equal to unity. (This is Squire and van der Tak's recommended value, and $\alpha = 1$ is shown by Brent to be consistent with the egalitarian value judgement that all generations be considered to make the same total contribution to social welfare.) The comparison reduces to a contrast between using the per capita growth rate g and the life expectancy growth rate λ as the SDR.

Brent's study presented estimates of g and λ for 120 countries. A 24-year period was used, i.e., between 1965 and 1989. The value for λ that produced the LEDR was calculated by assuming a smooth exponential rise in life expectancies between 1965 and 1989 such that $L_{1965}.e^{\lambda 24} = L_{1989}$. The range of estimates for λ was between 0.0591 per cent for Hungary and 1.6258 per cent for Oman. The range for g was between -2.8 per cent for Uganda and 7.0 per cent for the Korean Republic and Singapore.

An important practical difference of using the LEDR rather than the CRI is immediately obvious from considering these ranges. With the CRI, it is quite easy to obtain *negative* estimates for the SDR. Table 11.5 lists all the countries in Brent's sample of 99 countries for which growth data exists that have negative g values, and would therefore have negative SDRs. As we can see, there are 21 countries that would have a negative discount rate based on the standard consumption numeraire. But there are no cases in Table 11.5 of a negative SDR using the LEDR. In fact, in none of the 120 countries for which there is life expectancy data is there a negative value for the LEDR. The LEDR approach is therefore more consistent with the basic idea behind discounting, namely, that a unit today be worth *more* than a unit in the future.

A second difference between the CRI and the LEDR is in terms of how these rates vary with the income levels of countries. There exists a common expectation that, *ceteris paribus*, the SDR should be higher for low-income countries. A low-income country has more need for resources today and would therefore discount the future at a greater rate. The LEDR has this property, seeing that in the Brent sample it was significantly negatively correlated with per capita income. But the CRIs did not have this property; it was significantly positively related to per-capita income.

Table 11.5   Countries with negative CRIs (g's) but positive LEDRs

Country	Income per capita 1989 $s	CRI Growth rate (g) 1965–1989	LEDR (λ) 1965–1989
Ethiopia	120	−0.1	0.4583
Tanzania	130	−0.1	0.5443
Chad	190	−1.2	0.9968
Madagascar	230	−1.9	0.6152
Uganda	250	−2.8	0.2632
Zaire	260	−2.0	0.7754
Niger	290	−2.4	0.8156
Benin	380	−0.1	0.8090
Central African Rep.	390	−0.5	0.9094
Ghana	390	−1.5	0.5672
Zambia	390	−2.0	0.7597
Mauritania	500	−0.5	0.8857
Bolivia	620	−0.8	0.7597
Senegal	650	−0.7	0.7427
Peru	1 010	−0.2	0.8138
El Salvador	1 070	−0.4	0.5658
Jamaica	1 260	−1.3	0.4200
Argentina	2 160	−0.1	0.3043
Venezuela	2 450	−1.0	0.4390
Libya	5 310	−3.0	0.8963
Kuwait	16 150	−4.0	0.6705

Source: Brent (1993)

The LEDR as the pure time preference rate   The Kula and Eckstein approach to estimating the pure rate of time preference is to use the survival rate of Mr Average today. From a social, intergenerational perspective, it is not the fact that Mr Average today is mortal that is decisive. Mr Average in the future is also mortal. Hence, what is socially significant is the degree of mortality of different generations. That is, it is *differences* in generational mortality rate that should determine the pure time preference rate. The Brent study based on changes in life expectancies contained this intergenerational element. One could therefore use estimates of the LEDR to represent ρ in the CRI formula given by equation (11.12).

It was previously reported that the range of values for the LEDR in the full sample of 120 countries was between 0.0591 per cent and 1.6258 per cent. Thus ρ values based on the LEDR would lie comfortably within the 0 to 5 per cent range recommended by Squire and van der Tak. One then would be ensuring that future generations' interests would not be ignored in the determination of the SDR. Although not one of the 21 countries listed in Table 11.5 had an LEDR value greater than 1 per cent, it is interesting that even these low values were sufficient in 9 cases to convert a negative CRI figure into a positive SDR rate. Every country would have a positive SDR if we took the upper bound 5 per cent value in the Squire and van der Tak recommended range.

It would seem therefore that, in practice, one role for the pure time preference rate is to help to ensure that positive SDR rates emerge from using STPR formulae. Basing the value for ρ on the LEDR does provide a logically consistent basis for fixing pure time preference rate values. It is thus more satisfactory than just picking a value at random within the 0 to 5 per cent range.

11.3.4 The Farmers' Home Administration's SDR

Brent (1989) treated the problem of determining the SDR as a weight estimation exercise. A capital expenditure loan involves a cost today for a flow of future benefits. In deciding whether to give a loan or not, the public decision-maker is trading off current consumption for future consumption. The more loans that are passed, the less emphasis is being given to current consumption and the higher is the implicit SDR that is being used. The estimate of the SDR corresponds with the rate that, at the margin, distinguishes an approved loan from one that is rejected.

The Farmers' Home Administration (FmHA) in the United States received loan applications to purchase farms. Buying a farm involves an initial capital expenditure C_0 (which equals the value of the loan, plus other items of expenditure). In return, the farm produces a stream of future net benefits (profits), starting one year later, i.e., B_1. Assuming that the future net benefits are the same in each year (over an infinite horizon), the relevant CBA criterion would involve the difference between the present value of the future net benefits and the initial capital cost:

$$\Delta W = B_1/i - C_0 \qquad (11.15)$$

As we did when imputing the value of a statistical life (in Chapter 8), and finding the distribution weights (Chapter 10), we assume that past public expenditure decisions D were determined by the benefits and costs (where again $D = 1$ is a project acceptance and $D = 0$ is a project rejection). If this relation is linear, we obtain the equation:

$$D = A_0 + A_1(B_1/i - C_0) = A_0 + A_1(B_1/i) - A_1(C_0) \qquad (11.16)$$

where A_0 and A_1 are constants. In this equation, the benefits and the costs have the same coefficient because both components are in present value terms. This is, of course, the purpose of having a discount rate i.

Written as an estimation equation, relation (11.16) appears as:

$$L = N_0 + N_1 B_1 - N_2 C_0 \qquad (11.17)$$

The right-hand side variables of equation (11.17) are related to the right-hand side variables of equation (11.16) by $N_1 = A_1/i$ and $N_2 = A_1$. The dependent variable of (11.17) is the Logit L. It is related to the D of (11.16) as follows. Define with P the probability that the decision-maker will accept the farm loan application (i.e., $D = 1$). L is the logarithm of the odds $P/(1 - P)$.

The ratio of the two N coefficients in equation (11.17) produces $N_2/N_1 = i$. This means that if we regress the B_1 and C_0 on L, then the ratio of the two coefficients will produce an estimate of the SDR. The intuition behind this method of deriving an estimate of the SDR is this. The decision-maker has to compare a flow of future farm profits against the current cost of purchasing the farm. The decision-maker has to trade off the flow against the stock and this is precisely the role of the discount rate. So when a particular trade-off is chosen (i.e., implied from past decisions) this is the same as fixing a particular value for the SDR.

The data came from a sample of 153 individual FmHA files related to decisions made by county supervisors in New York State over the period 1978–84. The result was that the estimates for i were in the range 69–72 per cent. Obviously, the FmHA loans were riskier than most other government loans. Farmers who applied to purchase a loan had to be turned down from private sources of credit. But, this is a very large 'risk premium'.

The results of the FmHA study are interesting for two reasons:

i.   They cast doubt on the Staats survey summarized in section 11.1.4. Agencies might claim not to discount, but their behaviour might suggest otherwise. FmHA did not have an explicit discount rate, and yet they used a very high implicit rate when deciding to whom to give a loan .

ii. The range found (69–72 per cent) far exceeds the 25 per cent upper limit given in the Tresch quote presented in the introduction section. It seems that theorists need to make an allowance for 'individual risk'. A project with a given expected value should be valued differently according to the individual characteristics of the applicant (the person undertaking the investment). (See also Brent, 1991d.)

11.4 Final comments

The summary and problems sections conclude the chapter.

11.4.1 Summary

In the problems for Chapter 1, one could see that the size of the SDR was of prime political concern. The larger the discount rate, the fewer public investment projects that would be passed; hence the smaller would be the public sector relative to the private sector. Given that the SOCR is expected to be higher than the STPR, one should not be surprised that those who favour limiting the size of the public sector would be those who advocate the SOCR. However, our advocacy of the STPR was not on political grounds. We tried to argue that the STPR was the conceptually correct rate to use for discounting purposes in a second-best world.

The obvious rate to use as the SDR is the market rate of interest. But this is not correct when constraints other than production exist. This rate is also problematical when one questions the ability of individuals to make intertemporal decisions. Chapter 7 presented examples of individual estimates of discount rates. In this chapter we saw how these estimates would need to be adjusted if they ignore external benefits (the effects on the heirs of others). A way (formula) for checking whether to adjust the market rate upwards or downwards was presented.

Moreover, the individual rates would need to be replaced if one considered that myopia was a factor when individuals look into the future to assess benefits. This leads to the idea that a socially determined rate may be more appropriate than individual rates for social decision-making purposes. The STPR rate that is most often used in CBA recognizes that future generations are likely to be richer than current generations. A premium would then be given to the consumption of the current generation. The size of the premium would depend on just how much richer would be the future generation (which depends on the growth rate g) and how important we value income inequality (as reflected by the elasticity of the social marginal utility of income η).

In addition to including (as a multiple) g and η, many analysts recommend the use of a pure time preference rate ρ. This allocates a premium according to the generation in which any individual belongs. The current generation would prefer that a premium be given to their consumption because they may not live into the future. Essentially, determining ρ depends on how much importance one gives to this preference. If one dismisses the preference as individually rational, but socially irrational, then one would set ρ equal to zero. If one accepts the idea of democracy, then the current generation contains the only voters that exist.

A positive rate for ρ would then have to be acknowledged. Current practice fixes this rate by reference to individual survival rates.

The first case study showed that the idea that 'prevention is better than cure' prejudges social decision-making in the health-care field. In general, 'cure' comes later than 'prevention'. As such the relative desirability of cure depends on the size of the SDR one adopts. We saw that for the anti-malarial programme in India, when the SDR was 14 per cent or higher, cure was better than prevention.

As the SDR is just an intertemporal weighting scheme, one needs to explain how to estimate these weights. In the last chapter we saw that one could either use the 'a priori' or the imputational approaches. The second and third applications used the a priori approach in terms of how they fixed η and α (the elasticity of the social marginal utility of time). The final case study used the revealed preference approach.

The second application showed how the (authoritarian) STPR formula could be estimated for Canada and the United States. The values obtained were moderately low, at around 5 per cent for both countries. However, if one wished to apply the STPR formula to all countries, the third application showed that a very serious practical problem must be faced. If a country's growth rate is negative, the STPR must come out negative if ρ is ignored. For 21 countries (in a sample of 120) this was the case. Even if one did include a positive rate of pure time preference, it was shown that 9 countries still had a negative SDR using an STPR based on consumption (called the CRI). If one instead bases the SDR on a numeraire expressed in units of time (called the life expectancy discount rate LEDR), one would find a positive SDR for all 120 countries.

Thus, the third case study did double duty. It provided: (a) an alternative base to consumption for the STPR; and (b) an alternative method for estimating ρ when consumption was the numeraire. In either context, the logic underlying the STPR was adhered to. Just as we recognized that future generations would be richer than current generations (and therefore we should give a premium to current generations on this account), we also recognized that future generations were likely to be better off in that they will have longer life expectancies. A premium in addition to (or instead of) that given to the current generation for lower income should be included because of this life expectancy difference.

The last case study estimated the SDR that a policy-maker actually used. It came out with the disconcerting result that the rate used was very high (around 70 per cent). Certainly it was outside the range currently suggested by theorists. This study highlighted the fact that, if individuals are doing the spending, and the government project is one of providing the loan to facilitate that spending, then inevitably individual preferences are being included in the determination of the SDR. Individuals who are currently cash constrained are likely to have a high preference for current consumption. The SDR estimate could then be expected to be high. In the two-stage process, where the government is providing the finance and the individual is undertaking the investment, we need to distinguish project risk from individual risk. That is, the riskiness of a project depends on whom exactly is undertaking the project. In FmHA decisions, the high estimate for the SDR would be justified by the high individual risk associated with would-be farmers who were turned down for loans by the private sector.

11.4.2 Problems
The chapter has largely concentrated on the formulation of the STPR given in equation (11.12). This determines i as the product of the per capita growth rate g and the elasticity of the social marginal utility of income η. For simplicity, assume ρ is set equal to zero, in which case equation (11.11) is the operative formulation. Now we consider what difference it makes to consider separately the components of per capita consumption, equal to the ratio of aggregate consumption to the population level. In particular, we focus on the implications for the CRI formula of including the population growth rate p. Note that the per capita growth rate g is the *difference* between the growth rate in aggregate consumption G and the population growth rate p. The problems therefore explore the alternative formulations to equations (11.11) and (11.12) existing in the literature.

1. Layard (1972) shows that when social welfare depends only on consumption per head c, that the CRI becomes:

$$i = \eta g + p \qquad\qquad (11.18)$$

    where g is the rate of growth of per capita consumption and p is the rate of population growth. He also points out when social welfare depends on population times the marginal welfare from consumption per head, equation (11.11) results. Take equation (11.18) and replace g by $G - p$. What then is the essential difference in the two formulations when $\eta = 1$?
2. On the basis of your answer to question 1, how would you interpret the 2 per cent reduction that Cohn makes to the SDR?
3. Gramlich (1981) recommends using p as the SDR. Using equation (11.11), what assumptions are necessary to obtain $i = p$? Are these assumptions plausible? Using equation (11.18), what assumptions are necessary to obtain $i = p$? Are these assumptions plausible? Using equation (11.12) (i.e., now drop the assumption that $\rho = 0$), what assumptions are necessary to obtain $i = p$? Are these assumptions plausible?

11.5 Appendix
Given the emphasis in this chapter to equation (11.12), it is important to show how it is constructed from first principles. In particular, one needs to see where

the pure time preference rate ρ comes into the story, and how it comes about that it is added in the CRI formula.

Let $W(t)$ be the welfare function for any generation t. Assume that this is a function only of per capita income c in the form $W(t) = [1/(1 - \eta)] c^{1-\eta}$. Define the intertemporal welfare function W as the present value of all the generational welfare functions W_t:

$$W = \int e^{-\rho t} W(t) \qquad (11.19)$$

where ρ is the intergenerational discount rate.

The value of an extra unit of consumption is the derivative W_c. The SDR is the rate of fall in the value of W_c over time:

$$i = -\frac{dW_c / dt}{W_c} \qquad (11.20)$$

The denominator of equation (11.20) is equal to: $e^{-\rho t} c^{-\eta}$. The time derivative of this is on the numerator. Hence equation (11.20) is:

$$i = \frac{e^{-\rho t} \eta c^{-\eta-1} dc / dt + e^{-\rho t} \rho c^{-\eta}}{e^{-\rho t} c^{-\eta}} \qquad (11.21)$$

Equation (11.21) reduces to:

$$i = \eta\, c^{-1}\, dc/dt + \rho \qquad (11.22)$$

Since the growth rate in per capita consumption g is defined as $g = (dc/dt)/c$, equation (11.22) is equal to equation (11.12) in the text.

PART V

12   User prices

12.1   Introduction

We have the social services (education and health) in mind when we discuss the theory of user prices in this chapter. We first discuss models where user prices are set very low and excess demand exists. Hence we will be dealing with markets that do not clear. Some rationing will be taking place. An argument will be made showing how it is possible to increase efficiency and improve distributional objectives by raising user fees to consumers. Then we present the general CBA framework with user prices when an externality exists causing a wedge between the social and private demand curves. Cost recovery, which is the context in which the rationing model was developed, will be shown to be a particular case of the general CBA framework. The other issue to be discussed is how user prices affect the presumption in the literature that public investment must outperform the private sector by the extent of the MCF (first discussed in Chapter 9).

The first application shows that, not only is it possible in theory to increase efficiency and equity by raising user fees, it can also happen in practice. Then there is a study which develops and tests a rule to tell when user fees are optimal. The last application analyses a situation where there is no excess demand. Hence, raising prices will reduce usage. Changing user fees is then compared to alternative policy options in terms of their relative impact on usage.

12.1.1   Assumptions about user fees

As a preliminary to an analysis of user fees, it is useful to clarify how such charges were handled in the CBA framework outlined up to this point. It is necessary only to focus on the version without weights (either distributional or sectoral). From the starting point where one is seeking a positive difference between benefits and cost $(B - C)$, we subtracted repayments R from both categories to obtain: $(B - R) - (C - R)$.

In the criterion $(B - R) - (C - R)$, repayments are the product of price and quantity $R = P.Q$. This definition was not used earlier as neither P nor Q operated independently. In effect, we had both P and Q fixed at $\bar{P}$ and $\bar{Q}$. This meant that R was fixed $R = \bar{P}.\bar{Q}$.

P was fixed because prices were thought to be outside of the control of the person making the cost–benefit decision. Q was fixed in the sense that the CBA decision related to a given-sized project, where the choices were only whether to approve or reject that particular sized project .

For example, in the railway closure decision study by Brent (1979) previously discussed, the decision whether to discontinue a railway line was determined by the Minister of Transport; while rail fares were a matter for British Rail, an independent public enterprise. The Transport Minister could decide to close a line or leave the line open. The Minister could not vary the scale of operations (e.g., change the frequency of train services). Rail fares and number of trains to be run were considered 'quality of service' issues and within the domain of British Rail.

In this chapter we relax the constraints on P and Q in two stages. First, in section 12.1.2, we treat only one of the components as being fixed. The analysis starts out with the price being fixed, but this is transposed to fixing quantity. This is the cost-recovery framework. Second, in section 12.2.1 we allow both P and Q to vary and call this the general CBA criterion. From this we can determine the optimum price (i.e., user fee).

12.1.2   User fees and cost recovery

Jimenez (1987) provides a comprehensive analysis of the theory and practice of user prices (see also Katz, 1987). Thobani (1984) set up the basic model which was developed by Jimenez and this is summarized below.

For simplicity, there will be no private consumption costs apart from the user charge. In line with the economics of a mixed economy, we consider the government intervening in the context of a private market that is underproducing. This is due to an external benefit that private demand does not recognize (such as the benefits to others of receiving an inoculation for a contagious disease). Diagram 12.1 depicts the private market demand curve as D_P and the social demand (which includes the externality) as D_S. Average costs are assumed constant, so the marginal cost curve MC is shown as a straight line. The private market equilibrium would be at a quantity Q_P (where $D_P = MC$) and the social optimum is at Q_S (where $D_S = MC$). However, pricing policy is such that neither a private nor a social equilibrium exists.

The current user charge set by the government is the price $\bar{P}$ which is fixed well below costs. The government cannot satisfy everyone who wishes to buy the product at the price $\bar{P}$ because it has a fixed budget constraint. Define S as the total subsidy available to the government for this particular social service. This subsidy must cover the difference between what the output costs and what is received in revenues from the user charges, i.e., $S = C - R$. With revenues equal to price times quantity, the constraint can be expressed in per unit terms as:

$$\frac{S}{Q} = \frac{C}{Q} - \bar{P} \qquad (12.1)$$

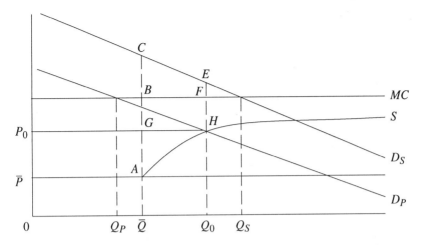

The diagram shows that it is possible to increase efficiency by raising using fees. Initially, we are at point A where there is excess demand. Then the user fee is raised to P_0. The net gain is the consumer surplus area $BFEC$, being the difference between the area under the demand curve and the area under the supply curve over the quantity range for which there is excess demand, i.e., $\bar{Q}Q_0$.

Diagram 12.1

Equation (12.1) states that the subsidy per unit is the difference between the cost per unit and the user price. It can be seen from this equation that, with costs and the subsidy given, quantity Q and price $\bar{P}$ are positively related. A rise in quantity lowers the subsidy per unit (on the left-hand side) and requires a rise in the user price (to lower the right-hand side) to satisfy the budget constraint. In other words, the government by fixing the quantity, fixes the user price (and vice versa). Let $\bar{Q}$ be the current rationed quantity that corresponds to $\bar{P}$.

The locus of prices and quantities that satisfy the budget constraint defines Jimenez's isosubsidy curve (which is called the 'supply curve' in Katz's model). It is drawn as the upward-sloping S curve in Diagram 12.1. It starts at point A, corresponding to the point $\bar{Q}, \bar{P}$, and continues as a rectangular hyperbola. The higher the user charge, the greater the quantity that can be financed from the fixed subsidy. Satisfying the S relation is the cost-recovery part of the analysis.

At $\bar{Q}$, the marginal social benefit is greater than the cost by the amount BC. There are therefore net benefits to be obtained from expanding output past $\bar{Q}$. To satisfy S, one must raise the user price as one increases output. That is, the increased charge is being used to fund the output expansion. Up to Q_0 there is excess private demand and the rising S curve can be exploited. Once this quantity has been exceeded however, consumers will not willingly purchase more at a higher price. An increased government subsidy will be required. With S

regarded as fixed therefore, Q_0 is the upper limit by which increases in user charges can be used to expand output and thereby increase social welfare. The net gain from increasing the user fee from $\bar{P}$ to P_0 is the area *FECB*.

So far, the argument has been that (when there is excess private demand) one can increase efficiency by raising user fees. What about the distributional effects? Must they necessarily be adverse? Katz points out that the answer to this question depends on the specifics of the rationing scheme used to impose $\bar{Q}$ as the initial quantity. Before dealing with a particular rationing scheme, we need to identify the income changes from the rise in user charges from $\bar{P}$ to P_0.

The rise in user price leads to an income gain and an income loss. The income loss is incurred by old consumers of quantity $\bar{Q}$. They have to pay more for the same quantity. Their consumer surplus is reduced by the amount of their extra payments equal to $\bar{P}AGP_0$. In efficiency terms, this amount is transferred to the producers of the subsidized service and would therefore cancel out. But, focusing only on consumer effects, this is an income loss. The income gain goes to the new consumers of the additional output $\bar{Q}Q_0$. The income gain is the area *GHEC* (the difference between the area under the social demand curve and the revenue charged $\bar{Q}Q_0HG$). (Again, *GHFB* of *GHEC* is a transfer to producers, which makes *BFEC* the only consumer effect that is not offset by a producer effect. This is, of course, why *BFEC* is the efficiency effect stated above.)

The distribution issue then is who are the new consumers receiving the income gain *GHEC* and who are the old consumers incurring the income loss $\bar{P}AGP_0$. Katz highlights the fact that many countries adopt a rationing scheme for education (especially higher education) that depends on certified exam results. All those receiving a score greater than some cut-off level are admitted to the subsidized schooling, while those below the level must go elsewhere (and forgo the subsidy). If there is a positive relation between getting a high test score and being a member in an upper-income household, then the incidence of the subsidy can be readily identified. The old consumers who receive the rationed quantity $\bar{Q}$ will be the upper-income groups and the new consumers will be from less well-off households.

The complete argument for raising user fees in markets with private excess demand is this. One can increase efficiency and also distributional equity when it is the high-income groups that benefit most from the low user fees (and thus receive most of the government subsidy).

12.1.3   User fees and the MCF
When one is dealing with pure public goods, it is logical to assume that user fees are zero, as the free-rider problem may prevent charges being made for the public good. However, even in health and education, there are many situations where pricing does in fact take place, and many more instances where user fees are absent, but where charges could be introduced. With LDCs currently having

severe fiscal problems, user fees are likely to be an increasingly employed policy option. In these circumstances, it is important to point out the vital link between user fees and the *MCF*.

Abstracting from distributional issues, the main justification for raising users fees is the existence of an *MCF* greater than unity. When taxes incur an excess burden over and above the revenues they produce, user fees are an alternative source of funds that could reduce the inefficiency of that taxation. One should therefore expect user fees to be important when the *MCF* is high. Nonetheless, there is an implication of this link between user fees and the *MCF* that has been ignored by most in the CBA literature. One must question the validity of the 'outperforming criterion' suggested by Browning (1976) and mentioned in Chapter 9.

The outperforming criterion was derived from the requirement that the welfare relation expressed in (9.3) be positive:

$$B - (MCF)\ C > 0$$

When we insert repayments into this expression, the CBA criterion (without distribution) appears as:

$$(B - R) - (MCF)(C - R) > 0 \tag{12.2}$$

Recognizing the existence of repayments makes a big difference as to how much outperforming one should expect by the public sector over the private sector. It will be recalled from Chapter 9 that Browning (1976), working with an estimate of the *MCF* equal to 7 per cent, argued that government projects should have benefits greater than 1.07 in order to be comparable to a project in the private sector (where taxes would not have to be raised and therefore no excess burden would exist). In Chapter 9, we raised one objection to this presumption, which was that the *MCF* might not exceed 1. Now, we have a second objection. With positive user fees (and even with an *MCF* greater than 1) the degree of outperforming is much less than the extent to which the *MCF* exceeds 1.

The easiest way of seeing this point is to reformulate equation (12.2) as:

$$\frac{B}{C} > MCF\left(1 - \frac{R}{C}\right) + \frac{R}{C} \tag{12.3}$$

It is clear from equation (12.3) that the degree of outperforming (i.e., the extent to which *B* should exceed *C*) is a function of the ratio of repayments to costs, and does not just depend on the value of *MCF*. With *MCF* = 1.07, the degree of outperforming is 7 per cent only if there are no user fees (i.e., $R/C = 0$). But, for example, when $R/C = 0.5$, the degree of outperforming drops to 3.5 per cent; and this drops to zero when $R/C = 1$. (A full discussion of the implications of user fees for the outperforming requirement is given in Brent, 1995b.)

12.2   CBA and user fees

The analysis in this section is based on Brent (1995a). (See also Kirkpatrick, 1979.) We first form the most general of all the CBA criteria used in this book. That is, distributional weights are added to the criterion with the *MCF* and user fees. The optimal user fee is derived from this criterion. Then we return to the cost-recovery setting to explain how this analysis should be reinterpreted when placed in the context of the general CBA framework.

12.2.1   Optimal user fees

Prior to this chapter, B, R and C, were to be interpreted as marginal concepts in that a project was a change in output and there were benefits, revenues and costs from this output change. Now, we consider B, R and C as corresponding to total changes from the project and we contemplate changing the scale of the project by another unit (leading to marginal benefits, revenues and costs). This is necessary because we are going to analyse the decision whether to charge a little more (or little less) for the social service and, clearly, variable magnitudes will change because of this adjustment.

In Chapter 9, we used the weight a_B to apply to any benefits that go to the private sector and a_C was the weight that was attached to costs incurred by the private sector. The ratio of the two sector weights (a_C/a_B) defined the *MCF*, and the welfare criterion was:

$$W = B - (MCF)\, C$$

Chapter 9 ignored user fees and distribution effects. As pointed out earlier, repayments R reduce both net benefits $(B - R)$ and net costs $(C - R)$. Attaching distribution weights to these net benefits and costs (again assuming that the beneficiaries are a low-income group and the taxpayers are high income) we form the welfare function with repayments and distribution:

$$W = a_2\,(B - R) - a_1\,(MCF)(C - R) \tag{12.4}$$

We can simplify the notation by dividing equation (12.4) through by a_2 (dividing W by a constant does not affect the rankings of projects) and writing the equation as:

$$W = B - R - \omega\,(C - R) \tag{12.5}$$

where ω is the one composite weight that combines the relative sector weights and the relative distribution weights. That is:

$$\omega = (a_1 / a_2)(MCF) = \frac{MCF}{a_2 / a_1} = \frac{a_C / a_B}{a_2 / a_1}$$

In equation (12.5), user prices are present via the relation $R = P.\bar{Q}$. However, it will be convenient to regard the government as setting the user prices by determining how much quantity to provide. Thus, (12.5) is optimized by changing quantity, seeing how they affect the determinants of a change in welfare, and stopping when there is no welfare gain left. The quantity change leads to marginal effects for all the variables in equation (12.5). Call MB the change in benefits due to the quantity change, MR the change in revenue, and MC is the marginal cost. The change in welfare from the output change ΔW will therefore show a gain when:

$$\Delta W = MB - MR - \omega (MC - MR) = 0 \tag{12.6}$$

In line with the welfare economic base to CBA given in Chapter 3, marginal benefits are given by the (social) demand curve. A point on this curve defines the social demand price P^*. Identifying MB with P^*, we can solve equation (12.6) for P^*, which is the definition of the optimal user charge. The resulting P^* (derived in the appendix) is a weighted average of the actual price P and the marginal cost MC.

$$P^* = \omega MC + P (1 - \gamma) \tag{12.7}$$

where $\gamma = \omega + (1/e_p) (1 - \omega)$. As in the Ramsey rule, the inverse of the price elasticity of demand plays a role in determining the optimal user charge via its effect on γ.

Equation (12.7) is the key one. It shows that the optimal user price is a function of four main ingredients. Two of these are fundamental to most analyses of shadow pricing, i.e., the existing price and the marginal cost. In terms of Chapter 4, P replaces the consumer demand price P_C and MC is the producer supply price P_p. Thus equation (12.7) has the same form as the general shadow pricing rule (4.3). The remaining two components are the price elasticity of demand and the (sectoral and distributional) weights. These last two components determine the extent to which the optimal user charge will be closer to P or MC.

Although equation (12.7) has the structure of earlier shadow pricing formulae, there is a very important conceptual difference. Previous shadow pricing theory identified the market price P that one *should* charge with the shadow price.

However, in the current context, we are trying to fix the shadow price when the existing price is not set optimally. The existing price could be non-optimal either because: (a) the social demand curve (for which P^* is a point) is different from the market demand curve (for which P is a point) due to the existence of externalities; or because (b) multi-tiered decision-making is taking place (and the lower tier sets P independently of the social requirement P^*). In either case, P is not on the social demand curve D_S and so P and P^* do not coincide.

The underlying logic of equation (12.7) can best be understood by focusing on the role of the price elasticity term e_p. There are two cases:

i.   First assume a unit price elasticity. This sets $\gamma = 1$, and hence $(1 - \gamma) = 0$. The optimal user charge is $P^* = \omega\, MC$. This is like the traditional marginal cost pricing rule, except that distribution is important. If the government values funds greater than it values income distribution (i.e., the MCF is large relative to a_2/a_1) then ω will be greater than 1 and user prices will be set above MC. Note that it is the existing funds from tax sources that are being considered here, not those from changing user fees (which are zero in this case).

ii. When the elasticity of demand is not unity, changing the user price will change revenue (up or down). Unlike the simple Ramsey rule, the size of the price elasticity may increase *or* decrease the social price depending on the value of ω. If $\omega < 1$, a higher elasticity raises the social price; while if $\omega > 1$, a higher elasticity lowers P^*. The reason for this is straightforward. When the price elasticity of demand is less than unity, any price increase will raise revenues. This revenue increase is important if, and only if, the government has a higher value on public income relative to distribution, i.e., ω exceeds unity.

12.2.2   The CBA criterion with cost recovery

We can regard the cost recovery analysis covered in section 12.1.2 as primarily concerned with the second bracketed term in equation (12.7). With the subsidy defined earlier as $S = C - R$, we can characterize cost recovery as keeping S constant when quantity is changed. For a fixed subsidy then, we wish the marginal subsidy MS to equal zero. As $MS = MC - MR$, setting this to zero implies:

$$MC = MR \qquad (12.8)$$

This result, that marginal revenue should equal marginal cost, is also the condition for profit maximization. This has prompted some (such as Creese, 1991) to suggest that cost recovery requires that decision-makers set user prices so as to maximize profits.

However, this interpretation ignores the first bracketed term in equation (12.7). Hence when the condition $MC = MR$ is inserted into equation (12.6), it leads to:

$$MB = MR \qquad (12.9)$$

Consequently, combining equations (12.8) and (12.9), and because $MB = P^*$, we obtain the familiar marginal cost-pricing condition:

$$P^* = MC \qquad (12.10)$$

The main conclusion from using cost-recovery objectives in the CBA framework is that one can ignore the weight term ω. In other words, ω is set equal to 1 in equation (12.6).

The finding that ω has no role to play is easy to explain. In the cost-recovery framework, the financial effect of altering Q is neutralized. There is no further transfer of funds from the private to the public sector. Income distribution will not be affected. Nor will there be any need to increase taxes or government borrowing. The issue is simply whether at the margin the social demand price is greater than the marginal cost.

It is important to understand that the cost-recovery literature here assumes that there is excess demand. Under these circumstances one may increase both P and Q and leave the subsidy unaffected. But the CBA framework explains *why* raising P and Q is worthwhile. With excess demand, as Diagram 12.1 shows, MB or P^* is greater than MC and an expansion in output is necessary to close this gap and satisfy (12.10).

12.3 Applications

In section 12.1, we explained how an increase in user fees could increase both efficiency and equity. A necessary condition for this result was the existence of excess demand. The first case study by Thobani (1984) explains how this result, and the necessary precondition, was relevant for primary and secondary education in Malawi. This analysis is within the cost-recovery framework where there was a fixed budget constraint. The remaining applications do not assume there is excess demand. The case study by Brent (1995a) uses the CBA framework presented in section 12.2 to assess whether the actual user charges imposed by the state governments in India for economic services were optimal or not. Without excess demand, any increase in user charges must expect to reduce the quantity demanded. Mwabu et al. (1994) calculate the price elasticities of demand for health-care in Kenya. The impact on the numbers treated is then compared with other policy options.

12.3.1   User fees within a fixed budget constraint

The Thobani rule is that if there is excess demand, there is scope to raise user fees and increase efficiency. Then afterwards, on a case-by-case basis, one can see if equity is sacrificed or enhanced. Thobani uses this two-step procedure to analyse the case for raising user fees in Malawi. He considers each of the three education sectors (primary, secondary and university) in turn.

i.   Primary sector   As can be seen from Table 12.1, the primary sector takes up the largest share of the Malawi expenditure budget. But, in terms of expenditure per student, expenditures are minuscule at 12 Kwacha (K) per annum (K1 = US$1.1). The tuition rate is K2, which means a subsidy of K10 per student. Although there does not appear to be any rationing, because anyone who is willing to pay tuition is admitted to primary school, excess demand is present in a quality rather than a quantity sense. The student–teacher ratio can be used to gauge the quality dimension.

Table 12.1   Education expenditures by category in Malawi (1979–1980)

Category	Expenditure (millions of K)	Percentage of total	Number enrolled	Expenditure per student (K)
Administrative	2.83	13.9	—	—
Primary	8.22	40.3	711 255	12
Secondary	3.00	14.7	14 317	209
University	4.74	23.2	1 620	2 925
Other	1.61	7.9	—	—
Total	20.40	100.0	729 741	28

Source: Thobani (1984)

The Malawi government has determined that a class size of 50 is optimal. With actual average class sizes equal to 66, rationing takes place in terms of restrictions in the access to teacher time. Universal primary education was a target that was not met even with the 66 class size. This target obviously clashes with the aim to lower the class size. With the existence of excess demand established, Thobani could recommend an increase in tuition to around K3–K4. This would improve efficiency in the primary education sector by hiring more teachers and purchasing necessary books and supplies.

It is true that raising the user fee for primary education will reduce enrolment. Thobani argues, however, that it will not be the lowest income groups who drop out. Highest enrolments (100 per cent) existed in the poorest northern region, above that of the richer central (51.5 per cent) and southern (56.2 per cent) regions. Thus there were pre-existing factors providing incentives for the richer groups not to go to school. A major factor here was the higher opportunity cost of a child's time in richer households. For example, a child could be used on the family farm. Since richer groups have a higher cost and a lower net return from primary education, it may be their children that have most to lose from any raise in tuition rates (which would lower their return even further).

ii.   Secondary sector   There was a lot of evidence of excess demand in the secondary education sector of Malawi. Only 1 in 9 of primary school graduates were enrolled in secondary schools. In order to enter a secondary school, one must pass the Primary School Leaving Certificate Examination. Because the return to secondary education was so high, many (around half) of the applicants had sat the test on a previous occasion. On efficiency grounds then, Thobani advocated a raise in rates for this sector. All the three main types of secondary school (grant-assisted and government boarding schools, and government day schools) charged a uniform tuition fee of K20. To cover books and supplies, Thobani suggested a rise in tuition to K30. Because the three types had wide divergencies in the boarding fees that they charged, it was suggested that boarding fees be raised to the level of the highest charger (in the range K75–K100).

The equity case for raising fees was the one identified in section 12.2. Rationing by test scores discriminates against the poor. For example, they would be less able to afford to repeat a year in order to retake the entrance examinations. Thus, it is likely that using user fees would not have any more adverse effects on the enrolment by the poor than the pre-existing rationing-by-exam system that is to be replaced. If, in addition, one employs (as recommended by Thobani) price discrimination in terms of allocating selective scholarships, then equity can be made to improve in parallel with efficiency.

iii.   University sector   The situation for the universities was much more different than for the other sectors. Due to the shortage of secondary school graduates, the private demand curve for higher education was well below that of the social demand. No excess demand existed. This was the case even though user fees were effectively *negative*, that is, tuition, and room and board, were free and, in addition, the students received pocket money of K12 per month .

Without the existence of excess demand, no case can be made for increasing fees that would not lower quantity. Thobani argued that the loss of enrolment could be minimized if the subsidy element (pocket money) were removed and board and lodging were charged. Then, by a system of scholarships for the poor and loans for the rich, tuition fees could be gradually introduced. There was a tradition of paying for the previous levels of education and this could be exploited in the university sector.

To conclude: secondary education in Malawi was a classical situation where the preconditions existed for raising user fees within the cost-recovery framework. Non-price rationing was severe, creating large excess demand. The primary education sector could also come under this framework, with rationing being in terms of there being a very high teacher–student ratio.

Discussion   There are two aspects of Thobani's analysis that are particularly noteworthy. They both revolve around the fact that Thobani's user fee recommendations were actually implemented.

i. Most of the time, there is no firm link between the outcome of a particular CBA evaluation and what is actually decided in practice. (Though, as we have seen in our coverage of railway closure decisions in the UK, and AFDC payments in the United States, there are many cases of a general correspondence between the underlying theory of CBA and real-world behaviour.) This is not necessarily a weakness of CBA principles, as the evaluation could still have helped clarify matters for the decision-makers, and made them more informed of the consequences of their actions. But when, as in Thobani's case, the evaluation led to actual policy changes, the claim that one needs to study CBA is more convincing. Thobani presented the results of his World Bank study to the government of Malawi in October and November 1981. In April 1982, tuition rates and boarding fees were raised for primary and secondary education to almost exactly those levels recommended by Thobani. (Fees were not introduced for higher education. But note that the excess demand requirement did not apply for this sector.)

ii. From the point of view of the rationale of cost recovery outlined in section 12.1, raising user fees (when there is excess demand) is only a necessary condition for greater efficiency. To be sufficient, the revenues that accrue from the rise in user fees must be devoted to expanding the quantity (or quality) of the relevant good or service. This condition was satisfied in the Thobani study as he noted that, even after excluding revenues for fees, the 1983 education budget showed a 20.9 per cent increase over 1982. This one-year increase is especially significant given the fact that in the eight-year period prior to the Thobani study, expenditure over the entire period rose by only 20 per cent (in real terms).

The Thobani case study makes a very important contribution to public policy analysis. It identifies the key ingredients for cost recovery when a fixed budget constraint exists. The analysis is simple yet insightful. It highlights policy options that one could easily ignore when using a traditional (market-clearing) demand and supply analysis. However, as explained in section 12.3, this type of analysis is not a complete CBA and cannot therefore take advantage of the wider implications of this framework. Let us consider three additional considerations that adopting CBA allows one to incorporate into the decision-making process.

i.   There is no scope for relaxing the budget constraint in the cost-recovery framework. Usually it will be the case that some extra funds would be made available if a strong justification can be found. The argument is that whether a tax increase is feasible or not depends precisely on what the extra tax revenue will be spent. In CBA, the *MCF* indicates how relaxing the government's budget constraint effects the social outcome at the margin. In the cost-recovery framework, the implicit *MCF* is infinite, which is a situation which will only rarely accurately describe the prevailing financial circumstances.

ii.   It is easy to see the main drawback in the Thobani mode of analysis. It is fine if efficiency and equity move in the same direction. But, if this is not the case, then a trade-off is required. This is precisely what is provided by the formal CBA criterion presented in section 12.2 (and what is missing from a cost-recovery analysis). Distribution weights are the vehicle by which the trade-off is expressed in CBA. In the Malawi context, one would (presumably) employ weights greater than 1 for effects on primary school students (living in poorer rural areas), and weights less than 1 for university students (who are the richer urban elite). The high primary school weight would not affect outcomes, as both efficiency and equity were furthered by raising user fees. In the university sector, however, a reduction in enrolment (which is an efficiency loss) has to be compared with a distribution gain (increased revenue would come at the expense of the rich). In this case, the low distribution weight would (at the margin) encourage an increase in fees (by fostering a distribution gain). The final result in a CBA (as to the desirability of raising university user fees) would then depend on whether the weighted distribution gain was greater, or less, than the weighted efficiency loss.

iii. Lastly, Thobani mentions in his study the 'compression effect'. This refers to the long-term beneficial effect on income distribution of expanding education. An increase in the supply of those educated lowers the wage for skilled labour. This reduces the wage disparity between skilled and unskilled labour, lowering income inequality. In a cost-recovery context this is an *ad hoc* argument that must be 'somehow' included in the overall equity assessment. In CBA, it is simply an intertemporal effect to be included in the analysis. As such, it is a discount rate issue. Alongside any current weighted benefits, there are discounted future benefits to add on. The size of the SDR indicates how important the future compression effect is in current terms.

12.3.2   CBA and user fees

Government subsidies in India were so large that (in the late 1980s) they amounted to around 15 per cent of national income. This level of subsidies was not thought sustainable. One contributing factor was the level of user fees charged for government goods and services. They were low and getting lower over time. So Mundle and Rao (1991) (and Rao and Mundle, 1992) did an analysis of user fees to see if their low levels could be justified. We focus on that part of their analysis concerning the pricing policies of the 14 main states. Most of the Indian subsidies were generated at the state level (equal to 62.04 per cent of the total subsidy in 1987–88). Because they found that those states in greatest need (for example, those with low income, high illiteracy or infant mortality rates) were not those that charged the lowest fees, Mundle and Rao recommended that user fees be raised in India.

Brent (1995a) used the data provided by Mundle and Rao, and applied this in a CBA framework. This allows one not only to say whether current fees can be justified or not, but it also indicates what is the optimal level of the fees. In this way one can quantify the magnitude by which user fees should be changed, as well as the direction of change.

The optimal user charge P^* was set out in equation (12.7) as a weighted average of the marginal cost MC and the actual price P:

$$P^* = \omega\,MC + P\,(1 - \gamma)$$

It will be recalled that ω was the composite weight that expressed the MCF as a ratio of the relative distribution weights (a_2/a_1), and γ combined ω with the price elasticity of demand e_p in the form: $\gamma = \omega + (1/e_p)\,(1 - \omega)$. Estimates of P and MC were derived from Mundle and Rao's data. Values of $-1/2$, -1 and -2 were tried for e_p. This leaves ω yet to be determined. As explained in the Brent study, the way that Mundle and Rao estimated their costs automatically included an allowance for the MCF. This means that only the determination of the distribution weights needs now to be explained.

The determination of the distribution weights   To estimate a_2/a_1, Brent basically followed the Squire and van der Tak (1975) approach outlined in Chapter 10. The weight for any state a_2 was an isoelastic function of the per-capita income of the state y_2, along the lines of equation (10.7):

$$a_2 = y_2^{-\eta}$$

This made the ratio of the weights take the form:

$$\frac{a_2}{a_1} = \left(\frac{y_1}{y_2}\right)^{\eta} \tag{12.11}$$

As explained in Chapter 10, the Squire and van der Tak recommended value of $\eta = 1$ for the inequality aversion parameter should be regarded as a strong social preference for inequality. As such, it should be regarded as the upper bound value. A less extreme (but still pro-poor) value of $\eta = 1/2$ was used as the lower-bound alternate.

The only problem left was how to specify the reference group (state) 1 used to fix a_1. Group 1 is the group that is financing the project (the state expenditures). Brent adopted two scenarios for a_1. One was termed *progressive* and the other *average*. In the former, it was assumed that the group paying the subsidy is in the position of the state with the highest per-capita income. In the latter scenario, it was assumed that the group paying the subsidy corresponds to a typical resident in a state at the average state income level.

Table 12.2   Relative income distribution weights

State	Per capita income: y_2	Average financing $a_2/a_1 = (2934/y_2)^{\eta}$		Progressive financing $a_2/a_1 = (5689/y_2)^{\eta}$	
		$\eta = 0.5$	$\eta = 1$	$\eta = 0.5$	$\eta = 1$
Andhra Pradesh	2 691	1.0442	1.0903	1.4540	2.1141
Bihar	1 848	1.2600	1.5877	1.7546	3.0785
Gujarat	3 527	0.9121	0.8319	1.2700	1.6130
Haryana	4 399	0.8167	0.6670	1.1372	1.2932
Karnataka	3 301	0.9428	0.8888	1.3128	1.7234
Kerala	2 913	1.0036	1.0072	1.3975	1.9530
Madhya Pradesh	2 398	1.1061	1.2235	1.5403	2.3724
Maharashtra	4 479	0.8094	0.6551	1.1270	1.2701
Orissa	2 199	1.1551	1.3342	1.6084	2.5871
Punjab	5 689	0.7181	0.5157	1.0000	1.0000
Rajasthan	2 226	1.1481	1.3181	1.5987	2.5557
Tamil Nadu	3 413	0.9272	0.8597	1.2911	1.6669
Uttar Pradesh	2 354	1.1164	1.2464	1.5546	2.4167
West Bengal	3 095	0.9736	0.9480	1.3558	1.8381

Source: Brent (1995a)

The estimates of the relative distribution weights are shown in Table 12.2 (Brent's Table 2). The average per-capita income for all the states was 2 934 rupees (Rs) in 1987. This sets $y_1 = 2\,934$ Rs in the average scenario for equation (12.1). The state whose income was closest to this average figure was Kerala with 2 913 Rs per capita. The state with the highest per-capita income was Punjab. In the progressive scenario $y_1 = 5\,689$ Rs. Bihar is the poorest state (with the highest weight) and Punjab is the richest (with the lowest weight). In the average regime, with $\eta = 1$, the range of values for the weights is between 0.5157 and 1.5877, which is a relative factor of 3.0787. With $\eta = 0.5$, the range is between 0.7181 and 1.2600, and the relative factor drops to 1.7546. In the progressive regime, with $\eta = 1$, the range of values is between 1.0000 and 3.0785, and with $\eta = 0.5$, the range is between 1.0000 and 1.7546. The relative factors are the same as for the average regime. The main effect therefore of assuming a progressive rather than an average financing scenario is that the range centres around 1.9630 rather than 1.0052 when $\eta = 1$ (and around 1.3859 rather than 0.9630 when $\eta = 0.5$).

Given that the differences in the weights are not very large, even with a high level of income aversion ($\eta = 1$) and with the assumption of progressive financing, Brent emphasized only the highest values for the relative distribution weights (shown in the last column of Table 12.2).

Actual and optimal user prices for economic services   With all the parameters set, the CBA framework was then applied to state expenditures in India. User fees were so obviously low (around 2 per cent of costs) for social services, that attention was given to economic services (where on average 25 per cent of costs were recovered by user fees). Economic services were split into 6 categories, namely, agriculture and allied services, irrigation, power and energy, industry and minerals, transport and communications, and other economic services.

Brent defined a 'project' as the expenditure by a state on a particular category of economic service. It was assumed that each rupee of per-capita state expenditure provides an equal unit of output of service to recipients. With 14 states, and 6 categories of economic service, there were 84 projects in total. For each project there was an actual price P. Using this information on P, and the marginal cost, equation (12.7) was then used to estimate the social prices P_*.

Table 12.3 (Brent's Table 5) records the main results. This corresponds to the case which gives the *least* difference between actual and social prices (and hence gives most support to existing pricing practices). Essentially, this involves using a high value for ω and having a negative $1 - \gamma$ value for *all* states. (Specifically: the distribution weights are those in the last column of Table 12.2; the price elasticity of demand was –2; and the *MCF* was 5.2.)

A situation where the actual price is above the social price is indicated with the footnote sign ¶ in Table 12.3. This corresponds to 'overpricing'. As we can

Table 12.3 Actual and social prices for economics services 1987–88 (rupees)

$$P_* = \omega MC + (1 - \gamma)P$$

State	Agriculture & allied		Irrigation		Power & energy		Industry & minerals		Transport & comm.		Other economic	
	P	P_*	P	P_*	P	P_*	P	P_*	P	P_*	P	P_*
Andhra Pradesh	11.53	37.94	17.17	23.61	17.91¶	−3.21	5.62¶	2.06	1.97	6.60	14.88¶	−11.10
Bihar	9.59	14.12	1.64	23.05	0.05	6.12	2.62¶	2.45	0.29	5.33	0.90¶	0.46
Gujarat	12.97	50.57	47.15¶	39.00	0.01	15.52	4.03	7.76	0.36	9.40	6.44¶	−2.45
Haryana	9.47	51.92	43.90	55.97	54.04¶	−16.26	0.87	5.55	81.71¶	−45.64	8.02¶	−7.16
Karnataka	23.00¶	21.88	28.75	31.80	23.27¶	13.21	6.84	7.44	0.18	14.84	6.32¶	−3.35
Kerala	18.58¶	12.15	3.77	23.95	8.07¶	−4.24	1.32	7.03	1.46	15.84	3.99¶	−0.65
Madhya Pradesh	63.24¶	−8.62	3.03	34.31	12.20¶	4.91	0.59	3.90	1.27	13.78	1.02¶	0.16
Maharashtra	72.07¶	−21.86	37.31¶	11.26	19.37¶	−7.15	1.10	7.08	0.87	10.23	0.92¶	−0.43
Orissa	23.44¶	12.11	2.35	34.64	6.41¶	−0.18	1.87	5.44	0.82	10.03	1.56¶	0.10
Punjab	7.95	51.86	21.54	69.51	8.09	122.39	2.46	11.92	36.05¶	−8.98	4.50¶	−6.14
Rajasthan	4.20	21.39	24.08	30.21	0.19	8.74	5.97¶	1.53	0.16	20.99	10.52¶	−3.64
Tamil Nadu	17.86	38.27	8.38¶	6.97	0.00	42.97	3.96	5.58	1.98	12.00	0.83	13.28
Uttar Pradesh	9.84	16.41	17.36¶	16.47	0.01	9.01	7.57¶	−1.19	0.63	−8.75	1.47¶	−0.06
West Bengal	8.37	24.06	4.52	14.45	0.68	5.94	1.98	4.72	0.83	12.70	0.74	0.91

Source: Brent (1995a)

see in the table, the number of projects where overpricing takes place is 34. Every one of the 6 types of project (i.e., category of economic service) had at least one state where there was overpricing. Only in West Bengal was there no instance where the actual price matched the social price. Nonetheless, even with all the assumptions working towards lowering the value of user prices in the social pricing equation, underpricing was the norm. For 50 of the 84 projects, the actual user prices were below their social counterparts.

The application of the CBA framework to India's state user-pricing experience does therefore, on the whole, support the Rao and Mundle conjecture that it is hard to justify the limited use of user pricing for state government services in India.

12.3.3   User fees and health demand

What critics of user fees for health and social services fail to understand is that even with zero user fees, implicit pricing still takes place in other forms. There are consumption costs involved with travelling to a school or clinic (in time and money). These consumptions costs help to explain why the rich are the groups who often gain the most from the government subsidies implied by zero user pricing. For example, by siting hospitals in towns, the richer urban areas receive greater access than the poorer rural areas. In the Mwabu et al. (1994) study of medical treatment in rural Kenya, varying the distance to the government facility was included as one alternative to user pricing. The other policy options were an across-the-board rise in incomes and changing the quality of the health service provided (varying the number of drugs available at a clinic).

Just as with the classic transport study by Foster and Beesley (1963) which introduced the concepts of generated and diverted traffic, Mwabu et al. were careful to distinguish 'demand diversion effects' (whereby patients transfer to private alternatives when user prices are raised) from 'demand reduction effects' (whereby patients cease to be treated by the formal health-care system). Mwabu et al. emphasize that those against user fees are usually more concerned with the demand reduction effects. In their analysis they basically focus on usage and how this is affected by user fees and other policy options.

The usage effects of user fees is, of course, an elasticity issue. What is involved then is an estimate of the demand curve for health-care treatment. Strictly, one is dealing with a *conditional* demand curve, as one seeks treatment only if one has a health-care problem. The 'quantity' being estimated is the probability of making a visit to the government facility (given that one is sick). The independent variables are: the charge at the government facility; the fees levied by other providers in the formal system (missions and private clinics); income and quality indicators (e.g., availability of aspirin, antibiotics and malaria drugs). The 'alternative' of leaving the formal health-care system was analysed as a separate *self*-provision (which includes going to traditional healers and retail shops).

The estimated elasticities (using the Logit technique referred to in earlier chapters) are listed in Table 12.4. We see that the own price elasticity for the government facility is very low at (–) 0.10. However, the own price elasticities are much higher in the other alternatives in the formal system. In fact, these are own price elastic, being (–) 1.57 for missions and (–) 1.94 for private providers. One important conclusion therefore of this study is that one cannot assume that because health-care is judged essential it must therefore be insensitive to price changes.

Table 12.4   Demand elasticities for health care in Kenya

Demand variable	Government	Mission	Private
Government fee	–0.100	0.023	0.023
Own fee	–0.100	–1.571	–1.937
Distance to government facility	–0.079	0.090	0.090
Distance to own facility	–0.079	–0.300	–0.204
No. drugs in government facility	0.118	–0.137	–0.137
Income	–0.006	0.293	0.319

Source: Mwabu et al. (1994)

Another important elasticity result relates to the distance 'price' variable. Distance reduces usage in all three parts of the formal health-care system. For government facilities, patients are around eight times more elastic for this consumption cost than for the explicit user fee. Cross price elasticities are positive, which means that missions and private providers are substitutes for government clinics. But their magnitudes are small.

Lastly, we need to comment on the estimates of the income elasticities. These establish that government facilities are inferior goods (the income elasticity is negative), while the other parts of the formal system are normal goods (their income elasticities are positive). As income grows with development, patients switch from government clinics to alternative providers. Over time one can therefore expect that health will be less of a drain on public resources.

Mwabu et al. use their elasticity estimates to simulate various policy changes. The four main policy alternatives were to: (1) raise user fees at government facilities by K10 shillings (Kshl0 = US$0.20); (2) reduce the distance travelled to government facilities by 20 per cent; (3) increase the number of drugs available at the government facilities by two; and (4) increase income by 20 per cent. The basis of comparison for the simulation was per 1 000 sick patients. The results are presented in Table 12.5.

Table 12.5   Policy simulations per 1 000 sick patients

Policy change	Government	Mission	Private	Self
1. Rise in user fees in government facilities from 0–10 Ksh	−97	+8	+28	+61
2. Reduction in distance to government facilities by 20%	+9	−1	−3	−5
3. Rise in the number of drugs in government facilities by 2	+19	−2	−6	−12
4. Increase in household income by 20%	−1	+2	+9	−10

Source: Mwabu et al. (1994)

Policy change 1 is what concerns us the most and this also has the greatest impact. The K10 shillings price rise would lead to a reduction of 97 (per 1 000 sick patients). Thirty-six patients would go elsewhere (8 to missions and 28 to private providers). This makes the demand reduction effect 61. This finding reminds us that it is the total demand curve that is relevant for CBA, and not just the part of the demand that is satisfied by government provision. Note that although the price elasticity is low at (−) 0.10, the relative reduction in numbers at public facilities is large. Of 1 000 sick patients, 536 would be at public clinics. The 97 patient decrease is an 18 per cent reduction in demand at government facilities.

Also of interest is policy change 4. The results mirror the earlier estimated income elasticity finding. A 20 per cent increase in income leads to 10 patients (per 1 000 sick patients) entering the formal health-care system (i.e., 'self' goes down by 10). In addition, 1 patient leaves the public sector, making an 11-patient rise to the non-governmental formal sector. The higher the income the more patients attend missions and private providers. It is clear then that making improvements at government health-care facilities would favour the poor rather than the rich.

Mwabu et al.'s study is very informative and should be viewed as complementary to a CBA evaluation. The study estimates that raising user fees by K10 shillings would reduce the number of visits by 61 (per 1 000 patients) to the formal health-care sector. Whether this is desirable or not depends on the size of the benefits lost for these patients, how important is the extra revenue that is collected (K6 100 shillings per 1 000 patients), and how large is the cost savings from serving fewer patients. The problems in 12.4.2 require that one draw all these ingredients together.

12.4 Final comments
For the last time, we close with the summary and problems sections.

12.4.1 Summary
In this chapter we recast the basic cost–benefit criterion, which was defined in terms of quantity changes, so that it could deal with judgements as to the adequacy, or otherwise, of user prices. The resulting criterion expressed what the user prices should be, that is, their social values, as a weighted average of the actual price and marginal costs. The weights reflected two major social concerns that worked in opposite directions. High actual prices would adversely affect those with low incomes. But, with a high premium on public income, any increase of revenues would make available valuable resources which could be invested and help the economy to grow. Cost recovery was seen to be a special case of this general framework; one where all the weights are equal to unity. In this situation, the social pricing rule was the traditional one of requiring that prices equal marginal costs.

It is clear then that the complete CBA criterion with user prices combines efficiency, budgetary and distributional concerns in one umbrella framework. User fees link all these three dimensions. That is, higher user fees cover costs, and reduce required subsidies, but they also place a burden on the poor. Thus, the way to appreciate CBA is as a means of combining a number of disparate concerns and extracting a compromise outcome.

Nowhere was this more evident than in the case study by Mundle and Rao related to user pricing by the states in India. Low prices led to a large budget deficit that placed an enormous macroeconomic burden on the economy. Concern for public revenue was therefore high and this was reflected in the choice of value for the *MCF*. On the other hand, low-income states may not be able to afford user fees that cover costs. There was a need to incorporate distributional considerations and the weighting procedure did just that. The optimum user fee is the one that provides the best balance between revenues generated and the distributional damage.

Without CBA, one is forced to *hope* that there are available policy options that can improve all objectives simultaneously. It is in this context that the contribution by the cost recovery literature can be best understood. When there is excess demand, efficiency can always be improved. When the rationing that caused the excess demand operates disproportionately on the poor (i.e., more disproportionately than relying on user fees), raising using fees can further efficiency and distribution. The Malawi case study revealed just such a situation. But note that even in this best case scenario, one's horizons in cost recovery are still limited. Necessarily, revenues are being held constant. One is not able to give consideration to increasing revenues no matter how large a value for the *MCF* one thinks appropriate.

When excess demand does not exist, raising user fees will decrease usage. How large this will be depends on the elasticity of demand. The Kenyan case study by Mwabu et al. showed that the price elasticity varied greatly among health-care providers, and was actually greater than 1 for missions and private providers. No simple expectations regarding elasticities should be made, even when essential social services are being considered.

We close the book by referring the reader to the problems. This shows, in a step-by-step fashion, how the general CBA criterion presented in this chapter can be applied to the Mwabu et al. policy situation to produce recommendations concerning the choice of user fees. The test of the usefulness of learning CBA principles is in their applicability.

12.4.2 Problems

Our optimal user-pricing rule (12.7) was derived from the welfare criterion given by equation (12.5). This welfare criterion can also be used, as with the analytical framework employed throughout the book, as a means of deciding how to move towards the optimum. That is, for a particular price change, one can use equation (12.5) to see whether the consequences are socially worthwhile. Note that if one keeps on accepting all price changes that provide positive net benefits according to criterion (12.5), and stop when these net benefits are zero, one will then have obtained the optimum user price that would correspond to P^* in equation (12.7). The problems below require that one test whether the K10 shilling user fee analysed by Mwabu et al. is a social improvement or not, and whether the price can be raised further still.

Assume throughout that average costs are constant at K10 shillings per person (visiting a health facility) and that distribution is not an issue (set $a_2 = a_1$ and hence make $\omega = MCF$).

1. In the Mwabu et al. study, originally there was no user fee at government clinics and there was to be a rise to K10 shillings. To keep matters simple, assume that prior to the rise, there were 1 000 patients treated in total (in all forms of health facility). After the price rise there were 939 patients in the formal health sector (61 dropped out). Draw the demand curve for formal health-care, assuming that it is a straight line between the old and new prices, and throughout the whole of its range. (That is, assume that for every K10 shilling rise in user fee, usage drops off by 61.) Calculate the loss of total benefits (B), the rise in revenue (R), and the cost saving C for the K10 shilling rise.
2. On the basis of the figures derived for B, R and C in question 1, and assuming the $MCF = 1$, apply criterion (12.5) to see whether or not the K10 shilling fee is a social improvement. By inspection of the demand curve, can you tell what is the optimum price P^* (when the MCF equals 1)?

3. Hereafter, assume that the $MCF = 1.1$. Is the K10 shilling fee now worthwhile? (Hint: note that the criterion (12.5) can be written also as: $B - (MCF)C + R(MCF - 1)$.)

4. Consider a further rise from K10 shillings to K20 shillings. Insert this new point on the demand curve drawn previously. Calculate the new values for B, C and R and thereby determine whether the K20 shillings fee is worthwhile. (Hints: the new quantity is 878, and the loss of B (the area under the demand curve) now consists of the loss of revenue (K10 shillings times 61) plus the consumer surplus loss (the triangular area equal to K305 shillings)).

5. Finally, consider a rise in the fee from K20 shillings to K30 shillings. Is this fee change worthwhile? On the basis of all your answers (from 3 onwards), what is the price range in which the optimum P_* must lie?

12.5   Appendix

Here we derive the optimal user price equation (12.7). The objective is to maximize social welfare as given by equation (12.5): $W = B - R - \omega(C - R)$. The first-order condition is:

$$\frac{dW}{dQ} = B' - R' - \omega(C' - R') = 0 \tag{12.12}$$

where the primes represent the derivatives with respect to quantity. Benefits are the area under the social demand curve. To obtain this we integrate under the social demand price (P_*) curve: $B = \int P_* dQ$. Differentiating B leads to: $B' = P_*$. Substituting P_* for B' in (12.12) and collecting terms in R' produces:

$$P_* = \omega C' + (1 - \omega)R' \tag{12.13}$$

Using the standard relation between marginal revenue and price, $R' = P(1 - 1/e_p)$, with e_p the price elasticity of demand, equation (12.13) becomes:

$$P_* - P = \omega C' - P\left[\omega + \frac{1}{e_p}(1 - \omega)\right] \tag{12.14}$$

Define $\omega + (1/e_p)(1 - \omega) = \gamma$ and substitute in equation (12.14) to obtain equation (12.7):

$$P_* = \omega C' + P(1 - \gamma)$$

References

Ahmad, E. and Stern, N. (1987), 'Alternative Sources of Government Revenue: Illustrations from India, 1979–80', Ch. 11 in Newbery, D. and Stern, N. (eds), *The Theory of Taxation for Developing Countries*, New York: Oxford University Press.

Arrow, K.J. (1963), 'Uncertainty and the Welfare Economics of Medical Care', *American Economic Review*, **53**, 941–73.

Arrow, K.J. and Lind, R.C. (1970), 'Uncertainty and the Evaluation of Public Investment Decisions', *American Economic Review*, **60**, 364–78.

Atkinson, A.B. and Stern, N.H. (1974), 'Pigou, Taxation and Public Goods', *Review of Economic Studies*, **41**, 119–28.

Atkinson, A.B. and Stiglitz, J.E. (1980), *Lectures on Public Economics*, New York: McGraw-Hill.

Bahl, R.W. and Lin, J.F. (1992), 'Automotive Taxation', Ch. 7 in *Urban Public Finance in Developing Countries*, Washington DC: World Bank.

Ballard, C.L. and Fullerton, D. (1992), 'Distortionary Taxes and the Provision of Public Goods', *Journal of Economic Perspectives*, **6**, 117–31.

Ballard, C.L., Fullerton, D., Shoven, J.B. and Whalley, J. (1985a), *A General Equilibrium Model for Tax Policy Evaluation*, Chicago: Chicago University Press.

Ballard, C.L., Shoven, J.B. and Whalley, J. (1985b), 'General Equilibrium Computations of the Marginal Welfare Costs of Taxes in the United States', *American Economic Review*, **75**, 128–38.

Barkley, P.W. and Seckler, D.W. (1972), *Economic Growth and Environmental Decay*, New York: Harcourt Brace Jovanovich.

Baumol, W.J. and Bradford, D.F. (1970), 'Optimal Departures from Marginal Cost Pricing', *American Economic Review*, **60**, 265–83.

Baumol, W.M. and Oates, W.E. (1971), 'The Use of Standards and Prices for Environmental Protection', *Swedish Journal of Economics*, **1**, 42–54.

Becker, G.S. and Murphy, K.M. (1988), 'A Theory of Rational Addiction', *Journal of Political Economy*, **96**, 675–700.

Ben-Akiva, B. and Lerman, S.R. (1985), *Discrete Choice Analysis*, Cambridge, Mass.: MIT Press.

Berry, R.E. and Boland, J.P. (1977), *The Economic Cost of Alcohol Abuse*, New York: Free Press.

Blomquist, G. (1979), 'Value of Life Saving: Implications of Consumption Activity', *Journal of Political Economy*, **87**, 540–58.

Boadway, R. (1976), 'Integrating Equity and Efficiency in Applied Welfare Economics', *Quarterly Journal of Economics*, **90**, 541–56.

Boadway, R.W. and Wildasin, D. (1984), *Public Sector Economics* (2nd edn), Boston: Little, Brown & Company.

Bohm, P. (1972), 'Estimating Demand for Public Goods: An Experiment', *European Economic Review*, **3**, 111–30.

Bowker, J.M. and Stoll, J.R. (1988), 'Use of Dichotomous Choice Nonmarket Methods to Value the Whooping Crane Resource', *American Journal of Agricultural Economics*, **71**, 373–81.

Boyle, M.H., Torrance, G.W., Sinclair, J.C. and Horwood, J.C. (1983), 'Economic Evaluation of Neonatal Intensive Care of Very Low Birth-Weight Infants', *New England Journal of Medicine*, **308**, 1300–307.

Bradford, D.F. (1975), 'Constraints on Government Investment Opportunities', *American Economic Review*, **65**, 887–99.

Brent, R.J. (1976), 'The Minister of Transport's Social Welfare Function: A Study of the Factors behind Railway Closure Decisions (1963–1970)', Ph.D Thesis, University of Manchester (unpublished).

Brent, R.J. (1979), 'Imputing Weights Behind Past Railway Closure Decisions Within a Cost–Benefit Framework', *Applied Economics*, **9**, 157–70.

Brent, R.J. (1980), 'Distinguishing Between Money Income and Utility Income in Cost–Benefit Analysis', *Public Finance Quarterly*, **8**, 131–52.

Brent, R.J. (1984a), 'A Three Objective Social Welfare Function for Cost–Benefit Analysis', *Applied Economics*, **16**, 369–78.

Brent, R.J. (1984b), 'On the Use of Distributional Weights in Cost–Benefit Analysis: A Survey of Schools', *Public Finance Quarterly*, **12**, 213–30.

Brent, R.J. (1986), 'An Axiomatic Basis for the Three Objective Social Welfare Function', *Economics Letters*, **20**, 89–94.

Brent, R.J. (1989), 'The Farmers' Home Administration's Social Discount Rate', *Applied Economics*, **21**, 1247–56.

Brent, R.J. (1990), *Project Appraisal for Developing Countries*, New York: New York University Press (also published in the UK by Harvester-Wheatsheaf Books).

Brent, R.J. (1991a), 'A New Approach to Valuing a Life', *Journal of Public Economics*, **44**, 165–71.

Brent, R.J. (1991b), 'On the Estimation Technique to Reveal Government Distributional Weights', *Applied Economics*, **23**, 985–92.

Brent, R.J. (1991c), 'The Numbers Effect and the Shadow Wage in Project Appraisal', *Public Finance*, **46**, 118–27.

Brent, R.J. (1991d), 'The Cost–Benefit Analysis of Government Loans', *Public Finance Quarterly*, **19** (January), 43–66.

Brent, R.J. (1991e), 'The Numbers Effect, the Form of the Welfare Function, and the Social Discount Rate in Project Appraisal', in Bhagwan Dahiya, S..

(ed.), *Theoretical Foundations of Development Planning*, Volume 5, *Project Evaluation*, New Delhi: Concepts Books.

Brent, R.J. (1992), 'The Consumption Rate of Interest and the Numbers Effect', *Public Finance*, **47** (3), 111–20.

Brent, R.J. (1993), 'Country Estimates of Social Discount Rates based on Changes in Life Expectancies', *Kyklos*, **46**, 399–409.

Brent, R.J. (1994), 'Shadow Prices for a Physician's Services', *Applied Economics*, **26**, 669–76.

Brent, R.J. (1995a), 'Cost–Benefit Analysis, User Prices and State Expenditures in India', National Institute of Public Finance and Policy, Discussion Paper No. 5, New Delhi.

Brent, R.J. (1995b), 'The Outperforming Requirement, User Prices and Cost–Benefit Analysis', Department of Economics, Fordham University.

Brookshire, D. and Coursey, D. (1987), 'Measuring the Value of a Public Good: An Empirical Comparison of Elicitation Procedures', *American Economic Review*, **77**, 554–66.

Brookshire, D.S., Thayer, M.A., Schulze, W.D. and D'Arge, R.C. (1982), 'Valuing Public Goods: A Comparison of Survey and Hedonic Approaches', *American Economic Review*, **72**, 165–77.

Brown, G. and Mendelsohn, R. (1984), 'The Hedonic Travel Cost Method', *Review of Economics and Statistics*, **66**, 427–33.

Browning, E.K. (1976), 'The Marginal Cost of Public Funds', *Journal of Political Economy*, **84**, 283–98.

Browning, E.K. (1987), 'On the Marginal Welfare Cost of Taxation', *American Economic Review*, **77**, 11–23.

Buchanan, J.M. and Stubblebine, C. (1962), 'Externality', *Economica*, **29**, 371–84.

Carrin, G. (1984), *Economic Evaluation in Health Care in Developing Countries*, New York: St Martin's Press.

Clark, W.B. and Midanik, L. (1982), 'Alcohol Use and Alcohol Problems among US Adults: Results of the 1979 Survey', in NIAAA, *Alcohol Consumption and Related Problems*, Washington DC: USGPO, 3–54.

Clawson, M. (1966), *Economics of Outdoor Recreation*, Washington DC: Johns Hopkins.

Coase, R.H. (1960), 'The Problem of Social Cost', *Journal of Law and Economics*, **3**, 1–44.

Cohn, E.J. (1972), 'Assessment of Malaria Eradication: Costs and Benefits', *American Journal of Tropical Medicine and Hygiene*, **21**, 663–7.

Constantatos, C. and West, E.G. (1991), 'Measuring Returns from Education: Some Neglected Factors', *Canadian Public Policy*, **17**, 127–38.

Cordes, J.J. and Weisbrod, B.A. (1979), 'Governmental Behavior in Response to Compensation Requirements', *Journal of Public Economics*, **11**, 47–58.

Creese, A.L. (1991), 'User Charges for Health Care: A Review of Recent Experience', *Health Policy and Planning*, **6**, 309–19.

Cropper, M.L., Aydede, S.K., and Portney, P.R. (1992), 'Rates of Time Preference for Saving Lives', *American Economic Review*, **82**, 469–72.

Cropper, M.L., Evans, W.N., Beradi, S.J., Ducla-Soares, M.M. and Portney, P.R. (1992), 'The Determinants of Pesticide Regulation: A Statistical Analysis of EPA Decision Making', *Journal of Political Economy*, **100**, 175–97.

Dasgupta, A.K. (1972), *Cost–Benefit Analysis: Theory and Practice*, New York: Harper & Row.

Deaton, A. and Muellbauer, J. (1980), *Economics and Consumer Behavior*, Cambridge: Cambridge University Press.

Diamond, P.A. (1975), 'A Many-person Ramsey Tax Rule', *Journal of Public Economics*, **4**, 335–42.

Diamond, P.A. and Mirrlees, J.M. (1971), 'Optimal Taxation and Public Production', *American Economic Review*, **61**, 8–27 (Part 2, **61**, 261–78).

Dorfman, R. (1972), 'Risk and Uncertainty in Cost–Benefit Analysis', in Layard, R. (ed.), *Cost–Benefit Analysis*, Middlesex: Penguin Books.

Drummond, M.F., Stoddart G.L. and G.W. Torrance (1987), *Methods For The Economic Evaluation Of Health Care Programmes*, London: Oxford University Press.

Dupuit, J. (1952), 'On the Measurement of the Utility of Public Works', reprinted in *International Economic Papers*, No. 2, London: Macmillan.

Eckstein, O. (1961), 'A Survey of the Theory of Public Expenditure Criteria', in *Public Finances, Needs, Sources and Utilization*, New Jersey: Princeton University Press, 439–94.

Feldstein, M.S. (1972a), 'Distributional Equity and the Optimal Structure of Public Prices', *American Economic Review*, **62**, 32–6.

Feldstein, M.S. (1972b), 'The Inadequacy of Weighted Average Discount Rates', Ch. 13 in Layard, R. (ed.), *Cost–Benefit Analysis*, Penguin Books, Middlesex, England.

Feldstein, M.S. (1977), 'Does the United States Save Too Little', *American Economic Review*, Papers and Proceedings, **67**, 116–21.

Fellner, W. (1967), 'Operational Utility: The Theoretical Background and Measurement', in Fellner, W. (ed.), *The Economic Essays Contributed in Honor of J. Bates Clark, Clark Essays*, New York: Wiley.

Fingarette, H. (1988), *Heavy Drinking*, Berkeley: University of California Press.

Fleming, J.M. (1968), 'Targets and Instruments', *International Monetary Fund Staff Papers*, **15**, 271–91.

Foldes, L.P., and Rees, R. (1977), 'A Note on the Arrow–Lind Theorem', *American Economic Review*, **67**, 188–93.

Forester, T.H., McNown, R.F. and Singell, L.D. (1984), 'A Cost–Benefit Analysis of the 55 MPH Speed Limit', *Southern Economic Journal*, **50**, 631–41.

Foster, C.D. and Beesley, M.E. (1963), 'Estimating the Social Benefits of Constructing an Underground Railway in London', *Journal of the Royal Statistical Society*, Series A, 46–56.

Fullerton, D. (1991), 'Reconciling Recent Estimates of the Marginal Welfare Cost of Taxation', *American Economic Review*, **81**, 302–8.

Fullerton, D. and Henderson, Y.K. (1989), 'The Marginal Excess Burden of Different Capital Tax Instruments', *Review of Economics and Statistics*, **71**, 435–42.

Gramlich, E.M. (1981), *Benefit–Cost Analysis of Government Programs*, New Jersey: Prentice-Hall.

Gray, T. and Olson, K.W. (1989), 'A Cost–Benefit Analysis of the Sentencing Decision for Burglars', *Social Science Quarterly*, **70**, 708–22.

Hanemann, W.M. (1984), 'Welfare Evaluation in Contingent Valuation Experiments with Discrete Responses', *American Journal of Agricultural Economics*, **66**, 332–41.

Hanemann, W.M. (1991), 'Willingness to Pay and Willingness to Accept: How Much Can They Differ?', *American Economic Review*, **81**, 635–47.

Harberger, A.C. (1968), 'Statement', in *Hearings Before the Subcommittee on Economy in Government of the Joint Economic Committee of the Congress of the United States*, Washington DC: United States Printing Office.

Harberger, A.C. (1978), 'On the Use of Distributional Weights in Social Cost–Benefit Analysis', *Journal of Political Economy*, (Supplement) **86**, 87–120.

Harberger, A.C. (1984), 'Basic Needs versus Distributional Weights in Social Cost–Benefit Analysis', *Economic Development and Cultural Change*, **32**, 455–74.

Harwood, H.J., Napolitano, D.M., Kristiansen, P.L. and Collins, J.J. (1984), *Economic Costs to Society of Alcohol and Drug Abuse and Mental Illness: 1980*, North Carolina: Research Triangle Institute.

Hau, T.D. (1986), 'Distributional Cost–Benefit Analysis in Discrete Choice', *Journal of Transport Economics and Policy*, **20**, 313–38.

Hau, T.D. (1987), 'Using a Hicksian Approach to Cost–Benefit Analysis in Discrete Choice: An Empirical Analysis of a Transportation Corridor Model', *Transportation Research*, **21B**, 339–57.

Hau, T.D. (1990), 'Electronic Road Pricing: Developments in Hong Kong 1983–89', *Journal of Transport Economics and Policy*, **24**, 203–14.

Hau, T.D. (1992a), 'Economic Fundamentals of Road Pricing: A Diagrammatic Analysis', *Policy Research Working Paper No. 1070*, Transport Division,

Infrastructure and Urban Development Department, Washington DC: World Bank.

Hau, T.D. (1992b), 'Congestion Charging Mechanisms for Roads: An Evaluation of Current Practice', *Policy Research Working Paper No. 1070*, Transport Division, Infrastructure and Urban Development Department, Washington DC: World Bank.

Haynes, P. and Larsen, C.R. (1984), 'Financial Consequences of Incarceration and Alternatives: Burglary', *Crime and Delinquency*, **30**, 529–50.

Hicks, J.R. (1943), 'The Four Consumers' Surpluses', *Review of Economics Studies*, **11**, 31–41.

Hirshleifer, J. and Riley, J.G. (1979), 'The Analytics of Uncertainty and Information – An Expository Survey', *Journal of Economic Literature*, **17**, 1375–421.

Hochman, H.M. and Rodgers, J.D. (1971), 'Is Efficiency a Criterion for Judging Redistribution?', *Public Finance*, **26**, 76–98.

Holtman, A.G. (1964), 'Estimating the Demand for Public Health Services: The Alcoholism Case', *Public Finance*, **19**, 351–8.

Horowitz, J.R. and Carson, R.T. (1988), 'Discounting Statistical Lives', Department of Economics, Discussion Paper 88–16, University of California, San Diego.

Horowitz, J.R. and Carson, R.T. (1990), 'Discounting Statistical Lives', *Journal of Risk and Uncertainty*, **3**, 403–13.

Hsiao, W.C. (1987), 'The Resource-Based Relative Value Scale: An Option for Physician Payment', *Inquiry*, **24**, 360–61.

Hsiao, W.C., Braun, P., Kelly, N.L. and Becker, E.R. (1988a), 'Results, Potential Effects, and Implementation Issues of the Resource-Based Relative Value Scale', *Journal of the American Medical Association*, **260**, 2429–38.

Hsiao, W.C., Braun, P., Yntema, D. and Becker, E.R. (1988b), 'Estimating Physicians' Work for a Resource-Based Relative Value Scale', *New England Journal of Medicine*, **319**, 835–41.

Hughes, G. (1987), 'The Incidence of Fuel Taxes: A Comparative Study of Three Countries', Ch. 20 in Newbery, D. and Stern, N. (eds), *The Theory of Taxation for Development*, New York: Oxford University Press (for the World Bank).

Irvin, G. (1978), *Modern Cost–Benefit Methods*, London: Macmillan.

James, E. (1975), 'A Note on Uncertainty and the Evaluation of Public Investment Decisions', *American Economic Review*, **65**, 200–05.

Jimenez, J. (1987), *Pricing Policy in the Social Sectors*, Baltimore: Johns Hopkins.

Jones, L.P., Tandon, P. and Vogelsang, I. (1990), *Selling Public Enterprises*, Cambridge, Mass.: MIT Press.

Joyce, J.P. (1989), 'An Investigation of Government Preference Functions: The Case of Canada, 1970–1981', *Journal of Macroeconomics*, **11**, 217–32.

Katz, M. (1987), 'Pricing Publicly Supplied Goods and Services', Ch. 21 in Newbery, D. and Stern, N. (eds), *The Theory of Taxation for Developing Countries*, New York: Oxford University Press.

Kessel, R.A. (1974), 'Transfused Blood, Serum Hepatitis, and the Coase Theorem', *Journal of Political Economy*, **82**, 265–89.

Kirkpatrick, C.H. (1979), 'Distributional Objectives and the Optimum Level of Road User Charges in Developing Countries: Some Results for Kenya', *Manchester School of Economics and Social Studies*, **47**, 139–59.

Knight, F. (1921), *Risk, Uncertainty and Profit*, reprinted, New York: Sentry Press, 1964.

Kula, E. (1984), 'Derivation of Social Time Preference Rates for the U.S. and Canada', *Quarterly Journal of Economics*, **99**, 873–82.

Layard, P.R.G. and Walters, A.A. (1978), *Microeconomic Theory*, New York: McGraw-Hill.

Layard, R. (ed.) (1972), *Cost–Benefit Analysis*, Middlesex: Penguin Books.

Little, I.M.D. (1957), *A Critique of Welfare Economics* (2nd edn), Oxford: Oxford University Press.

Londero, E. (1987), *Benefits and Beneficiaries*, Washington DC: Inter-American Development Bank.

Loury, G.C. (1983), 'Efficiency and Equity Impacts of Natural Gas Regulation', in Haveman, R.H. and Margolis, J. (eds), *Public Expenditure and Policy Analysis* (3rd edn), Boston: Houghton Mifflin.

Lowson, K.V., Drummond, M.F. and Bishop, J.M. (1981), 'Costing New Services: Long-term Domiciliary Oxygen Therapy', *Lancet*, **i**, 1146–9.

Marglin, S.A. (1968), 'Objectives of Water Resource Development: A General Statement', in A. Maas (ed.), *Design of Water Resource Systems*, New York: Macmillan.

Marshall, A. (1924), *Principles of Economics* (8th edn), London: Macmillan.

Mayshar, J. (1990), 'On Measures of Excess Burden and their Application', *Journal of Public Economics*, **43**, 263–89.

McNeil, B.J., Weichselbaum, R. and Pauker, G.(1978), 'Fallacy of the Five-year Survival in Lung Cancer', *New England Journal of Medicine*, **299**, 1397–401.

Millward, R. (1971), *Public Expenditure Economics*, London: McGraw Hill.

Mishan, E.J. (1976), *Cost–Benefit Analysis*, (3rd edn), New York: Praeger.

Mitchell, R.C. and Carson, R.T. (1989), *Using Surveys to Value Public Goods: The Contingent Valuation Method*, Washington DC: Resources for the Future.

Moffit, R.E. (1992), 'Back to the Future: Medicare's Resurrection of the Labor Theory of Value', *Regulation*, **10**, 54–63.

Mooney, G.H. (1986), *Economics, Medicine and Health Care*, Sussex: Harvester-Wheatsheaf Books.

Morrison, S.A. (1982), 'The Structure of Landing Fees at Uncongested Airports', *Journal of Transport Economics and Policy*, **16**, 151–9.

Mundle, S. and Rao, M.G. (1991), 'The Volume and Composition of Government Subsidies in India', *Economic and Political Weekly* (May).

Musgrave, R.A. (1969), 'Cost–Benefit Analysis and the Theory of Social Goods', *Journal of Economic Literature*, **7**, 126–44.

Musgrave, R.A. and Musgrave, P.B. (1989), *Public Finance in Theory and Practice*, (5th edn), New York: McGraw-Hill.

Mwabu, G., Ainsworth, M. and Nyamete, A. (1994), 'Quality of Medical Care and Choice of Medical Treatment in Kenya', *Journal of Human Resources*, **28**, 838–62.

Newbery, D. (1988), 'Charging for Roads', *The World Bank Research Observer*, **3**, 119–38.

Ng, Y-K. (1983), *Welfare Economics*, New York: Macmillan.

Orr, L.L. (1976), 'Income Transfers as a Public Good: An Application to AFDC', *American Economic Review*, **66**, 359–71.

Pauker, S.G., and Kassirer, J.P. (1975), 'Therapeutic Decision Making', *New England Journal of Medicine*, **299**, 1397–401.

Pearce, D.W. and Nash, C.A (1981), *The Social Appraisal of Projects*, New York: Halstead.

Phillips, L. and Votey, H. (1975), 'Crime Control in California', *Journal of Legal Studies*, **4**, 327–49.

Pigou, A.C. (1920), *The Economics of Welfare*, London: Macmillan.

Pogue, T.F. and Sgontz, L.G. (1989), 'Taxing to Control Social Costs: The Case of Alcohol', *American Economic Review*, **79**, 235–43.

Pouliquen, L. (1970), 'Risk Analysis in Project Appraisal', *World Bank Staff Occasional Papers*, No. 11, Washington DC: World Bank.

Prest, A.R. and Turvey, R. (1968), 'Cost–Benefit Analysis: A Survey', *Economic Journal*, **75**, 683–735.

Ramsey, F. (1927), 'A Contribution to the Theory of Taxation', *Economic Journal*, **37**, 47–61.

Rawls, J. (1971), *A Theory of Justice*, Cambridge, Mass.: Harvard University Press.

Rao, M.G. and Mundle, S. (1992), 'An Analysis of Changes in State Government Subsidies: 1977–87', National Institute of Public Finance and Policy, New Delhi.

Ray, A. (1984), *Cost–Benefit Analysis,* Baltimore: Johns Hopkins.

Reutlinger, S. (1970), 'Techniques for Project Appraisal under Uncertainty', *World Bank Staff Occasional Papers*, No. 10, Washington DC: World Bank.

Rundell, O.H., Jones, R.K. and Gregory, D. (1981), 'Practical Benefit–Cost Analysis for Alcoholism Programs', *Alcoholism: Clinical and Experimental Research*, **5**, 497–508.

Samuelson, P.A. (1954), 'The Pure Theory of Public Expenditure', *Review of Economics and Statistics*, **36**, 350–56.

Samuelson, P.A. (1955), 'Diagrammatic Exposition of a Theory of Public Expenditure', *Review of Economics and Statistics*, **37**, 350–56.

Schelling, T.C. (1968), 'The Life You Save May Be Your Own', in Chase, S.B. Jr (ed.), *Problems in Public Expenditure Analysis*, Washington DC: Brookings.

Schriver, W.R., Bowlby, R.L. and Pursell, D.E. (1976), 'Evaluation of Trade Readjustment Assistance to Workers: A Case Study', *Social Science Quarterly*, **57**, 547–56.

Sen, A.K. (1972), 'The Social Time Preference Rate in Relation to the Market Rate of Interest', Ch. 10 in Layard, R. (ed.), *Cost–Benefit Analysis*, Middlesex: Penguin Books.

Singh, B., Ramasubban, R., Bhatia, R., Briscoe, J., Giffin, C. and Kim, C. (1993), 'Rural Water Supply in Kerala, India: How to Emerge from a Low-level Equilibrium Trap', *Water Resources Research* (forthcoming).

Smith, V.L. (1980), 'Experiments with a Decentralized Mechanism for Public Good Decisions', *American Economic Review*, **70**, 584–99.

Smith, V.L. (1991), *Papers in Experimental Economics*, Cambridge, Mass.: Cambridge University Press.

Squire, L. and van der Tak, G.H. (1975), *Economic Analysis of Projects*, Baltimore: Johns Hopkins .

Staats, E.B. (1969), 'Survey of Use by Federal Agencies of the Discounting Technique in Evaluating Future Programs', in Hinricks, H. and Taylor, G. (eds), *Program Budgeting and Benefit–Cost Analysis*, California: Goodyear.

Stason, W.B. and Weinstein, M.C. (1977), 'Allocation of Resources to Manage Hypertension', and 'Foundations of Cost-Effectiveness Analysis for Health and Medical Practices', both in *New England Journal of Medicine*, **296**, 732–9 and 716–21.

Stuart, C. (1984), 'Welfare Costs per Dollar of Additional Tax Revenue in the United States', *American Economic Review*, **74**, 352–62.

Swint, J.M., and Nelson, W.B. (1977), 'The Application of Economic Analysis to Evaluation of Alcoholism Rehabilitation Programs', *Inquiry*, **14**, 63–72.

Tarr, D.D., and Morkre, M.E. (1984), 'Aggregate Costs to the United States of Tariffs and Quotas on Imports: General Tariff Cuts and Removal of Quotas on Automobiles, Steel, Sugar, and Textiles', *Bureau of Economics Staff Report to the Federal Trade Commission*, Washington DC.

Thaler, R. and Rosen, S. (1975), 'The Value of Saving a Life', in Terleckyj, N.E. (ed.), *Household Production and Consumption*, New York: NBER.

Thobani, M. (1984): 'Charging User Fees for Social Services: Education in Malawi', *Comparative Education Review*, **28**, 402–23.

Thompson, M.S., Read, J.S. and Liang, M. (1984), 'Feasibility of Willingness to Pay Measurement in Chronic Arthritis', *Medical Decision Making*, **4**, 195–215.

Tideman, T.N. and Tullock, G. (1976), 'A New and Superior Process for Making Social Choices', *Journal of Political Economy*, **84**, 1145–60.

Torrance, G.W., Boyle, M.H. and Horwood, S.P. (1982), 'Application of Multi-attribute Utility Theory to Measure Social Preferences for Health States', *Operations Research*, **30**, 1043–69.

Tresch, R. (1981), *Public Finance: A Normative Theory*, Texas: Business Publications.

Turvey, R. (1963), 'On Divergences Between Social Cost and Private Cost', *Economica*, **30**, 309–13.

UNIDO (1972), *Guidelines for Project Evaluation*, New York: United Nations Industrial Development Organization.

Usher, Dan (1986), 'Tax Evasion and the Marginal Cost of Public Funds', *Economic Inquiry*, **24**, 563–86.

Vinod, H. (1988), 'Dynamic Benefit–Cost Ratio Criterion for Practical Sequential Ranking to Encourage Cost Control and Self Help', *Indian Economic Review*, **23**, 263–74.

Watson, P.L. and Holland, E.P. (1976), 'Congestion Pricing: The Example of Singapore', *Finance and Development*, **13**, 20–23.

Weisbrod, B.A. (1968), 'Income Redistribution Effects and Benefit–Cost Analysis', in Chase, S.B. (ed.), *Problems in Public Expenditure Analysis*, Washington DC: Brookings.

Weisbrod, B.A., Test, M.A. and Stein, L.I. (1980), 'Alternative to Mental Hospital Treatment', *Archives of General Psychiatry*, **37**, 400–405.

Whittington, D., Briscoe, J., Ximming, M. and Barron, W. (1990), 'Estimating the Willingness to Pay for Water Services in Developing Countries: A Case Study of the Use of Contingent Valuation Surveys in Southern Haiti', *Economic Development and Cultural Change*, **38**, 293–311.

Wildasin, D.E. (1984), 'On Public Good Provision with Distortionary Taxation', *Economic Inquiry*, **22**, 227–43 (the errata to this paper appears in the January 1985 issue).

Williams, A. (1983), 'Cost–Benefit Analysis: Bastard Science? And/Or Insidious Poison in the Body Politick?', in Haveman, R.J. and Margolis, J. (eds), *Public Expenditures and Policy Analysis* (3rd edn), Boston: Houghton Miflin.

Willig, R.D. (1976), 'Consumer Surplus Without Apology', *American Economic Review*, **66**, 589–97.

World Bank (1990), *Dams and the Environment*, Washington DC: World Bank.

Zerbe, R.O. and Dively, D.D. (1994), *Benefit–Cost Analysis*, New York: Harper Collins.

Index

Index 333

quality adjusted life years, in CUA 15,
16

railway closures
compensation tests on 44–6
determinants of 45
distribution weights in 261–2
Ramsey, F., and Ramsey Rule 80, 85–8,
91
in airport landing fees 94–6
calculation of 105–6
in physicians' services 100–102
and shadow prices 259
and user fees 299–300
Randall 155
Rao, M.G. 306, 313
Rawls, J. 247
Ray, A. 241
recreation, cost–benefit analysis of
hedonic pricing 196–8
travel cost method 185–8
redistribution in-kind
objective of 243
in rail closures study 261–2
Rees, R. 169
rehabilitation in crime control 194
reservoir example of risk (Dorfman)
159–61
resource based relative values system, in
shadow prices of health-care
97–100
Reutlinger, S. 159
revealed preferences
applications to CBA 19–20
in distribution weights 249–52
basic principles 249–50
estimating weights 250–52
social discount rate in 285–7
and statistical life 205–6
Riley, J.G. 163
risk 158–83
applications 170–80
alternative time horizon lengths
178–80
diagnostic decisions 173–5
lung cancer treatment 170–73
mortality risk, discount rates for
175–7
costs of 161, 165, 181–3
definitions and concept 159–60

and social discount rate 167–70
Arrow–Lind theorem 168–9
present certainty equivalent value
168
rate adjustment 169–70
see also uncertainty
risk aversion 162–3
risk neutrality 162–3
diagnostic decisions and 173–5
road licensing system (Singapore),
external effects of 123–5
Rodgers, J.D. 244
Rosen, S. 191
Roy 105
Rundell, O.H. 118, 120

Samuelson, P.A. 132–4, 136, 138
San Francisco Bay Bridge study 70–72
Schelling, T.C. 191
Schriver, W.R. 40–41
Scitovsky Paradox 34–5
SDR see social discount rate
Seckler, D.W. 37
Sen, A.K. 274
Senegal 284
Sgontz, L.G. 116, 125–7
shadow prices 79–106
and accounting ratios 81–2
applications
airport landing fees 94–6
health-care provision 91–4
Medicare 96–100
physicians' services 100–102
in competitive markets 82–4
definition 80–81
deriving, methods of 84–90
Lagrange multipliers 84–5, 104–5
producers' prices 88–90
Ramsey Rule 85–8, 105–6
gasoline price study, distribution
weights in 259–61
MCF as 230
and optimal commodity taxation 81
Singh, B. 65–6, 149
Smith, V.L. 136, 144, 149, 150
social CBA 4
social discount rate (SDR) 4–5, 267–90
alternative concepts of 271–2
SOCR as 271